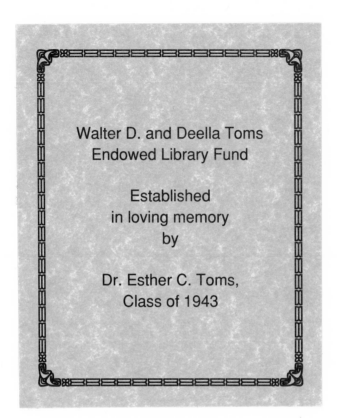

Walter D. and Deella Toms
Endowed Library Fund

Established
in loving memory
by

Dr. Esther C. Toms,
Class of 1943

NATIVE AMERICA TODAY

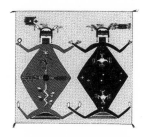

NATIVE AMERICA TODAY

A GUIDE TO COMMUNITY POLITICS AND CULTURE

BARRY M. PRITZKER

ABC-CLIO

Santa Barbara, California
Denver, Colorado
Oxford, England

Ornament on title pages and chapter opening pages is a twentieth-century Navajo rug. The motif of Mother Earth and Father Sky is taken from the sacred sand paintings.

Library of Congress Cataloging-in-Publication Data
Pritzker, Barry.
  Native America today : a guide to community politics and culture / Barry M. Pritzker.
    p. cm.
  Includes bibliographical references and index.
  Summary: Describes the political structure of some of the Native American tribes of North America, as well as their social conditions and their relationship to the U.S. government.
    ISBN 1-57607-077-8 (alk. paper)
    1. Indians of North America—Politics and government. 2. Indians of North America—Government relations. 3. Indians of North America—Social conditions. [1. Indians of North America.] I. Title.

E98.T77 P75 1999
970'.00497—dc21   99-052306
                                                                          CIP

05 04 03 02 01 00 99   10 9 8 7 6 5 4 3 2 1

ABC-CLIO, Inc.
130 Cremona Drive, P.O. Box 1911
Santa Barbara, California 93116-1911

This book is printed on acid-free paper ∞.
Manufactured in the United States of America.

To my family,
and to all who struggle against injustice

CONTENTS

CONTEMPORARY ISSUES

CONTEMPORARY PROFILES OF TRIBES AND GROUPS

DOCUMENTS: ACTS OF CONGRESS, EXECUTIVE ORDERS, COURT DECISIONS, LAWS, AND RESOLUTIONS

ACKNOWLEDGMENTS

This book would be far less complete had the following people not been so generous with their time and energy: Larry Sievers and the Chukchi Sea Trading Company for technical assistance and permission to use material from the company's website; Frank Tyro, media/public TV director, Salish Kootenai College Media and Teleproductions Center; The Confederated Salish and Kootenai Tribes for the biography of Michael (Mickey) Pablo; Leah Dorion, curriculum and publishing coordinator at the Gabriel Dumont Institute of Native Studies and Applied Research; the National Indian Law Library, Boulder, Colorado, for material on tribal constitutions; Bill Henderson for material on the Canadian constitution; Yvon Gesinghaus, general manager of the Musgamagu Tswataineuk Tribal Council, for background and permission to use the resolution on salmon farming in British Columbia; Hank Bear for insight into the battle over resource control in New Brunswick; Russ Imrie, webmaster of the Costanoan-Ohlone Indian Canyon Resource, for support and permission to use material from the excellent website; and Robert Jaeger and Daisy West, at the Bureau of Indian Affairs, for material on tribal constitutions. Special thanks are due Daisy West, without whose very generous assistance and encouragement this project might not have been fully realized.

I would also like to express appreciation to Gary Night Owl for publishing *Wotanging Ikche*, or *Native American News*, a weekly cyberjournal of news and information for the Native American community and their supporters. Thanks are also due to Indian and Northern Affairs Canada for statistics and the First Nations chart (Appendix II). I have also used statistics from the U.S. Department of Commerce, Economics and Statistics Administration, Bureau of the Census.

I would particularly like to thank Kwegsi for his contributions to the article on the Mi'kmaq struggle to gain control of their natural resources. He not only provided information about the logging controversy but, more importantly, confronted me with my own cultural biases and underscored the importance of choosing my words carefully. His thoughtful words helped me to better understand both the insidious dynamic of governmental oppression of native people and the terrible human cost of this course of action.

Todd Hallman, my editor at ABC-CLIO, enabled this project from the beginning. Liz Kincaid, Libby Barstow, and especially Connie Oehring provided their usual high level of production expertise and assistance. I would also like to recall with gratitude the 1982 Summer Institute of the Newberry Library's Center for the History of the American Indian and the generosity of the students and community of the Taos Pueblo Day School in the fall of 1977. Finally, I would like to thank my wife, Carol Batker, for all of her help. Her professional work on ethnic women writers, as well as her activism and commitment to social justice, has inspired me and informed my own thinking. This book has benefited from her insightful comments and countless other expressions of support.

While I have received a great deal of assistance from many generous and thoughtful people, I alone am responsible for the shortcomings of this book. My sincere apologies to those whom I may offend through errors of omission, commission, or insinuation.

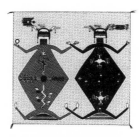

INTRODUCTION

Who are Native Americans? Despite all the books, movies, and television specials, most non-natives have no idea. Our images harken back to Hollywood stereotypes of "savages" either "noble" or "vanishing," or both. If we ever think of contemporary Indians, it is in terms of giant casinos, romantic notions of spirituality, or dire poverty. These images, as far as they go, are not false: Indian people do operate casinos, enjoy a rich religious and ceremonial heritage, and suffer disproportionately from poverty and its attendant social ills.

However, many Indians and Inuit (Eskimos) are also major players in local, regional, and national economic, political, and environmental decision making. In fact, native people today—teachers, lawyers, engineers, planners, artists, entrepreneurs, and others—influence life in North America to a degree not seen in centuries. Today's diverse Indian and Inuit communities embrace wealth and poverty, traditionalism and cutting-edge modernity, ongoing struggle and hard-won success. The answer to the question "Who are Native Americans?" is that they include the poverty-stricken and casino-owning people depicted in the newspapers as well as the dam operators, resource managers, businesspeople, activists, and planners who are not so well publicized.

This book is meant to provide insight into some of the political, cultural, and economic issues of interest and concern to people living in contemporary, rural Native American communities. Although many native people (about three-quarters in the United States) live in cities, I have chosen to focus mainly on rural communities because such communities, with their land bases (in most cases), form the heart and soul of native identity for many people. In this book, the method of looking at each issue with respect to three different communities is meant to suggest the complexity and the diversity of native societies themselves. Were I to look at each issue with respect to 50 different communities, 50 different scenarios would be revealed.

As a supplement to the main entries in the Issues section, I have included a selection of documents on contemporary issues. These include tribal resolutions, Indian court decisions and proclamations, U.S. and Canadian laws and court decisions, executive orders, and acts of Congress. The documents shed additional light on some of the themes addressed in the first part of the book. In particular, readers may get a sense of the extent to which the lives of native people in both countries are entwined with the law and local issues. Especially when read in conjunction with the Issues section, the documents also reveal the tension between native desires for sovereignty and the upholding of treaty rights on the one hand and the determination of U.S. and Canadian governments, on the other hand, to try to control their native populations.

Several biases are built into both the selection of and the material supporting my topics. For instance, I have relied almost exclusively on the written word for information. Given that the book is about a great diversity of cultures without a strong written tradition, such an approach of necessity has excluded some material relevant to this study.

Since few books and articles exist about the most recent developments and trends, I turned to that most contemporary of communications media, the Internet. Like society at large, the number of native World Wide Web sites has exploded over the past few years. Because electronic information is notoriously unstable and undependable, one must be careful to distinguish the factual from the bogus—especially, perhaps, where culturally sensitive material is concerned. Still, in some cases I have chosen to include a topic not necessarily because it is more immediate or more significant to more people but simply because there is a computer-literate constituency that has provided electronic information on the subject. Underlying the entire project, of course, are my own personal political and cultural biases as a middle-class, non-native man.

Statistics may provide a context for or reveal a small part of the lives of contemporary native people. As of August 1997, the official native (Indian and Alaska Native) population of the United States stood at 2.3 million, or 0.9 percent of the total population. Native people are younger than the population at large: In 1990, the median age of native people living on reservations was 22 years, while the U.S. median age was 33 years. In 1997 about half of all natives living in the United States were under 27 years old. About 26 percent of Alaska Natives were Indian and another 12 percent were Aleuts in 1990. The rest were Eskimos. The total native population living in the United States is expected to grow to 2.4 million in 2000 and up to 4.4 million in 2050, when it would represent nearly 1.1 percent of the entire population.

Of the 557 federally recognized tribal entities in the United States, 220 are in Alaska. Another 150 or so are in various states of petitioning for federal recognition. About 30 tribes are recognized by a state but not by the federal government. Reservation land in the United States totals about 55 million acres, or roughly 2.4 percent of the aboriginal holdings. Of the 55 million acres, roughly 80 percent is tribal trust land that ranges in size from less than one acre to the more than 25,000-square-mile Navajo reservation. The rest is privately owned by non-natives. Almost half of all people living on Indian reservations are not Indians.

Indians are not, on the whole, a healthy group. The attempted suicide rate among adolescent Indians, at one in six, is four times the general rate for teens. Tuberculosis is 7.4 times greater among Indians, diabetes 6.8 times greater, and alcohol mortality 6 times greater than for all other races combined. In late 1994, about one in three American Indians and Alaska Natives aged 15 or older reported having a disability.

Other indicators are equally troubling. The median family income of Native Americans living in the United States in 1993 was $21,750, or roughly two-thirds that of the population at large. The per capita income of Indians residing on reservations and trust lands in 1989 was almost $4,500. About 66 percent of American Indians 25 years old and over had graduated from high school in 1990, about 9 percent below the national average. About 9 percent had graduated from college compared with a national rate of 20 percent.

At least 27 percent of all Indians live below the poverty level, according to 1990 Census Bureau figures. This number increases to more than half for reservation Indians. The unemployment rate on some reservations regularly reaches 90 percent. Many reservations endure conditions similar to those in Third World countries. On the other hand, the number of native-owned businesses in the United States increased 93 percent between 1987 and 1992, to over 102,000. These firms took in $8.1 billion in 1992, up 115 percent from five years earlier.

Canada's total aboriginal population increased between 1986 and 1991 by 43 percent, to over one million people.[1] Most of the increase came from Bill C-31 registrants[2] and nonstatus Indians. The average income for all aboriginal people rose 31 percent between 1986 and 1991, compared to an increase of 7 percent for non-natives.The income for on-reserve registered Indians decreased slightly during the period, while of all aboriginal groups this one had the highest percentage of its income coming from government payments. Overall unemployment among aboriginal people fell slightly during the period to 19 percent, a figure still almost double that of non-native people.

As of December 31, 1995, there were almost 600,000 "registered" Indians and 608 bands in Canada. (This number is projected to increase to 900,000 by 2015.) This was a relatively young population, with 76 percent under 40 years of age and 50 percent under age 25. Almost 60 percent of Indians lived on-reserve. Only 10 percent of these bands had populations exceeding 2,000, and 6 percent had populations under 100. Life expectancy had increased significantly, from 59 years for men and 66 years for women in 1975 to 69 years

---

1. All Canadian data courtesy of Indian and Northern Affairs Canada.

2. Bill C-31 provided for the recognition of people formerly excluded because they had a native mother but a non-native father.

for men and 76 years for women. Between 1981 and 1993 the infant mortality rate dropped in half, from 22 to 11 infant deaths per 1,000 live births.

In Canada, the proportion of Indian children graduating from high school more than doubled between 1985 and 1995, from 31 percent to 73 percent. Enrollment in postsecondary institutions tripled. The percentage of Indian students being educated in band-controlled precollege schools more than doubled during the period, from about 20 percent to 54 percent. A corollary statistic relates to native languages: In 1991, over 50 percent of on-reserve registered Indians reported speaking an aboriginal language as their first language, up roughly 3 percent from five years previous.

North of 60° North (Northwest Territories [NWT] and Yukon), roughly 43,000 people identified themselves in 1991 as having aboriginal origins. This number is approximately 50 percent of the total number of people living north of 60° North. Educational levels in the region increased significantly, at least between 1986 and 1991, although the rate for non-natives still remained between four (Yukon) and 15 (NWT) times higher. Similarly, unemployment among natives was 24 percent in the NWT and 25 percent in Yukon, while among non-natives it was four and 9 percent respectively. Average family incomes in the NWT were up from about $40,000 in 1985 to close to $56,000 in 1990.

Beyond statistics, however, or perhaps beside them, are the lives of real people. The key to even the most basic understanding of native communities is to move beyond stereotypes to the realization that native people are making change happen for themselves today. Military conquest, mass murder, disenfranchisement, relentless cultural attacks, exploitation, and neglect have been the lot of virtually all North American native societies. This treatment has left grim legacies, and despair, hopelessness, poverty, and dependence are deeply rooted in many communities. Yet, even here, in many cases, great strides are being made. Far from having vanished into the sunset, native people across North America are defending their rights, revitalizing their cultures, and attempting to live with dignity *as native people* in the twenty-first century.

I have chosen to cover the following topics: arts and crafts, economic development, education, gaming, health, identity, land (re)acquisition, media, mining, natural resource control, representation, sacred sites, and sovereignty. These seemed to me to be important examples of matters that affect native people today. It is important to note that the categories are fluid in their definition. That is, I have discussed the Chukchi Sea Trading Company in terms of economic development, but I could just as easily have used it to illustrate an important aspect (marketing) of native crafts. Other categories that are more or less interchangeable are gaming and resource control, economic development and most others, education and identity, and identity and representation. Except for a very few exceptions, I have tried to focus specifically on native communities, leaving it to other books to provide insight into broader policy issues or the interplay between native people and the dominant society.

I discuss the issue of crafts with reference to Zuni Pueblo, the Pomo people, and the Catawba Nation. Although my economic development section focuses on the Tlingit, the Inupiat, and the Seminole, I could have used other groups to illustrate any number of angles related to this issue. One aspect I did not mention specifically is the right of tribes to choose environmentally unfriendly economic projects. In Utah, for instance, the Skull Valley Band of Goshute Indians (Western Shoshone) has signed a lease with a private company for a high-level nuclear waste storage facility on the reservation. The band has the support of the Bureau of Indian Affairs (BIA) but emphatically not that of the state of Utah.

Another economic development angle is the legacy of mismanagement and environmental destruction caused by government control of tribal assets. In Oregon, for instance, the Confederated Tribes of Coos, Lower Umpqua, and Suislaw have crafted a plan to take over management of up to 95,000 acres of federal land. The plan's centerpiece is the repair of environmental damage caused by generations of clear-cutting. The overall goal is both to restore economic self-sufficiency and to revitalize the tribal culture. In addition to practicing selective logging, the tribe hopes to gather and market other forest products, such as berries (jam) and mushrooms. Their approach—blending traditional values with modern ecosystem management and business practices—underlies many native economic ventures.

All of my education examples—Menominee, Mohawk, and Métis—center on aspects of local control and innovation. Tribal schools and colleges have blossomed over the past generation. The main advantage of tribal schools is that most instantly replace a curricular focus that is often oppressive and demeaning with one that is supportive and affirming. Furthermore, such schools often emphasize traditional culture, especially language, in order to strengthen tribal cohesiveness and identity. The tribes themselves often control the curriculum even in reservation schools still run by the government.

Unfortunately, most non-natives teach about native people in ways that remain simplistic, stereotypical, demeaning, and downright false. Even those teachers who consider themselves well-intentioned often lack the training or the materials to improve; others lack also the motivation. Native education needs to be raised to still higher levels. Partnerships could be developed between native and non-native schools, for instance, so that non-native students could actually meet or talk with their native peers. Computer technology could play a major role in this type of exchange. The Cradleboard Project, designed by the musical artist Buffy Sainte-Marie, incorporates (in fact, pioneers) many of these innovative ideas.

Gaming is a hot topic in Indian country. I discuss issues such as gaming's relative benefits to Indian groups, corruption, factionalism, and conflicts with non-native neighbors in terms of the operations of three tribes: the Mashantucket Pequot Tribal Nation, the Oneida Nation, and the Prior Lake (Shakopee) Community. I have largely omitted the whole area of conflicts with state and federal authorities, such as the opposition faced by the Coeur d'Alene tribe in its 1997 effort to conduct an Internet gaming operation. Also in 1997, the Seminole Tribe of Florida, long a determined advocate of Indian gaming, sued the Interior Department in an effort to force it to permit full-scale casino operation on any Indian land in the country. The Indian Gaming Regulatory Act of 1988 mandates that states negotiate in good faith with tribes that wish to begin gaming operations. Yet, for various reasons, some states (such as Florida) have refused to do so, resulting in more legal challenges and conflict.

Selected native health issues (suicide, domestic violence, and diabetes) are discussed with reference to the Standing Rock (Lakota) Reservation, the Anishinabe community at Leech Lake (Minnesota Chippewa Tribe), and the Pima people respectively. A look at the Lumbee tribe, the Costanoan/Ohlone people, and the Colorado River Indian Tribes reveals aspects of the "identity issue;" that is, the highly complex questions related to how and why native people see themselves as native people and who has the authority to rule on the legitimacy of individual and group identity. The struggles of the Lakota people, the Lubicon Cree, and the Western Shoshone Nation reveal something about the meaning of land (re)acquisition for native people.

Montana State University offers a film program for Native American students called Native Voices, in which students are encouraged to learn the technical, artistic, and business aspects of film and to use the medium to explore various political and social issues of concern to them personally. Salish Kootenai College, one of the media examples in this book, operates a television station that serves both telecommunications students and, in a different way, the Flathead Reservation at large. KTNN, one of the Navajo Nation radio stations, is an example of a native media outlet that succeeds by meeting the needs of a culturally and politically diverse and physically widespread constituency. In a departure from community-based examples, I have also highlighted telecommunications organizations with regional, national, and international audiences to illustrate more far reaching contemporary native media issues.

The effects of mining, not all of which have been negative, are often extreme. For instance, mining royalties are an important part of some tribes' income. But mining is almost always accompanied by environmental devastation, serious health problems, and economic exploitation, as the Navajo, Menominee, and Cree examples illustrate. The Menominee are trying to avoid those effects by waging a fierce battle against a proposed local mining project. In other cases, such as that of the Innu people of Labrador, native communities are working—or trying to work—with government officials to negotiate mutually agreeable terms for a mining project to proceed. Mining is an extremely controversial and occasionally divisive issue almost everywhere it exists in Indian country.

Native communities have long sought to control their own natural resources. Traditionally, the federal governments in both Canada and the United States have exercised this prerogative, resulting in the loss to the tribes of billions of dollars in royalties or direct income and, not infrequently, the chance to continue basic subsistence activities. In almost all cases, the quest for control over natural resources means long and expensive legal battles. The Southern Ute Tribe, for example, has just lost an important court battle over the natural gas within coal beds beneath tribal lands. Non-natives own the surface and mineral rights, but the Utes own the coal, which was split off from the rest of the mineral rights early in the twentieth century.

There are also often religious implications as well, as in the case of the Yakama Nation, which continues to fight for its treaty right to harvest salmon. The Mi'kmaq of Canada's Maritime Provinces have sought to control land they regard as unceded, mainly as a way to bring in some desperately needed cash. The Osage Tribe profited handsomely from its oil resources, but today the complexities related to resource control threaten tribal unity and possibly even the existence of the tribe itself.

Representation is the only category I have approached completely from a pan-Indian perspective, for all native people are affected by non-natives who pass themselves off as Indian for profit, by historically inaccurate depictions of native people in educational curricula and in the popular culture, and by hurtful caricatures in the guise of team mascots. None of these issues may be as pressing, as, say, economic development or sovereignty, but where in the rank order of importance does one place human dignity? The problem of the negative representation of native people is at the same time a very old and a very contemporary one; like all forms of racism, it will take a special, perhaps more personal, kind of solution.

I discuss the issue of the protection of sacred sites in terms of the San Carlos Apache community, the Wyandotte Tribe/Wyandot Nation, and the Colorado River tribes, the latter of whom seek to stop a nuclear waste dump on land they consider sacred. Similarly, the Modoc, Pit River, and Shasta people oppose CalEnergy's plans to build two geothermal energy plants on Medicine Lake, fearing widespread environmental destruction of a traditional sacred area. In almost a reversal of this theme, the Makah Indian Tribe recently resumed the ancient practice of whaling, an activity with strong religious elements, only to be vehemently opposed by non-native conservationists. The Nuu-chah-nulth people in British Columbia also defend their right to hunt whales.

In Montana, Indians are mobilizing to preserve sacredness of another kind. In early 1999, a delegation of native people began a 507-mile walk from South Dakota to Montana in an effort to protect the slaughter of the last wild bison herd. The herd is under attack from Montana officials, who claim that bison spread a disease called brucellosis that can cause cows to abort. Over 1,000 head of bison were slaughtered in 1996–1997; the state Department of Livestock sold many of these for a profit of hundreds of thousands of dollars. The Indians, for their part, reject the claim that the bison are a real threat to the cattle industry. They have asked (in vain) for the bison to be transferred to their herds rather than killed. They used the walk to build awareness of the plight of the bison and to reinforce their own traditional knowledge and spirituality.

Closely related to the issue of sacred sites are those of repatriation and religious freedom. Congress passed the National Museum of the American Indian Act in 1989 and the Native American Graves Protection and Repatriation Act (NAGPRA) in 1990. Both of these laws mandate, under certain circumstances, the repatriation of millions of human remains and cultural artifacts from U.S. museums receiving federal support. NAGPRA also increased the protection of native grave sites on federal and tribal land and outlawed trafficking in native remains. Under these laws, thousands of remains and artifacts have been returned to Indian groups. Yet some museums have proven less than fully cooperative, and a deep division has developed between those people favoring accessibility for further study and those favoring a dignified reburial.

Congress also passed the American Indian Religious Freedom Act (AIRFA) in 1978. Yet, in practice, Indians have often been denied the religious freedom enjoyed by other Americans. For instance, the U.S. Supreme Court has ruled that adherents of the Native American Church may be discriminated against for their sacramental use of peyote. Indian prisoners are routinely denied the opportunity to perform sweats and other religious and spiritual practices. As the examples in this book illustrate, Indians are often denied access to sacred sites outside of reservations that, in any case, are desecrated on a regular basis. In its *Lyng v. Northwest Indian Cemetery Protective Association* (1988) and *Employment Division v. Smith* (1990) decisions, the U.S. Supreme Court effectively eviscerated AIRFA. Most of its policy recommendations, in any case, had been ignored.

Finally and, in many ways, most importantly, comes the issue of sovereignty. In some ways, this one encompasses all the rest, for it goes to the heart of the ability of native groups to make decisions for themselves. In the United States, recognized Indian groups enjoy a "government-to-government" relationship with the federal entity, but what exactly does this mean? In practice, it means that tribes have varying amounts of autonomy (mainly tax and certain regulatory exemptions) over their own people and within their own communities. However, it is invariably U.S. (as opposed to tribal) courts and political bodies that regulate tribal autonomy, and, in any case, the United States has always claimed the authority to abrogate any treaty made with Indian nations unilaterally if it so desired.

Native sovereignty is a more fluid question in Canada than in the United States. It is also more complex in some ways, because of the ongoing issue of Quebec's special status. Although the Meech Lake Accord—the proposed constitutional recognition of special status for Quebec but not for Canada's aboriginal people—was defeated in 1990, essentially by Manitoba's lone native legislator, the issue of special status for Quebec remains a hot-button issue with regard to First Nation sovereignty. Native groups perceive that their own status could be threatened by Quebec's actions and have pushed for resolution of their grievances with federal officials. Constitutional recognition of First Nation governments was proposed in the 1993 Charlottetown Accords (it was rejected in a national referendum) and continues to be a very controversial—and as yet unresolved—political issue. This book looks at the issue of sovereignty as it plays out in three groups: the Quinault Nation, the Onondaga Nation, and the Inuit people of eastern Canada.

The topics I have chosen are not definitive. Many other important changes are taking place on family, local, state, provincial, regional, and national (that is, among and between native nations and the United States and Canada) levels. In the summer of 1999, representatives from two leading native groups, the National Congress of American Indians (in the United States) and the Assembly of First Nations (in Canada), planned to merge their organizations. Creating a formal alliance of North American tribes and First Nations will strengthen their political power and, by the way, fulfill the dream of the great Shawnee war chief, Tecumseh. In Canada, Bill C-31, passed in 1985, was designed to rectify a part of the Indian Act that stripped official "status" from native women who married non-natives (although native men who married nonnatives kept their "status"). However, the bill provides for a "reduced status" in such cases and raises the possibility that within just a generation or two offspring from such marriages could lose their native status—and with it, a range of protections—entirely. The question of "status" in Canada touches much deeper social, cultural, and political issues of native identity.

Also in Canada, a historic agreement was recently reached between the Nisga'a Nation, the federal government, and the government of British Columbia. For years, British Columbia refused to treat with native groups, a situation ripe with profound injustice and political and economic uncertainty. The Nisga'a were extremely tenacious, however, with their legal challenges. The compromise—under which the Nisga'a retain title to roughly 7,200 square miles of land (roughly 8 percent of their traditional territory) as well as $190 million in cash and various benefits—is being hailed by the Nisga'a as a victory and by some other First Nations (as well as the British Columbia Liberal party) as a swindle.

In the United States, in a development that may have profound significance for Indian groups, a federal judge has issued a contempt citation to government officials for "delay and deceit" regarding the accounting of federal trust funds for Indian tribes. These are funds properly belonging to the tribes that have been controlled by the federal government for over 100 years. The February 1999 citation, which was directed toward the secretary of the interior, the secretary of the treasury, and the head of the BIA, preceded a lawsuit that was ongoing as of the summer of 1999. In that suit Indian groups allege that the government has mismanaged the funds to the point that billions—perhaps tens of billions—have simply disappeared. Allegations have also emerged of the willful destruction of records relevant to the case.

Tourism is another complicated contemporary issue that affects native nations in various ways. For instance, the Navajo Nation has been criticized for its development along Lake Powell for, among other things, making sure it has clean drinking water while many wells on the Navajo Nation have been contaminated by mining activity. Some reservations, such as the Umatilla (Oregon), the Blackfoot (Montana), and the Oneida (Wisconsin), welcome tourists, including a growing number of Europeans, who want to learn about contemporary Indian life and get a view of Indian history that differs markedly from what they may have learned in school. Tourism can be a boon for reservation economies but, as is often the case, economic gain must be balanced with possible environmental destruction or profanation of religious ceremonies.

Language is also a subject with tremendous cultural implications. Somewhere between 50 and 60 percent of aboriginal Indian languages once spoken in what is now the United States still exist. Of the roughly 175 Indian languages that are still spoken, perhaps as few as 20 are still spoken by parents to babies. Speakers of traditional tribal languages are overwhelmingly old. California is perhaps the classic example: Although as many as 50 Indian languages are spoken there, none is used fluently by children. Since language is bound closely together with culture—it both reflects and helps shape the ways in which a person views the world—loss of language means in a very real way loss of identity. Among nearly every native group, various efforts are underway to save and revitalize traditional languages.

Many of the worst abuses of the past, such as mass murder, have eased or in some cases stopped altogether. The Sun Dance and the potlatch are no longer prohibited by law. Government officials no longer kidnap Indian children and force them to attend boarding schools meant to destroy their culture and sense of pride in themselves. Many important aboriginal rights, such as those relating to subsistence activities and political decision making, have been acknowledged. Readers should understand, however, that, in general, oppression and exploitation of Native Americans have not stopped. Not only is there still a great deal of anti-Indian prejudice among society at large, but the U.S. and Canadian governments continue in many ways to subvert legitimate treaty rights and to exert other pressures on native people to give up their culture, traditions, and resources.

Native Americans were here thousands of years ago and will be here as long as North America supports human life. Today, in part by drawing on their rich cultural heritage, Indian and Inuit people are holding non-native governments to their treaty responsibilities while empowering themselves and their people on a scale unprecedented in modern times. I hope this book will provide some insight into this process and into the dynamism of today's native cultures.

NATIVE AMERICA TODAY

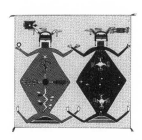

CONTEMPORARY
ISSUES

ARTS AND CRAFTS

The production of art and crafts resonates strongly among native people, in part because it is so connected to cultural identity and, in many cases, religious practice. Often the mere presence of native artists makes an important political statement about the resistance of a people's values to usurpation by the dominant culture. If all art has a strong cultural component, it is important to think about the ways in which Indian arts and crafts are significantly different from those created by other Americans.

There are many issues relating to craft production among native people. What follows is a look at only three specific societies. With the Zuni, a people highly identified with art, one may come to understand that core cultural and spiritual values are expressed through artistic design, execution, and display. Naturally, as Zuni society continues to evolve, so do artistic techniques and themes, yet the place and meaning of art remain central. It is no coincidence that at Zuni, art production is nearly ubiquitous.

Pomo basketry shares a similar relationship with cultural identity. Yet, unlike Zuni art, which has evolved throughout the ages within a relatively stable environment, Pomo basket making barely survived the depredations committed against the people, and it continues to be threatened by a loss of access to traditional resources as well as various forms of environmental pollution. Both technique and materials have remained basically unchanged for generations. Like Catwaba pottery, the very existence of this craft plays a crucial role in the people's identity.

Perhaps alone among eastern tribes in the United States, the Catawba have retained a prehistoric pottery technique. Catawba potters, like Pomo basket makers, tend to use the old materials and techniques, whereas Zuni artists, perhaps because their society is so much more traditional, feel freer to incorporate new materials and designs. Similarly, like Pomo basketry, but unlike Zuni art, Catawba pottery is made only by a select few. Still, Catawba potters have led the way backward, as it were, to anchor a revitalized modern culture in ancient tradition.

Zuni weaving, pottery, and jewelry; Pomo basketry; and Catawba pottery are just a few examples of contemporary native art and craft production. Each tradition is unique to its own society. However, by looking at materials, form, technique, cultural implications, production, marketing, and other issues, it is possible to gain insight into an activity of prime importance to many of today's native communities.

ZUNI

While most Native American groups have artistic traditions of one form or another, and many continue to be recognized for their fine arts and/or crafts, the Zuni of New Mexico are one of the few groups instantly associated with this activity. Many non-natives received their first introduction to Zuni arts and crafts through the Fred Harvey Company, a southwestern firm that sold large amounts of Indian crafts to tourists from the late nineteenth century to about 1940. Later the Indian Arts and Crafts Board (IACB), established in 1935, played a major role in promoting the development of Zuni and other Indian arts and crafts. In its early days, this federal entity mounted exhibitions, encouraged high standards, and helped set up tribally owned crafts cooperatives. It now functions mainly to protect trademarks and discourage fraud. The IACB also administers three federal museums.

A Zuni Indian weaves a blanket on the Zuni Reservation in New Mexico. Zunis both make a living and reinforce cultural values through the manufacture and sale of their arts and crafts. (L.L.T. Rhodes/Photophile)

Weaving is one of the most ancient of Zuni arts. Textiles were finger or loom woven and decorated with paint or embroidery. Finished products included a variety of items, such as clothing, straps, and bags. Ancient raw materials such as plant and animal fibers were largely replaced in about 700 when cotton arrived from the south and west. In the sixteenth century the Spanish brought sheep, which provided wool, another new material. The Spanish also introduced metal knitting needles and new design forms. Later commercial cloth and synthetic dyes became available as raw materials.

As non-native goods became increasingly available to Indians, however, native crafts and manufacture tended to languish. By the early twentieth century, the Zuni produced only a few handspun and handwoven items, mainly for their own use and for interpueblo trade. Although Pueblo weaving had declined dramatically, it was soon to undergo a revival, thanks mainly to the work of the Indian Arts Fund in Santa Fe and the IACB. Today, Zunis are again engaged in textile production, although this activity remains a very time- and labor-intensive craft, and its vitality at Zuni remains in doubt.

Pottery and basketry are also very old crafts. Ceramic production also declined dramatically in the early to mid-twentieth century, in part because a prominent Anglo trader discouraged the sale of pottery to tourists. However, a pottery revival began in the 1970s and '80s. Formerly a female activity, Zuni pottery is now made by both women and men. Perhaps more than other Zuni crafts, pottery making and its associated tasks, such as clay gathering, are connected with prayer and proper behavior.

Since few elder potters remain, many Zuni potters now learn their craft in schools and from a few experts. Daisy Hooee Nampeyo, for instance, a Hopi potter married to a Zuni, teaches Zuni-style pottery. Jennie Laate, an Acoma potter who married into the Zuni Pueblo, was given permission to make pottery in the Zuni style and taught traditional pottery technology at Zuni High School from 1973 to 1989. She instructed as many as 2,000 students in the full range of traditional pottery techniques.

Interestingly, perhaps the most well-known of Zuni crafts, silver work, is the least traditional. Zuni have been making jewelry—mainly drilled and carved shell and stone—for about 1,000 years. It was not until the 1830s, however, that the people began making brass and copper jewelry, and not until about 1870 that they began working with silver, a skill they learned from Mexican people. Many of today's Zuni jewelers use silver to frame intricate patterns of small turquoise, coral, and jet settings, a style that reflects prehistoric artistic traditions. Zuni jewelry techniques include needlepoint, mosaic, inlay, petit point, and cluster.

For many Zuni, wearing their jewelry intrinsically confers prestige and worth. Although most Zuni art is sold outside the pueblo, it embodies a fundamental expression of Zuni values. Characteristics of Zuni jewelry include an extremely tight fit of stone into setting, which may reflect the tightness of Zuni society as well as its precision, order, and clarity. Each stone occupies a particular niche, without which the whole would be not only incomplete but fundamentally flawed. In the same way, Zuni society is a horizontally structured one in which each member (and each artist) occupies a definite and valued niche. Each is an expert and an authority within that niche but makes no claims to authority in other areas.

The production of Zuni jewelry is primarily based on the family unit, where a husband and wife operate as a team and their children serve as apprentices. Most Zuni jewelry is produced at home. The emphasis is on continuity and excellence as well as specialization within a particular family.

The process of acquiring raw materials and distributing finished product has changed over the years. Raw materials, for example, are far easier to acquire than they once were. Dealers might come to Zuni bringing materials from anywhere in the world. They may buy a household's—or several households'—entire production of crafts, while other people, known as buyers, engage in smaller, more personal transactions, and may be looking for more unusual pieces. Few pieces are generally sold directly to tourists, despite the relatively high profit margin.

In addition to shops and galleries, other major avenues of exposure to Zuni crafts include the Museum of Northern Arizona in Flagstaff and the Santa Fe Indian Market. One interesting question that arises out of this structure is whether or not Zuni art that is sold almost exclusively to non-Zuni—and includes design styles suggested at least in part by the marketplace—ceases in some way to be Zuni. Few Zuni believe that it does.

An ongoing problem that both debases Indian art and cheats the artist out of just compensation is the counterfeiting of Zuni and other Indian art. Copies often look authentic and sell for a fraction (as low as 1 or 2 percent) of the real thing. In the late 1990s, Indian art in the United States generated close to $1 billion in sales, but at least 40 percent of all Indian arts and crafts sold in the Southwest is said to be fake. New Mexico legislators helped pass a 1990 federal law that mandates the identification of all imported "Indian-style" jewelry and crafts. However, these identification labels are often removed by unscrupulous merchants, and enforcement of the law is minimal.

The Zuni government is working to develop a certification process to protect both the tribe and individual artists. Even this project, however, is running into trouble. A town in the Philippines has renamed itself "Zuni" and so stamps its fake Zuni crafts. Also, a textile importer in India calls his line "Zuni" in order to trade on the reputation of that name. Even Navajo manufacturers have taken to copying some Zuni art styles. In addition to being of non-native workmanship, fake Indian arts and crafts often contains poor quality or synthetic materials.

Zuni place a high priority on increasing individual income, enhancing educational opportunities, and improving living conditions. Toward these ends, the people have used part of their $50 million in land claims compensation to start and/or support several businesses, including Pueblo of Zuni Arts and Crafts. With stores on the pueblo and in San Francisco and outreach into museums and galleries worldwide, this organization is a major force in promoting contemporary Zuni arts and crafts. Drawing on ancient traditions, the

Zuni people are poised to use their hard work and talent in the service of accomplishing their collective and individual goals.

POMO

The Pomo have been weaving baskets in north-central California for at least a thousand years. Before non-natives arrived, Pomos made beautiful baskets for their own practical and ceremonial use as well as for trade. Like virtually all California Indians, however, the Pomo suffered terribly during the nineteenth and twentieth centuries. Outright slaughter, dispossession, forced attendance at boarding schools, and racism interfered with the crucial generational transfer of weaving knowledge and skill.

The non-native market for Pomo baskets began in the 1890s, and from about 1890 to 1920 nearly every Pomo woman was engaged in weaving baskets for the non-native trade. In recent years, pesticide use, which affects plants, animals, and people's health, has emerged as a serious challenge to Pomo basket makers. Still, contemporary Pomo baskets are once again considered to be among the finest in the world.

Pomo basket makers traditionally included both men and women, although women concentrated almost exclusively on fine basketry, whereas men tended to make items such as fish traps and cradles. Pomo baskets varied in shape from the flat-plate form to spheres and various sized cones. The unusual elliptical, or boat-shaped basket, is also a traditional Pomo style. Patterns were equally varied and tended toward the asymmetrical and discontinuous. As for purpose, there were carrying baskets, medicine baskets, baby baskets, gift baskets, ceremonial baskets, prayer baskets, and more. Baskets were often buried with a corpse.

Contemporary techniques are very similar to the ancient ones. Weavers twine and coil their baskets, using the plaiting technique only to make handled seed beaters. In twining, the Pomo use plain and twill techniques. They generally use two weft elements, although the use of three allows them to create plain, braided, or latticed twining. Coiled baskets begin with a single rod or a three-rod triangulation of willow shoots. Superfine weaves may include up to 50 or more stitches per inch, although 18 is more common. As in the past, coiled baskets often have elaborate decorations in feathers and/or shell beads and pendants. Susan Billy, grandniece of master weaver Elsie Allen (1899–1990), is one of the more well known contemporary basket weavers.

Most weavers of contemporary coiled baskets use traditional materials such as willow (stripped or with the bark left on) as well as colored fibers: sedge grass root (white), bullrush root (black), and new redbud shoots (reddish-brown). Their materials are natural and always gathered (dug), never purchased. This approach presents various access problems, since the materials are frequently on land owned by non-natives. Craftspeople also often find that necessary plant materials have been destroyed because they stood in the way of either roads or new, artificial watercourses. (In the mid-1980s, a key source of basketry plants was lost when a Pomo valley was flooded to create Lake Sonoma. Elsie Allen, then in her eighties, led a group of Pomo women and other people in inventorying the valley's plants and transplanting some to private land.) In addition to plant materials, basket makers use items such as abalone, feathers, and clam-button beads for decoration.

Pomo basket weavers choose willow shoots, which they pick in early spring, for their uniformity. The shoots are smoothed by scraping or by forcing them through holes. The weavers know how to encourage tight-packed stands of bulrush by digging older plants with long rootstocks. The split bulrush fibers are dyed black by burial in wet ashes; different colors can be obtained by varying the type of ash, the materials that are added to the ash (anything from walnut hulls to rusty nails), and the length of burial. Skilled weavers pick Western redbud shoots in various weather conditions to obtain different colors and then process them to obtain the weft material.

Contemporary feather basket construction presents even more problems, however, as most birds that were formerly trapped for their feathers (such as the pileated woodpecker or meadow lark) are now protected by law. Many are also dying out as a result of pesticide poisoning. Women who make these baskets today must use either the feathers of game birds such as mallard and pheasant, which are not traditional, or find well-preserved dead birds. Few, if any, use feathers or any other materials that have been artificially dyed.

Pomo women also make beaded baskets using black, red, white, and yellow beads. The patterns on these baskets often imitate those of coiled baskets. As wild birds (for feather baskets) become less and less accessible, it may be that beading baskets will become more popular.

The liberal use of pesticides and herbicides in Pomo country endangers not only birds and plants but the weavers themselves, as well their children, since they are directly exposed to unsafe levels of the poisons through hand gathering and by the custom of passing plant material through the mouth to prepare it for weaving. Pesticides are no longer sprayed on some of our national forests, but the toxic cumulative effects of years of application remain, and private landowners, especially timber companies, are generally unresponsive to such concerns. As a result, human and other animal communities of the lower Klamath watershed have experienced elevated incidences of cancer, respiratory ailments, and deformities.

Indians have been meeting for years to try to stop the ground and aerial spraying but the state of California, through its Indian Dispute Resolution Services (IDRS), has not even considered this course of action. At the very least, Indian people are pressing for notification of pesticide application plans, advance notice of spray dates, involvement in review processes for nonroutine permitting, monitoring of drinking water sources, community health surveys, and health care worker training.

One group taking the lead on this and other such issues is the California Indian Basketweavers Association (CIBA). CIBA's goals include a variety of actions on the pesticide issue; working with public agencies on appropriate land management policies, such as those that allow for Indian access to native plants and encourage the restoration of natural habitat; and educating native and non-native communities about Indian basket weaving and gathering practices. Some of their action items have been met; others are still under negotiation.

In 1996, Pomo basket makers joined with other Native American craftspeople to open the American Indian Contemporary Arts Gallery (AICAG) in San Francisco. The AICAG is just one of many art galleries to feature Pomo baskets. In 1997, members of the Pomo tribe traveled to Australia as part of the Northwest Native Basketweavers Association to attend the first International Indigenous Basketweaving Conference.

Pomo basket weavers have always been naturalists, since they had to know exactly where and when to gather the precise raw materials they needed. Today they are also environmentalists. Deeply committed to continuing the ancient art of basketry, Pomo weavers try to make other people understand the need for legal protection for plants central to a native people's continuing culture. They also try to stop or at least restrict the use of highly toxic pesticide and herbicide application. It is an uphill battle on both fronts, yet the people persevere.

CATAWBA

In the east, people of the Catawba Indian Nation of South Carolina are using their ancient and continuous pottery traditions to rediscover and revitalize their culture. Once a powerful group of Indians, their origins are not entirely clear. The Catawba language is a remote branch of Siouan. The archaeological record indicates that the people have been in South Carolina for at least several thousand years, yet at least one tradition has them living in the north or northwest (upper Ohio Valley or Canada) until about the mid-seventeenth century.

If the Catawba did originate in or near the Ohio Valley, they would have been part of one or more of the Mound Builder cultures. (In any case they would have felt Mound Builder influence, although they appear not to have engaged in a period of active mound building.) Adena, Hopewell, and Mississippian cultures influenced the Ohio Valley and the Southeast from about 1,000 B.C.E. until the early sixteenth century. These cultures evolved rich artistic traditions, including pottery. Information and material exchange operated freely, if inconsistently, throughout the entire region from the eastern Great Plains to the Atlantic coast.

The Catawba may be the only eastern Indian group to retain the late Mississippian pottery tradition. Today, Catawba masters create pottery using nearly pure aboriginal technology. Only acknowledged Catawba Indians are allowed to learn the ancient traditions. Tools, techniques, and know-how have been handed down within families in an essentially unbroken process throughout the centuries. The sole non-native technological innovation—

squeeze molds—may have been learned from eighteenth-century Moravian settlers.

Pottery begins with the clay. Catawba Indians dig two types—fine pipe, or "gold," clay and coarse "pan" clay—from specific sites on and near their reservation. Like the construction methods themselves, clay sites and composition are of crucial importance. Whereas commercial potters' clay is separated, refined, and then remixed, the clay that goes into Catawba pots reflects the region's unique geology. Its properties contribute to the distinctiveness of Catawba pottery and in turn help to connect people with the land.

With raw materials in hand, Catawba potters process, construct, and design their wares according to the ancient methods. They beat, mix, and strain the clay; form it into coils; and then hand shape the piece, using both modern and ancient tools. After the piece has dried slightly, it is scraped and "rubbed," or polished, with heirloom bone and stone tools. Pots are slowly heated, often in a kitchen oven, and then baked in open outdoor fire pits. The final products are usually of a mottled red, gray, and/or black color, resembling highly polished wood.

The Catawba custom of selling utilitarian pottery to non-native planters, begun more than 200 years ago, continued into the twentieth century. However, warfare, disease, famine, loss of land, and other disasters began taking their toll on the people as early as the seventeenth century. Many Catawba left the area for Oklahoma and the far west in the nineteenth century. In the 1950s, the last native Catawba speaker died, and the tribe was officially terminated in 1962. From a high of perhaps 20,000 people in the sixteenth century, the population had declined to about 50 people in the early twentieth century. Finally, in 1993, the federal government rerecognized the tribe and paid it $50 million as a settlement for its land claims.

The settlement sparked the massive Catawba Cultural Preservation Project (CCPP), complete with a staff of archaeologists and historians. In many ways, pottery revitalization, already underway at the time of the settlement, serves as a cornerstone for cultural renewal. Younger tribal members learn from older ones, a process that supports the survival not only of ancient craft techniques but of the culture as a whole. In turn, CCPP supports the pottery tradition; for example, it helps to provide the funds to purchase ancient clay sources and brings to light, in part by reacquiring ancient pots, ancient styles and designs that contemporary potters incorporate into their repertoire.

From a low of only six master potters in the 1980s, Catawba pottery has recovered to the point where there were about two dozen active potters in the late 1990s, as well as more than 60 tribal members with some personal knowledge of the craft. The many types of Catawba pottery include cooking and effigy pots, wedding jugs, pitchers, eastern style peace pipes, and smoking pipes. Wares bring prices of between $10 and $500 or more. Late-twentieth-century potters include Georgia Harris, Nola Campbell, Viola and Earl Robbins, Evelyn and Susan George, Mildred Blue, and the Canty family. Catawba potters have also helped to reestablish "traditional" pottery, defunct since about 1900, among the eastern Cherokee in North Carolina.

Today there are many manifestations of the living tradition of Catawba pottery. The Catawba Pottery Association (CPA), active since 1976, sponsors classes to help keep the traditions alive. It also participates in the Schiele Museum's permanent Catawba Village Exhibit and in local Indian festivals. Master potters instruct students; other potters hold formal classes for children. In 1997, the tribe had its first pottery exhibit west of the Mississippi River, at Santa Fe's Institute of American Indian Arts Museum.

Although Catawba pottery traditions have survived intact for centuries, prior to the 1990s both they and the people were in a decline that might have been irreversible. At the turn of the millennium the population has grown to roughly 3,000 people, and these people are more aware of their heritage than Catawba have been for generations. The potters, in particular, have rediscovered their people's creativity. Always in the vanguard, they continue to help a renewed people dissolve the barriers between past and present and look proudly toward the future.

ECONOMIC DEVELOPMENT

Given the general history of exploitation, loss of resources, and enforced dependence, economic development is a particularly challenging problem for many native communities. Whether located in Canada or the United States, these populations are often far from markets. Many lack marketable resources, and even if they do not, they are hampered both by a relatively poorly educated work force and a dizzying array of regulations that tend to keep them from making their own decisions. In some cases, there is ambivalence about the meaning of economic development: There is no question that jobs and cash are needed, yet there is also an unwillingness to undermine traditions that run counter to individualism, materialism, and, in many cases, environmental destruction, the hallmarks of capitalist development.

The Tlingit people of southeastern Alaska have a long tradition of prosperity. The separation from their aboriginal traditions began more than 200 years ago; by 1900, many Tlingit were comfortable with non-native economic activities and beliefs. Even though the Alaska Native Claims Settlement Act (ANCSA) stripped away their aboriginal land title in 1971, they have continued to prosper by forging a robust and varied economy based on their valuable traditional resources (fish and forests) and other business ventures.

Although whaling and sealing are still a way of life in parts of northern Alaska, a group of isolated Inupiat people has found a way to market local crafts to a worldwide audience. This electronic solution to local cash-flow problems, while unusual and extremely small-scale (unlike the extensive Tlingit and Seminole economies), has the potential to be duplicated in other remote native communities.

The Florida Seminole, in contrast, have a double tradition of struggle. They were battling the U.S. Army to a standstill when the Tlingit were receiving tribute from lesser Indian nations. Fiercely independent, the Seminole refused to surrender, even if it meant fashioning a new and difficult economy deep in the swamps. They have no history of prosperity, such as that of the Tlingit, nor do they have the need, like the Inupiat, to reach out to distant places for economic opportunity (although—why not?—they do operate a cybermarket of their own). The Seminole have taken advantage of a contemporary "natural resource"—Florida's booming tourist and retirement populations—and a relatively well educated population to create a diversified economy worth $100 million a year.

Despite their successes, both the Seminole and the Tlingit, as well as most other native groups, must still deal with regulations that are really vestiges of the people's dependent and subjugated status. Powerful interests fight against the tribes, sometimes overtly, sometimes behind the scenes, to retain their unfair share of tribal resources, even if that means keeping the people dependent and poor. Increasingly, native people are becoming more educated and politically savvy, trends that augur well for increased and innovative economic activity. Yet geographical, educational, political, and philosophical obstacles remain to be overcome before native communities can return to anything like the economic independence they once knew.

TLINGIT

Independent sea people and prosperous traders from time immemorial, the Tlingit were visited and influenced by Russians and Spaniards as early as the mid-eighteenth century. After the United States purchased Alaska in 1867, Tlingit culture came under increasing attack. Since the government prevented Indians from filing legal claims, Tlingits saw little or none of the hundreds of millions of dollars of gold associated with the Juneau and Klondike gold rushes. Some jobs were available with commercial fishing and canning companies. Some Tlingit also worked as hop pickers into the twentieth century, but living standards had fallen dramatically since the days of independence.

The definitive event in modern Tlingit history was the 1971 Alaska Native Claims Settlement Act. Among the act's many provisions were those establishing twelve regional corporations and hundreds of village corporations. These entities were created to receive and manage the monetary and real resources conveyed to the people by ANCSA. Each person of at least one-quarter native descent on December 18, 1971, became a member of a regional corporation and received 100 shares of stock. Assets of the regional corporations included cash (roughly $440 million), the subsurface rights to all 22 million acres of village corporation land, and outright ownership of an additional 16 million acres of land.

Sealaska, one of the regional for-profit corporations, is intended to be a key part of Tlingit economic development. With corporate headquarters located in Juneau, its primary areas of activity are fisheries, investment, land development, and logging, but Sealaska also has business interests that range from plastics manufacturing to limestone mining. The corporation earned over $25 million in 1997, its thirteenth straight profitable year. In 1997 Sealaska was the third-largest Alaska-based business and the second-largest native corporation. At the end of 1995, the corporation owned total assets worth $320 million, not including resources received through ANCSA.

While depending primarily on logging, Sealaska is also committed to addressing issues not faced by many other timber harvesters. These include balancing jobs and profit with a concern for the land, including uses considered traditional by the Tlingit and Haida people, and protecting native sites such as cemeteries and subsistence use areas. Sealaska continues to clear-cut, while at the same time investigating alternative methods such as selective logging and selective helicopter logging.

Approximately 16,000 people held shares in Sealaska in the mid-1990s. These are people born before December 18, 1971, as well as their descendants who received shares through inheritance or gifting. Shareholders may receive a number of important benefits, including dividends, scholarships, internships, and jobs. Descendants born after December 18, 1971, are not presently enrolled as shareholders, although the current shareholders are free to admit them at any time. To date, votes on this issue are about evenly divided. The question of shareholder descendants remains an open and pressing one.

In 1997, Sealaska disbursed $9.5 million in dividends to its shareholders. Up to 35 percent of net earnings, averaged over a five-year period, is made available for dividends from operating profits. Up to 50 percent of the earnings of the shareholder permanent fund, averaged over five years, is also available for distribution. Some shareholders also receive a portion of certain ANCSA revenue sharing funds that Sealaska receives from other regions. There is also an elders' fund that distributes money to shareholders who have reached their sixty-fifth birthday.

Sealaska also contributes to the local economy by means of activities such as its $150,000 investment in the Southeast Vocational Training and Resource Center, part of an educational and training program run by the Central Council. Sealaska spends more than $70 million annually doing business in southeast Alaska and manages the region's largest private land holdings. In addition to its economic activities, Sealaska commits important resources to language study, scholarships, and a legislative agenda meant to benefit the Tlingit and Haida people. ACE—advocacy, culture and education—has become a new division of Sealaska and an important part of its overall mission.

Among the entities funded by Sealaska Corporation is Sealaska Heritage Foundation (SHF). A nonprofit organization, SHF uses its own funds and grant money to fund a variety of activities. For instance, it provides scholarships to shareholders, their descendants, and Native Americans living in southeast Alaska. Other SHF projects include recording and translating Tlingit oratory, support for contemporary Tlingit theatre, and support for language and curriculum study. SHF funds help make it possible for people to study aspects of traditional knowledge; the funds also support a biennial Native American cultural festival in Juneau.

Of course, Sealaska is not the only or even the primary way most Tlingits earn a living. Tribal corporations also play important roles in some local economies. One Tlingit tribal corporation, Kake, located in the village of the same name, is achieving its two main goals—profitability and creating jobs—by fashioning a diversified economic program. Like Sealaska, its primary activity is logging, but the corporation is also involved in real estate, fisheries, building and road construction, bioremediation, and even bow and arrow construction. It employed about 200 people in the mid-1990s and was primarily responsible for the town's success in exchanging its chronic unemployment for a labor shortage.

That profit is of primary importance may be seen in Kake's involvement in clear-cutting old growth and in supporting the logging industry by building access roads. Fisheries activities take advantage of the town's location near the fishing grounds. With fishermen able to off-load their catch in Kake, the corporation responded by reopening an abandoned cold-storage plant and marketing and transporting the fish itself.

In fact, Kake Tribal is well known regionally and even internationally for creating a lunch meat from chum salmon called salmon ham, or Alaskan Delight. The meat tastes like smoked turkey or ham and is almost completely fat free. It may be found on the shelves of national discount stores and supermarkets.

Economic diversification also allows the corporation to provide jobs to the roughly half of its members who live away from the village. For instance, plans to export its growing expertise in bioremediation could allow it to participate in the cleanup of sites in Puget Sound, thus offering jobs to members who live in that region.

The Central Council of the Tlingit and Haida Indian Tribes of Alaska also administers several economic enterprises. Among these are the Tlingit and Haida Steel Industries and a nonprofit organization, Tinaa Corporation, which promotes native self-sufficiency and economic independence through the development of small businesses. Tinaa's services include the Tinaa Fund, a microenterprise loan fund. The council's Economic Development Program promotes and facilitates sustainable economic development strategies in the tribal communities of southeast Alaska. Its Vocation Training and Resources Center has trained hundreds of students in jobs that are both viable and compatible with traditional values. In 1997, the center's resources were augmented when the council received a $2 million grant from the Department of Housing and Urban Development to construct a job training, entrepreneurship, and library resources services facility.

Some more rural Tlingit continue the traditional activities of hunting, fishing, and gathering. Drawing upon great and ancient traditions, others earn a living through art, especially wood carving and weaving. The Tlingit, especially those living in more urban areas, have also achieved success in any number of professional fields and in business.

INUPIAT

The Inupiaq Eskimo people, or Inupiat, are not a tribe at all but people who define themselves in terms of geography and language. Their name comes

A classroom in Point Hope, Alaska, home to the Chukchi Sea Trading Company. Artists and craftspeople in this isolated village have found a way to market their wares to a worldwide audience. (Clyde H. Smith)

from the dialect of the Inuit, or Eskimo, language (Inuktitut) that they speak. The other group of Eskimos in Alaska, located south of the Inupiat, speak the Yup'ik dialect. Despite their similar languages, Inupiat and Yup'ik cultures differ from each other in many important ways.

Point Hope, Alaska, is located in northwest Alaska, along the Chukchi Sea, 330 miles southwest of Barrow. It is one of the oldest continuously occupied Inupiat Eskimo sites in Alaska. Many people in Point Hope still depend on traditional subsistence activities such as whaling and sealing. Complete plumbing is a rarity, and fewer than half of all households have a telephone. The only year-round access is provided by a state-owned airstrip. Marine and overland transportation provide seasonal access. More than 90 percent of the village's roughly 725 residents are Eskimo. The cash economy is based on government jobs as well as art and craft manufacture.

Caroline "Kerm" Kingik is an Inupiat Eskimo who lives in Point Hope. A woman with a long-standing interest in Eskimo art, she knew that artists from her village had trouble selling their work because of a paucity of potential customers. (No roads connect Point Hope with the rest of the world.) Local artists were forced to make contact with and arrange for shipment to—

and payment from—shops that catered to the tourist market in cities far from their homes.

Many of these artists continue to live primarily in a subsistence economy, but today even people who catch what they eat must have some cash. Selling their art is one of the few ways that these people were able to get enough cash to supplement their traditional lifestyles. Kingit is not only an expert in Eskimo art but a shrewd businesswoman as well. She understood that both supply and demand existed; the only thing missing was an effective marketing system. The answer: a virtual store, located on the World Wide Web.

Her initial knowledge of computers came from her job as a child welfare case worker. Since her children used computers at school, and her husband was learning as well, the family purchased a home computer in 1993. Before long the family realized one of the central facts about the Internet, which is that almost anything can exist in cyberspace and is therefore accessible to anyone with the proper equipment (which, today, means at least tens of millions of people worldwide).

Two years later, Kingit and her husband, David Welch, formed the Chukchi Sea Trading Company (CSTC). Aside from the family computer, start-up expenses amounted to about $1,000. Planning was key to the venture's success: finances, website design, server sites, advertising, marketing, legal issues, and more were worked out with great care. The company's website is basically an electronic catalog, with rich graphics and links to relevant historical and cultural information.

All of the items for sale at the virtual CSTC are based on traditional form and design. Although non-natives first appeared in Inupiat territory over 200 years ago, many traditional skills have never been lost, and many have also been adapted for modern life. Eskimos still sew clothing such as mukluks and fur hats; these, as well as dolls, yo-yos, parkas, and other fur clothing are available. Dolls were traditionally used during the fall ceremonies to depict certain past events in puppet-like performances. Yo-yos are made from sealskin and polar bear, often with beaded rawhide tops.

Depending on location, whales and caribou played a central role in Inupiat life. Like the bison hunters of the Great Plains, the Inupiat used every part of the animals and made them the basis of many religious ceremonies and beliefs. Although plastic and lightweight alloys have replaced baleen in everyday life, native artists of the far north continue to use whale parts for jewelry, scrimshaw etchings (the style was influenced by Boston whalers of the last century), masks, and baskets. Bone from the spines of bowhead whales appears primarily in masks and figure carvings.

Walrus ivory was also a key raw material in traditional Inupiat culture. Today, walruses are still killed for food and skins. CSTC customers can purchase headmounts as well as various ivory jewelry and gift items, with or without scrimshaw designs. The material may be new, old, or ancient mastodon ivory.

Although Kerm Kingik and David Welch run CSTC as a for-profit business, they insist that their primary goal is to showcase the beauty and quality of Eskimo arts and crafts as well as the history and culture of the Inupiat people. Their chosen medium—cyberspace—means that they will reach a worldwide audience, of which few—if any—will ever visit Point Hope, Alaska.

SEMINOLE

The Seminole Tribe of Florida is an example of a growing number of Indian groups with successful and diversified economic development. The Seminole, who were never formally defeated in three wars with the United States, took refuge in the swamps of central and south Florida, where they were able to retain their independence. Until the beginning of World War I, the Seminole economy was dominated by hunting, trapping, and trading. Everglades denizens such as alligators (hides), birds (plumes), and otters (pelts) furnished trade goods for the Seminole.

At that time, however, state and federal authorities implemented a massive agricultural development project. The first step was to begin draining the Everglades. This blow was soon followed by another: The land boom of the 1920s led directly to the displacement and impoverishment of many of Florida's Indians. During the Depression years, most Seminole relocated to federal reservations in the south, where many—perhaps two-thirds—exchanged their religious beliefs for Christianity and their tradi-

Ah-Tah-Thi-Ki Museum director Billy Cypress (center) stands among lifelike mannequins that help illustrate Seminole life at the Big Cypress Reservation in Florida, 1997. (AP Photo/Gregory Smith)

tional education for non-native–style schooling. The Seminole economy also experienced a commensurate shift, as cattle herding and low-end wage labor soon replaced trade as the most important activities.

It was not until the late 1970s that the Seminole economy began to show serious signs of life. The sale of tax-free cigarettes at reservation smoke shops proved highly profitable but not as profitable as high-stakes bingo. These ventures, especially the latter, underlie the Seminole economic revival and general success of the 1990s.

By 1998 the Seminole Tribe of Florida employed almost 3,000 people, including almost 1,000 Indians, in numerous tribal enterprises. Their business interests are located on six reservations and also include an off-reservation aircraft company. The tribe purchased more than $24 million in goods and services from over 800 Florida vendors in 1997. It pays about $3.5 million in federal payroll taxes and has a gross annual income of more than $100 million.

While gaming is the tribe's bread and butter, tourism is also important. Some of the most successful enterprises are located at Big Cypress Reservation. There, the Ah-Tah-Thi-Ki ("to learn") Museum has served since 1993 as an educational resource for both tribal members and non-natives. Interested visitors will learn a great deal about Seminole culture from rare artifacts, interactive exhibits, theatres, and archives. The museum's expansion plans include adding an auditorium and a dining area. The museum offers four levels of membership.

Also at Big Cypress is the Billie Swamp Safari, at which visitors may tour 2,000 acres of swamp wilderness. Transportation is provided by "swamp buggy," motorized vehicles with balloon tires, and by airboat. The attraction also offers complete camping facilities, including the opportunity to sleep in a traditional Seminole chickee (an elevated structure with thatched roof and open walls); campfire stories told by "real Indians"; a store; a café; and a full-service restaurant.

Similarly, Big Cyprus Hunting Adventures offers tourists the chance to hunt game on over 3,000 acres of tribal land. Depending on the season, species available for hunting include hog, bear, wild turkey, snipe, quail, and deer. Every effort is made to ensure a comfortable and successful adventure. The enterprise offers a variety of hunting packages. Finally, 600-acre Big Cyprus Citrus Grove was developed with a $1.5 million grant from the Administration of Native Americans (ANA) as well as financial assistance from the Bureau of Indian Affairs. The grove operates under the direction of the tribe's governing council.

Other reservations contain similar businesses. The Sheraton Four Points Inn in Tampa is a tribal enterprise. Also in Tampa, the tribe provides a tourist complex complete with "authentic" Indian village, a museum, and a crafts and gift shop. Hollywood, Florida, boasts Historic Okalee. This village museum, created in 1960 but closed in 1987, reopened to tourists in 1998. Brighton features a rodeo arena, a turtle hatchery, and Brighton Citrus, 150 (soon to be 235) acres of prime citrus groves. Seminole Brand Ropes is located at Immokalee, as are various tourist-related enterprises.

Seminole gaming may be found in Tampa, Hollywood, Immokalee, and Brighton. Hollywood Seminole Bingo, which opened in 1979, was the first high-stakes operation in the country. The tribe added to its extensive gaming operations in 1996 when it helped launch the *Seminole Empress*, a 465-foot ferry cruising between Tampa and St. Petersburg and Cancun, Mexico. The tribe owns not the ship itself but its casino management contract. The ship holds 850 passengers and 245 cars. It also contains a discotheque, a dining room, conference facilities, a swimming pool, and, of course, a large casino. In 1999, the tribe was still trying to negotiate a gaming compact, as defined by the federal Indian Gaming Regulatory Act (IGRA), with the state of Florida. (Florida is one of only five states not to have either a compact or an arbitrated solution.) The tribe seeks permission to introduce Class III gaming (poker and slots), a move that could be worth hundreds of millions of dollars.

Off-reservation tribal enterprises include Micco Aircraft Company, manufacturers of the Micco SP20 custom aircraft. The *Seminole Tribune*, "Voice of the Unconquered," is published every two to three weeks. Finally, the tribe hosts a "cyber-market," at which on-line tourists may purchase a variety of crafts including dolls, baskets, and clothing; books; videos; music; and even food and cleaning products. The tribe's business successes have not eliminated adversity; in fact, some tribal elders maintain that wealth contributes to stubborn problems such as inequality, the loss of traditions, and substance abuse. Still, with a diversified economy, and poised to expand its lucrative gaming operations, the Seminole Tribe of Florida has turned its swamp into a gold mine.

EDUCATION

Western-style education has never been easy for many Native Americans. A traditional focus on oral rather than written communication positions many native students, particularly those closer to their ancient customs, as less prepared to handle the conventional reading and writing–based curriculum. A host of other obstacles may confront native students seeking educational success. These include poverty, poor health, a lack of role models, and poor self-image, helped along in part by curricula that either ignore their culture or, more likely, treat it as though it were something shameful.

Antipathy, or even hostility, toward mainstream education is also an element in the educational equation. The parents and grandparents of many Indian students attended government- or church-run boarding schools that actively sought to destroy their sources of cultural strength and inspiration. Such schools sought to convince Indians that members of "their race" were incapable of succeeding academically. Many boarding schools produced in their students an association between education and repression and even physical violence. Negative attitudes toward American-style education were often passed down to children and grandchildren.

Furthermore, in contrast to the "American" white-middle-class model, which emphasizes learning based on reading and writing, many Native Americans learn primarily by observation and direct experience. Studies suggest that Indians also tend to be less sequential and more holistic in their approach to learning. This mismatch of learning styles and cultural expectations has often resulted in underachievement, high drop-out rates, absenteeism, and a host of other problems for Indian students. In order to combat this situation, tribes began fighting for control of their own educational processes and curricula, a battle that was won to a significant degree by 1980.

Great strides have been made in recent years in the field of Native American education. The Menominee examples demonstrate several new approaches, including using tribal-oriented themes in the classroom, giving teachers more flexibility with how they meet state standards, and greatly increasing the role of parents and elders in community education. At the College of the Menominee Nation, the emphasis is on programs that focus on the tribal economy—specifically, casino management and forestry.

The Mohawk people of Akwesasne and Kahnawake take these innovations even further. At the Akwesasne Freedom School, for example, the entire curriculum is based on Mohawk culture and traditions. In a move designed to strengthen cultural knowledge and identity, virtually all classes are conducted in the Mohawk language. Yet the school insists that its students are at least as well prepared to enter the next level of education as are students from traditional schools.

In Saskatchewan, Canada, the Gabriel Dumont Institute (GDI) shows the way to meet the educational and professional needs of the area's large Métis population. Most of its programs are community based, and most feature a hands-on component. Unlike many native-oriented schools, GDI does not feature a strong traditional language component. Still, the institute has been highly successful in serving a historically neglected native population.

The best teachers, native and non-native alike, increasingly discover and root out culturally offensive and historically inaccurate educational material or use it as a lesson in racist stereotyping. Unfortunately, not all teachers are good, and in any case, native students still face a formidable array of obstacles to classroom success. Nevertheless, with the strong trend toward local control over curricula and educational programs, and more and more native people becoming educators, educational levels among native students at all levels, including the professions, are on the rise.

MENOMINEE

In 1990, Menominee County, Wisconsin (the Menominee Reservation), was the thirteenth poorest county in the United States. In the early 1990s, the Kenesha Primary School, plagued with the usual problems of an "at-risk" population, embarked on a project to transform its educational strategy. First, it adopted an integrated curriculum based on the whole language approach to language arts. This structure also allowed the teachers to assume more responsibility for educating their students by giving them the opportunity to create high-interest, tribal-oriented themes that would drive the curriculum. The faculty had a great deal of flexibility within the requirement that it satisfy various state guidelines for measuring learning.

Simultaneously, the school took a big step toward increasing parental involvement—and thus, according to many studies, the success of its students—by asking parents to determine the issues on which the school should focus. Administrators and faculty began to plan their curricula to emphasize issues deemed important by parents. These included traditional tribal values, perhaps especially respect for self, others, and the environment. Teachers who themselves may not have properly understood tribal values began a program of self-education.

Parents and elders were invited into the classroom to share their stories and generally facilitate the articulation between education and community life. At the same time, students used their increasingly positive identity as

Menominee Indians and their strengthening academic skills to study the world outside of the reservation. By the late 1990s, the Kenesha Primary School had made important strides in its overall goal of strengthening student educational achievement.

Higher education poses similar obstacles for Indian students. In response to their growing awareness of the problems and their understanding of possible solutions, Indians began creating tribal colleges. The first of these, Navajo Community College, opened in 1968. As of the late 1990s there were over 30 tribal colleges and universities. The College of the Menominee Nation (CMN) opened in 1993. Funded largely by casino profits, it functions on the twin concepts of learning by doing and community service.

CMN promises its students an experience based on the "history, traditions, values and aspirations" of the Menominee Indian Tribe as well as the opportunity to "achieve a significant position in the world's economy and social structure." In the late 1990s, almost all students came either from the Menominee or the nearby Stockbridge-Munsee reservations. Once dormitories are constructed, the school expects to enroll a much more diverse student body. CMN is a member of the American Indian Higher Education Consortium.

In the late 1990s, CMN offered associate degrees transferrable, if desired by the student, toward BBA (Bachelor of Business Administration) degrees at the University of Wisconsin–Green Bay. The two schools had also begun an expanded partnership that included offering accredited courses over the Internet and were considering offering Internet courses that would allow students to earn associate, baccalaureate, or masters degrees in certain program areas.

Reflecting the reality of the Menominee economy, CMN is the only Wisconsin college at which students can get a college degree in casino management. Courses include gaming ethics, gaming law and compacts, advanced gaming accounting, and supervision and surveillance of casino games. The school's president in 1998, a nun, pushed for the casino curriculum in part to counter the misperception that Indians cannot manage their own casinos.

In fact, non-Indians have tended to manage these establishments since casino gambling became widespread on Indian reservations in the early 1990s. Outside management companies often take between 30 and 60 percent of the profits as their fee. Tribes who manage their own operations can retain a greater percentage of the profits. They could then be in a stronger position, as many tribes desire, to create businesses that are not connected to the gaming industry. As the Menominee see it, this would be the proper path to true economic independence and social stability.

Other majors at CMN, such as computer operations and forestry and natural resources management, are also geared to reflect life on the reservation. In fact, the Menominee Sustainable Development Institute (MSDI), part of CMN, is a reflection of and a homage to the central role of the forest in the lives of the Menominee people, as well as the ability of the people to live in a sustainable fashion for millennia. MSDI is dedicated to examining Menominee achievements in sustainable forestry and applying those lessons to the larger model of sustainable development.

The two institutions, CMN and MSDI, work together at all grade levels to encourage Menominee students both to understand their people's long-standing commitment to environmental sustainability and to help meet the need for educated professionals in business and natural resource management. Employing innovative educational approaches and linking them directly with values, identity, needs, and strengths, Menominee leaders have created the means by which their people—individually and collectively—might achieve success in the twenty-first century.

MOHAWK

Mohawks living at Akwesasne (St. Regis Reserve) and at Kahnawake have created unique educational institutions that grew out of separate, though related, needs faced by the people of each community. The Haudenosaunee (Iroquois) in general, and the Mohawk in particular, have traditionally taken their status as sovereign nations very seriously. Modern battles (some of them armed) over these issues with Canadian officials began in the 1960s. In 1979, the people of Akwesasne founded the Akwesasne Freedom School, and the people of Kahnawake opened the Kahnawake Survival School, in order to ensure that their children would have the opportunity to be educated in a way that emphasized Mohawk language and culture.

The crisis that precipitated the creation of these schools centered around the issue of Quebec independence. Beginning in the mid-twentieth century, the people of Quebec began to see in the growth of English, Protestant Canada a threat to their identity as a French and Catholic entity. In 1976, the Parti Québécois came to power in the province with the promise to take steps, up to and including secession, to protect the province's special status. The Provincial Assembly soon passed a program for the separation of Quebec from Canada. Bill 101, part of this plan, imposed special regulations on native children attending school outside of their communities.

The Mohawk (and other native people in Quebec) opposed Bill 101 on the grounds that it attacked their sovereignty by recognizing the right of provincial authorities to legislate culture and education for First Nations. Mohawks labeled the bill a violation of the Two Row Wampum Treaty and other agreements between sovereign nations. Community leaders and school committee members held meetings and decided to take matters into their own hands.

The Akwesasne response to this turmoil, and to the general and ongoing attack on their culture, especially in the public schools, was to found the Akwesasne Freedom School (AFS). The Mohawk Nation runs this independent school that includes grades prekindergarten through eight. AFS is self-funded, with most of the budget coming from the community of Akwesasne. Its multidisciplinary curriculum is based on the Mohawk Thanksgiving Address, which itself reflects the people's inextricable connection with and fundamental responsibility to their own traditions, to the earth, and to all life.

The school's slogan, "Two Worlds for One People," reflects its fundamental goal of instilling confidence in students while preparing them to live successfully as Mohawk Indians and responsible citizens of the world. Parents play a key role at AFS, as do Mohawk elders and wise native people of other cultures. School administrators expect their graduates to have gained at least as much knowledge as they would have in public school and, in addition, to be prepared to help their people to achieve autonomy in a dualistic society. Even beyond these lofty goals, AFS sees itself as helping to effect a change in the hearts of native people living throughout the hemisphere.

The cornerstone of education at AFS is language. In 1985, AFS began a unique immersion program to increase the numbers of children fluent in Mohawk. All instruction—speaking, reading, and writing—is conducted in the Mohawk language with the exception of the final semester, in which English is used in order to help ease the transition to public school. Each school day begins and ends with a student reciting the Thanksgiving Address in Mohawk from memory.

Other subjects include the usual lineup and are covered as far as possible in a manner that underscores Mohawk identity. For instance, science is future oriented, reflecting the Mohawk ideal of responsibility for seven future generations. Major themes, such as aspects of nature and celestial bodies, are taken from the Thanksgiving Address. Both Mohawk tradition and contemporary events play a key part in the investigation of the social sciences. All students study the traditional fifteen ceremonies and celebrate them in the Longhouse.

The Freedom School suffered a crisis in 1984 when people learned of a direct threat posed by the seepage of toxic wastes from a nearby factory. Enrollment quickly dropped, and the school was forced to relocate. The process of evaluation and planning took time, however. A new 6,000-square-foot facility will be located on 157 acres of land, but as of the late 1990s the new school was not yet complete.

The Kahnawake people responded to the educational and sovereignty crisis in a similar way, opening the Kahnawake Survival (High) School (KSS) on September 11, 1978. KSS was the first native-controlled school in Kahnawake. Its name reflects the feeling that the people would not survive without a school designed for their needs. The school seeks to educate Mohawks to the idea that they share a common destiny and can and should shape that destiny with pride and a strong sense of identity. The school boasts a new science center, a fully equipped computer center, a middle school complex, a Mohawk language center, arts and carpentry facilities, a sports complex, and other buildings and centers used for administration, assembly, and so on.

The school's curriculum parallels the provincial curriculum while providing a strong component of Mohawk language and culture. The new middle school features an innovative instructional program that centers around the homeroom teacher, who both teaches and provides a strong adult role model for the children. One of the main purposes of this type of arrangement is to foster a strong sense of community and cooperation while maximizing parental involvement. The school offers four terminal degrees: an academic diploma, a vocational diploma, a vocational certificate, and a life skills certificate.

In the 1960s, some Kahnawake residents began a controversial drive to "purify" the Mohawk bloodline. The band council passed a law in 1981 stating that only Mohawks are permitted to live on the reserve. By the mid-1990s, the council had taken the concept of survival a further and more literal step by evicting people with less than 50 percent Mohawk blood. A group of residents also began protesting outside the homes of non-Mohawks.

This controversy has profound educational as well as social and political implications. Schoolchildren have begun arguing with each other over who is "more Mohawk." Furthermore, in 1995 the band council voted to expel up to 30 children from its schools because they were judged to have an insufficient percentage of Mohawk blood.

The action was promptly criticized by the school board chair, Josie Curotte, who took the council to task for requiring the board to enforce political decisions rather than educate students. Bucking the council, the Kahnawake School Board decided to use less restrictive requirements, allowing students to attend Mohawk schools if they are registered with either the band or the federal government. The latter entity defined any Indian as "status" who has at least one aboriginal parent.

Acting on their beliefs in the value of their own culture and of their political sovereignty, Mohawk at Akwesasne and Kahnawake have created unique educational institutions and programs. They are indeed preparing their students to live successfully as Mohawk and as citizens of the world. Since the early 1970s, dropout rates have plunged from about 80 percent to about 10 percent. In these two schools, the Mohawk have found both freedom and survival, based on teaching excellence, community involvement, and cultural integrity.

MÉTIS

The Métis Nation of Saskatchewan (MNS) is determined to promote the twin goals of Métis self-government and Native American revitalization. Toward this end, the MNS has created an educational arm, known as the Gabriel Dumont Institute of Métis Studies and Applied Research (GDI). This Métis-owned "native cultural institution controlled by native people" is a center for scholarly research, teacher training, administrative development, and distance learning. Its constituency is based in, but not bounded by, the central Canadian plains.

Gabriel Dumont was a leader in the Métis resistance of 1885. Although illiterate, Dumont spoke six languages and was a highly skilled rider, marksman, hunter, and fighter. In the 1870s, Dumont opened a ferry across the

South Saskatchewan River and became a leader of his community. As such he was active in seeking Métis representation to the Territorial Council and fighting for rights such as schools, land title, and land grants. He served the Métis provisional government by commanding a small army in 1885. Escaping to the United States, he later returned to Saskatchewan, where he died in 1906.

GDI sees itself as a cutting-edge innovator with a practical purpose, namely, "the design, development and delivery of specific educational and cultural programs and services." All education and training are fully accredited. All programs are sensitive to Métis culture and offer a Métis studies component. Most are community based and, where possible, include an applied practicum phase. Furthermore, programs provide comprehensive academic as well as personal support services to students.

While the institute works cooperatively with other educational partners, such as the Universities of Saskatchewan and Regina, it maintains both its independence and its Métis identity. Its various departments and programs include Dumont Technical Institute (DTI), Gabriel Dumont College, and the Saskatchewan Urban Native Teacher Education Program (SUNTEP). Due to recent budget cuts, the Gabriel Dumont Community Training Residence, a fourteen-bed facility serving female offenders in transition from incarceration to their homes and families, was forced in 1996 to cut its formal ties with GDI.

Curriculum Development, Research, and Library and Information Services form the heart of GDI's Core Services Division. These sections receive preferred status because they constitute the most effective and fundamental means for GDI to fulfill its mandate of promoting and renewing Métis culture. One of the most ambitious of GDI's recent curriculum development projects has been creating a comprehensive compact disc (CD-ROM) about Métis life in Canada. Other recent curriculum projects include the publication of a Métis *Veterans Book*; a Métis music tape project, based on the traditional songs of the Métis of western Canada; various historical books, atlases, curriculum guides, and videos and the Alfred Reading Series translations into Michif (the Métis language), Cree, and French.

GDI's SUNTEP is a pioneer in local teacher education and a highlight of the institute's overall programming. SUNTEP programs are held in cities that include Prince Albert, Saskatoon, and Regina. Each regional program provides many opportunities to link teacher education with Métis culture. For example, participants organize and facilitate cultural camps also attended by elders, and they present cultural workshops, Métis theatre performances, and electronic projects to local schools and even national and international organizations. SUNTEP staff is also involved in creating integrated math, health, and physical education programs.

The total number of SUNTEP graduates since the program's inception in 1980 is nearing 500. Most graduates (roughly 90 percent) are able to find employment as teachers immediately following completion of the program, especially since the program enjoys an excellent reputation in the region. GDI views SUNTEP as an ideal way to address the chronic need for native teachers and to help break the cycles of poverty, welfare dependence, and race and gender inequality.

The DTI works with the Saskatchewan Institute of Applied Science and Technologies and provincial community colleges to provide basic adult education. Established in 1992, its courses of study include preparation for the general equivalency diploma as well as training in office management, business administration, and computer repair. Financing and job placement services are an integral part of the program.

Other key GDI programs include the Management Studies Program, in partnership with the University of Regina (where students may obtain a two-year diploma in administration); the Métis Management Program (Yorkton, Regina, Meadow Lake), which offers certificates in administration and in continuing education (administrative development); the Métis Social Work Program (offers a certificate of social work in conjunction with the University of Regina), which trains people who plan a career in social work with Métis communities; the Métis Entrepreneurial Program, provided as a means to stimulate sustainable business development in the Métis community; and the Heavy Equipment Operator Training Program.

GDI, which is the first Métis-controlled education system in Canada, is funded in part by Saskatchewan Education and the provincial government. Its operating budget in 1996 was almost $1 million of a total budget of over $3 million. Plans for the future include offering courses in Michif; offering courses via distance learning systems; and, if funding is sufficient, physical growth. It is already serving as a model for other institutions: In 1998, the Manitoba Métis Federation created the Louis Riel Institute along the lines of GDI. This institution is scheduled to provide a full range of programs and services beginning in 2000. As the Métis people continue to take their rightful place in Canadian society, institutions like GDI will be at the forefront in providing them with the means to succeed.

GAMING

Gambling is an ancient and integral part of many Native American cultures. In 1988, Indian casinos grossed about $100 million a year. Ten years later they brought in more than $6 billion. For a few tribes, gaming has provided an excellent source of employment and income. Tribes with successful gaming operations have used profits to do the following: make per capita payments, provide loans for other tribal businesses, diversify the tribal economy by buying or developing other businesses, reacquire land, and fund a variety of health and human services programs, scholarships, and recreational activities.

Contrary to myth, however, only a small percentage of Indians benefit from casino gaming. A more typical example of tribal casino gaming is that of the Oglalas of the Pine Ridge Reservation. Their facility has created over 100 local jobs. It brought in about $1 million in 1997, yet per capita payments that year amounted to just $38, and that community remains among the poorest in the United States.

Only about 5 percent of tribes are involved in gaming at all. Furthermore, gaming is often a mixed blessing, at best, for native communities. Casinos work best for small tribes located near urban or tourist centers. This description fits all three tribes in this section but relatively few others. Foxwoods, the resort and casino owned by the Mashantucket Pequot, has succeeded spectacularly. The other two tribes, Oneida and Shakopee Dakota, also run successful casinos. Like the Pequot, they must deal with non-native neighbors who both welcome job creation and spin-off economic benefits and resent the "rich Indians'" nontaxable land.

Although Turning Stone, on the Oneida Nation, is a successful casino, the Oneida exemplify the internal divisions that can accompany Indian casino gaming. That tribe is split over the very question of whether or not the people should be involved with gaming. Objections are based on several grounds, including the potential for corruption and violence, the opposition of this kind of gaming to traditional values, and the idea that casino gaming may lead inevitably to stricter governmental controls, further compromising tribal sovereignty. Opposition to gaming among some Oneida has occasionally turned ugly.

The Shakopee Dakota also run a profitable operation, but its value to the tribe stops there. Since Indian tribes often are not able to manage these enterprises properly, more than 70 percent hire outside management companies. Some of these companies are known to squander profits and/or desecrate Indian cultures and traditions. Allegations such as these have surfaced in connection with the Mystic Lake casino. Charges of corruption have severely shaken the Shakopee tribal government. The situation has dragged on, unresolved, for years, hamstringing tribal operations, generating lawsuits, and creating deep divisions within the community.

As Indian gaming continues to grow, so do the controversies surrounding it. Associated legal, cultural, financial, and moral issues, including tax revenues, regulations, and competition with state lotteries, continue to dog the industry. The success of a few tribes lends support to the efforts of non-natives who are not favorably disposed to Indians to cut federal support for and to impinge on the sovereignty of all tribes. Indian gaming is a complicated issue with many implications still to be properly worked out.

PEQUOT

Decimated by war and disease in 1637, by the early twentieth century the Mashantucket (Mushantuxet, or Western) Pequot were widely considered to have become extinct. Their population had declined to roughly 10 people. Most of the old ways had long since been forgotten. Basket making, one of the few remaining traditional crafts, had virtually disappeared, since most of the practitioners had died. The community's economic failure was ensured by a Connecticut law that prevented Indians from engaging in economic activities on their own land.

In the early 1970s, with only one person living on Pequot land, the state of Connecticut was making plans to turn the reservation into a park. That resident, Elizabeth George Plouffe, fought a one-woman battle to protect her land and her legacy. She urged any remaining Pequot to return to the reservation. Her grandson, Richard Hayward, moved back at that time and, with others, began researching Pequot land transfers throughout the years. Convinced that many of those transfers had been conducted fraudulently, these people filed suit on behalf of the tribe in 1976. The resolution of this lawsuit was the 1983 Mashantucket Pequot Indian Land Claims Settlement Act. According to its terms, the people received formal federal recognition and a land settlement of 214 acres in Ledyard, Connecticut. It was on this land that the tribe, with the help of a $65 million loan from a Malaysian family (in exchange for a continuing share in the profits), established a high-stakes bingo operation in 1986, followed in 1992 by the Foxwoods Resort Casino.

Within just a few years, Foxwoods had become the most profitable casino in the world. Annual revenues approached or perhaps exceeded $1 billion. The 2.5-million-square-foot complex consists of 15 restaurants, two luxury hotels, almost 4,000 slot machines, a spa, a salon, a concert hall, and an amusement park. A new hotel–convention center–casino opened in 1997, and in that year Foxwoods welcomed about 45,000 visitors daily. In the late

The original entrance of the Mashantucket Pequots' Foxwoods Resort Casino—one of the most successful Indian gaming complexes, this casino takes in an estimated $1 billion a year. (Courtesy of the Foxwoods Resort Casino)

1990s, the Pequot were Connecticut's second-largest employer and its largest taxpayer (roughly $125 million annually).

With an enrolled population of just 318 (1995), the Mashantucket Pequot have become fabulously wealthy. Each member is entitled to a house, a well-paying job (including training if necessary), free education through graduate or professional school, free child care, and free heath care. Parents who elect to stay at home with their children also receive a significant salary plus medical benefits. These benefits are over and above the dividend checks received by all tribal members, as owners of the casino. The reservation itself, consisting of little but woods and a couple of trailers as recently as the mid-1980s, now boasts new houses, extensive athletic facilities, a child development center, a health care facility, and a multimillion-dollar community center.

The $135 million Mashantucket Pequot Museum and Research Center opened in August 1998. The library's collections focus on the history of northeastern Indians. The library also tells the story of the Pequot people, a tribe once believed to have been destroyed in 1637 but later recognized as having retained many of its traditions well beyond that time. In addition to being a significant research center, the facility serves to educate and inform the general public about the history of the Pequot and other regional native peoples. It is also the primary—and, in most cases, the public's only—access to tribal members.

Recently, with competition looming and simply as a sound economic strategy, the tribe has begun to diversify its investments. These now include high-speed ferry service between New York and southeastern Connecticut, several hotels and other real estate, a shipyard, and a mail-order pharmaceutical company as well as part ownership of two Rhode Island golf courses. Activities also include a perfume venture and waterfront development in nearby Norwich. The tribe is considering expanding its ferry service to LaGuardia Airport and, beyond that, constructing a major transportation hub that would link trains, ferries, and highways.

The tribe also gives millions away in charity, to causes from the Smithsonian Institution's new American Indian museum and the Special Olympics to local playgrounds, churches, and baseball teams. In 1997 it returned $578,000 in federal housing aid, saying it should be sent to Indian groups who really needed the money. Although the tribal council is moving toward a greater degree of management control, casino and financial managers include high-powered executives from companies such as Xerox, Pepsi, and Hilton Hotels Corporation.

Despite the tremendously positive effect Pequot industries have had on the local and state economies, the people's relationship with non-natives is not always smooth. Residual racism against both Indians and blacks (many Pequot are dark skinned) is certainly a factor. Some neighbors complain bitterly about "rich Indians" taking their land. The issue of sovereignty also rankles. State officials and even regular citizens are reluctant to cede the control over Indian life that they have exercised for centuries. Some want the Pequot to pay more in taxes and for services, while some oppose the casino for moral reasons. Of course, there is opposition to Indian successes on the national level as well. Pequot lawyers and lobbyists join other representatives from other Indian tribes in Washington to battle the possible imposition of new restrictions on Indian gaming and to ensure that they survive the anti-Indian sentiment that periodically flares in Congress.

The Pequot cope with their share of internal dissent as well. Lighter-skinned tribal members, for instance, are overrepresented among the tribe's governing elite. Few Pequot object to being in the gaming business, but continuing allegations of greed, racism, and favoritism suggest that the newfound wealth may be contributing to divisions within the tribe. Perhaps it is not surprising that factions and internal rifts are magnified by public exposure generated by their wealth. The question of just who or what is a Pequot remains compelling among this very diverse and contemporary group of people.

Although in 1998, the Mashantucket Pequot were the wealthiest Indian tribe in the United States, Foxwoods now faces competition from the Mohegan Sun casino. Other New England tribes are also hoping to open casinos in the near future. Other challenges include improving relations with their neighbors, using their position as important players in regional economic

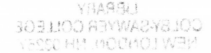

planning and development to best effect, and continuing to manage their own affairs wisely, all while solidifying tribal unity. For the moment, the Mashantucket Pequot are certainly poised for continued success.

ONEIDA

In New York, the Oneida Indians also faced a severe crisis. Once masters of roughly 6 million acres of territory that stretched from Lake Ontario to the upper Susquehanna River—and, with their fellow members of the Iroquois League (the Cayuga, Mohawk, Onondaga, and Seneca [and later Tuscarora]), east to west from the Hudson River to the Illinois River and north to south from the Ottawa River to the Tennessee River—their land had been reduced in the early 1990s to just 32 acres in central New York. Most of the 25 or so families on the reservation lived in squalor. Jobs were scarce. Aside from a few elders, most of the people had forgotten their traditional culture.

The Turning Stone Casino Resort has changed this picture dramatically. The casino opened in 1993 and soon generated over 2,000 jobs, guaranteeing full employment for tribal members. The casino is fully owned, although not managed, by the Oneida Nation. The once-destitute tribe financed the $10 million in construction costs with profits from a six-year-old bingo operation as well as bank loans. Highly profitable slot machines are illegal in New York, but the 68,000-square-foot casino does use "virtual slotless" machines, a computer-generated game similar to one-armed bandits. It also features over 150 gaming tables, a luxury hotel, five dining rooms, and six retail boutiques. In 1996, daily attendance at Turning Stone averaged about 7,000 people. When it opened, Turning Stone was unique among East Coast casinos in setting the minimum age to place a bet at 18 rather than 21. Alcohol is banned at Turning Stone.

The benefits to the Oneidas have been profound. While the nation does not make per capita payments, it does provide higher education, health care, elder care and child day care, a language and cultural center, an agricultural center, a new community center, recreational facilities, and supplements to federal social service programs. New and upgraded housing is also provided with funds matched with federal dollars. Oneida housing also comes with a proviso for some personal contribution, either financial or in kind, in order to counter the idea that handouts are possible, even from one's own people. The Oneida seem determined not to let dependence on tribal largesse take the place of dependence on federal funds.

Gaming has made other economic ventures possible, such as Oneida Textile Printing, a new recreational vehicle park, and an agricultural business. The people also plan to add a large hotel and golf course to their casino complex. Gasoline and cigarette sales remain important economic activities. As of 1997, the Oneida Nation was the biggest employer in Oneida and Madison Counties.

Neighbors are delighted at the economic boom brought by the casino. At the same time, they are fearful that the Oneida will begin buying up nearby land and taking it off the tax rolls. Indeed, the nation's "original" 32-acre landholding had by 1996 grown to almost 4,000 acres. Furthermore, the Oneida have sued for the return of several hundred thousand acres of nearby land they maintain was taken from them by fraudulent means. Like the Pequot, however, the Oneida have attempted to smooth relations with their neighbors, in part by contributing money to local causes, including the Red Cross and the town of Verona for renovation of its town hall.

Like many Indian casinos, Turning Stone is not without controversy. In 1997, the Oneida notified the state lobbying commission that, as a sovereign nation, they considered themselves exempt from lobbying disclosure rules. Their position, according to their lawyer, is that "the power to deal with and regulate the Oneida Nation is exclusively a federal matter, and state laws and regulations do not apply to the nation unless Congress has specifically delegated such power to state governments." In response, there has been some feeling within the state legislature favoring seizure of the casino on the grounds that the tribe has refused to comply with state gaming and lobbying laws.

Perhaps the greatest challenge to the casino has come from within. Some members of the Oneida Nation who are bitterly opposed to gambling have moved to shut down operations altogether. Dismissed by federally recognized tribal representative Ray Halbritter as simply jockeying for power, the dissenters went so far as to file (unsuccessfully) for a temporary restraining order. They maintained that the casino never received proper approval from the National Indian Gaming Commission and, further, that any agreements signed by Halbritter were invalid since he had been replaced earlier by the Grand Council of Chiefs of the Haudenosaunee Confederacy. This small but vocal group also strongly opposes Halbritter on the grounds that his decision-making style is near dictatorial in nature and, further, that he is more interested in profit than in the interests of the Oneida people. They also accuse him of pocketing a significant percentage of the casino take.

Opponents further charge that the roughly 1,100 members of the Oneida Indian Nation never had the opportunity to vote on whether or not they actually wanted the casino and would have rejected it if they could have. Many of these opponents believe that the casino does not exist for them at all but rather for the development of the local (non-native) economy. In fact, two years after the casino opened, and eight years after the tribe began its bingo operation, ostensibly to raise money for a fire department after local firefighters failed to respond to a fatal fire on the reservation, there was still no tribal fire department, and about two dozen nation members still lived in rundown trailers.

Two years after the Nation opened Turning Stone, it announced plans for another casino, at least twice as big as Turning Stone. Its location in the Catskills would place it less than 100 miles from New York City. The deal looked sweet to local businesses and county officials, which stand to gain millions of dollars and thousands of jobs if the casino is approved by state and federal officials. Almost as soon as it had announced the proposal, however, the Oneida faced the prospect of competition from the St. Regis Mohawk, who announced their own plan to build a casino at the same site. Furthermore, the governor is on record as opposing Indian casinos on the grounds that they do not pay local or state taxes. Among other hurdles, the legislature—and the voters—would have to legalize casino gambling in the state, a move that would also serve to expose the nation to competition from other quarters as well.

In 1994, Turning Stone was one of the 10 most successful Indian casinos in the nation. Its prospects look good, but the Oneida people remain divided over the issue of gaming. Some traditionalists decry casinos as destroying what little remains of traditional culture. Others claim to place sovereignty over profits, even if it means damaging or destroying the casino. Tribal representative Ray Halbritter's position on this issue is that "you can't act like a sovereign nation until you have economic independence." The people must find a way to resolve this classic dilemma of Indian gaming.

SHAKOPEE MDEWAKANTON DAKOTA

Like most Indian casinos, Mystic Lake, owned by the Shakopee Mdewakanton (Santee) Dakota community of the Prior Lake Reservation in Minnesota, makes money. In fact, it does so well that in 1994 every enrolled adult member of the community was paid about $400,000 out of casino profits. Such high payments were possible because the community's population, at around 300 (1998), is small, while the casino's location near the Twin Cities—and the Mall of America—is favorable.

The casino took in roughly $500 million in bets during the year ending in September 1993. At that time it enjoyed a profit margin in excess of 50 percent. When it opened in 1992, the casino boasted 1,000 slot machines and 76 blackjack tables. The draw averaged 12,000 people a day. Capitalizing on its success, tribal leaders decided quickly to build another casino—Dakota Country—adjacent to the first one. The complex provided about 4,500 jobs in 1994.

For years, tribal leaders sought to keep the specifics of its per capita payments a secret out of fear of a possible adverse reaction by local non-natives and even less successful Indian groups. Neighbors such as the Prairie Island Sioux and the Lower Sioux, for instance, make far smaller per capita payments, along the lines of $25,000 a year. In any case, not all Indian tribes elect to spend their casino profits on per capita payments. Chippewa bands who own casinos in northern Minnesota choose to invest profits in community projects such as schools and roads.

While some tribes manage their gaming operations directly, Mystic Lake Casino is run by a tribally owned company called Little Six, Inc. The tribe has no control over Little Six except through a semi-independent tribal gaming commission. This arrangement has generated intense internal conflict. The hub of the controversy is a powerful rivalry between the former head of

Little Six and his cousin, the tribal chair. While personal in nature, the rivalry also highlights a key debate about casino profits: Who gets to share them, and how?

Little Six has maintained that, while the casino does not pay taxes per se, it does pay the equivalent of taxes to the tribal government. According to a formula that was common in the mid-1990s, the management company retains a percentage of the casino's profits, and the tribal government claims the rest. The tribe spends most of its share on individual payments. About one-third is used for various projects, and a small percentage goes toward an education fund.

This arrangement has been a prescription for trouble, with each "side" maneuvering to bolster control of its share of the profits. Toward this end, the chair, for example, has been accused of changing the rules of enrollment in order to increase the number of people eligible for payments and thus the amount of money under his control. The enrollment controversy, in which tribal enrollment standards have been significantly lowered, is the largest and one of the most bitter in recent memory. Chairman Stanley Crooks counters that he is only trying to share the wealth more equitably and accuses Little Six of mismanagement, improper personal relationships with employees, and shortchanging tribal members.

In fact, newspapers reported in the mid-1990s that Indians who work at the casino complex were more likely than non-Indians to be given low-paid, low-skill jobs and twice as likely to quit their jobs or be fired. Indians are overrepresented in part-time jobs, which constitute about half of all jobs at Mystic Lake. A part-time classification means that employees receive no benefits regardless of the number of hours they work. Of the casino's 11 departments, only one—housekeeping—reported employing more Indians than non-Indians. A corroborating report issued in 1994 by the Native American Political Association, of Mesa, Arizona, alleged that Little Six hired relatively low numbers of Indians, provided little or no training, was unsuccessful in retaining and promoting those Indians it did hire, and permitted an atmosphere of intimidation and inequality between Indians and non-natives.

The allegations regarding improper relations with employees on the part of the Little Six chief executive officer have had significant repercussions. A lawsuit by a former employee charged that her ex-boss, the former head of Little Six, coerced her into having sex with him and fired her when he learned she was pregnant. Tribal attorneys argued that casinos are not subject to state or federal law. In 1996, the state Supreme Court agreed, ruling that the Mystic Lake casino was immune from the sexual harassment lawsuit. The decision meant, in effect, that Indian gambling establishments enjoyed the same immunity from suits as do tribal governments. The decision has been appealed to the U.S. Supreme Court.

While some tribal members hailed the decision as an affirmation of tribal sovereignty, others see it differently, saying that tribes who behave irresponsibly and then seek to thwart justice on the grounds of sovereignty claims just play into the hands of their enemies. According to this view, opponents of

Indian sovereignty are just waiting to build public sentiment against Indians so that they can mount a legal or legislative challenge. Among others, the Anishinabe writer Gerald Vizenor has warned that the element of greed renders sovereignty and gambling incompatible. Critics maintain that tribes that continue to combine sovereignty with mismanagement, incompetence, and injustice create a divisive and destructive force in both native communities and society at large.

Anti-Indian feelings can run high in Minnesota, and non-native bar, restaurant, and resort owners have lobbied hard against Indian gaming, claiming that it deprives the state of needed tax revenue and hurts their own businesses. Some Minnesota lawmakers have proposed creating four state-run casinos designed to compete directly with Indian-owned establishments such as Mystic Lake. Scott County, where Mystic Lake is located, has proposed building toll roads around the casino. The government says it needs the money to maintain the heavily traveled roads near the casino, but Indians see the plan as another anti-Indian attack. Despite its obvious success in the 1990s, the Shakopee community faces many challenges in its gaming operations.

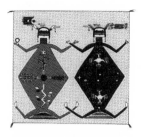

HEALTH

Compared to other racial or ethnic groups in North America, Native Americans must be said to suffer from poor health. Yet, among the leading causes of death in the United States for all races, the only category in which Native Americans and Alaska Natives outrank the U.S. population at large—by almost 400 percent—is that of accidents and their adverse effects. In the United States, inadequate funding and a lack of many essential medical services are just two of the many problems that continue to plague the Indian Health Service. Many native health problems, such as malnutrition, violence, and substance abuse, can be traced to the effects of poverty combined with the legacy of mass murder, land theft, cultural attacks, disenfranchisement, and dependence.

Suicide, an extreme example of self-directed violence, is examined in terms of the Standing Rock community, where in recent years it has grown to epidemic proportions. Colonialism and assimilationist policies have shattered traditional family structures that, in times past, served to hold Lakota society together. Other government actions destroyed economic self-sufficiency. The most innovative programs at Standing Rock today are those designed to address the suicide epidemic.

Leech Lake, Minnesota, is an example of a community in which violence is more outwardly directed. The Anishinabe people who live there suffer many of the same health and economic problems as does Standing Rock, although the severity is somewhat less. Both groups have focused on solutions that include creating task forces and holding healing rituals. Leech Lake has also, through the tribal community college, instituted workshops on how to overcome societal racism and the anger and frustration that often accompany this form of hatred. Furthermore, Leech Lake has created a communities of nonviolence program that its supporters hope will serve as a national model to combat domestic violence.

One serious health problem that appears in many native communities is perhaps most pervasive among the Pima—a high incidence of diabetes and obesity. The causes of these problems are complex but probably include an element of self-directed violence. That is, while genetics and hormonal imbalances almost certainly play a role, poor diet and lack of exercise are also strong contributing factors. Pima responses to diabetes and obesity are more behavioral and psychological than community based, yet the overall health of the group is a theme running through all three examples.

Another theme appears in the following examples of native health issues. Among all of these groups, and many others, the people are discovering for themselves how best to meet the challenges posed by their problems. Native people often recognize that outside influence of one sort or another has been a major part of their health (and other) problems. At the same time, they harbor no more illusions about living in the past than does any other group. Increasingly, the answer is to draw on the many strengths of their traditions while fashioning contemporary solutions to community health problems, all the while acknowledging and trying to address broader and deeper issues such as racism and unemployment.

STANDING ROCK LAKOTA

In 1990, Indians suffered an average suicide rate 95 percent higher than that of the general population. (On some reservations this figure approached 400 percent.) While accidents are by far the leading cause of death among natives aged 15–44, suicide is tied with chronic liver disease and cirrhosis for second place (it is a clear second among ages 15–24). The Standing Rock Reservation in North Dakota and South Dakota experienced at least 40 suicide attempts in late 1997 and early 1998, in which six teens lost their lives. Similar patterns may be seen in Canada, among First Nations such the Davis Inlet Innu (Newfoundland) and Birdtail Sioux (Manitoba).

While tribes tend to have their own unique patterns of suicide and suicide rates, some generalizations may be instructive. Indians tend to commit suicide in adolescence, whereas in the general population suicide peaks both at that time and in old age. Furthermore, it is primarily young Indian men who kill themselves, mostly with a firearm or by hanging. Suicide attempts by Indian women tend to be less successful and are often a result of drug overdoses.

Other factors that influence Indian suicide include the loss of a parent or significant caretaker and attendance at boarding school. Studies are inconclusive on the relationship between traditionalism on a reservation and the suicide level. That is, a sense of tradition can help to provide meaning and purpose but can also, in the face of continued and ongoing lack of opportunity, throw into greater relief the contrast between Indian identity and more mainstream versions of success. Not surprisingly, a correlation appears to exist between poverty (including unemployment and school drop-out rates) and levels of aggression, including aggression directed against the self.

Alcohol and other drugs have had an extremely negative impact on the Lakota people (as they have on many native people and non-natives alike). Substance abuse (like suicide itself) may be traced, at least in part, to the disruption of the family, the effects of poverty (including ill health, a sense of helplessness, and a lack of opportunity), generations of culture change, a con-

Lakota youth shooting hoops on the Pine Ridge Reservation (South Dakota), 1999. For young Lakota Indians on reservations such as Standing Rock and Pine Ridge, sports are not enough to offset the difficulties of inadequate economic development and a legacy of oppression. (AP Photo/John Gaps III)

certed effort on the part of dominant cultural institutions to demonize and denigrate native culture, and a position of powerlessness within the dominant culture. For some groups, the stark contrast between the activities and purpose of traditional life and the enforced idleness and lack of purpose of contemporary reservation life has never adequately been resolved.

Like many native people, the Lakota traditionally enjoyed, in addition to "full employment" and a great deal of political independence, a complex and highly supportive family structure. (The term "family" itself must be seen in this context as a colonialist construction, valid mainly because of the position of Indian tribes versus the federal government, which, by virtue of its human services policies, can literally mandate the structure of families today.) The basic unit was the *tiyospaye*, a word that may be defined as a band but that is more properly a kinship unit based on an extended family structure. The *tiyospaye* functioned to regulate the number of children, support children who lost parents through divorce or death, and care for the elderly (who in turn transmitted cultural norms to the children). Thus it was through the *tiyospaye*, rather than the nuclear family, that the Lakota maintained cultural balance and continuity.

When the bison were killed and the Lakota defeated, in the late nineteenth century, the federal government moved strongly to suppress or eliminate Lakota culture. Missionaries and boarding schools—including their practice of the forced removal of children from their homes—had a particularly deleterious effect on traditional structures such as the *tiyospaye*. Poverty, want, and sickness demoralized the people as age-old support systems began to erode. The government continued to remove Indian children from their families well into the twentieth century. The *tiyospaye* have survived the onslaught on Lakota culture but in a weakened form, unable effectively to counter the influence of poverty, chronic unemployment, and a host of resulting social ills.

As late as the 1950s, Standing Rock knew a measure of independence. In 1960, however, a federal dam project flooded 5,000 acres of the reservation's most productive croplands, turning farmers into welfare recipients. Today, economic and social conditions remain extremely difficult at Standing Rock. Substandard housing was made even worse by a federal repair budget that dropped by one-third in the mid-1990s. The unemployment rate in 1997 hovered around 75 percent (while North Dakota had the nation's lowest un-employment rate—1.9 percent).

In March 1998 there were over 150 children on the Standing Rock Reservation on suicide watch. These people were being both monitored and counseled. Unfortunately, school-based programs are largely ineffective, since so many teens have stopped attending school. Many young men on the Standing Rock Reservation see their future in the bleakest terms. Gangs have flourished and with them all sorts of violent behavior. Teens reach out desperately for support by forming suicide pacts and swearing silence among outsiders. In the view of many of Standing Rock's teens, suicide may be seen as an ultimate act of freedom from oppression and hopelessness.

The Standing Rock Reservation is currently employing a number of strategies to fight the suicide epidemic. A Suicide Task Force has been in charge of identifying the problems and devising and implementing solutions. Some, such as community meetings, hot lines and support groups, and parental training, have been borrowed from other groups who are or have been in a similar situation. Week-long summer camps have been established. These are based on the idea that healthy bodies make healthy minds. Seeking to establish a sense of unity and hope, they provide attendees with counseling and various traditional activities as well as healthy food and exercise.

Furthermore, the American Indian Movement (AIM) provided help in bringing in a corps of psychologists and counselors to help with the crisis. AIM also proposed to set up a pen-pal system so that Indian youth could get support from other Indian youth. An organization called the Native American Women's Health Education Resource Center, operated under the auspices of the Native American Community Board (NACB), offers programs to address various health-related issues.

The strategy of the various task forces and community groups has been to look at the situation in as positive a light as possible. They are trying to strengthen feelings of pride, cooperation, and cohesiveness among community members. One method is to bring not only psychologists but also tribal leaders, traditional healers, elders, teachers, students, and parents together to address the issues in a holistic, mutually supportive way.

As of early 1999 the immediate crisis at Standing Rock had eased, but conditions there, and in many other native communities, remain extremely difficult. On some level, what is needed is employment, or at least empowerment and the realistic prospect of employment. Until this happens, communities will continue to be faced with severe challenges to the health of their members.

PIMA

Pima Indians in the United States suffer the world's highest rates of diabetes (Type 2, or non-insulin-dependent diabetes mellitus [NIDDM]). The Pima diabetes rate is roughly 50 percent among those over 35—about eight times the national average. Their levels of obesity are among the highest in the world. The two medical conditions are separate but related. Both can be life threatening; diabetes, in particular, often results in blindness, limb loss, and the need for kidney dialysis.

While diabetes and obesity are common among minority groups—especially Indians—in the United States and among some aboriginal peoples throughout the world, they seem to be especially pronounced among the Arizona Pima and, as well, among their neighbors, the Tohono O'odham (Papago). (Mexican Pimas, once part of a unified Pima tribe, have normal or unexceptional rates of both diabetes and obesity, a fact at least partly attributable to their semitraditional diet and relatively high levels of physical activity.) Researchers began studying NIDDM among Pima Indians of the Gila River Reservation in Arizona in the 1960s. Since then, Pima have been involved in several longitudinal studies concerning diabetes and obesity.

Pimas were desert farming people. (They still are, but now they raise crops for sale or for livestock feed rather than for their own consumption.) Their traditional diet, consisting mainly of maize, pumpkins, and beans and supplemented by desert animals (deer, jackrabbits, fish) and other plants (mesquite and screw bean, cholla buds, saguaro fruit), was high in carbohydrates and fiber and low in fat. Foods such as melons and wheat joined the ancient food complex in the sixteenth century.

This traditional (or semitraditional) diet continued into the early twentieth century, when non-natives diverted the Pima people's water supply and destroyed their traditional agriculture. Especially since the 1950s, the Pima have eaten a "typical American" diet, that is to say, one relatively high in fat, calories, and processed foods. Pimas have exhibited high levels of diabetes and obesity only since the 1950s. The fact that rates between 1981 and 1988 were greater than between 1965 and 1972 suggests that environmental factors (such as diet and lack of exercise) play a significant role in the twin problems.

There are several risk factors for NIDDM in Pima Indians. Parents with diabetes—especially parents who acquired the disease at an early age—are more likely to have children with diabetes. The highest risks, both for obesity and diabetes, are to those children whose mothers were diabetic during pregnancy. Thus, by the time these children reach child-bearing age they are more likely to be obese and diabetic, therefore having diabetic pregnancies and passing along a high predisposition for the two conditions to their own offspring. (A related observation that needs more study is that NIDDM among Pima Indians is more prevalent in women of reproductive age who have never been pregnant than in those who have experienced at least one pregnancy.)

Similarly, while a causal link between obesity and diabetes has never been established, the two conditions are strongly related. Both diabetes and the degree of obesity have increased since the early part of this century. Furthermore, the strongest predictors of diabetes in children are two obese, diabetic parents, while diabetes develops much less frequently in thin Pimas, even among those with diabetic parents. However, the reported association of NIDDM with menstrual irregularity is more pronounced in less obese women.

Diet, too, plays an important role in NIDDM. In fact, many scientists hold to the "thrifty genotype" factor as a strong contributor to both obesity and diabetes among the Pima. According to this idea, Pimas evolved a genetic tendency to store fat in times of plenty against the lean times that are inevitable in the desert. When their diet in the mid-twentieth century went from roughly 15–20 percent fat to 40 percent fat, this genetic advantage became a liability.

The idea of a genetic component gained credibility when studies revealed that many American Indian tribes (including Seminole, Seneca, Choctaw, Cherokee, and San Carlos Apache) have very highly elevated incidences of diabetes, as do other indigenous Asian groups such as Micronesians and Polynesians. Diabetes is also unusually frequent among Mexican Americans with genetic ties to Indian groups. Scientists postulate a correlation between high levels of diabetes and Asian-aboriginal heritage, possibly because such groups carry a diabetes-susceptibility gene (as yet hidden), perhaps the so-called thrifty gene, which in the past may have given them a selective advantage.

Furthermore, a 1997 study revealed a link between the incidence of NIDDM and infant feeding methods. That is, people who were exclusively breastfed had, especially during the first two months of life, experienced significantly lower rates of NIDDM than those who were fed formula from a bottle. One possible explanation cited for this conclusion is that bottle feeding tends to result in overfeeding, since after about five minutes of sucking a breast the fat content of the milk declines precipitously. There may also be hormonal responses to the different foods that impact insulin sensitivity and general responses to food later in life. This study also has implications for the observation that diabetes rates seem to have risen dramatically during the latter twentieth century, since breast feeding was more common earlier in the century.

Despite a great deal of study, scientists in the late 1990s remain unclear as to the precise nature and mode of inheritance of the genetic factor. Most remain in the dark about just why the incidence of diabetes is so high among Pimas in the United States. They do know that the development of diabetes in Pimas is similar to that of other populations. They also know that while obesity and dietary changes are linked to diabetes, there are groups who experience these conditions who do not contract diabetes. (Blood samples of full-blood Pima Indians have been sent to over 200 laboratories worldwide. The fact that these samples are poorly tracked, if they are tracked at all, has led some people to speculate that they could be acquired and used by hate groups to develop biological weapons to target specific ethnic or racial populations.)

NIDDM appears to be caused by both environmental and genetic factors. Drugs, diet, and exercise all appear to be important weapons in the fight against diabetes among the Pima. The disease may very well be subject to other forms of intervention, although the precise nature of these interventions remains unknown, and none of the voluminous research to date has materially helped Pimas to decrease their rates of diabetes or obesity. Prevention is still the ultimate goal. One strategy that interests many scientists is to try to delay the disease's onset. The idea is that reducing or eliminating diabetes during pregnancy will result in a decreasing number of cases. In the future, gene therapy may also play a key role.

Like most Americans, Pimas are well aware of what constitutes a healthy diet. A new Pima wellness center includes a weight room and a gymnasium. However, also like most Americans (among whom obesity levels are also rising sharply), this knowledge is not sufficient in itself to reverse chronic weight problems. Most Pimas tend to think of diabetes as inevitable, uncontrollable, inherited, and incurable and thus are not generally motivated to engage in ameliorative practices. It is possible to see the rise of the diabetes epidemic as the latest event in a continuum marked by the loss of self-sufficiency and the substitution of dependency. Any realistic goal of encouraging the Pima, the Tohono O'odham, and other Indians to see NIDDM as controllable and even, to a degree, preventable should probably be linked with strategies to empower the peoples' sense of what is possible in their lives.

LEECH LAKE ANISHINABE

In 1999, a U.S. government study found that American Indians were twice as likely as a member of the population at large to become victims of violent crime. As telling as this figure is, it is misleading in that some reservation communities experience homicide rates up to 20 times higher than the national average. Some social scientists speculate that the only reason Indian homicide rates are not higher is that violence among Indians is so often turned inward, in the form of high suicide rates (see the earlier section on the Standing Rock Lakota, for instance). Rates of domestic violence, including child abuse, are equally high.

Other socioeconomic indicators in Indian communities are equally disturbing. The maternal mortality rate is roughly 40 percent higher than the

U.S. average, and the infant mortality rate is also significantly elevated. Deaths from accidents are three times the national average. Indians are six times more likely to die from alcohol-related causes and two to three times as likely to drop out of school. Many rural communities still lack indoor plumbing and electricity.

Furthermore, unemployment averages between ten and eighteen times the national average. This chronic high unemployment contributes to a serious diminishing of hopes and expectations for the future. One very personal and immediate result of poverty, and one that most Americans are unfamiliar with, is hunger. Most Americans do not understand, or do not choose to understand, the sense of desperation and helplessness that can grow out of such conditions.

Indians must also deal with factors that exacerbate the link between violence and poverty. Many Indians still suffer the effects of having been the targets of mass murder; of having their religion and culture brutally repressed; of having been made to feel ashamed, in government and church-affiliated boarding schools, for example, of their identity; of ongoing racial discrimination; and of a complicated legacy of dependency and colonialism. Many Indians today are estranged from their Indian identity—they no longer know or are only in the process of rediscovering what it means to be an Indian. Despite the fact that they may speak English and watch the latest television shows, many feel that they do not fit in to the dominant mass-market consumerist culture. Even though many Indians can count on the support of strong kinship ties, this position leaves them very much in a psychological no-man's land.

Despite the link between violence and poverty, the causes of reservation violence are complex. Nor are solutions simple and easy to achieve. Most likely, a variety of strategies, some unique to particular communities, will be necessary to combat the problem of reservation violence. Increasing economic opportunity is certainly a key component of any successful approach. Self-determination in the context of sovereignty is another: It is the only way out of decades, if not centuries, of crippling economic and political dependence. Passage and enforcement of laws banning racial discrimination—as well as a genuine change in attitude on the part of racist non-natives—would reduce pressure from the outside and open economic opportunities. More local strategies include various forms of family intervention, changes in school curricula and textbooks, and cultural revival.

The Leech Lake (Ojibwe) Reservation, located in Cass Lake, Minnesota, had a 1997 per capita income of $14,000 and an unemployment rate in excess of 30 percent. Levels of violence had reached the point at which the people decided they were no longer tolerable. While self-determination and other such broader policy goals are beyond the scope of any single community, Leech Lake has initiated a comprehensive program aimed at preventing violence. One important component—the creation of communities of nonviolence—was initiated in 1997 by the Leech Lake Women's Services Program (WSP). Under this system, a network of existing services tried to ensure that victims—and potential victims—of domestic abuse understood both their needs and their rights. By using preprogrammed cellular phones, a trained advocate from a Community Response Team would be able to intervene in an abusive situation throughout the 1,000-mile community in a timely fashion.

The WSP builds on a variety of services already available to women in particular and families in general, such as substance treatment and programs aimed at preventing family violence. WSP's director, Helen Condo, would like to see the Community Response Team used as a model for prevention projects that would empower communities. She considers the program's emphasis on personal responsibility for gaining knowledge of resources and strategies for assistance as important in building self-esteem. It is also, she notes, an antidote to historical government policies aimed at destroying Indian families.

Leech Lake Community College has attacked another pillar of violence in the community by sponsoring a training program called Undoing Racism. The purpose of the program is to train people to develop specific skills to challenge social, political, and economic structures in which legitimacy and power are always defined as non-native or, more specifically, white. Like the Community Response Team, Undoing Racism seeks to assist the individual in understanding a situation and in gaining the tools necessary to challenge and then change that situation. The training program has helped to reinforce the need to create a community environment that emphasizes tribal, as opposed to mainstream, values.

Every year the tribe holds a week-long Circle of Wellness Gathering that focuses on a holistic conception of health. Tribal members learn about healthy lifestyle options and reinforce positive aspects of their culture at various workshops, exhibits, and ceremonies. They may improve their gardening skills, discover practical nutritional options, participate in exercise programs such as a walk/run in memory of deceased loved ones, and receive free trees to plant. The gathering is also an occasion to honor tribal elders and, in an effort to empower people to act against domestic violence, to honor survivors of this particular social ill.

Finally, in response to the community's social problems as well as its political ones (see the Anishinabe tribal profile in the "Contemporary Profiles of Tribes/Groups"), the people at Leech Lake have been holding a series of healing rituals, part of which included cleansing feasts. The rituals were held under the supervision of a traditional teacher, or medicine man. One very specific problem the people are trying to resolve is a perception that tribal politicians are denying money and services to people in need.

Like many contemporary native communities, Leech Lake has chosen to acknowledge its social problems and take definite steps to alleviate them. Their approach is holistic, focusing both on members of their own community and on aspects of the dominant society that are known to contribute to violence among and toward native people. Indian communities like Leech Lake are developing innovative antiviolence approaches that may serve as examples to others and that serve ultimately to empower their own people.

IDENTITY

To a very great extent, the issue of identity supersedes all others in importance for Native Americans. (Paradoxically, it can also be seen as among the least important as well!) Before the late fifteenth century, of course, everyone in the Western Hemisphere (with the brief exception of Norse visitors) was a Native American. Today, the question of who is an Indian, Inuit, or Alaska Native is not always easy to answer, yet it often carries tremendous economic as well as psychological implications. Blood quantum, or percentage of "Indian blood," is the most commonly used—and, in some ways, the most pernicious—indicator. This standard varies from group to group, however, and in any case begs the main issue: Who gets to answer this question, and why?

The question of whether or not one is a Native American is related to that of whether the tribe or First Nation with which one is associated is federally recognized. This is a hotly contested area that shows no signs of cooling. The Lumbee people, for instance, are federally recognized but only partially— that is, they do not receive all of the government benefits to which federally recognized tribal entities are entitled. Their quest for full recognition has as much to do with money and politics as any determination based on the facts. However, they are opposed not only by the federal government but also by some other Indian groups.

Although, unlike the Lumbee, the Costanoan/Ohlone people of California have unquestioned aboriginal antecedents, the two groups share a perception on the part of non-natives of a tenuous connection with their past. The Costanoan/Ohlone were once declared to be "extinct," yet they still exist, possessing rich traditions, an active community life, a strong Indian identity, and a determination to achieve federal recognition. Their struggle rests as much on questionable treaty proceedings in the mid-nineteenth century as on having to "prove that they are Indian."

Among the people of the Colorado River Reservation, identity means something else—how can one be a "Colorado River Indian" when this "tribe," created by the U.S. government, did not exist before 1865? These people have no formal recognition problems—that is, unlike the Lumbee or the Costanoan/Ohlone, no one doubts that they are Indians. But are they Mojaves, Chemehuevis, Hopis, Navajos, or members of the Colorado River Indian Tribes (CRIT)? Can they be both, say, Mojave and CRIT? If so, do they have a primary identity, and why and when do they separate one identity from the other? If not, what happens to cultural heritage and traditions—and does it matter?

In all of these cases, the key question of who gets to answer these questions is somewhat ambiguous. Indian groups who seek or have federal recognition must have a document, such as a constitution, which specifically addresses the question of identity. In almost all cases, the group itself is the sole arbiter of who is and who is not a member. Yet, at least in the case of federally recognized tribal entities, constitutions must be approved by the federal government. In Canada, the issue of native identity is highly charged as well. The Constitution Act of 1982 addressed and was supposed to resolve this issue, but a wide range of legal questions remains that impact people in very specific and definite ways.

Official recognition is unimportant to many native people for the simple reason that they do not need the government to tell them who they are. Yet, few are naive about the legal, financial, and even cultural implications of issues of recognition and identity. These battles will continue to be fought in federal and tribal courts for the foreseeable future. They will also be negotiated by individuals and community subgroups, who, despite their deep personal involvement, often do not have any easy answers.

LUMBEE

Identity has always been an issue for the roughly 50,000-member Lumbee Tribe of Cheraw Indians. Located in the marshlands of North and South Carolina since at least the mid-eighteenth century, the tribe is officially recognized by the state but not completely by the federal government. That is, existing federal recognition specifically excludes the right, enjoyed by almost every other federally recognized tribe, to receive federal services. For better or worse, recognition confers a measure of legitimacy on a tribe's political sovereignty and even, perhaps, on its racial identity. However, as Indian tribes know well, official recognition is based in part on an essentially arbitrary perception of reality on the part of federal officials, a perception to which the tribes themselves may or may not—voluntarily or involuntarily—adhere.

The Lumbee case casts light on the key issues of contemporary Indian identity: Who is an Indian? What is a tribe? Who gets to decide? More amorphous, but perhaps no less important, is the issue of "Indianness"—that is, not who, but what, is Indian. This is a question that resonates for many ethnic and racial groups because it is so central, and yet so elusive, a component of both individual and group identity. Paradoxically, perhaps, the issues are intimately related: Not only does full federal recognition confer certain tangible benefits, but to some degree it also influences the people's sense of their own identity.

Lumbee ancestry may include members of early English colonies, such as the "lost" colony of Roanoke. Most likely the Lumbee are descended from an-

A Lumbee father and son photographed in 1979. Most members of the roughly 40,000-member tribe live in Robeson County, North Carolina. They have been fighting for federal recognition for years. (Corbis/Ed Eckstein)

cient Siouan-speaking groups such as the Hatteras, Saponi, and Cheraw. When first encountered by non-natives in the early eighteenth century, the Lumbee were living as free frontier farmers with no discernible Indian customs or traditions within living memory. The only evidence to suggest a native ancestry was their own oral history and a skin color that was darker than that of the local English and Scots.

The people remained relatively isolated until non-natives, pressed for space, began appropriating Lumbee farmland. In at least a tacit recognition of their Indian status, the state of North Carolina disenfranchised the Lumbee in 1835 along with other "persons of color." After the Civil War, in an effort to avoid the worst of southern segregation, the Lumbee sought an official status as neither "white" nor "Negro." They also initiated a quest for recognition as an Indian tribe at that time. In 1885 they obtained state recognition under the name of Croatan Indians of Robeson County. The group also obtained control over its own school system at that time.

Other "official" names followed for the Lumbee. In 1911, at their request, their name was changed to Indians of Robeson County. Two years later, however, having found this name unsatisfactory as well, mainly because it lacked distinctiveness, the people were designated Cherokee Indians of Robeson County. This name arose from the intermarriage between some Lumbee and Cherokee during the Revolutionary War. In the early 1950s, the group almost became the Siouan Indians of Lumber River. This inability to settle on a single name is evidence of confusion on the part of both state officials and the Indians themselves as to the proper identity of these people.

The Lumbee Indians of North Carolina became an "official" tribe in 1953, when the state conferred recognition under that name. Federal recognition followed three years later. However, in the recognition act the government included a termination-era clause specifically excluding the Lumbee from receiving benefits or services to which federally recognized tribes were normally eligible. In a 1987 decision, the Bureau of Indian Affairs declined to consider full recognition. The matter was taken up with Congress in 1988 and subsequently, but to no avail.

Complicating the Lumbee petition is the existence of other aboriginal groups in and around Robeson County who are pursuing independent federal recognition. While small, these groups, most of whom call themselves Tuscarora, insist on their own political identity. They have opposed complete federal recognition of the Lumbee on the grounds that their identity would be in danger of being subsumed into the dominant group (Lumbee). This dynamic has tended to dilute the Lumbee's claim to tribal unity and thus identity, in the eyes of outsiders, a situation that does not help their quest for full federal recognition.

Other factors also complicate the Lumbee drive for full recognition. These include the opinion of many non-natives (and not a few Indians) that the Lumbee are not "real" Indians, the large size of the Lumbee population (and thus the financial impact of recognition), and a lack of political history (treaties or reservations) with the federal government (or even the state). Even other Indian tribes, such as the Cherokee, feel threatened by the possibility of full Lumbee recognition.

Despite their lack of success in official circles, most Lumbee never doubt that they are an Indian tribe. The people maintain their identity mainly by means of a close-knit community, or series of mainly Lumbee communities in and around Robeson County, North Carolina. Kinship networks remain strong and an important focus of Indian self-awareness. They are maintained, even among Lumbee in Baltimore and other locations, by intermarriage and by coming together at life-cycle events, homecomings, and other important times. While the people lost control over their school system in the 1960s, their former teaching college has become the Pembroke campus of the University of North Carolina and remains a hub of Lumbee activity.

The other key locus of community identity is the near-universal membership in one of over 100 all-Indian Protestant churches located in Robeson County. Religious doctrine varies among the churches but membership does not. Many churches sponsor the homecomings that mark Lumbee life. The churches' social role in Lumbee life is just as vital as their religious one.

The Lumbee operate the North Carolina Indian Cultural Center in Pembroke, North Carolina. New projects will include trails and improvements to an amphitheater as well as restoration of the home of the nineteenth-century Lumbee hero Henry Berry Lowery. Local cultural events include the Lumbee-Cheraw powwow and an annual Native American Wild Game Festival. A local newspaper also fosters cohesiveness within the community.

The Lumbee have been struggling with the politics of identity for a long time. Their sense of themselves as Indians is based not on anything as crass as blood quantum (normally a key component of racial or ethnic identity) or even traditional customs and religion. It is about a way of looking at life, a sense of the past. Most Lumbee would welcome the infusion of federal dollars that would come with full recognition. On some level, they do not need the federal government to tell them they are Indians. But, especially having been mistreated for so long for the very reason that they were Indians, at the root of their petition is a quest for both validation and respect.

COSTANOAN/OHLONE

When is extinct not extinct? For years, particularly in the early twentieth century, many anthropologists and historians considered the Costanoan/Ohlone people to be "ethnologically extinct" because, in their view, they were no longer an identifiable culture. That is, the non-native "experts" observed no Costanoan/Ohlone territory and no language, no discernible traditions, and no people who any longer considered themselves Costanoan. However, in the late twentieth century several thriving Costanoan/Ohlone bands have petitioned the federal government for official recognition. Did these people return from extinction?

The answer is no—and yes. Traditional Costanoan[1] culture remained relatively intact during more than a century of contact with non-natives beginning in the mid-seventeenth century. However, in the late eighteenth century the Spanish built seven missions in Costanoan territory, which stretched from San Francisco Bay to south of Monterey Bay and inland to the edge of the central valley. The Costanoan people attempted armed rebellion to preserve their culture but in this were unsuccessful. Missionization largely destroyed traditional Costanoan/Ohlone culture as well as the culture of other regional Indian groups.

By the early nineteenth century, the Costanoan population had fallen by roughly 80 percent as a consequence of disease, hardship, and general abuse. Survivors intermarried with other Indian groups brought by force to the missions, such as Yokuts, Esselen, and Miwok, as well as with non-natives. In 1821, the missions were secularized and taken over by Mexicans. What remained of traditional culture was repressed, diluted, and generally forgotten. However, some Costanoan families maintained their identity even throughout all the generations of hardship.

In the early twentieth century, some Costanoans still spoke the dialects of Chochenyo, Mutsun, and Rumsen. Furthermore, these people retained enough of their identity as Costanoans to want to ensure the survival of what was left of their culture. In the mid- to late twentieth century, Costanoan/Ohlone land claims activity, combined with successful efforts to save old burial grounds, led to the creation of the Ohlone Indian Tribe and the Pajaro Valley Ohlone Indian Council and to a general revival of the people. Ohlone culture reemerged in the 1980s and '90s as multifaceted and vigorous.

Despite the existence of several treaties, no land had ever been officially designated as Costanoan prior to the twentieth century. In 1911, a Costanoan man named Sebastian Garcia obtained an allotment of about 150 acres at Indian Canyon, near Hollister, California. This was one of the places to which Costanoan people had fled to escape the persecution of Spanish missionaries. In 1980, Garcia's great-granddaughter, Ann Marie Sayers, applied under the 1887 Indian Allotment Act for an additional 123 acres in Indian Canyon.

Eight years later, and after a great deal of work, she received "trust patent" to the land. Since then, Sayers and groups of friends and allies have

---

1. The word "Costanoan" is of Spanish derivation and refers to Indians of the coast, specifically those who lived between Monterey and the Golden Gate. The word "Ohlone" comes from the name of one such group formerly located near present-day San Mateo County, California. "Ohlone" is also the word that native Indians of the Bay area have used to describe themselves in the twentieth century. Although the terms Costanoan and Ohlone are used interchangeably today, many people prefer the latter term, with the understanding that by choosing the name of one "Costanoan" group they are not obscuring the culturally and linguistically diverse character of their ancestors' societies.

restored parts of the land, conducted traditional purification rituals there, and made it a center of life for Costanoan/Ohlone life. Since an upstream corporation currently diverts much of their water, the people of Indian Canyon have also been engaged in an effort to prohibit such activity under a strong and legally enforceable Native American Free Exercise of Religion Act and other laws. The museum at Indian Canyon and the Carmel Valley Indian Cultural Center, established by Rumsen Costanoans, are centers of Costanoan activity such as the revival of basketry, language, and mythology.

Costanoan/Ohlone people work to protect ancient burial sites and for the return of Indian remains. In a highly controversial case, the people in 1990 successfully negotiated with Stanford University for the return of ancestral skeletal remains. The Ohlone Indian Tribe holds title to the Ohlone Indian Cemetery in Fremont, California, as a result of another struggle over ancestral remains. In fact, the importance that they give to this kind of work is one key reason (other than justice) that the various Costanoan/Ohlone groups are pressing for federal acknowledgment: Under the Native American Graves Protection and Repatriation Act (NAGPRA), remains can be returned from museums and collections only to federally recognized groups.

The people also play an active role in supporting the rights and working for the cultural and political revitalization of all California Indians. In June 1998, for instance, Costanoans challenged a Bureau of Indian Affairs (BIA) policy that would terminate the government's responsibility for all trust lands held by California Indians who are not federally recognized. They also actively support, through lobbying and raising public awareness, the recognition struggles of the roughly 35 California tribes whose petitions remain pending before the BIA. Indian Canyon itself, the only "Indian country" within the original Costanoan/Ohlone territory, is also a place where anyone of Native American heritage can come to hold ceremonies on traditional and sacred land.

Another aspect of contemporary Costanoan culture is the annual storytelling festival sponsored by the Indian Canyon Nation of Costanoan people. In 1998, the two-day event featured five storytellers, a play, and music. Profits were directed toward the Village House at Indian Canyon. Other activities sponsored or promoted by Indian Canyon included a World Cultural Festival, a women's ceremony, several powwows, and annual events such as a candlelight vigil to remember the 1860 massacre at Indian Island (Eureka), an Indian basket market, Ohlone Days, and a California Indian conference.

Communications plays a large part in contemporary Costanoan culture. A newsletter, *Noso-n* (Mutsun for "in breath so it is in spirit"), keeps the people informed about important activities. The Costanoan/Ohlone people also have an outstanding site on the World Wide Web that helps them to link with each other, with people interested in assisting them with their work, and with academics, other professionals, and the interested general public in the United States and around the world. With the help of consulting professionals, Ann Marie Sayers and others are in the process of reviving the Mutsun language by creating a dictionary.

Sayers, with the help of University of California–Santa Cruz students, has also opened a library at Indian Canyon. The library contains material on California Indians in general but focuses on Costanoan history and culture. Included are more than 100 cassettes of Costanoan elders recalling tribal history and culture. Library workers have also created a computerized data bank based on the 1928 California Indian census. This project will help people determine valuable information about their ancestry, including Indian descent and/or tribal membership and land claims information.

For years, the Ohlone were told that their people had become extinct. However, by redefining their history, taking control of ancestral sites, and fighting for the protection of their rights and natural resources, the people have rejected extinction. They have reestablished their tribal identities and reclaimed their identity, their heritage, and their future. Far from having disappeared into history, the following Costanoan groups were fully functioning Indian tribes and had applied for federal recognition as of early 1999: Amah Band of Ohlone/Costanoan Indians, Costanoan Band of Carmel Mission Indians, Costanoan/Ohlone Indian Families of the San Francisco Bay, Indian Canyon Band of Costanoan/Mutsun Indians, Muwekma Indian Tribe, Costanoan Ohlone Rumsen-Mutsun Tribe, and Ohlone/Costanoan-Esselen Nation. Their petitions are in various stages of consideration.

COLORADO RIVER INDIAN TRIBES

Like some other Indian groups, the Colorado River Indian Tribes (CRIT) have been a coherent community for only a relatively short period of time. CRIT's constituents—Mojave, Chemehuevi, Navajo, and Hopi—are from distinct Indian groups with ancient cultures, yet actions undertaken by the U.S. government have combined some members of these groups into a new tribe. The formation of CRIT has forced the constituent members to adapt to a new identity. This process has taken and will continue to require a good deal of adjustment. On the other hand, political and cultural formation among native people has always been fluid to a greater or lesser extent. The creation of CRIT merely provides a modern focus on an ancient dynamic.

In fact, one of the constituent members of CRIT, the Chemehuevi, is itself a relatively recent political creation. Originally the most southerly group of Southern Paiute (an anthropological designation that encompasses a diverse group of linguistically and culturally related peoples), the proto-Chemehuevi drifted south toward Mojave territory in the eighteenth century. In the early nineteenth century they occupied the former territory of one Mojave group as well as that of the Pee-Posh (Maricopa) Indians. Having relocated to the Colorado River, this group adopted a crop-based economy and began to think of itself as a political entity distinct from both the Paiute and the Mojave.

In 1865, the federal government created the Colorado River Indian Reservation (CRIR) as well as the political entity called the Colorado River

Indian Tribes. At the time only Mojave and Chemehuevi people lived in the area. Following World War II, however, the government relocated a number of Navajo and Hopi families onto the CRIR, ostensibly to provide them with better opportunities for farming than they had at home. The government had previously insisted that a portion of the CRIR must be reserved for "colonization." CRIT rejection of this action in 1952 was ignored by the Interior Department. Finally, in 1964, Congress agreed to halt the colonization of the CRIR.

The formation of CRIT and its development as a distinct tribe have been difficult for tribal elders, who were and are especially concerned about the preservation of ancient cultures, traditions, and identities. Circumstances on the CRIR have favored the Mojave culture: The reservation is located on aboriginal Mojave territory, and the Mojave population of CRIT is greater than the combined populations of the other three tribes. Therefore, the Mojave have tended to dominate the political and cultural life of the reservation.

Today, traditional conceptions of individual identity have changed, as has the community's sense of itself. Intermarriage and propinquity have worked to create what is in effect a multicultural (intertribal and interracial) tribal membership. On one level, that which values continuity with the pre-CRIT past, tribal identity has become separated from name and geography. The location of identity has turned inward, toward kinship ties and a knowledge of language and cultural practices. Elders' groups have grown in importance, as younger people increasingly appreciate their value as a vital link to the past and older people feel that their message is being received. More and more students are studying their people's history and material culture. Legal codes reflect the issue of identity in terms of cultural instruction and enrollment.

Furthermore, a tribal museum and a combination library and archive help to preserve the heritage of the constituent tribes. Here, documents and artifacts from the Chemehuevi, Hopi, Mojave, and Navajo past are stored and displayed. The archive consists of original and reproduced documents, photographs, and video and audio tapes of oral histories. The documents include personal correspondence, government documents, and the professional work of social scientists. The facility is free and open to tribal members as well as the general public.

On another level, of course, CRIT has been around for more than 130 years and members definitely view themselves as members of a unified political and even cultural entity. All economic activities, including tourism and recreation, agriculture, small business, light industry, and government, are conducted without regard to national origin. In fact, these activities all help to promote and further tribal unity.

The tribes are justifiably proud of both their unity and progress and recognize that the two are inseparable from one another. Pioneers in multiculturalism in the United States, members of the CRIT have learned that maintaining identities on different levels need not be mutually exclusive or divisive. Like all multicultural communities (and virtually all communities *are* multicultural), the people of CRIR understand that their strength lies not only in their land and other natural resources but perhaps especially in the unique contributions in its own constituent groups and individuals and the dynamism with which these elements interact with and reinforce each other.

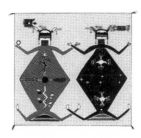

LAND (RE)ACQUISITION

Native Americans, especially those living on reserves or reservations, tend not to view land as a commodity. Connections with the land are long and deep. Creation itself is associated with specific locations on the contemporary map. Food came from the land, and with it, all religion, healing, and spirituality. One reason for the Indians' dispossession is that their concept of land use and "ownership" so differed from that of non-natives. Time after time, native people testified that they had no idea that the treaties they signed took away their lands so completely and irrevocably. When they did sign, knowing that they were giving up their lands on some level, it was almost always under conditions of extreme pressure and accompanied by deep humiliation and shame.

Even today, with relatively few native people able to engage in traditional subsistence activities, especially in the United States, the land retains its profound importance. It is still strongly linked with origin, identity, religion, and economy, and it is also linked with various crucial legal rights. In 1999, Native Americans controlled roughly 2.5 percent of their aboriginal land. Many groups spend a great deal of time, money, and energy trying to reacquire control of lands that are legally still theirs or lands that have been taken from them by often unscrupulous means.

Possession of the Black Hills in South Dakota is a classic case. By any reasonable standard, insofar as they can be said to belong to anybody, they belong to the Lakota people. After excruciating legal battles, federal courts agreed, and awarded the people cash for their land claim. However, unlike most native groups, Lakota tribes have refused the money and insist on return of the land. Some members of Congress have tried, unsuccessfully, to acknowledge the Indians' "ownership" of the hills and arrange for a partial return. In the meantime, non-natives have so polluted parts of the Black Hills that at one point the U.S. government considered labeling the Lakota holy site a National Sacrifice Area. This long and tragic saga has yet to be resolved.

In Alberta, Canada, the political details differ but the result is similar. Federal and provincial authorities have permitted non-native companies to extract billions of dollars worth of resources from unceded Lubicon Cree land. The mining activities have caused extensive environmental pollution and have spread poverty, despair, and sickness among a people who were recently self-sufficient. In fact, at one point, dispossession and environmental destruction threatened to wipe out the people entirely. After a hard fight, the Lubicon Cree will probably get some of their land back, but because of the pollution, it is unlikely that they will regain the economic independence they enjoyed just a generation ago.

The Western Shoshone Nation claims a great deal of Nevada by right of aboriginal possession, never having ceded its land in any treaty. Like the Lakota, these people have been offered and have refused monetary compensation. The Western Shoshone have so far managed to avoid the environmental contamination suffered by the Lakota and Lubicon Cree people, although non-native mining companies have their eye on the land. Federal courts have ruled on the issues, reversed themselves, and re-reversed themselves so many times that the people are no longer waiting for even a "victor's justice." For the crime of grazing cattle on their unceded land, they have been subject to a regular campaign of arrest and property seizure.

All three cases illustrate the tenacity with which native people continue to fight for their land. Many non-natives cannot understand why, for instance, the Lakota, many of whom suffer severely from poverty, will not accept an award now worth almost a half-trillion dollars for the grossly polluted Black Hills. In part, the answer lies in what it means to be a Lakota, a Lubicon Cree, a Western Shoshone, an Indian. As native educational levels rise, and as the people grow more sophisticated in dealing with U.S. and Canadian institutions, native legal experts will increasingly challenge the murky or downright fraudulent nature of so many treaties. This may mean that they will begin to reverse the long history of their exploitation and reacquire some of the land to which they are, by legal agreement, entitled.

LAKOTA

The case of the Black Hills is among the most well known and infamous land grabs in U.S. history. The struggle over the Black Hills was at least partly responsible for the destruction of the Seventh Cavalry in 1876 and for the slaughter of thousands of Lakota and other Indians in the late nineteenth century. More recently, it serves as a rallying point for Indian patriots for whom, as they demonstrate every day, land can never be exchanged for money. These people, mainly Lakota Indians, have refused compensation for the Black Hills and expect some day to reacquire them.

The Black Hills have meant different things to different people. The Lakota were not the first native group whose territory included the Black Hills, nor were they the first who regarded the hills as sacred. (Other groups include the Kiowa, Kiowa-Apache, Comanche, Cheyenne, and Arapaho.) They were, however, the last native group to do so and certainly the most powerful and determined to retain them. Lakotas traditionally observed a correlation between certain features of the hills and the stars and based their

Three Lakota chiefs—from left, Vincent Blackfeathers, Spencer Westerton, and Isaac White Face Sr.—in July 1999. Lakotas have been insisting that the U.S. government return the Black Hills under the terms of the 1868 Fort Laramie Treaty. (AP Photo/J. Scott Applewhite)

mythology and their seasonal movements on these associations. For the Lakota, the Black Hills, or Paha Sapa, are the heart and soul of their very identity.

Non-natives have a different perspective on the hills. In the 1860s, having suffered defeat at the hands of Red Cloud and other Lakotas in alliance with Cheyenne and Arapaho warriors, the United States signed the Fort Laramie Treaty of 1868. The treaty established the boundaries of Sioux country and obligated the United States to respect those boundaries unless three-fourths of adult male Indians of signatory tribes desired a change. At the time of the signing the Dakota (Sioux) people were a sovereign nation in every sense of the term and were recognized as such by the United States.

Shortly thereafter, however, and in violation of the treaty, Gen. George A. Custer led an expedition into the Black Hills in which gold was discovered. Unable to persuade the Indians to cede the hills, the government, again in violation of the treaty, simply pulled the army away and allowed miners to swarm into the hills. The Battle of the Little Bighorn/Greasy Grass (1876) was to a large extent an effort by the United States to seize the Black Hills by force and by the Indians to defend their rights under the Fort Laramie Treaty.

The Lakota won the battle, but they lost the war. Failing again to obtain the necessary number of signatures, the U.S. Army pursued a "total war" policy against the Lakota, destroying villages, killing noncombatants, and forcing leaders to surrender. For its part, Congress simply passed the Black Hills Act of 1877 and unilaterally appropriated 7.7 million acres of the Black Hills. (The act also appropriated tens of millions more acres of Dakota land.) Non-native mineral and energy companies went on to extract tens of billions of dollars worth of gold, uranium, timber, and other resources from the Black Hills. Pollution of the hills by heavy metals and nuclear waste is so severe and widespread that the government at one time considered labeling them part of a National Sacrifice Area.

The treaty signatories—Rosebud, Oglala, Cheyenne River, Standing Rock, Lower Brulé, Crow Creek, Santee, and Fort Peck Dakota—have never recognized the legality of the Black Hills Act. In 1923, as soon as they had obtained the statutory authority, the Indians sued the United States for return of the Black Hills. No firm decision was forthcoming until 1974, when the Indian Claims Commission (ICC) ruled that the U.S. seizure of the hills was illegal because, in violation of the Fifth Amendment, the government had neither compensated the Indians nor obtained the land fairly and honorably.

The ICC mandated compensation of $17.5 million plus 5 percent interest. A year later the Court of Claims reversed this decision, based on a legal technicality pertaining to the compensation issue, but it left open the possibility of a payment—without interest—on the fairness issue. In its decision, the court concluded that "a more ripe and rank case of dishonorable dealings will never, in all probability, be found in our history."

In 1978, Congress acted to allow the courts to consider the case without regard to the legal technicality, and the following year the courts reinstated the award of $17.5 million plus interest—$122.5 million. The United States promptly appealed, but in 1980, the Supreme Court upheld the ruling. Significantly, the court never spoke to the issue of whether or not the land could be returned, since this was generally considered to be in the purview of Congress. Since the Lakota have never seriously considered accepting the award in lieu of the land, the money remains in a Treasury account, gathering interest. Efforts to reoccupy the hills and to force the hand of the United States by appealing to international law have proved fruitless.

Unlike much land claimed by Indians, about 1.3 million acres of the Black Hills is still "owned" by the United States (as opposed to private interests) and thus could be returned by it. Since only Congress has the authority to "return" land, the Lakota succeeded in having a bill introduced in 1985 that called for financial payment *and* land return. The so-called Bradley bill would "reconvey full title" to roughly 750,000 acres of the Black Hills to the Lakota Nation. It would also reconvey partial title to tens of thousands of acres more, including several sacred sites. In an explicit acknowledgment that the Lakota never ceded title to the hills, payments were to be considered "damages" rather than "compensation."

The South Dakota congressional delegation and state officials strongly opposed the bill, and it was withdrawn in 1990. Another reason for the bill's failure was opposition within the Lakota ranks. Some leaders drew up a competing bill calling for significantly greater compensation as well as near total political sovereignty over all reservation lands. That bill, too, died in 1990.

The 1990s have brought mainly inertia to the fight for the Black Hills. A few Lakotas have called for moving beyond the impasse. They argue that true liberation from over a century of dependence and despair will only be achieved through economic independence and urge their compatriots to use the award monies, valued in 1997 at $424,000,000, to buy more land, perhaps in the Black Hills, or to trade their money for federal lands in the Black Hills. Some call for uniting behind a new bill and using the money for a massive lobbying campaign.

In fact, the Fort Peck (Montana) Assiniboine Sioux in 1997 were the first to break ranks, voting overwhelmingly to accept their share of the settlement money. Embattled Sioux Council Chair Raymond "Abby" Ogle maintains that the people will never get the land back, but his opponents claim that he needs the money to cover unwise loans. Furthermore, the Great Sioux Nation Treaty Council has raised questions about Ft. Peck Sioux's being party to the land claim in the first place.

Meanwhile, the Black Hills remain the center of the universe, the most sacred place on earth, for the Lakota people. Opposition remains nearly unanimous to continued development of the hills, including a proposed 100-million-dollar resort by actor Kevin Costner and a massive stone sculpture of their great leader Crazy Horse. Whether or not they ever reacquire the hills, most Lakota people today stand behind the words of Crazy Horse: "You do not sell the land the people walk on."

CREE (LUBICON)

The 500-member Lubicon Lake Cree Nation, located in northern Alberta, Canada, was pursuing a land claim with the Canadian and provincial governments when oil was discovered on tribal land. Until that time, the Lubicon people had been a small group of isolated Indians living fairly traditionally. Their main camp was located near Lubicon Lake, called Prairie Lake by the people themselves. Within a decade of the 1979 onset of drilling, the people's ability to hunt and trap was shattered, their land became poisoned, and their health declined sharply. Dependence and despair took the place of self-sufficiency. The Lubicon Cree lost battle after battle for control over their land, but they have never surrendered the war.

The land issue revolves around the "official status" of the Lubicon people as well as the federal transfer of Lubicon land to the provincial government in 1930. Canada maintains that Treaty Eight (1899) gave them the right to transfer the land. However, the Lubicon Cree maintained that they were one of a number of bands that were "overlooked" during the treaty process and deny that they ever signed Treaty Eight. In any case, in 1939 the Canadian government agreed to recognize the Lubicon people as a separate band. Part of the deal included a 25.4-square-mile reserve.

For various reasons, including the onset of World War II, the Indians' isolation, and government foot dragging, the claim was never resolved. Formal recognition—without a land claims settlement—finally took place in 1973. When an all-weather road into the Lubicon area was completed in 1979, oil drilling began in earnest. Oil companies obtained hundreds of leases from the provincial government. They and their affiliated industries built an extensive infrastructure of roads and pipelines. The companies drilled more than 400 wells within a 15-mile radius of the Little Buffalo Lake Community, the main Lubicon settlement. Within 10 years more than 100 companies were active in the area. Between 1979 and 1996, more than $8 billion in resources had been extracted from Lubicon land.

Seeking to stem the tide, the band in 1980 sued Canada, Alberta, and various oil companies for the promised reserve and $1 billion in compensatory damages as a result of oil drilling and associated detrimental activities. The claim was based on aboriginal title or, if this were rejected, on Treaty Eight (since the band was in the Treaty Eight area) privileges or, if this were rejected, on the grounds that the reserve they were promised was never delivered. While the case was in litigation, however, development continued and, in fact, expanded dramatically.

Without consulting the Indians, Alberta leased 11,000 square miles of land, including all of the Lubicon Cree's traditional territory, to Daishowa-Marubeni International of Japan. In 1990, Daishowa built a bleached kraft pulp mill in the area. The mill is the largest in Canada and consumes over 4 million trees per year. At this rate of deforestation, the Lubicons' return to their traditional life may be impossible. The mill also releases massive amounts of toxic organic compounds into the ecosystem.

Industrialization has been almost a complete disaster for the Lubicon Cree. Most of the game that the people hunted and trapped has been either shot intentionally by industry workers or has declined owing to loss or poisoning of habitat. Annual income fell by over 90 percent between 1979 and 1995; welfare dependency, virtually unknown before the oil wells and logging, reached 95 percent in the mid-1980s. Health problems abound, and living conditions, as a result of poverty and neglect, are among the worst in Canada. In 1984, the World Council of Churches felt compelled to warn the Canadian government that it courted genocide in this matter. In 1990, the United Nations formally charged Canada with a human rights violation with regard to its treatment of the Lubicon Cree.

Equally as serious, at least in terms of cultural survival, has been the effect of industrialization on the transmission of skills, knowledge, and lore having to do with the people's traditional life. And, since they were largely based on hunting and trapping, ceremonialism and religious faith have also undergone a parallel crisis. In place of the continuity of a sense of place and belonging, growing numbers of people, mainly the young, are experiencing alienation and despair. Unable to participate in either their traditional lifestyle or the modern world, many people have fallen victim to the social problems, such as alcoholism and suicide, that plague so many poor and struggling communities.

On the other hand, since the disaster is of such recent occurrence, many Lubicon Crees still derive a great deal of strength and inspiration from their close connection with the land. Led by their elders and their energetic chief, Bernard Ominayak, the people continue to press for a just resolution of the situation. For instance, a boycott of a Shell Oil exhibit of Indian art at the 1988 Olympics led to renewed negotiations. They have also organized a support network that is international in scope and that has achieved significant results. The highest profile activity of this network has been a boycott of Daishowa Corporation. After holding the clear-cutting at bay for seven years, organizers ended the boycott in 1998 after Daishowa, citing losses of more than $14 million, agreed to cease logging operations in the disputed area until after the issues were resolved between the Lubicon people and both the national and provincial governments.

There have been some hopeful signs that the land claims issue might be resolved. Formal negotiations resumed in 1995 and were given an additional boost in 1998. The Lubicon people are asking for 157 square miles of land, $72 million for housing and services, and around $33 million for development. They also want $120 million from Ottawa and Alberta in compensation for the removal of forestry and energy resources. Issues impeding progress include the government's refusal to provide meaningful compensation for irreparable damage to the people's way of life, disagreements over the size of the band (and thus the size of the payments), and Canada's possible reluctance to settle because of the implications for the cases of other similarly small, "unrecognized" bands who have fallen through the cracks of national native policies.

In February 1999, negotiators announced a draft agreement on the key issue of band membership—the Lubicon people want all band members to have recognition under the Indian Act, while the government is concerned about extending that status to "too many" people. Negotiations continue to finalize this agreement and also to resolve outstanding disagreements on reserve land and community development. For the first time in 60 years, a resolution to the tragedy of Lubicon Lake Cree may be at hand.

WESTERN SHOSHONE

In Nevada, two elderly sisters named Dann refuse to pay grazing fees to the Bureau of Land Management (BLM) on the grounds that the land belongs to their people, the Western Shoshone Nation (WSN). The government denies their claim, confiscates their cattle, and issues eviction notices. Meanwhile, transnational companies prepare a massive gold mining operation on the land. Leaders of the WSN organize a defensive occupation. Underlying the whole controversy are the twin issues of treaty interpretation and the very identity of the Western Shoshone people. A look at the positions of the Western Shoshone, the BLM and the Interior Department, the courts, and other parties to the dispute reveals important aspects of the politics of Indian land (re)acquisition.

Traditionally, the people now known as Western Shoshone had no tribal identity at all. The largest unit of group identity among these people was probably the extended family or the band, although the people also came together on occasion in larger groups. Shoshones did not recognize private property but rather moved freely over the vast distances needed to support their existence in a precarious environment.

In 1863, the chiefs of some Western Shoshone bands signed a "treaty of peace and friendship" with the U.S. government. Ratified in 1869, the Treaty of Ruby Valley forms the basis of the Western Shoshone claim to two-thirds of the state of Nevada and parts of other states as well. Meanwhile, although perhaps as many as two-thirds of Western Shoshones continued to live in at least a semitraditional way apart from any reservation well into the twentieth century, non-native encroachment gradually led to a general loss of land. In the 1930s, the United States stepped up its hitherto half-hearted project of recognizing Western Shoshone bands and leaders of its own creation. A number of Western Shoshone governments were created under the Indian Reorganization Act (IRA).

Also in the 1930s, one group of Western Shoshones began legal action to pursue their land claim. For various reasons (including personal financial gain), the attorneys for this group, the Te-Moak Bands (itself an IRA creation), stipulated land loss owing to encroachment and pressed in the 1940s for compensation instead of the land itself. A split developed within the Te-Moak Bands Tribal Council over the issue of land versus compensation. At no time did this group represent a majority of Western Shoshone people. However, for its own purposes the United States recognized the Te-Moak Bands Tribal Council as the exclusive representative of the Western Shoshone people and blocked traditionalist groups from participating in the claims process.

The Indian Claims Commission (ICC) weighed in on the case in 1962, agreeing that the Western Shoshone had lost their land title. The date arbitrarily decided on for the loss—July 1, 1872—was only three years after the adoption of the Treaty of Ruby Valley, a period when the non-native population of Western Shoshone country was minuscule, certainly not enough to have taken over the entire territory. By 1979, the U.S. Court of Claims (the ICC had been disbanded a year earlier) had decided (without Western Shoshone input) on a figure of $26 million in compensatory funds and prepared to settle the Western Shoshone claim.

Meanwhile, in the 1970s and early '80s, nationalist strength within the Western Shoshone groups grew to the point where the Western Shoshone Nation was proclaimed in January 1984. Five years later its governing body, the Western Shoshone National Council (WSNC), consisted of 18 groups.

The WSNC's organizational statement (constitution) gives it the power to deal with issues that affect the Western Shoshone people as a whole, thus establishing, for the first time, a true Western Shoshone nation. The WSNC never desired compensation for the disputed land. In fact, in 1976 even the Te-Moak Bands Council switched its position, joining those who rejected a monetary settlement and claimed full title to the land.

Since the mid-1980s, however, the unity of the WSN has broken down. (Some people maintain that the group consists of a small number of Western Shoshones and their non-native supporters.) In the late 1990s, Western Shoshone groups are represented by tribal councils. These, in turn, reflect many interests, such as those of wealthier cattle owners, for whom the amount of past-due grazing fees might exceed what they would receive as a per capita share of judgment funds, and those people who would prefer to receive their share of these funds on a per capita basis. Many Western Shoshones do not even live on a reservation; these people have still different needs and interests.

Enter the Danns. For generations, the Dann family had allowed their horses and cattle to graze on land outside their 800 acres located in Crescent Valley. In May 1974, the BLM advised Mary and Carrie Dann of its intent to sue them for grazing fees that the Danns had refused to pay, since they did not recognize BLM authority over the land. Legal challenges to this action provided a venue for the judicial hearing of the Western Shoshone land claim. The one court that examined the case on its merits, the Ninth Circuit Court of Appeals, found in 1978 no evidence to support the government's claim that the Western Shoshones' aboriginal land rights had been extinguished.

In 1980, a district court ruled that Western Shoshone title had been good until December 1979, when the tribe had received compensation for the land from the Court of Claims (the award had been accepted by the secretary of the interior but not by the WSN). An appeals court ruled in 1983 that the Danns (the Western Shoshone) had never lost title to their land, either in 1872 or in 1979. However, two years later the U.S. Supreme Court ruled that the Western Shoshone had no standing owing to the loss of their title by gradual encroachment, *as found by the ICC*, a technicality that effectively halted further judicial consideration of the case on its merits. The ruling left room for the Danns to claim *individual* aboriginal rights, a claim that was upheld in 1986. However, although the ruling allowed the Danns to use the land, it did not acknowledge title based on the Ruby Valley Treaty.

Finally, on appeal, the Ninth Circuit Court reversed itself in 1989 and ruled that the people *had* lost title to the land in 1872. This decision allowed the BLM to continue its actions against the Danns. In 1992, in an effort to resist the BLM, the WSNC "nationalized" the Danns' cattle. This action by a sovereign nation should have provided the full protection of international law, but the BLM, citing legal rulings barring the WSNC from standing in the land claims case, refused to recognize its authority. Later that year armed BLM agents seized over 40 of the nation's horses.

Stymied by the U.S. government, the Danns in 1993 took their case to the Inter-American Commission on Human Rights, an arm of the Organization of American States (OAS). They seek an impartial hearing over the issue of Western Shoshone ownership of the disputed land, which Western Shoshones call Newe Sogobia (roughly "the people's earth mother"). Their ongoing fight won them the 1993 human rights award from Sweden's Right Livelihood Foundation. In 1993, and again in 1998, the OAS formally requested that the United States stay its actions against the Western Shoshone pending a full investigation by that body. The United States has declined to comply with the OAS ruling.

Meanwhile, in 1996, the Canada-based Oro Nevada Mining Company bought the nearby Dean Ranch, a purchase that surrounds the Dann land with 93,000 acres of company land including mining claims. The Indians hold that the mines will further damage and deface sacred land protected by treaty. They noted that one drill site was located on a Western Shoshone cultural and spiritual encampment where an annual gathering took place. The Interior Department, which oversees mining regulations and is also charged with protecting the interests of Indian tribes, has ignored Western Shoshone concerns. After drilling 37 holes, Oro Nevada withdrew from the valley in 1997, at least temporarily.

In March 1997, the WSNC sought an injunction against further invasions of their land and breaches of their sovereignty by either the United States or private mining companies pending resolution of the land dispute. Their legal tactics escalated to a lawsuit in late 1998, by which means the nation hopes to resolve the outstanding issues once and for all. The Interior Board of Land Appeals (IBLA) imposed a stay on BLM actions against the Danns in August 1998, giving further credibility to the Indians' claims.

The 1979 land claim "award" is the focus of a great deal of controversy. In 1998, members of four tribes in question—Te-Moak, Duckwater, Ely, and Yomba—voted on the distribution of funds (valued at $105 million). The result was overwhelmingly in favor of per capita payments. However, tribal representatives against 100 percent per capita payments, and concerned about the resolution of land issues, have sought to reverse this vote by questioning its legality.

Fines against the Danns and the WSN in 1998 amounted to over $500,000. Even Western Shoshones who do not necessarily support the WSN believe strongly that they maintain key rights under the Treaty of Ruby Valley. (One reason that so many voted to accept distribution of the land claims fund was their belief that receipt in no way compromises their rights under that treaty.) Some of these people are more interested in translating their rights into land for housing than for running cattle. The Western Shoshone have a compelling land claims case and grievance against the BLM. Right now, the government holds the land, the money, and a Supreme Court decision in its favor, but even this may not be enough to thwart the aspirations of a determined people.

MEDIA

Like anyone else, Native Americans may establish careers in communications. However, as a group they tend to face several obstacles, such as relatively low education levels, poor access to resources, and outright discrimination, that people who are not members of minority groups do not generally have to confront. On the other hand, native people enjoy particular opportunities to serve their communities (few reserves or reservations have radio or television stations that directly serve Indian populations) or to work in the growing field of Native American media.

KTNN, the Voice of the Navajo Nation, has an enormous range (as it must, to reach the huge Navajo Reservation). It provides news and entertainment, in English and Navajo, to a widely scattered and diverse community, many of whom do not have television, telephone service, or even electricity (many people tune the station in on car or truck radios). Its on-air personalities and eclectic, Navajo-language programming are all part of the draw.

Several colleges, such as Salish Kootenai College (SKC), offer programs specifically designed to meet the needs of Native American students. At SKC, a television station provides technical training as well as a range of services, including Indian programming and satellite links, to the Flathead Reservation. Unlike KTNN, whose audience is mainly Indian, SKC-TV directs its largely educational programming as much toward non-natives as Indians, although there are some shows specifically designed for the latter. Despite their ties to tribal governments, both KTNN and SKC-TV have established a functional independence.

On a far larger scale, and outside of any one community, northern Canadian networks and Native American Public Telecommunications (NAPT) provide a wide range of technical opportunities as well as highly innovative programming to regional, national, and worldwide audiences. NAPT's mission also includes an overtly political element: to empower native people in the use and control of all types of information technology. Though different in both scope and design from KTNN or SKC-TV, like these stations NAPT and the Canadian entities exist primarily for key native constituencies, some of which, until recently, have been quite isolated.

While native people still face more obstacles than do non-natives in entering many fields, Native American media—radio, television, newspapers, electronic information and publishing—provide significant professional opportunities for training, creative expression, and employment. The media also provide a chance for wider and more meaningful communication among native groups and between natives and non-natives. These developments have already improved life for many Native Americans.

NAVAJO

Indian radio stations are still something of a rarity. With fewer than 30 in the United States (Canada has many small "bush" stations), it follows that most Indian communities lack access to radio programming specifically designed to meet their needs and interests. This situation is particularly hard on Indian people who speak only or primarily their native language and who perhaps are also elderly and isolated. Such stations that exist take their missions seriously—but, for many, their on-air personality is far from that.

One of the more interesting Indian radio stations is KTNN-AM, broadcasting out of Window Rock, Arizona, capital of the Navajo Nation, since 1986. Roughly half of its on-air personalities are women and, to judge from their radio personae, wild women at that. KTNN jocks receive marriage proposals by the score and, in fact, delight in "romancing" their audience. The women's punchy, familiar, down-home style is one reason that the entertainment publication E! Online selected KTNN as the number-one station in the United States.

Although owned by the Navajo Nation (or perhaps because of this fact), KTNN considers itself representative of the community at large. That is, KTNN is not an official organ of the Nation, nor is it a place to receive only the government's perspective on news and public affairs. The station's motto, "We hold nothing and no one sacred," reveals an intensely independent ethos. In fact, Tazbah McCullah, general manager of KTNN, once aired a controversial show that focused on the marriage problems of former Navajo Nation president Albert Hale. Hale could have fired McCullah and other KTNN staff, although, out of respect for the station's independence, he did not.

The station's format is as eclectic as its politics. Depending on the time of day, listeners might tune in to traditional and avant-garde Navajo music (including B. Johnson, Vincent Craig, the Chinle Valley Singers, and the Sweethearts of Navajoland), other Indian bands (such as Brule, Sharon Burch, Casper, Clandestine, Fun-

The logo of one of the larger Navajo radio stations, KTNN. (Reproduced with the kind permission of KTNN)

maker, Haida, Poetic Justice, Red Earth, and XIT), bilingual news, powwow music, country music, jazz, reggae, rock, and bluegrass as well as live music and a range of talk shows.

KTNN's mission to serve its audience leads to work that most radio stations never need to consider, because other stations operate to serve a particular demographic segment of the population, whereas KTNN aims at the entire population of a huge geographic area. Discussions about sex and family issues coexist with more traditional news and information. The station must accommodate the needs of the roughly 6,000 people in the community who speak only Navajo (programmers also consider the various regional dialects of the Nation's members). Respect must be shown to listeners who might prefer to hear something—perhaps a geographical feature—referred to by its Navajo name, which might have spiritual or religious connotations, rather than its English name, which, for some, might be associated with colonialism and oppression.

Because many people depend on KTNN not only for entertainment but as a crucial—and, in some cases, the only—source of news and information, the station maintains a full-time news department. Only about one-quarter of Navajo households have telephones. Of the households with television, most get only commercial stations from nearby cities like Albuquerque and Farmington, although NNTV (Navajo Nation TV), a low-power television station, has recently gone on air. With the exception of NNTV, these outlets provide little, if any, coverage of Navajo issues. On the other hand, almost everyone owns an AM radio, if only in a car or truck. Distances are large on the reservation, and the roads are rough. Many people spend a good deal of time in their vehicles in order to get supplies, go to meetings, visit, and so on.

Technologically, KTNN is up to date. The studio is fully computerized and digital. It operates continuously over a clear-channel radio signal at 50,000 watts on 660 MHz to a very wide audience: During the day its signal covers southeastern Utah, southwestern Colorado, and much of northern Arizona and New Mexico; at night it includes up to 13 western states and northern Mexico, and listeners sometimes call in from as far away as Canada. If the range seems unusually large, it is: In 1984, KTNN received the last 50,000-watt clear permit to be issued in the United States. Unlike most stations, clear channels have only one other station in the country with the same frequency. This greatly facilitates a very wide signal area at night, when the AM signals skip around the atmosphere. Thus, these permits were extremely valuable.

KTNN is not the only radio station in the area. The Navajo Nation also owns all-country KWRK, which operates out of Window Rock. KGAK, in Gallup, converted to an all-Navajo format in late 1998. That is, programs will be broadcast in both Navajo and English, but programming will focus on the Navajo Nation. Another station, Farmington-based KNDN, has had an all-Navajo format since 1957. Perhaps its signature is an open mike policy that allows Navajo people to go on air, almost at any time, to talk about issues of interest or concern to them or to keep in touch with family members.

In 1999, Navajo Nation president Kelsey Begaye announced plans to construct a full digital infrastructure within the Navajo Nation. A first step, and one dependent on emerging Federal Communications Commission policy, would be the operation of one or more low-power radio stations with a strictly Navajo focus. It is unclear whether this plan will materialize or, if it does, what effect it might have on KTNN. In any case, KTNN, the Voice of the Navajo Nation, seems to have captured a unique and valuable niche in community life and is probably here to stay.

SALISH AND KOOTENAI PEOPLE AND AIHEC

Tribal television stations are even scarcer than radio stations. There were just a handful of Indian-affiliated television stations in the mid-1990s, located in such places as Metlakatla, Alaska; Lame Deer, Montana; Cherokee, North Carolina; and Fort Yates, North Dakota. In many ways, the facilities at Salish Kootenai College in Montana illustrate some of the problems and possibilities in Native American television broadcasting. Their Media and Teleproductions Center is home to Salish Kootenai College television, or SKC-TV, a low-power public television station whose four transmitters serve about 90 percent of the Flathead Reservation in Montana through ultrahigh frequency (UHF) broadcast and cable systems.

The station's audience is the general population of the reservation. While approximately 80 percent of the community is non-native, most of the station's roughly three hours per week of local programming focuses on Indian themes. This is because station managers believe that nearby commercial television stations, plus other non-native media, do a good job covering non-Indian issues. Despite this imbalance (and despite the presence on the reservation of various white-rights organizations), the station has served as an effective bridge builder between Indian and non-native residents of the Flathead Reservation.

Public Broadcasting Service (PBS) shows comprise the core of SKC-TV's programming; other shows have included Salish and Kootenai language classes, "Good Medicine" (a health show), overviews of tribal council meetings, "Montana Serenade" (music), "Cookin' with the Colonel" (native foods), and a variety of special and community events. Local schools such as the Two Eagle River School have also produced and aired their own shows. SKC-TV also produces, under contract for nonprofit and governmental organizations, programs such as the recent educational series on acquired immunodeficiency syndrome (AIDS) for Indian audiences.

One of the station's most important services is its connection with the American Indian Higher Education Consortium (AIHEC) and its Distance Learning Network (DLN). The DLN, based at Northwest Indian College (Bellingham, Washington), was established by AIHEC member colleges (including Salish Kootenai College) to address the lack of access to educational opportunities among native populations. DLN was established in the early

1990s, before the federal commitment to developing a national technology infrastructure. However, the network remains technologically appropriate, since some areas have either no telephone service at all or service that is inadequate for Internet support.

The Department of Commerce provided funding for AIHEC to install a satellite receiver station as well as a transmission station at the SKC Media and Teleproductions Center (as well as at other AIHEC colleges). According to its mission statement, the DLN exists to develop national and regional interactive telecommunications networks linking tribal- and Bureau of Indian Affairs (BIA)–operated schools in order to deliver enhanced and expanded postsecondary educational services for Indian people throughout the United States.

SKC-TV produces distance education uplinks and accesses downlinks for AIHEC over its Satellite Network. In the spring of 1998, the DLN broadcast nine courses, including "American Indian Law and Tribal Rights," that originated at SKC. The DLN also produced or transmitted several teleconferences on subjects including technology careers, technology in the classroom, and aspects of child advocacy law. Some colleges have taken the lead in integrating DLN satellite communications and the Internet to share local community cultural programming. In the future, DLN would like to produce programming that would include entertainment, intercollege student council, native education news, elders' assemblies, and cultural and language classes via a dedicated satellite channel.

Far more than a television station that happens to be located on an Indian reservation, SKC-TV offers students opportunities on many levels to become involved in the station. Classes in photography and video production are linked with the station's facilities, and students may gain further professional knowledge and training by serving as interns at the station. In fact, students are a vital resource in developing and maintaining facilities and systems.

Salish Kootenai College is also involved, through two of its faculty members (1998), in the National Computational Science Alliance; the AIHEC is one of the alliance's 60 research partners. This group is developing a National Technology Grid that will be used to solve problems collaboratively on a national, multidisciplinary scale. Funding for the alliance's activities is provided through the National Science Foundation (NSF). The SKC participants are funded through the Alliance for Minority Participation of the NSF.

Like many PBS stations, SKC-TV is funded through viewer memberships and local business underwriting (these contributions came to roughly $25,000 in 1998, or about 50 percent of the total budget, a figure that underscores the strength of Indian businesses on the reservation as well as the station's popularity among non-natives). SKC-TV also receives funds from the Confederated Salish and Kootenai Tribes (roughly $17,000 in 1998). Despite the tribal council's willingness to contribute matching funds, it has little input into programming decisions, partly because the station's licenses are held by the college (although the tribal council appoints the college's board of directors) and partly because of the station's solid overall reputation.

SKC-TV is currently a two-person operation. It has neither the staff nor the funds to become a community-access station, although, because it is a low-power station, its less than $200 a month operational costs are far lower than if the station converted to a full-power facility. Still, its small size notwithstanding, the station is an integral part of the Flathead Reservation, a resource upon which thousands of people count every day, and a model for both Indian and non-native community media.

AIROS, NATIVE AMERICA CALLING, AND NAPT

Tribal newspapers and radio and television stations will always play a vital role in their communities, but Native American telecommunications also exist on a national scale. In the north country, the Canadian Broadcasting Corporation (CBC) and Television Northern Canada (TVNC) play a dominant role. In 1995, CBC North TV went daily with news gathered and produced in the north and distributed to almost 100,000 people in the Northwest Territories and the Yukon.

TVNC is a nonprofit corporation that distributes local, aboriginal television and cable vision programming over an area of roughly 2.5 million square miles. It reaches an audience of 100,000 in 97 communities who speak 15 aboriginal languages. In 1999, TVNC began full transmission into the Aboriginal People's Television Network (APTN), a national television network by and about native people living in Canada. There are also a number of other native television organizations, such as Inuit and Cree Radio and TV Community Broadcasters (Nunavik, Arctic Quebec).

Organizations such as NAPT and American Indian Radio on Satellite (AIROS) have also been leaders with a variety of native-produced and -distributed programming. Not only do these groups reach out to Indians who may not have access to tribal media (in 1999 there were only 25 native radio stations in the continental United States, with another 10 in Alaskan native communities) and help build a national Indian consciousness, they also serve as places where native people can receive professional training and build careers in the growing telecommunications industry.

NAPT, whose slogan is "Empowering, Educating and Entertaining through Native Media," is an umbrella organization that receives major funding from the Corporation for Public Broadcasting (CPB). NAPT was founded as Native American Public Broadcasting Consortium in 1976 but changed its name in 1995 to reflect the fact that its focus had moved beyond public television and radio. Its overarching goal is to support tribal sovereignty. As a media group, it works toward achieving this goal by encouraging the awareness of tribal histories, cultures, languages, and aspirations through the fullest possible participation of American Indians and Alaska Natives. In other words, NAPT strives to be proactive and grassroots based, rather than paternalistic and management directed like so many non-native organizations have traditionally been.

NAPT provides training opportunities to encourage Indians and Alaska Natives to produce quality programs. It also promotes increased control and use of information technologies by native people. In fact, NAPT helps to create awareness of national telecommunications policies and provides leadership in developing such policies that are favorable to Native Americans. Finally, NAPT actively reaches out to native communities and Indian organizations in an effort to build partnerships to develop and implement telecommunications projects.

Although NAPT does most of its work in radio and television, it is not limited to these media. One of its projects is the maintenance and operation of IndianNet, the first national Indian-owned interactive information network. IndianNet provides a number of important services to the native (and non-native) community, including graphic design, the development of websites, and the hosting, storing, and marketing of client home pages. (Clients in early 1999 included Futures for Children, the Alliance of Tribal Tourism Advocates, and Small Business Ballpark.)

NAPT initiated the Tribal Infrastructure Information Project (TIIP) in 1994 to create a plan for a national demonstration project for American Indian tribal governments to participate in the National Information Infrastructure. The six tribes initially participating in the project (Sisseton Wahpeton Sioux Tribe, Eastern Band of Cherokee Indians, Standing Rock Sioux Tribe, Southern Ute Indian Tribe, Turtle Mountain Chippewa Tribe, and Campo Band of Mission Indians) received further training through California State University at Monterey Bay.

One of NAPT's more recent and high-profile initiatives is the award-winning "Native America Calling," a live, daily, national call-in radio show that explores contemporary issues concerning Native America and its neighbors. Listeners may tune in on the radio or become part of a truly international community by catching the program live on the World Wide Web. The show is based in Albuquerque, New Mexico, but regularly goes on tour to sites such as the Alaska Federation of Natives Convention; the National Museum of American Indian Film, Video and Radio Festival; the Canadian Aboriginal Festival; and the National Congress of American Indians Convention.

Recent programs on "Native America Calling" have included "New Agers in Indian Country," "The Cassini Probe of the National Aeronautics and Space Administration," "Indian National Finals Rodeo," "The Alaska Native Claims Settlement Act," "Homophobia in Native America," "Spider Woman Theatre," "Children of Alcoholics," "Gambling Our Sovereignty," "Crisis in Chiapas," and "Bones Controversy," a program about a dispute over the repatriation of Indian remains. Guests have included Kevin Gover (new BIA director), Suzan Harjo (activist), Tim Giago (editor of the newspaper *Indian Country Today*), Oren Lyons (Onondaga leader), Buffy St. Marie (entertainer), Michael Trujillo (Indian Health Service director), and Ada Deer (Menominee activist and former head of the BIA). The show airs Monday through Thursday with a special Wellness Edition on Fridays.

"Native America Calling" is distributed by AIROS. Founded in 1993, AIROS is a national distribution system for native programming through Native American and other public radio stations as well as the Internet. AIROS is the only public radio satellite distribution system exclusively carrying native programming. Furthermore, AIROS programming operates 24 hours a day, seven days a week. AIROS also provides RealAudio archive files and allows visitors on the World Wide Web to access a week's worth of programs at any time.

"Native America Calling" is AIROS's flagship program, but there are others as well. "AlterNative Voices," originating from KUVO-FM in Denver, features native music, interviews, and news. "The Infinite Mind" is a weekly show that explores the mind and mental health. "Native Sounds–Native Voices," an award-winning music show, is produced in two formats: a national edition and various regional productions. It showcases the many aspects of native music not easily available (or not available at all) in the mainstream radio marketplace. "Different Drums" (KBBI, Homer, Alaska) is another award-winning music program. Finally, "New Letters on the Air" features interviews with authors who are, or who write about, Native Americans. The best of the shows heard over AIROS underscore the diversity of native cultures across North America.

NAPT supports a number of other projects as well. The Public Television Program Fund is available to both native and non-native independent filmmakers to produce programming for national distribution on PBS. Ongoing projects (early 1999) include Indian cowboys, Osage ballerina Maria Tallchief, and the Iroquois roots of democracy in the United States. Vision Maker Productions promotes feature films and teleplays based on original material written by Native Americans. It also funds documentaries on Indians and Alaska Natives who lived in the past or are alive today. The quarterly *Vision Maker* newsletter features news about telecommunications issues impacting Indian country as well as information about productions, opportunities, festivals, project updates, and conferences. NAPT is also one of five Lead Information Centers established to represent special populations for the 2000 census.

Finally, Vision Maker Video (VMV) is a definitive listing of authentic Native American videos. Its award-winning collection, regularly reviewed by tribal experts and scholars, is made available for distribution to educational institutions. VMV programs include titles such as "Keepers of the Water" (Menominee and Chippewa protection of the Wolf River), "Dancing with Photons "(Navajo physicist Fred Begay), "Apache Mountain Spirits," "I Am Different from my Brother" (Dakota Name Giving), "The New Pequot," "American Indian Artists," "Sacred Buffalo People," "The Treaty of 1868," and "Native American Architecture."

MINING

Mining is a more or less specialized aspect of natural resource control. In this study, mining is used loosely to include not only mineral extraction but that of water resources as well. Mining, being an inherently dirty industry, is associated with unique problems—and opportunities. It has been linked with extreme environmental degradation, with gross corruption, and, in some cases, with profits as well. Profits gained through extraction of resources such as oil, coal, natural gas, and minerals located on Indian lands in the United States have largely been managed by the federal government. Perhaps not surprisingly, it is these profits, along with those related to land sales, now totaling tens of billions of dollars, that are at the core of the allegations of fraud and mismanagement leveled against the Interior and Treasury Departments (see the discussion in the Introduction).

Particularly emblematic of both problems and opportunities are the mining operations in the Southwestern United States. There, especially on the Navajo Reservation and at Hopi and Laguna Pueblos, cancer among uranium miners and their families and the permanent pollution of vital water resources have become a way of life. In the Four Corners region, coal mining has created an almost unimaginable degree of environmental destruction and a human rights drama that involves forced relocations. It is also a major source of cash for the Navajo and other Indian nations.

In Wisconsin, the Menominee Nation has taken a good look at the Four Corners situation and at other mining operations located on Indian land. Thus informed, it has chosen to forego any profits that might accrue to it from a proposed metallic sulfite mine. The Menominee, and the nearby Mole Lake Sokaogon Chippewa, have taken the lead in opposing the mine, preferring instead to protect their birthright, the Wolf River, and its associated recreational economy. The Indian people have been working very closely with like-minded non-natives and grappling with the shifting politics within the state legislature.

A look at how Cree groups in Canada have fared with the James Bay Project reveals other important aspects of the mining issue. Like the Navajo, the Cree agreed to the project but only when they had no practical choice. In some ways they have fared better than the Navajo in terms of benefits. In some ways, however, they have fared worse, in that an enormous chunk of their land is lost forever and a huge number of people have been displaced. They have also experienced the pollution and sickness that so often accompany mining operations. More recently, their position has moved closer to that of the Menominee but for somewhat different reasons. Like the Menominee and the Mole Lake Chippewa, Cree groups oppose further mining operations in part to protect their birthright, but unlike the U.S. Indians, who also have an eye toward the tourist industry, the Cree use their water and forest resources mainly for subsistence activities.

In most cases, mining has not become much, if any, more environmentally friendly in recent years. Many mining leases remain terribly exploitative, although, through organizations such as the Council of Energy Resource Tribes (CERT), tribes are increasingly renegotiating to their advantage. (Among the Navajo, for instance, coal royalties have risen from the Bureau of Indian Affairs–negotiated 15¢ per ton to up to $3 per ton.) Despite their growing political power and sophistication, native groups still have a great deal of difficulty opposing vested interests in government and industry. Too, the people continue to be subject to forced relocation—again, the situation at Big Mountain on the Navajo Reservation is especially tragic and egregious.

NAVAJO

Mining on Navajo land may be seen against a backdrop of the destruction of an effective native economy. According to internal statistics, the Navajo people were virtually self-sufficient in 1920. In 1940, a majority of the Navajo made a living from stock raising and agriculture. Eighteen years later, following generations of government-imposed economic and political policies, fewer than 10 percent of the Navajo made their living from stock raising or agriculture. The major economic activity has become mining, specifically of uranium and, later, coal.

Navajo Indians who agreed to open their lands to uranium mining did so in large measure out of patriotism. Unfortunately, despite evidence gained as early as the early 1940s regarding the toxic effects of radiation, nobody—neither the Atomic Energy Commission, which for years bought all of the uranium; nor the mining companies, which operated the mines; nor the Interior Department, which was charged with responsibility for the health and welfare of American Indians—ever informed the Navajo that the mines were dangerous or ensured that the most basic safety measures (such as providing ventilation) were followed. Beginning in the 1960s, when people and livestock began to die by the thousands, these (or their successor) entities fought to weaken proposed health and safety standards and evade responsibility and compensation.

Uranium ore on Navajo land was first extracted in 1922. Mining boomed in the 1940s and supplied part of the material that went into the first atomic weapons. Navajo leaders (particularly Peter MacDonald, who founded CERT and later landed in prison on federal corruption charges) ultimately allowed

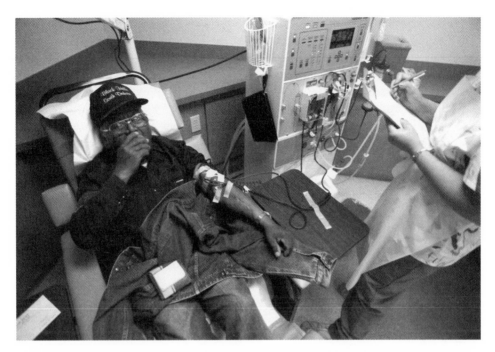

Former uranium miner Joe Kee Nez takes medication while undergoing kidney dialysis in Shiprock, New Mexico, July 22, 1997. Congress passed the Radiation Exposure Compensation Act in 1990 to help uranium miners. But Nez and other Indian miners suffering from cancer and other ailments blamed on radiation exposure haven't seen a penny. (AP Photo/Eric Draper)

over 1,000 uranium mines and mills on Navajo property. In addition, vast (some larger than 30,000 acres) coal strip-mines and plants have been or are currently in operation. The Navajo Nation's leaders, with encouragement from the U.S. government and the energy industry, essentially traded their people's health and safety, not to mention the sanctity of their lands, for greater employment, political power, and a considerable cash inflow.

For years, Navajo (and other) uranium miners dug ore in small "dog holes." When they blasted, toxic dust and gases filled the air. They ate food tainted with uranium oxide and drank the radioactive water of the mines. At the end of the day, their clothes—indeed, their bodies—were covered with radioactive material, spreading the poison within their very homes (some of which were, in fact, constructed of radioactive debris). Pay at Kerr-McGee mines was $1.60 per hour (two-thirds the off-reservation rate), without the housing and subsidized meals that non-natives often received. People who complained about working conditions or who talked about their health problems were summarily fired.

Furthermore, horrific accidents have occurred. In 1979, a United Nuclear dam at Churchrock, New Mexico, gave way and released more than 100 million gallons of highly radioactive water into Rio Puerco de Oeste. Hundreds of mines, many in areas where cattle graze and children play, remain open and unprotected against intrusion or the escape of radioactive gases or dust. Huge piles of radioactive waste (tailings) lie similarly exposed. Rainfall and inadequate reclamation have caused the contamination to spread over a large portion of western New Mexico and eastern Arizona. Radioactive water from the region will eventually find its way into the Colorado River and from there into the San Joaquin Valley, the country's largest source of fruits and vegetables.

Throughout the 1980s, serious efforts, notably by former interior secretary Stuart Udall, were made to secure some relief for Navajo miners. Although the government—under the Federal Tort Claims Act—was able to escape legal liability for the damage done to Navajo miners, it did pass the Radiation Exposure Compensation Act (RECA) in 1990. RECA came with a formal apology and promised "compassion" payments of $100,000 to certain uranium miners or their families. However, various provisions, including its administration by the Justice Department—which had fought the Navajo bitterly for years—rendered the act virtually useless.

In particular, the documentation required for a successful claim includes "official" marriage licenses that often do not exist, since the marriages took place under tribal auspices. Sick miners (or their widows), many of whom do not speak English, have had to travel great distances and sort through a bizarre maze of bureaucratic requirements. Furthermore, strip miners, open-pit miners, and mill workers are ineligible for compensation under the act, as are people who got sick by their proximity to contaminated sites. By 1993, of the 600 miners who had been tested by the Justice Department, only five had qualified for the payments. In 1998, the rejection rate for Navajo claimants exceeded 50 percent.

Coal mining is also responsible for catastrophic human and environmental damage. Peabody Coal operates the world's largest surface coal mine on the Navajo reservation. A slurry pipeline uses between two and three million gallons of aquifer water daily, causing entire ecosystems to dry up. Mining operations have destroyed sacred sites, medicinal plants, and wildlife habitat while leaving a legacy of destruction and pollution of land, air, and water resources. Perhaps not surprisingly, given the amounts of money involved, such operations have also been associated with years of corruption, political dissension, and human rights violations. These situations are being investigated by the United Nations Special Rapporteur on Religious Intolerance.

Coal mining in the area is at the root of another human drama as well. In 1962, a non-native "leader" cobbled together an ersatz Hopi tribal council and persuaded the tribe to file a lawsuit to gain title to coal-rich Navajo lands. When it succeeded, the Hopi began to lease the land to Peabody Coal; their action forced the Navajo council to follow suit. In 1974, in an effort to consolidate the mineral holdings, the U.S. government arbitrarily defined part of the Navajo reservation, including Big Mountain and the sacred Black Mesa, as Hopi property and ordered people on the "wrong" sides (100 Hopi and 10,000 Navajo) to relocate.

Most people gave in to the pressure of forced stock reductions, payments and fines, and physical intimidation as well as to the promise of benefits and a

Strip mining takes place at a Navajo-owned coal mine in New Mexico, 1969. (Corbis/Adam Woolfit)

new home. Many of those who moved, however, live as virtual refugees. Stripped of their land and thus the possibility of subsistence grazing, they are thrust suddenly into a cash economy that many do not understand or have any use for. Today, about 3,000 Navajo, many of them old and poor, have refused to sign the Accommodation Agreement and relocate. They have been subject to livestock impoundments and forced evictions that threaten their fragile economies, their spiritual connection to the land, and their very lives.

In 1985, the Navajo—and all Indian tribes—won an important victory when the Supreme Court ruled (*Kerr-McGee Corp. v. Navajo Tribe*) that the Navajo could impose taxes on energy companies operating on the reservation without the approval of the secretary of the interior. In 1996, following widespread Navajo testimony against the project, an administrative judge denied Peabody Coal's petition to renew the permit for its massive Kayenta mine. The judge found that Peabody Coal was guilty of numerous willful violations of various laws. The judge also found the Office of Surface Mining (OSM) to have failed in properly overseeing environmental compliance of the mine. The OSM, which supported the petition, is a part of the Interior Department, which is charged with a trust responsibility toward Indians in the United States.

The results of Navajo mining have been varied. The Navajo Nation's budget increased dramatically, from about $1 million in 1954 to about $12 million in 1958, primarily as a result of energy income. Today, the Hopi Tribe and the Navajo Nation receive about $40 million in income from coal mining alone, and mining generates jobs for Indian people. However, the overall benefit to individual Navajos has been much less clear. In 1990, their average per-capita income was $2,400, and the unemployment rate was 32 percent. Many Navajo continue to live without running water, electricity, roads, or telephones. Rural residents regularly charge Navajo environmental and other government officials with insensitivity (at best) to their needs. Neither has the nation been successful in using its financial resources to achieve long-term economic development.

Ongoing revelations continue to underscore the extent to which the Navajo were considered expendable in the service of mining. In 1997, the Navajo Uranium Radiation Victims Committee (NURVC) presented a report to the Navajo Nation Council that told of radiation experiments conducted in 1960 in which radioactive material was added to tuberculosis medicine and injected into Navajo patients at the Ft. Defiance hospital. The ostensible purpose was for scientists to be able to use a Geiger counter to follow the course of tuberculosis medicine as it ran through a patient's body. The report noted that Navajo people not suffering from tuberculosis were also injected with the material. The NURVC is also assisting Navajo coal workers with the federal Black Lung Act, and it is involved in efforts to reform the federal RECA.

MENOMINEE

The 223-mile Wolf River is at the heart of the Menominee Nation's battle with Nicolet Minerals Company (NMC), a wholly owned subsidiary of Rio Algom. For thousands of years, the river has been the heart of Menominee territory, which once encompassed 10 million acres of land in roughly the northeast quadrant of Wisconsin. The river appears in many Menominee legends and has enabled many traditional subsistence and cultural practices. In part because of its connection to wild rice, a unique local food source and the source of the nation's name, the Menominee people consider the Wolf River "the lifeline of existence."

Today, in addition to its historical and cultural significance for the people, the river is a key recreational site and bastion of the local tourist economy. In fact, it is one of the last clean, large white-water trout streams in the midwest. The 27 miles of the river within the Menominee Reservation have also been designated an Outstanding Water Resource and a National Wild and Scenic River.

In 1976, the Exxon Corporation announced that tests had uncovered important deposits of zinc, copper, lead, silver, and gold along the river. With Rio Algom, it formed the Crandon Mining Company (CMC) in 1993 and the following year submitted an application to the Wisconsin Department of Natural Resources to extract 55 million tons of heavy metals from the site. (A prior application, with different partners, had been submitted in 1982 but withdrawn four years later.) If and when the company is allowed to be in operation, it would like to concentrate operations in the town of Nashville, Wisconsin, located in the Wolf River watershed and home of another Indian tribe, the Mole Lake Sokaogon Chippewa. CMC became Nicolet Minerals Company in 1998.

The proposed metallic sulfite mine has been controversial for a number of reasons. Its likely negative impact in the regional environment directly threatens Chippewa treaty rights that guarantee access to traditional foods on ceded land. Opponents further allege that the operation would generate roughly 44 million tons of tailings, crushed rock, and water treatment sludge. Half of this debris would be dumped back in the mine with no liners or control technologies; the other half would be permanently stored above ground in a tailings landfill the size of 350 football fields reaching 90 feet high.

Other lingering socioeconomic, environmental, and political questions include the effect of mine dewatering on the Wolf River watershed, the risk to clean air and water of both above- and below-ground storage of toxic waste materials, and charges of undue influence in the process by Exxon, CMC, and NMC. Despite the owners' assurances of major economic benefits with no negative effects, most mining projects are associated with rural poverty. They are also susceptible to a boom-and-bust cycle that results in little or no positive long-term socioeconomic impact.

Finally, opponents allege "numerous inconsistencies, inadequate sampling methods, and conceptual discrepancies" in the groundwater model used by CMC to predict impacts. Local residents point to Exxon and Rio Algom's environmental track records as a cause for further concern. At best the project poses serious potential problems; a worst-case scenario, which would include major toxic waste spills and cleanup costs, is a recipe for disaster.

In 1995, the Mole Lake Chippewa obtained Treatment-as-State (TAS) status from the U.S. Environmental Protection Agency (EPA). TAS status allows the tribe to set its own water quality standards and grant certain permits. In 1998, the Wisconsin attorney general brought suit against the EPA in an effort to force it to rescind Mole Lake's TAS status. This move, which, if successful, would greatly facilitate the mine's permitting process, effectively put the state in the position of trying to stop one of its communities from protecting its own drinking water and cultural resources. The Indian community and the town of Nashville have been cooperating on this issue ever since 1997, when Nashville began actively to oppose the project.

In January 1998, in support of a proposed mining moratorium bill, the Menominee Nation issued a 28-page report to the state legislature detailing the project's social, cultural, economic, and environmental problems. Later that month, the Republican majority removed the most meaningful parts of the bill and, in a late-night special session, voted to send the bill to the senate without giving the public a chance to lobby their representatives for a reconsideration. At the same time, Rio Algom purchased Exxon's share in Crandon Mining and changed CMC's name to Nicolet Minerals Company, vowing to continue the project and build "an environmentally sound and technically superior operation."

The final version of the bill, signed into law in April 1998, requires mining companies to prove that there is a similar North American mine that had operated for 10 years and had been closed for 10 years and did not pollute the water. The actual impact of the law will be determined by its interpretation by various state agencies, such as the Department of Natural Resources (DNR). The Menominee Nation has pointed out that the moratorium law would never have passed without the support of grassroots organizations, including Indian tribes. In the summer of 1998, it joined with forty coalition groups and 25 state legislators in demanding that the Wisconsin DNR stop the permitting process until the company complies with the new law.

As of early 1999, NMC had yet to meet the moratorium law's requirements, despite signs that DNR was willing to waive or unilaterally modify at least some of the criteria. The legislature of the Menominee Nation has passed a law banning sulfide metallic mining within its boundaries without the consent of two-thirds of its eligible voters. The Nation stands firm in opposing the project, calling for enforcement of all environmental protection laws. It vows, in the words of its mission statement, to "exercise its sovereign rights and responsibility to protect and ensure for future generations [the] Menominee environment and natural resources." For its part, NMC expects to receive its permits by 2001 and to begin mining three years later.

CREE

In 1999, roughly 12,000 Cree and about 7,000 Inuit lived in the James Bay watershed of northern Quebec. These people have made their living based on hunting, fishing, and trapping for thousands of years. The James Bay wilderness is home to the world's largest caribou herd. Rich in biodiversity, James Bay is one of the Northern Hemisphere's most important waterfowl habitats and contains thousands of marine mammals such as seals and beluga whales.

In the early 1970s, Hydro Quebec and its owner, the Province of Quebec, announced a massive hydroelectric scheme. The James Bay Project was intended to provide for Quebec's power and allow it to base its economy on the export of electricity. As originally envisioned, the project would flood over 10,000 square miles of subarctic wilderness. Engineers planned to construct over 400 dams and dikes to alter the flow of 19 rivers. Power would be generated by nine power stations. The fact that the land was being occupied by its original and rightful "owners" was never even considered. In fact, project promoters never even bothered to consult the residents.

The James Bay hydroelectric project was allowed to proceed over the objections of the Indians of Quebec Association, the predecessor of the Grand Council of the Crees (1974). In 1975, Cree groups living in Quebec reluctantly signed the James Bay and Northern Quebec Agreement (JBNQA). According to its terms, the natives ceded over 400,000 square miles of land. In exchange, they were promised a cash settlement of over $230 million and special concessions, including land ownership of over 2,100 square miles,

A dam spillway at James Bay, Quebec, Canada. In 1975 eastern Cree and Inuit groups ceded over 640,000 square kilometers (380,000 square miles) of land for the James Bay Hydroelectric Project. Additional hydroelectric projects are generally opposed by First Nations because of the massive environmental destruction, physical displacement, and cultural loss associated with them. (Corbis/Karen Tweedy-Holmes)

subsistence rights on over 20,000 square miles more, and a veto over mineral exploitation. The agreement also called for an environmental review to be completed on all future projects before work would be allowed to commence.

In the mid-1990s, the first phase of the James Bay Project, also known as James Bay I (JBI) or LaGrande (after the LaGrande River), was completed. Three major rivers were diverted to flood over 7,000 square miles of Cree hunting territory. The world's largest hydroelectric complex, JBI comprises five reservoirs, nine dams, and over 200 dikes. Its eight power houses have a power output of 15,244 megawatts of electricity, enough to power a city of nearly 6 million people. The entire project was conceived and finished without an environmental review.

Roughly 40 percent of the local native people lost their livelihood as a result of the resulting wildlife destruction and environmental contamination. Flooding released bacteria that transformed naturally occurring, insoluble mercury into soluble, toxic methyl mercury that poisoned the fish on which the people depend. Other contaminants caused an epidemic of childhood diarrhea. Jobs promised by Hydro Quebec turned out to be mostly of the low-wage, menial variety. Moreover, not all of the money called for in the agreement was allocated. Hunting and fishing remain the most important economic activities for the Cree. However, many Crees no longer able to hunt or fish did find work in new Nation-owned enterprises such as the Cree airline, construction, and canoe manufacturing.

The project's next phase, James Bay II, was to flood almost 700 square miles of the Great Whale river basin, located north of JBI. Twenty-three power stations would produce another 28,000 megawatts of electricity, much of which was slated to be exported to the United States. Completion of this project would destroy virtually all of the remaining Cree hunting grounds. Construction was to begin in 1991.

Local Crees met many times to determine, if they could, their position on Great Whale. Businesspeople spoke in its favor, citing the possibility of economic development. Some people suggested taking a hard line against it but only as a negotiating position. Others were completely against the project, in part because they believed that people displaced by the resource destruction would become virtual refugees.

Furthermore, the Cree (and many non-natives) maintain that the electricity is not needed. Quebec is one of the most wasteful and inefficient electricity consumers in the world. Studies by private consultants have revealed that the province could save more than twice Great Whale's proposed generating capacity by implementing simple conservation measures. In 1989, the people, unwilling to follow the path of their fellow Cree to the south, voted to reject the project categorically and to refuse any and all funds offered as compensation.

Their action did not deter the government. Although the Supreme Court mandated an independent federal environmental review of the project, Quebec officials believed that under the JBNQA they had the authority to complete the full James Bay project without Cree approval. However, the Cree, judging that the courts ultimately would not deny the wishes of the government, made a strategic decision that the fight over Great Whale would be at least as important in the United States as in Canada. Toward this end, the Cree embarked on a public relations campaign.

Environmental and native-rights activists in the United States responded. Sympathetic articles appeared in newspapers and magazines. Students pressured universities to sell off Hydro Quebec bonds. In 1990, Maine backed out of a contract worth $9 billion. Vermont voted to reduce (but not eliminate) its purchase of James Bay power. In 1992, the project suffered a major defeat when New York State, probably responding more to an electricity glut than to public pressure, pulled out of a $17 billion contract. The state subsequently canceled another multibillion-dollar contract.

With the environmental review underway, Inuit groups affected by Great Whale decided in 1994 to settle with Hydro Quebec. The province's roughly 7,000 Inuit agreed to accept more than $500 million in compensation for environmental destruction and the loss of their subsistence activities. Although the Inuit disapproved of the project, they reasoned that since they could not stop it they might as well influence the way it impacts their people. The Inuit also won the right to name two members of the five-person committee evaluating the project, and they were to receive funds for infrastructure improvements and job training. Cree leaders were unhappy with the agreement, fearing that it gave the Inuit a stake in seeing the project through to completion and would undermine their own efforts to stop it.

However, events later that year made the Inuit agreement seem premature. First, the Cree informed the government that, should Quebec ever succeed in its much publicized goal of separating from Canada, the Cree, by virtue of their status as a sovereign nation, might decide to remain part of the federation. In November, the long-awaited environmental review was released and was immediately attacked for serious procedural flaws. Under mounting pressure, Quebec announced that it was "indefinitely shelving" the Great Whale project. Native groups remained cautious, noting that the project had not been canceled outright as many had hoped. In fact, some believed that delaying while quietly obtaining authorization to proceed is one of Hydro Quebec's strategic plans.

Indeed, Indian leaders were informed in the summer of 1997 that Hydro Quebec was reviving Great Whale, albeit in a modified form. The plan now is to divert up to 16 rivers, including the Great Whale and Rupert, into the LaGrande project. The project would flood sacred Lac Bienville, the headwaters of the Great Whale River and a major wildlife sanctuary. It would also flood the home of the world's largest caribou herd and destroy key Cree trapping grounds. In 1998, the Quebec government invoked emergency powers that allowed Hydro Quebec to avoid environmental reviews for this and future unspecified projects.

Attention has also turned to Hydro Quebec's projects slated for the traditional and unceded territory of the Innu. In 1998, the Innu community of Uashat-Maliotenam accepted a package worth more than $60 million in compensation for damages caused by the Sainte-Marguerite III (SM3) project, including environmental destruction, mercury poisoning, and loss of subsistence activity. The Innu are also expected to gain as much as $50 million in economic spin-offs, such as construction contracts, from the project. However, representatives from Innu organizations in Newfoundland (Innu Nation), Labrador (Mamit Innuat), and Quebec have announced that they will oppose future development projects that do not have the consent of the Innu people, such as the $10 billion Lower Churchill River project and the Voisey's Bay mining project. Talks on the future of that project began in mid-1998 between the Innu Nation of Labrador and the government of Labrador.

Looming over the entire issue is Hydro Quebec's Grand Canal project, a $100 billion plan to dam the mouth of James Bay to create a huge lake. Water from this lake would be channeled through existing waterways and new canals to regions as far away as the Southwest in the United States and possibly even Mexico. Hydro Quebec officials insist the time has come to move forward and talk about welcoming the Cree as business partners. The Indians, however, stand firm in their virtually unanimous opposition to the destruction of their birthright and their way of life.

NATURAL RESOURCE CONTROL

Many native communities contain extremely valuable natural resources. Government officials have always been aware of the value of resources such as fish, water, and timber. The existence of others, such as oil and uranium, was largely unknown when the reservations and reserves were created. In any case, the U.S. and Canadian governments often moved to exploit native resources quickly and, with some exceptions, with little (or no) input from or compensation to the native communities themselves. Non-native governments usually claimed native resources whether or not they had bothered to go through the motions of "acquiring" them according to their own laws. The results, as predictable as they were ugly, have included widespread environmental pollution, destruction of subsistence and cultural activities, increasing dependence, population dislocation, and, in many cases, a sharp decline in overall native health.

Today, Indians, Inuit, and Alaska Natives are engaged in all-out battles for control of their natural resources. They have taken on this fight for economic and spiritual reasons and because they are increasingly able to assert their legitimate treaty rights. For instance, despite years of ruinous overfishing and poor management by non-natives, salmon has regained its honored place in the lives of many Columbia River and Puget Sound tribes. The celebrated 1974 Boldt decision formally upheld fishing and other resource rights of the Yakama and other tribes. In 1999, the U.S. Supreme Court declined to review a 9th Circuit Court ruling upholding treaty rights that allow 17 western Washington tribes to take shellfish on state and privately owned tidelands and beaches in Puget Sound and other inland waters. Yet, despite these victories, state and federal authorities continually seek to chip away at those rights, and the tribes are forced to maintain continual vigilance.

In southeast Canada, the struggle between the Mi'kmaq Indians and provincial and national authorities also reveals both the lengths to which non-native governments will go to retain control of Indian resources and the determination of native people to reassume that control. A people desperately in need of jobs, the Mi'kmaq have been legally denied the right to draw upon their forest resources because the government claims those resources for itself. The Mi'kmaq have waged a furious legal battle contesting Canada's claim. Furthermore, in an echo of the Osage Nation, whose government is elected by a minority of its people, the Mi'kmaq (and all First Nations) have a government imposed on them from the outside. Canada will only recognize the band councils it created (and not traditional governmental structures), entities that tend to support its positions. The people await what could be called their own Boldt decision with a mixture of hope, impatience, and anger, in that they know that they should not have to rely on Canadian courts to "give" them what is already theirs.

For the Osage Nation, once made fabulously wealthy from their oil resources, the issue of resource control is more an internal matter. Unlike the Yakama, Mi'kmaq, and most other tribes, only a small number of Osage may legally benefit from the tribe's oil wealth. This "in" group wants desperately to remain closed. However, since there is some evidence that the government can cease to recognize the Osage tribe once the last of this group dies, sharing the wealth becomes as much a matter of survival as one of fairness. Meanwhile, the federal government plays a key role here too. In the form of the Interior Department, it approves all major tribal decisions. Hardly a disinterested party, the government would directly benefit from the tribe's destruction, since in that case it would probably acquire Osage oil wealth for itself.

Authority over natural resources is slowly and unevenly shifting from the U.S. and Canadian governments to native governments. However, in cases where native people have reacquired control over their resources, debate often rages over how to exploit natural resources, how to divide income or royalty payments, or even whether to exploit the resources at all. The positions of traditionalists—those who recognize a religious obligation to protect the earth and a way of life—and "progressives"—those who prioritize the promise of jobs and money—are not easily reconciled. As much as any single issue, debates over natural resource control have the potential to serve as a catalyst for Native American renewal.

YAKAMA

The Yakama Nation in Washington, a conglomeration of formerly independent bands and groups of the western Plateau region, grew out of the treaty negotiations of 1855. According to that treaty, the Yakama ceded almost 11 million acres of land in exchange for a million-acre reservation and other considerations. The treaty also allowed the people to continue to fish and gather plants at their usual subsistence locations. The issues relating to resource control both on the reservation and on the adjoining treaty lands have remained controversial ever since.

Yakamas and other Indian people have always taken great care to steward their land, animal, and water resources. Fish—particularly salmon and steelhead trout—are not only a food source but the linchpin of Yakama religious life. Fishing has been the lifeblood of Columbia River Indians from time immemorial. However, a number of factors, including the construction of massive dams and irrigation projects, the growth of off-shore fishing fleets, and the explosion of sport fishing, led both to the Indians' losing access to their traditional fisheries and to a sharp decline in the actual fish run. By the 1960s, the situation had become critical. In 1965, the Yakama, a relatively conservative people, felt compelled to protect their fisheries with armed patrols. Non-natives, meanwhile, had long sought clear title to the Indian land.

Various lawsuits culminated in a landmark 1974 ruling (*U.S.* v. *Washington*, the so-called Boldt decision) that held that treaty Indians possess a unshakable legal right to fish at all "usual and accustomed" places both on and off the reservation. The ruling further held that Indians enjoy a similar right to participate in regional fisheries management and to possession of half of the annual fish harvest. Vigorous state resistance abated only when the U.S. Supreme Court upheld the essence of the ruling in 1979. Anti-Indian feeling remains high, however, and tribal members must still cope with some governmental and individual opposition, including physical intimidation.

The Boldt decision marked both an economic and a cultural turning point for many Northwest tribes, including the Yakama. However, the Supreme Court allowed the state to regulate the Indian fish harvest. In 1986, in a celebrated case involving several Yakama men arrested for violations of state fishing regulations, the U.S. Supreme Court upheld the federal authority over Indian fishing even on the reservation. This decision ensured that Indians would not be free to manage their resources in the careful, sustainable way that is their custom. It also paved the way for the state to further restrict Indian fishing.

In general, the government may regulate tribal fisheries only when it has shown that it can not mitigate a safety or conservation concern in any other way and only after it has taken "reasonable" steps to avoid this action. Just what constitutes "reasonable" is, of course, open to interpretation. The tribes argue that, by taking regulatory authority out of their hands, the court effectively compels the state not only to conserve fish but to ensure the continued viability of tribal salmon fisheries.

In a 1997 development that overshadowed the previous regulatory debates, however, the government placed the upper Columbia River steelhead salmon on the Endangered Species List. The Yakama and other nearby tribes, such as the Umatilla, Warm Springs, and Nez Percé, protest that this action may be disastrous to regional tribes' salmon fisheries. They claim that the government is demanding that the Indians bear the brunt of conservation efforts while sparing big financial interests like irrigators and dam operators.

Meanwhile, along with grazing, farming, and especially timber, fishing has once again assumed an active position within the Yakama economy. It provides a focus of tribal identity, a source of jobs and cash, and an opportunity for professional development. In an effort to cooperate on matters pertaining to their common interests, the state and Indian tribes are working together to an unprecedented degree on regulatory and management issues. For instance, along with the Washington Fish and Wildlife Department, the Nation currently operates one of the largest fishery conservation programs in the United States. The tribe is currently experimenting with an innovative program, called the Yakama-Klickitat Fish Production Project, designed to strengthen the genetic diversity of salmon—and increase their numbers—by returning hatchery fish to the wild. The Yakama Nation also participates in regional planning and management agencies such as the Columbia River Inter-Tribal Fish Commission.

Other issues of natural resource control have also arisen recently. In 1997, a Yakama Indian was acquitted on charges that he killed two elk out of season off the reservation, on the grounds that this activity was permitted under treaty. However, the prosecutor in the case still hopes to seek a conviction under (elk) conservation laws, an action that would prompt a ruling on whether or not the treaty supersedes state efforts to conserve the elk population. Many Yakama Indians also take seriously treaty provisions allowing them to harvest plants such as camas and bitterroot on the roughly 9 million acres of nonreservation treaty land. Collecting these plants is a part of Yakama spirituality and an important source of cultural transmission and stability. In 1991, the Yakama Nation launched an ambitious Wildlife Mitigation Plan, under which they plan to buy back land and restore wildlife habitat, in hopes of returning salmon to the Toppenish and Satus Creeks. This project involves a delicate balance of compromise with various outside interests.

Like the question of access to and control of water resources, the issue of Indian fisheries remains, to a considerable degree, in flux. Furthermore, with excessive logging and overgrazing destroying critical fish breeding grounds, the positive developments of the past generation may have occurred too late to save the salmon fishery at all. However, at the turn of the millennium it is clear that the Yakama Nation is once again an active manager of its own natural resources.

MI'KMAQ

The Algonquian Mi'kmaqs of southeast Canada live in a region of rugged forests, lakes, and rivers. Fishing is an important economic activity, as is logging. Despite the existence of these economic resources, however, and in common with many First Nations, years of political subjugation, economic exploitation, and cultural attacks have left the Mi'kmaq with chronic unemployment and many of the social problems that often accompany poverty—suicide, substance abuse, and dependency.

One of the ironies of Mi'kmaq life is that the majority of their territory is covered with a valuable natural resource—forest. Although the Mi'kmaq regard it as their unceded territory, the province claims almost all of this land. Consequently, almost all logging is carried out by large, politically connected, non-native companies. The Mi'kmaq contend that the dominance of these companies is squeezing out local companies, both Indian and non-native. They have long sought a greater share of the local logging operations and have recently moved to exercise control over their forest resources.

Since the issue of land ownership hinges largely on treaty interpretation, there is a question of which side gets the "default" advantage. In other words, which side is assumed to have land ownership unless proven otherwise? The First Nations' position is that, since they (obviously) did not give up their sovereignty so that the British could restrict their trade forever, they must be considered to have all titles and rights not formally ceded. They point to treaties signed in 1752 and 1760–1761 that guarantee Mi'kmaq (and Maliseet) people the right to harvest and trade with whomever they wish. They also point to historical precedent such as the Proclamation of 1763 and even legal precedent as formulated in cases such as Calder, Sparrow, and Delgamuukw (see Documents section). The First Nations make the point that, since treaties are made between sovereign nations, any changes must be made only upon the mutual consent of both parties and not arbitrarily by one of them.

However, in a move designed to place First Nations at a severe disadvantage, federal and provincial officials have managed to place the onus on the First Nations to prove their title—that is, to claim the default advantage. Not surprisingly, Canadian courts have agreed with their position. Furthermore, for the simple reason that Canada controls an enormous police/military power, legal battles are and will continue to be fought in Canadian courts, with all of their cultural, legal, and political biases, rather than under the auspices of First Nations or an impartial third party.

Modern conflicts between Canadian officials and Mi'kmaqs over natural resource control began in the 1950s. In the 1990s, Mi'kmaqs from New Brunswick as well as the Quebec community of Listuguj moved to assert control over their forests. Contending they would rather work than receive welfare, the people made it clear that while they were not mounting formal legal action regarding ownership of their vast ancestral lands, they did intend to support themselves in a dignified manner. Parallel goals included the ability to manage their own resources in ways that they deemed appropriate, such as eliminating clear cutting in favor of selective logging and ensuring all forest protection regulations were followed uniformly.

In 1996, a man from the Pabineau Reserve named Thomas Peter Paul began harvesting bird's eye maple, a hardwood commonly used in the dashboards of certain expensive cars. He was arrested and charged with illegal logging on crown lands. He maintained that he had a treaty right to harvest timber on unceded Mi'kmaq land. While two lower courts agreed with him, an appellate court ruled against him on both legal and procedural grounds, holding in part that there was not enough evidence introduced to show title to the land by First Nations. The Supreme Court declined to review the case.

However, because the 1997 Delgamuukw Supreme Court ruling requires Canada to negotiate "in good faith" with First Nations on land claims issues, an interim agreement was cobbled together between New Brunswick and the band council chiefs. In exchange for a cessation of the protests by the Indians, New Brunswick gave the Mi'kmaqs plots of land to log. Plot size was determined on a per capita basis. Although negotiations over logging remain ongoing, many Mi'kmaqs remain unsatisfied with the interim agreement on several grounds. They object to the state "giving" them what they regard as theirs by right and to the fact that the framework for the negotiations excludes the possibility of resolving the ultimate question of land title.

One of their main objections, and one that is found among many Indian groups in Canada, concerns the tension between imposed governmental political structures and pre-Canadian traditional governments. Many Mi'kmaqs view the band council, a creation of the Indian Act, as illegitimate, while they grant the traditional Mi'kmaq Grand Council (MGC) the proper authority to represent their people. Since national and provincial authorities in fact created the band councils, they prefer to negotiate with the councils rather than the MGC. Thus is the issue of control of economic resources closely linked with that of political representation.

Meanwhile, in Quebec, a similar logging crisis began in 1992 when the MGC applied to the minister of natural resources (MNR) for permission to log a particular section of timber. The following year, permission not having been forthcoming, the council approved a harvest on Crown lands behind the Listuguj reserve. The ministry objected, and years of fruitless negotiations followed. Finally, the MCG in 1998 unilaterally authorized Mi'kmaq companies to harvest the logs.

Mi'kmaq loggers were able to sell the logs to a mill in New Brunswick until, in mid-July, the Quebec government pressured the mill to stop accepting "illegal" Listuguj logs. The Mi'kmaqs took the next step by occupying a sawmill in the Gaspé region and erecting a blockade on a logging road. The provincial government countered by sending in a negotiator in order to defuse the escalating situation.

In late July, the MGC formally claimed jurisdiction over its traditional territory. When negotiations stalled, Quebec responded by threatening to dismantle the blockade and end the occupation by force. The Indians addressed this development in two ways. Officially, they noted that Section 35 of the Canadian constitution as well as recent Supreme Court decisions mandate that disputes over sovereignty, land, and resources issues must be settled by negotiations and not by violence. Secretly, some occupiers also began to assemble defensive weapons to be used in the event of an attack.

By early August, Quebec officially kept its police-action option open but had offered the Mi'kmaq a deal, worth roughly $1,000,000 and signed by the band council, whereby 110 more jobs would be brought to the reserve and about 13,000 cubic yards of wood would be available for logging. At first the deal was turned down, mainly by the protesters who, by and large, supported the traditional MGC. However, several days later an agreement was announced. Under its terms, the number of new jobs remained the same (110) but the amount of wood available to Mi'kmaq loggers was raised to 40,000 cubic yards. Significantly, this binding agreement was supported by the MGC.

Of the land open to Mi'kmaq loggers, half would be available to Jigug Enterprises, a nonprofit corporation established for the Mi'kmaq people, and half to private Mi'kmaq logging companies. Organizers of the protest admitted that they settled for less than one-quarter of the 209,000 cubic yards they originally demanded but maintained that the deal was a good start and that it was obtained without violence. Furthermore, the Indians noted that the additional timber allocated to them under the agreement came from non-native forestry companies operating in the region. This development spurred hopes that the companies, which to date had never hired an Indian logger, might finally be open to including Indians in the industry.

The issue of Mi'kmaq resource control remains very much unsettled. Although negotiations continue, many Mi'kmaq people see federal and provincial officials as unilaterally imposing the context and the agenda of those negotiations. Lawyers for the First Nations still hope for a Supreme Court review of the Thomas Peter Paul case and continue to maintain that it is possible to reconcile the sovereignty of all nations involved. Meanwhile, despite evidence that its forests could not sustain even less intensive levels of logging, New Brunswick has stepped up this activity.

Osage

The Osage people of northeastern Oklahoma were once known as the "richest people in the world." The tribe's wealth came primarily from a combination of two circumstances: the discovery of oil beneath its reservation in 1896 and the ability to retain its mineral estate collectively when the reservation was allotted in the early twentieth century. The tribe has remained wealthy through the years by retaining control of the mineral estate. However, the original legal provisions regarding this resource have led to questions about who will continue to control the oil. This question is closely related to that of the identity and, in fact, the very existence of the Osage tribe itself.

The 1906 Osage Allotment Act, which overrode the 1881 Osage Constitution, remains at the core of the resource control–identity–existence issue. According to the provisions of the act, the reservation's surface area was divided among the 2,229 tribal members at that time. Furthermore, the mineral estate, while remaining tribally owned, could only be shared by the original allottees or their designated heirs. These people, known as "headright holders" or shareholders, received and continue to receive royalties from the production primarily of oil and gas. But many people, citing a number of legal opinions, believe that the tribal role itself includes *only* the original allottees and that the federal government will have the option of derecognizing or terminating the Osage tribe—and, thus, taking control of Osage oil—following the death of the last original allottee.

The Osage people were transformed by the discovery of oil. While the tribe certainly became very wealthy, money was not all that the petrodollars brought. Corruption, fraud, substance abuse, and violence were other results of the infusion of wealth. Tribal politics became almost completely consumed by the issues of oil leasing and royalty payments. The tribal government acquired a vested interest in maintaining the status quo, but it failed to note, or at least to recognize effectively, the growth of a very large group of Osages who held no headright. Since nonholders are legally barred from voting in tribal matters or holding office, this group of people became increasingly alienated from the tribal government.

By around 1990, this disenfranchised group of Osage had grown to over 10,000 people (out of a population of almost 15,000, including about 4,000 not listed on the census rolls). Two related problems were coming to a head: the question of the disenfranchised majority and the concern that when the last original allottee died the government might move to dissolve its trust responsibility and not recognize any Osage people, whether they owned a headright or not. The tribal council approached the situation with extreme caution: It recognized the problem of having the tribe controlled by a minority of its people, but it also wanted desperately to protect the rights of shareholders. It feared that broadening the membership roles would allow nonheadright owners to share in the mineral estate.

In 1992, a federal judge held in a lawsuit (*Fletcher* v. *U.S.*) that parts of the original 1881 constitution were valid and could be used to change the membership rules to include people not listed among the original 2,229 headright owners. The judge's opinion allowed a 1993 referendum to determine whether or not to alter or replace the tribe's governmental structure. The result was the creation of a new entity, known as the Osage Nation, under which all tribal members could vote and hold office. The old Tribal Council became known as the Mineral Council. The Nation held a constitutional election in 1994 in which 66 percent of *all* Osages voted. A second election was held in 1996.

However, the old tribal council appealed the ruling, and in 1997 an appellate court overturned the original decision. The court ruled that the judge disregarded U.S. policy granting sovereign immunity to Indian tribes. As a result, the federal government effectively dissolved the Osage Nation and restored the Tribal Council of the Osage Tribe of Oklahoma. (For its part, the Osage National Council, governing body of the Osage Nation, was appalled that the courts effectively disenfranchised up to 13,000 of the 17,000-member tribe. It vowed to appeal, in part on the grounds that the Tribal Council established by the 1906 Osage Allotment Act was itself a spurious entity created by the U.S. government in contravention of the Osage Constitution of 1881.)

Meanwhile, the Osage Shareholders' Organization (OSA) weighed in by accusing the Tribal Council of corruption. The group alleged that the council allowed energy companies to withhold hundreds of thousands of dollars in oil royalties and that the council covered up its illegal acts by refusing to provide tribal members (that is, shareholders) with relevant information. There have also been allegations of missing tribal trust funds to the tune of $177 million. The OSA has also lined up strongly behind the move to open membership roles, on the grounds that shareholders and nonshareholders alike will lose their rights if the United States effectively terminates the Osage tribe when the last allottee dies.

Following the federal government's mandate, a new chief was elected in a June 1998 election—by roughly 2.5 percent of the Osage population. As of early 1999 there had been no resolution of the issues of tribal membership or governance. Some Osage insist that the federal government will not simply terminate the Osage once the last original allottee dies (in mid-1998 there were only 20 such people alive, the youngest being 92 years old). Others consider this view naive in the extreme.

Some tribal members are circulating a petition that is meant to preserve the Osage Tribe by means of a new membership roll. They insist that their initiative is not designed to have any impact on the minerals estate, only to open up the membership and governance structures. The Tribal Council has expressed support for an expanded membership. However, the petitioners maintain that the council is dragging its feet and that, out of fear of losing both its political control and the shareholders' control over the mineral wealth, it does not want to prepare a new membership roll.

There is some irony that the issue of the tribe's mineral estate is so central to the tribe's political problems. Scientific evidence strongly suggests that the oil supply may be running out and could be exhausted as early as 2007 if no new reserves are discovered. Of course, there are other factors affecting the supply and availability of Osage oil, including the role of new technology in locating and extracting reserves and the relative price of oil. These uncertainties are pushing the tribe toward greater economic diversification but also ensure that the issue of control over natural resources will be a major one for the foreseeable future.

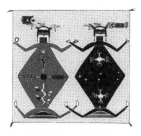

REPRESENTATION

Representation is an issue not easily illustrated with reference to individual communities. Therefore, unlike the other entries, this one has a pan-Indian focus. Representation affects every Native American to a greater or lesser extent, for it is here that, for many people, political and economic abuse meets personal humiliation. For a people who have lost so much throughout the years, dignity is an especially valuable resource. It is exactly this resource, such an important factor in meeting so many contemporary challenges, that suffers through various forms of misrepresentation.

Non-natives regularly represent themselves as native for reasons of personal profit or power. Obvious examples include New Agers who perform "Indian" religious ceremonies, people who charge for "Indian-style" healing, and entrepreneurs who make and sell fake Indian crafts. These activities involve a great deal of economic exploitation. Moreover, by purveying false notions of spirituality, ceremonialism, and knowledge, the people behind such activities also engage in cultural debasement.

Other forms of misrepresentation are equally offensive in different ways. The typical Thanksgiving story is only the most well known of the many historically inaccurate, culturally demeaning, and politically self-serving depictions of Indians in school curricula and among society at large. Thanksgiving may appear to be benign, and, in fact, the surface story is obviously a positive one. But happy histories often mask important conflicts that are equally, and perhaps even more significantly, a part of the story.

Sports mascots, which mock and trivialize native history and culture, remain pervasive in U.S. society. While many high schools and colleges have abandoned these racist caricatures, many have not. Professional sports have proven to be especially recalcitrant. Non-natives remain oblivious—at best—to the anguish many native people feel when confronted with sports mascots. As is the case with forms of spiritual and economic exploitation, it is far more convenient for non-natives to think of Indians in terms of a murky past full of honorable enemies than as contemporary people with rights and sensitivities that may conflict with theirs.

Native Americans struggle for political, economic, and even cultural justice. People for whom it is not an issue may have trouble understanding, but the struggle for dignity is an equally important and challenging part of the lives of many Native Americans. In many cases it is an intensely personal struggle, perhaps the one most able to be eased by a personal commitment on the part of non-natives.

Spirituality

The phenomenon of ersatz Indian spiritualists—non-natives who represent themselves as Indians for the purpose of gaining fame, money, and power—goes to the heart of the very complex issue of native representation. In fact, there is a lot of money to be made in the "Indian biz": Sales of books, ceremonies, workshops, and the like that purport to convey some sort of "Indian" knowledge are worth millions of dollars a year. But for most native people, the main problem with this type of activity is not the money that accrues to the impostors. Much more important are questions of cultural appropriation, blasphemy, and even survival.

Non-native appropriators of native spirituality and ceremonialism are known by a variety of names, such as "whiteshamans", "members of the Wanabi tribe," and "plastic medicine men." They may be seen within the New Age movement, the men's movement, the environmental movement, and even the "neopagan" movement, or within no movement at all. Specific examples abound. Anglo groups like Phoenix's infamous Kachina Klub or Prescott's Smoki People perform Hopi ceremonies. (Protests forced the Smoki people to stop performing their version of the Hopi Snake Dance.) Non-native artists represent their wares (crafts, music, ceremonial paraphernalia) as being of Native American origin. Non-natives organize pseudo "tribes" and take on "typical" Indian names. Fake Indian sites are posted on the World Wide Web for commercial purposes. Radio personalities and electronic chat hosts gather a following by claiming to dispense "Indian" knowledge.

Perhaps the most egregious example of this phenomenon is the relatively widespread practice of selling participation in "genuine Indian" ceremonies, as well as its corollary: representing oneself as an "Indian" medicine man or healer. For a fee, one can participate in a "sweat lodge ceremony" (or purchase a prefab sweat lodge itself, for that matter), a "sun dance," or a "vision quest." To understand the effect of this type of activity on many native people, one can imagine non-Catholics dressing as priests, offering their version of a Mass, and claiming to be the real thing.

The rise of this sort of activity is fairly recent, even though the general practice of stereotyping native people for profit is not new. Indian mascots (discussed later) are a venerable tradition in this country, and certainly Edward Curtis and other photographers tried to make money by selling their particular version of "Indianness." But neither the mascot-identified institutions nor artists like Curtis claimed to *be* Indian. In "Indian" performances at fairs, Wild West shows, and other such popular attractions, which have a fairly long pedigree, some performers have always been Indians, as are, today, some of the people castigated for misusing Indian culture.

With the exception of the Wild West show and Boy Scout–fantasy theme, Indians in the United States did not have much cachet among the general population before the 1960s. It was the crosscurrents of that tumultuous decade—call to consciousness, spiritual reawakening, hippie culture, social justice, back to the land, Red Power—that came together to alter the popular image of Indians. Mass marketing, that sine qua non of U.S. identity, helped fuel the trend. Suddenly, and for decades following the 1960s, fantasy became reality, as millions of non-natives began to find real value in what they imagined as a sort of generic, romanticized "Indian" spirituality.

The charitable view among many Native Americans of the attraction to non-natives of "Indian spirituality" is that the dominant culture is undergoing a spiritual crisis. Since Indians have been struggling for centuries against the onslaught of a culture to which many could not easily relate, there is a degree of sympathy for this explanation. However, this scenario is fraught with many ironies, not the least of which is that a society that has so consistently abused native people should now be reaching out to them for its salvation.

Many Indians who speak out against "whiteshamamism" note that in any case there is no such thing as "Indian" anything! "Indian," an appellation coined by Christopher Columbus, is a racial term. The "Indians" were never a nation or a coherent culture but rather a myriad of cultures, each with its own ceremonies and religion. To represent a piece of jewelry or a ceremony as "Indian" (as opposed to, say, Yurok, Laguna, or Creek) is just as ridiculous (and offensive) as the old Westerns in which every Indian wore a Lakota war bonnet, inhabited Monument Valley, Arizona, and was either bloodthirsty, stoic, or both.

Furthermore, Indians, no matter what their culture, do not as a rule charge money to heal. "Do Not Pay to Pray" has become a rallying cry against such practices. If payment is involved, the chances are excellent that the ceremony or healer is unauthentic and thus a sacrilege against the real thing. A Lakota group has officially "declared war" on "all persons who persist in exploiting, abusing, and misrepresenting the sacred traditions and spiritual practices" of their people (see Documents section). Native people do not care to see their religion desecrated any more than other groups do.

As if one were needed, Indians also have another compelling reason to protect their spiritual practices against hucksters, charlatans, and profiteers. In the words of Tulalip activist Janet McCloud, "First they came to take our land and water, then our fish and game. Now they want our religions as well." In this view, cultural appropriation is synonymous with racism, and both are tools that one group uses to exploit another. Carried to its logical end, this perspective underscores an attitude among some non-natives that, since Indians no longer exist, they (the non-natives) are free to claim and thus literally to define contemporary Indian identity. (This reasoning partly underlies the drive in Tennessee to loosen the criteria for official recognition, an action that could give minority "status"—and thus access to certain programs—to almost anyone.)

Another related danger to Indian people is that Indian impostors undermine the already difficult process of cultural transmission. Especially in this age of total mass marketing and worldwide communication without boundaries, Indian identity, especially among the young, may actually be shaped more by some self-styled, non-native ersatz "Indian" than by that person's tribal elders. Given the history of the non-native effort to erase Indian cultures, many people view this effect as particularly painful.

These criticisms raise several important questions: Who has the authority to say what is or is not permissible regarding native religious practice, and why? Can a Makah speak only for other Makah on the subject? Does blood quantum have any bearing on who may represent themselves as an Indian? Is there a "politically correct" line that must be adhered to regarding the appropriation of Indian culture?

There are many definitions of "Indian," including legal ones, but in the end common sense should probably prevail. Being Indian is part blood and part culture. In matters of religion and cultural practice, a person is more likely to be legitimate if she or he is a member of a federally recognized (or at least recognizable) tribe, is part of an Indian community, is proceeding with respect and not for profit or self-aggrandizement, and does not claim to speak for all Indians. None of these criteria is meant to be definitive (tribal membership is particularly problematic), but taken together they may suggest a standard of appropriateness.

Since Indians do not speak with one voice, there can be no easy answer to the question of whether there is a "correct" position on this issue. Traditional groups, including elders and religious leaders, generally condemn any attempt by any person or group to profit from Indian religious practice or to conduct ceremonies other than in the traditional manner and for tribally recognized purposes. If there is a consensus, it is that non-natives who claim to be sympathetic to "Indian culture" would be best advised to get to know some Indians, educate themselves about some of the real issues Indians struggle with, and ally themselves with legitimate activist groups. As for personal spiritual growth, many paths are available that do not exploit others.

THANKSGIVING

In Massachusetts, an activist group—United American Indians of New England (UAINE)—has taken on one of the most popular stereotypes of Native Americans. History textbooks tell how the Pilgrims arrived on these shores in 1620 from Holland, from whence they had fled seeking religious freedom. They did not know how to survive in the new land and might well have starved to death if not for the kindness of the local Pokanoket Indians, who showed them how to plant and what to eat. When the first harvest came in, the two groups sat down in peace and friendship to celebrate the first Thanksgiving dinner.

A Native American protestor from the United American Indians of New England (UAINE) scuffles with police officers in Plymouth, Massachusetts, in November 1997. UAINE is a controversial group that has won concessions from the town of Plymouth regarding the presentation of local Indian history and culture. (AP Photo/Jim Rogash)

Come late November, classrooms all over the United States (including some located on reservations!) are decorated with pictures of smiling Indians and happy Pilgrims. However, while the event in question may well have been marked by thanksgiving and interracial harmony, some people question its simplistic representation. In an alternative view, the Pilgrims came to this country not to find (much less establish) religious freedom, which they already enjoyed in Holland, but as part of a commercial venture. One of the first things they did was to rob Pokanoket graves and steal the Indians' winter provisions. Furthermore, while UAINE would agree that the Pilgrims were given considerable assistance by the Pokanoket people, members of the group note that the only thing the Indians got in return was unremitting persecution, land theft, disease, and genocide.

Moreover, many historians believe that the first Thanksgiving must be seen in the context of the main event in seventeenth-century interracial history: King Philip's War. In 1675, Metacom (or King Philip)—son of Massasoit, the Pokanoket leader who welcomed the Pilgrims in 1620—and his people had been so abused by the English that they launched an all-out war to retake their land. They nearly succeeded. Thanksgiving had been suspended during the war but resumed in 1676, when the Pokanokets had been nearly wiped out and soldiers entered Plymouth carrying Metacom's head on a pole.

The Thanksgiving holiday, however, is not about real events that unfolded between Indians and non-natives in seventeenth-century New England. It is supposed to commemorate an idealized moment frozen in our national consciousness, a moment of cooperation and interracial tranquility. From there, the national mythology concerning Indians and non-natives jumps to "Indian wars" of the mid-nineteenth century and from there to today, when Indians have more or less disappeared and the Pilgrims' benevolent vision has been fulfilled.

Every Thanksgiving since 1970, UAINE and its supporters have staged a National Day of Mourning in Plymouth, Massachusetts. UAINE is a loose coalition of activists led by Moonanum Roland James, a Gay Head (Aquinnah) Wampanoag (most Pokanoket descendants are now called Wampanoags), and Mahtowin Munro, a Lakota Dakota. UAINE's origins stretch back to 1970, when James's father, Wamsutta Frank James, was invited by Pilgrim descendants to speak on the occasion of the 350th anniversary of the Pilgrim arrival in North America. When they got wind of the content of James's speech, however, the group insisted on its revision. James refused and did not attend the event. Instead, as word of the incident spread, he and others gathered at Cole's Hill in Plymouth and declared Thanksgiving to be a National Day of Mourning.

Since the early days of the protest, UAINE has used the Day of Mourning to link events of the past with contemporary issues affecting American Indian and Inuit people. Speakers routinely speak out in support of Leonard Peltier, a Anishinabe/Lakota man widely considered to be unjustly imprisoned on a double murder charge. They refer to new stereotypes of Native Americans, noting that, especially in southern New England (home to the Pequots' hugely successful Foxwoods casino), many people now think of Indians as rich, whereas many native people in the United States continue to live in poverty. Speakers also decry the ongoing attacks against the religious practices, economic activities, and dignity of contemporary native people.

Moreover, the group makes common cause with other people oppressed by what it considers the values imported by the Pilgrims and their cultural descendants. Explicitly repudiating the myth of Euro-American superiority and inevitability expressed in holidays such as Thanksgiving and Columbus Day, UAINE has extended its umbrella to embrace other racial and ethnic minorities, homosexuals, and poor and working-class white people. Its vision is ultimately one of building a coalition not to restore some mythical Indian paradise but both to acknowledge a history of the United States very different from the mainstream version and to create a new society based, to a greater extent than today's, on tolerance, justice, and opportunity.

For years, the UAINE protest and the traditional Thanksgiving celebrations in Plymouth coexisted uneasily but peacefully. In 1995, however, UAINE members dumped sand and seaweed on Plymouth Rock. In 1997, marchers were met by Plymouth police who ordered them to disperse and then began using force, including pepper spray, to back up their demand.

More than two dozen people were arrested on a variety of disorderly conduct and unlawful assembly charges.

The officers defended their actions on the grounds that the group was marching without a permit. UAINE observed that they had marched for 28 years without a permit. They observed that non-native brutality against Indians in Plymouth was nothing new and, further, drew parallels between anti-Indian activities related to both the Pilgrims' commercial interests and the importance of the tourism industry in today's Plymouth. In fact, they maintained that the incident only underscored the existence of the continuing mistreatment of native people.

The case was finally resolved in October 1998 in a historic settlement. Both police and protesters were officially cleared of wrongdoing. Protesters agreed not to sue the town for injuries received, while Plymouth agreed to pay $100,000 for education about Native American history, $20,000 as payment of UAINE's legal fees, and $15,000 for two plaques, one honoring Metacom and the other presenting "alternative" views of Thanksgiving. The right to demonstrate peaceably on Thanksgiving Day without a permit was also formalized.

The Plymouth police are not the only ones who question the motives and the actions of UAINE. The Mashpee (Massachusetts) Wampanoag explicitly distanced themselves from UAINE in 1998. In their view, UAINE, once truly representative of local Indians, now espouses an extremist political agenda that only incidentally includes a few generic "Indian" issues. They note that UAINE refused to meet with local tribal organizations and does not focus on the contemporary concerns of real Wampanoags, such as federal recognition for the Mashpee tribe, hunting and fishing rights, or the Aquinnah gaming initiative. Other New England Indians reject UAINE as well.

In any case, UAINE and its supporters will continue to gather on Cole's Hill in Plymouth on the fourth Thursday in November. In 1998, organizers planned a peaceful demonstration free of drugs and alcohol. Most fundraising and merchandise sales were prohibited. A potluck social followed the National Day of Mourning. The groups' slogan underscores its contemporary message of self-representation: "We are not vanishing. We are not conquered. We are stronger than ever."

MASCOTS

The issue of mascots—the adoption by school and professional sports teams of native images or slogans—is not one that affects many Native Americans on a day-to-day-basis. However, while indicators such as economic output, incidence of malnutrition, mortality rates, and college diplomas are readily quantified, human dignity is not so easy to measure. For people who feel their self-respect is under attack by the use of sports mascots, the matter is indeed important.

Cleveland Indians fans celebrate the win of the 1995 World Series. Many people, Indians and non-natives alike, consider mascots such as this one to be racist and demeaning. (AP Photo/Mark Duncan)

The Cleveland Indians, Atlanta Braves, Florida State Seminoles, University of Illinois Fighting Illini, and Washington Redskins are just some of the hundreds of professional, college, and high school teams that have adopted native-type mascots and slogans. Most such mascots are accompanied by caricature images and symbols, such as tomahawk chops and generic, "Indian-style" music and dance. Since the controversy over sports mascots surfaced in the 1960s and '70s, several institutions—notably Stanford University, Dartmouth College, Marquette University, Syracuse University, Miami University (Ohio), and the University of Oklahoma—have dropped their offensive slogans and images. Most, however, remain reluctant to change.

For many native people and some non-natives as well, the use of Indian-type mascots sends messages that are both historically misleading and personally offensive. The "adoption" by non-native institutions of Indian symbols is designed with many purposes in mind. The institutions wish to link a view of Indians as savage, hostile, or aggressive with their sports teams. A related association is that of Indians as noble, worthy adversaries, a view that gained currency when Indians ceased to be thought of by the non-native population as a military threat. Proud, dignified, and relentless in battle: What could be a better image for a sports team?

However, when sports teams appropriate or create Indian images they send another message as well: that "Indians" are at the service of the teams or have somehow acquiesced in or given their blessings to the main business of the day, which is, after all, entertainment. Pregame or halftime pageantry often ritually links the Indian figure with the team in question. Both the team members and, not incidentally, the partisan audience are allowed to bask in the identification with ersatz or generic "Indian" values. Finally, the Indian figure leads or participates in some unifying event, such as the singing of the national anthem, symbolically affirming both the triumph of the dominant culture and native acquiescence in the outcome of the historical process (read the attempted genocide of their people).

Indian mascots are historically misleading in other ways as well. Who are Chief Wahoo, Chief Illiniwek, Chief Osceola, and the other Indian team mascots? Osceola, at least, had a historical identity: a Seminole leader (although not a chief), he opposed the removal of his people from their homeland, fought U.S. troops, and died while in prison after having been seized under a flag of truce. The others are mere fictions, as are most of the so-called Indian dances and music associated with the mascots. The creation of ersatz Indians and Indian cultural symbols to entertain largely non-native audiences may be understood in conjunction with the traditional Thanksgiving celebrations and New Age "Indian" ceremonies already discussed. All undermine the history, the identity, and even the contemporary existence of Native Americans.

It is easy to equate the practice with racism, and thus to understand the pain felt by many Indians over the use of Indian mascots, by switching metaphors. Would the Cleveland baseball franchise consider calling its team the Jews? Could one imagine a team called the Washington Blackskins—or, worse, a racial slur equivalent to "redskin," such as "darky"? Would the U.S. public accept (and would teams present), say, a Sambo image in place of the grinning, bucktooth Chief Wahoo? Would bands feel free to evoke musical images of warfare (stereotypes of Indians in Hollywood Westerns come immediately to mind) and imagined ceremonial themes of any other racial or ethnic group save Native Americans? Would university administrators defend

109

parodies of African dance as they do "buck and squaw" parties held by certain fraternities and sororities?

The use of Indian-type mascots has many defenders, not all of whom are non-native. The Seminole Tribe of Florida is on record as supporting Florida State University's caricature of Chief Osceola and its appropriation of the Seminole name for its sports teams. Not surprisingly, however, the various efforts to retain Indian-type sports mascots are led by non-natives. At the University of Illinois, for example, the chair of the Board of Trustees called Chief Illiniwek "an extremely important symbol for the university," noting furthermore that "[were she] a Native American person [she would] be complimented." Beyond this defense of the practice itself, officials opposed to change cite fears of an alumni or fan backlash that would have a negative impact on financial contributions (to the school) as well as a loss of merchandise sales. They offer this excuse despite evidence that schools who have dropped offensive mascots have suffered little or no impact on fund raising.

Opponents of Chief Illiniwek note the origins of the chief in a 1926 halftime charade designed to make fans feel good about themselves; the costume and war bonnet in a huckster's 1930s association of football and Custer's defeat at the Little Big Horn; and the proprietary logo from a freelance graphic designer in 1981. They point out that the Illini, who were not in any case a tribe but rather a loose association of bands, were a farming people who only fought to defend themselves. Joe Gone of the university's Native Student Association noted in 1997 that, "there is no need to remember Indians of the past. There are some 30,000 Indians in Illinois [today] and this university serves damn few of them."

Like happy images of Pilgrims and Indians or of "shamans" selling "genuine Indian" ceremonies, Indian-type sports mascots serve the desires of non-native people at the expense of Indian dignity and self-respect. The battle repeats itself generation after generation, as Indian children look at mascot caricatures and feel ashamed. When well-meaning non-natives are able to reject self-serving attitudes represented by such statements as "If I were an Indian I would feel honored" and take their cue from real native people, the latter will be free from a demeaning and destructive form of exploitation.

SACRED SITES

It is perhaps not surprising, given the differences in fundamental assumptions that still obtain between mainstream society and many native people, that conflicts over places the latter consider sacred remain intense and ongoing. Attachments to natural areas or resources do not involve romantic notions of the past but are often central to native identity and culture here and now. Among native people, religion and place are traditionally inseparable. For many non-natives, on the other hand, religion is something in a box (a church, which may be built anywhere), while land is nothing more than a commodity. There is a tendency for non-natives to see the former view as primitive, naive, and even subversive, which it is, of course, to the extent that it runs counter to capitalist notions of private property and the market economy.

Examples of the conflict abound. The San Carlos Apache have been praying atop Dzil Nchaa Si An, known to non-natives as Mt. Graham, for centuries. They recognize this place as the home to sacred spirits and the mountain itself as a sentient being. They are losing a fierce battle to prevent a consortium of groups, including the University of Arizona and the Vatican, from building a massive telescope complex on the site. Complex environmental issues are involved, as well.

In California, a coalition of tribes has banded together to stop the creation of a nuclear waste dump in Ward Valley, charging that environmental damage caused by construction and possibly contamination would threaten the sacred desert tortoise (not to mention the drinking water of millions of people). For the San Carlos Apache it is the mountain that lives, for the Colorado River tribes, the tortoise: The principle is the same. As with Mt. Graham, the Indian tribes have been able to enlist the help of people who object to the project strictly for environmental reasons. The main supporters of the dump have been the state of California and the nuclear industry, while Mount Graham is strongly backed by the federal government, a university, and powerful foreign interests. In both cases, the tribes have the determination of David going up against a powerful Goliath. Goliath seems to have the upper hand in Arizona, whereas in California David just might pull off a victory.

In Kansas, the controversy over sacred sites assumed an intertribal cast when the Wyandotte Tribe of Oklahoma threatened to build a casino on land

SACRED SITES

considered sacred by their relatives, the Wyandot Tribe of Kansas. Unlike the previous two examples, environmental considerations play little or no role in this controversy, nor do powerful outside interests (except possibly the state of Kansas). Sovereignty is a key issue here, but in a very different way than in the cases described above. In fact, this situation belies the myth of the essential sameness of all native groups, since the Wyandottes are perfectly willing to destroy one of their sacred sites—but only on their own terms.

These examples illustrate some of the different ways that native groups view sacredness and sacred sites. They also reveal what can happen when native religious practice conflicts with non-native desires. In both the United States and Canada, native religion and religious sites enjoy more legal protection than ever before. However, this is not saying much, since the traditional governmental stance toward native religion has been active opposition. In conflicts between native and non-native interests, even concerning religion, the latter almost always win. The struggle for native people over protecting their sacred sites remains very much an uphill one.

SAN CARLOS APACHE

With a coalition of supporters, the San Carlos Apache people have been seeking to halt construction of a Large Binocular Telescope (LBT, nicknamed "Columbus") on 8.6 acres atop 10,700-foot Mt. Graham, located in the Pinaleño Mountains about 100 miles northeast of Tucson, Arizona. The proposed $80 million telescope, featuring two mirrors about 26 feet in diameter, would be one of the world's most powerful of its type. The University of Arizona (UA) is chief sponsor of the telescope project. Two smaller telescopes on the same site are already on-line.

The financial and political strength of telescope supporters is impressive. Partners include the Vatican and Germany's Max Planck Institute. The church hopes to convert to Catholicism any life forms that may be discovered as a result of the telescope's use. It has also vowed, in the words of the Jesuit Vatican representative, to "suppress [the Apache religion] with all the force that we can muster."

Daring to oppose this powerful international consortium, the small San Carlos tribe claims that the project is defiling sacred ground without their consent and threatening their cultural survival. They consider the mountain to be a home to ga'an, sacred mountain spirits who taught the Apache their religion and their methods of healing. Ga'an are especially important in ceremonies such as the girls' coming-of-age ritual. The San Carlos Apache regard the mountain as a living organism whose powers will be harmed by the telescope project. Mt. Graham is also a source of medicinal herbs sacred to the Apache.

Mt. Graham (or Dzil Nchaa Si An, "Big Seated Mountain," in the Apache language) was originally part of the Apache reservation but was stripped by executive order in 1873 and now "belongs" to the U.S. Forest Ser-

112

An Apache Sunrise Ceremony, 1994. Apaches from the San Carlos community have opposed the telescope project on Mt. Graham in Arizona for years. Most recently they have insisted on being allowed to pray there as they have for centuries. (1994 Scott S. Warren/Tom Keller & Associates)

vice. In 1983 parts of the Pinaleño Mountains were withdrawn from the Arizona Wilderness Bill and designated an astrophysical research area. The following year UA proposed building 18 telescopes on the high peaks collectively known as Mt. Graham.

From the beginning, the project raised concerns among environmentalists. Due to its isolation from other boreal forests over 9,000 years ago, Mt. Graham contains five life zones and is known as a "sky-island," or isolated peak. As such, it is home to 18 unique life forms, such as the red squirrel, once considered extinct but now known to number perhaps several hundred individuals. A wide range of environmental groups, as well as sympathetic student groups, joined in opposition to the telescope project. In 1988, UA's own Office of Arid Lands opined that the land in question was too sensitive to be developed.

For its part, UA decided to become the first U.S. university to challenge in court Native American cultural values and religious rights. The university took the position that it had always worked closely with the San Carlos Apache on the siting and development of the telescopes and that the Indian opposition was unwarranted. Furthermore, it contests the Indians' claims to the mountain's sacredness, basing the opposition on alleged letters from tribal members locating the home of the *ga'an* on another mountain.

In an implicit acknowledgment of the project's environmental destructiveness, Congress in 1988 had passed, without hearings or Apache input, special legislation allowing the construction of three telescopes *in a specific location* and exempting the first phase of construction from further environmental review. In 1990, the San Carlos Tribal Council formally opposed the project and allowed Ola Cassadore-Davis to form the Apache Survival Coalition (ASC), a group composed of Apache medicine people and their supporters.

In 1991 the ASC filed suit in U.S. District Court to halt the telescope project. The group alleged that the project violated the American Indian Religious Freedom Act (AIRFA), the First and Third Amendments to the Constitution, the National Environmental Policy Act, the National Historic Preservation Act (NHPA), and the National Forest Management Act. (In 1988, in its Lyng decision, the U.S. Supreme Court essentially reduced AIRFA, an act of Congress, to the status of a nonbinding policy statement.) Since the original lawsuit was filed, the San Carlos Apache Tribal Council has passed four resolutions supporting the ASC and requesting that the telescopes be removed.

The ASC's lawsuit was dismissed in 1992 and an appeal rejected in 1994. However, in 1992 and 1993, the university realized that it had made a siting error and moved to change the location of the LBT. The Indians claimed the movement was arbitrary because no ethnographic study was conducted (on the new site), and they were not consulted in any case. A new lawsuit was filed, and in August 1994, a federal district judge ruled that the final phase was not exempt from federal laws because its site had been moved from that approved under the original plan. In 1995, the year the National Council of Churches passed a resolution supporting the Indians' opposition, the appeals court agreed with the demands of project opponents and ordered a new environmental review.

In an effort to circumvent the court's ruling, Arizona Republican Representative Jim Kolbe sponsored legislation allowing the project to continue and exempting it from all federal environmental law. Ironically (perhaps), his rider replaced provisions for an important study of acquired immunodeficiency syndrome (AIDS) among American Indians. The bill was passed and signed into law in April 1996. Later that year, the appellate court ruled that Congress was justified in passing legislation blocking any further environmental review.

The Apache Survival Coalition then told the court, in April 1997, that the U.S. Forest Service had violated the NHPA by moving the site 1,300 feet without having consulted the Apache Indians. The coalition asked that the sponsors be required to conduct a study, in conjunction with the San Carlos Apache, on the religious and cultural significance of the site. The Forest Service held that the change in siting did not require a new study. A federal appeals judge in July of that year upheld on a technicality a lower court's refusal to halt construction, ruling that the ASC had waited too long to file its suit.

Lawyers for the coalition said the group would consider further appeal and would also try to block the project by having the site placed in the National Register of Historic Places. (The President's Advisory Council on Historic Preservation found in 1996 that the project violated the NHPA.) In August 1998 a group of San Carlos Apache and other native people held religious observances on the site in violation of UA's requirement that they not visit without a "prayer permit." As of early 1999, construction was proceeding. The university hopes to begin operating the first of the two mirrors in 2001.

MOJAVE

In the southwestern United States, the Mojave and Indians from four other tribes—Chemehuevi, Cocopah, Quechan, and Colorado River Indian Tribes (CRIT)—have formed a coalition called the Colorado River Native Nations Alliance (CRNNA). The group's purpose is to oppose the siting of a 1,000-acre "low-level" nuclear waste dump in Ward Valley, located in the Mojave Desert near Needles, California.

The project has its origins in the 1980 Low-Level Radioactive Waste Policy Act, which shifts the burden for disposal of "low-level" waste (which may contain cesium, strontium, plutonium, and other extremely radioactive and long-lasting elements) to the states. The California Department of Health Services (DHS) licensed the project in 1994. However, since the site is located on federal land, the licensure meant little until or unless the land was transferred by the U.S. Department of the Interior (DOI) to the state.

The Indians reject the dump because of its direct threat to their culture, their economies, and, indeed, their lives. The spiritual significance of Ward Valley to the people is immense. One key reason is that the valley is home to the endangered desert tortoise. This animal, which can live as long as a century, plays a central role in the religion of CRNNA members. Considered a sacred teacher, the tortoise appears in the Mojave language through song cycles, in myths and legends, and in clan names.

Desert tortoises that inhabit Ward Valley are largely free of a fatal respiratory infection that, along with habitat destruction, has cut the total desert tortoise population in half over the past decade. In addition to its being a key desert tortoise habitat, Ward Valley is an important location for traditional medicinal plants. Ward Valley also lies adjacent to Spirit Mountain, mythological homeland to the Colorado River tribes who consider themselves guardians of the entire region.

Furthermore, a major aquifer runs directly below the site, which is located just 18 miles from the Colorado River. All five Indian tribes are sovereign nations that hold water rights presently used for agriculture and economic development as well as for domestic and recreational purposes. The Indians (and their allies) believe that radioactivity from the dump could quite possibly seep through to the aquifer and contaminate the Colorado River, which is the major source of their water as well as that of 22 million other people who live in the Southwest and Mexico.

The emblem of the Coalition to Save Ward Valley hangs on the framework of a teepee at the coalition's permanent encampment on the site of a proposed nuclear waste dump in Ward Valley, in the Mojave Desert about 20 miles west of Needles, California, February 15, 1996. Designed by Huna Smith, a local Chimehuevi Indian, the emblem depicts an endangered desert tortoise in midmeltdown with the nuclear radiation symbol on its shell. (AP Photo/ Reed Saxon)

Since the Ward Valley project is specifically designed to poison their land, the Indians consider any DOI support to be in violation of its fiduciary and trust responsibilities to the tribes. Moreover, the tribes cite two executive orders that they say the project explicitly violates. One is Executive Order 13007, which calls for the protection of Native American sacred sites on federal lands. The other is Executive Order 12898, Federal Actions to Address Environmental Justice in Minority Populations and Low-Income Populations.

Dump proponents believe that Ward Valley is needed to store waste generated by the use of nuclear medicine, nuclear power, and biotechnology research. They reject the safety arguments as well as those that concern Indian sacred land. Although former California governor Pete Wilson was a key advocate for the dump, approximately 200 cities and towns, including Los Angeles and San Francisco, have voiced their opposition, in part because of the threat to Indian sacred land. Senator Barbara Boxer and a number of California congressional representatives are also on record as opposing the project.

The dump's proposed managers, US Ecology (formerly Nuclear Engineering Corporation), plan to bury the waste in 55-gallon drums placed in shallow, unlined trenches recovered with vegetation. Scientists are divided on the issue of safety. Three U.S. Geological Survey (USGS) scientists describe the site as not having been demonstrated as safe for the proposed use, while the chief of nuclear waste hydrology of the USGS has described the risks as insignificant. US Ecology operates three other dump sites, all of which leak radioactive material (two are Superfund sites). A 1998 report by the nonpartisan General Accounting Office was highly critical of the safety record of US Ecology's parent company, American Ecology. The same report called into question American Ecology's assertion that only a few ounces of plutonium would be stored at the site, noting that the true amount could go as high as 124 pounds.

When Interior Secretary Manuel Lujan agreed to approve the transfer of the federally owned Ward Valley to the state (in 1993), the tribes and their supporters sued; out of that suit came the designation of 6.4 million acres, including the Ward Valley site, as critical habitat for the protected desert tortoise. The court found the transfer illegal and halted the proceedings. The project was further delayed in 1995, when the public learned that US Ecology had failed to report that its nuclear waste dump in Beatty, Nevada, similar in design to the one proposed for Ward Valley, experienced leakage and water contamination far more widespread than expected. This revelation caused the deputy secretary of the interior to call for a Supplemental Environmental Impact Statement (SEIS). It also encouraged opponents to initiate a vigil on the site.

The new interior secretary, Bruce Babbitt, had rescinded the transfer, but in May 1995 the Clinton administration agreed to support the land transfer pending resolution of the various lawsuits. As a preliminary step it ordered tests to determine the possibility of radioactive waste migration using tritium that had contaminated the valley's soil as a result of nuclear tests of the 1950s and '60s. In January 1998, the DOI issued permits for drilling and tritium testing. By now, the project's opponents had set up an encampment on the site.

With drilling and testing about to begin, the government demanded that the opponents' encampment be moved. The CRNNA's response was to launch a full-scale occupation. Among its demands were an end to further testing, face-to-face meetings with Secretary Babbitt, and explicit federal acknowledgment of its position. The occupation began on February 12, 1998. It was specifically nonviolent, with no weapons permitted on-site. Two days later the DOI ordered the occupiers to vacate the site. In response, the occupiers established a semipermanent camp known as Silyaye Aheace village and proceeded to hold religious and other ceremonies there. They and their supporters also put pressure on government officials to oppose the project, a demand to which the Clinton administration agreed in May.

On June 5, the DOI lifted its eviction order and withdrew its drilling permits. It also announced that it would formally oppose transfer of the site to the California DHS. This last position was taken in part because of a ruling by top California legislators that DHS had no authority to purchase the land and, in fact, that the governor violated state law by accepting $500,000 from US Ecology for the purchase. In response, the tribes removed their security roadblocks and cancelled their "red alert." They did, however, vow to continue the vigil until the project was permanently canceled.

In April 1999, a federal judge ruled that the United States does not have to turn over the land in question to the state of California. In June Governor Gray Davis declined to appeal that decision, although he also kept the project at least technically alive by not withdrawing the state's application to the DOI requesting the land transfer. Meanwhile, legislation authored by two Republican congressmen that would force the federal land transfer and exempt the dump from all existing environmental regulations remains pending. The SEIS and all testing have been indefinitely postponed. California legislators warn their constituents of a possible $1 billion increase in energy prices if the dump is built. Mexican legislators from border states are on record as opposing the project. Silyaye Aheace Village still exists, and the CRNNA remains firm in its determination to stop the project once and for all.

WYANDOTTE

Disagreements over the exploitation of sacred Native American ground do not always feature non-natives as major players. The Wyandotte Tribe of Oklahoma has proposed building a casino near the site of an old Huron cemetery located in Wyandotte County, Kansas. Many groups, including the Wyandot Nation of Kansas, four other Kansas Indian tribes, and virtually the entire Kansas government, vehemently oppose this idea. The controversy centers around issues of ownership of the disputed property, federal recognition of Indian tribes, treaty rights and sovereignty, the profitability of gaming, and the meaning of sacred in a native context.

The dispute has its origins in the breakup of the Wyandotte tribe in the 1860s. The Wyandottes, themselves descendants of the old Huron Confederacy, were removed from the state of Ohio to Wyandotte County, Kansas, in 1842. The tribal organization was dissolved in 1855. At that time the Wyandottes instead were encouraged to become U.S. citizens by taking their land in severalty. A cultural and political split developed, with the more acculturated people choosing citizenship and land allotments and the more traditional remaining noncitizens.

In 1867, the latter group, numbering about 200 people, relocated to the new Indian Territory (Oklahoma). The Wyandotte Tribe of Oklahoma was created in 1937 and rerecognized (they had been terminated in the 1950s) in 1978. The Wyandot Nation of Kansas, officially recognized by the state of Kansas, has petitioned for federal recognition. The two groups have had a troubled relationship ever since their split well over 100 years ago.

The "Huron cemetery" in Wyandotte County, Kansas, was reserved as a "public cemetery" under the 1855 treaty. It is listed in the National Register of Historic Places. Only the Wyandots continued to use the cemetery well into the twentieth century, and they have vigorously defended it against various development proposals. However, both tribes have claimed ownership of the property. In the 1950s, the Wyandotte Tribe proposed moving the graves to Oklahoma and selling the land for commercial development. In this they were successfully opposed by the Wyandot Nation of Kansas as well as by local non-native organizations. However, in 1994 the Wyandottes proposed moving the bodies in the Huron cemetery and building a casino on the site. In 1996, the Bureau of Indian Affairs (BIA) approved the tribe's request that the site be taken into trust status so that the Wyandottes could establish a gaming facility, in accordance with the provisions of the 1988 Indian Gaming Regulatory Act.

Vigorous opposition to the Wyandotte plan has been led by their relatives, the Wyandots of Kansas. In their view, as articulated by Chief Jan English, a casino located on or adjacent to the cemetery would disturb its sanctity. "Imagine our relatives lying here," said one member, "looking up at the floor of a casino." Furthermore, the Wyandots claim greater control over the cemetery than the Wyandottes on the grounds of continuous use.

There are a number of other interested parties as well. Fred Thomas, chairman of the Kickapoo Tribe, questioned the motivation of the BIA in approving the application of an out-of-state tribe when the Kickapoo had been trying for some time to get the BIA to put land in trust on its own reservation. He questioned whether the disputed land even had reservation status to begin with and submitted that the BIA was siding with commercial interests at the expense of the public interest, since the latter also had an interest under other federal laws in preserving the cemetery.

Presumably it was not the proposed casino but either the site or the potential competition that bothered the Kickapoo, since they opened their own gaming establishment, Golden Eagle, in 1996. Development of the cemetery was also opposed by the other Kansas Indian tribes with gaming compacts—the Prairie band of Potawatomi, the Iowa, and the Sac and Fox. These groups tried to open casinos in 1994 but were successfully opposed by the state.

State officials have been reluctant to back the Wyandotte plan in the face of so much Indian opposition. Governor Bill Graves is on record as opposing the project on the grounds that no Kansas land other than that owned by its resident tribes qualifies as "Indian lands" under the federal Indian Gaming Act. Kansas Senator Sam Brown in 1997 won an amendment to the DOI's appropriations bill designating the disputed land as a cemetery and declaring that it could never be used for any other purpose. The Wyandottes maintain that this law is unconstitutional because the tribe is protected by sovereign immunity.

For their part, the Wyandottes stood firm on what they consider solid legal ground. According to a letter to the mayor of Kansas City, dated August 29, 1997, Chief Leaford Bearskin maintains that the tribe has always had a right to build at the cemetery. He said that the tribe had delayed in deference to the city's wishes but, owing to federal funding cutbacks, it could no longer afford not to build a casino there. He noted that the facility over the cemetery was intended to be temporary and that the tribe would abandon the site if an alternative could be found. One such site, an old racetrack, was blocked by a bankruptcy judge.

A major development in the controversy occurred in July 1998, when the two tribes agreed that the site would only be used for burial or related religious or cultural activities. The agreement would prohibit any economic development on, over, or under the cemetery. It also called upon the Wyandots to withdraw from a lawsuit challenging the federal government's designation of the cemetery site as Wyandotte reservation land. The agreement must be approved by the DOI in order to have the force of law.

The two tribes consider it binding between themselves in any case. However, were DOI not to approve the agreement, the Wyandots would probably not drop out of the lawsuit. There is also a clause in the agreement that permits the Wyandotte Tribe to open a casino at the site of the Scottish Rite Temple, which is adjacent to the cemetery. The Wyandots would certainly oppose such a plan but for the moment are focusing on more positive and hopeful aspects of the agreement.

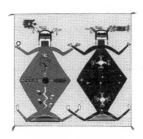

SOVEREIGNTY

Sovereignty is perhaps the single most contested issue of all. It also underlies most other contemporary concerns. True sovereignty, of course, entails complete political independence and self-rule. Yet, while the word is often used in connection with Indian tribes and First Nations, all native people remain subject to some extent to the laws of the United States or Canada.

Representative of the many complex aspects of the issue of tribal sovereignty is the debate over judicial and legislative jurisdiction. It is the position of virtually all native governments that they should have jurisdiction over all people, native and non-natives, on their territory. In the words of Trudell Guerue, chief judge of the Rosebud Sioux Tribal Court in 1988, "Tribal courts should have jurisdiction over non-Indians and over all crimes because everyone should be subject to the laws of the locale he is in. If I go to Denmark, I'm subject to the laws there, so if someone comes here he should be subject to our laws. . . . [This] is nationalism at its most basic. . . . It is our land and we should be in control" (quoted in Sharon O'Brien, *American Indian Tribal Governments* [Norman: University of Oklahoma Press, 1989], p. 152).

However, both Canada and the United States continue to reserve for themselves the right to determine the scope of native sovereignty. Formerly popular ideas such as Manifest Destiny and the White Man's Burden may appear to be relics of the past, but both countries continue to base their claims to control native life on such equally racist conveniences as the Doctrine of Discovery and *terra nulla*. In Section 35(2) of the 1982 constitution, the Canadian government attempted once again to define the issue of native identity and the scope of native rights, recognizing, for the first time, the "aboriginalness" of Métis and Inuit people as well as Indians. Recent U.S. Supreme Court cases, such as *Brendale v. Confederated Tribes and Bands of Yakima* (1989), in which the court severely limited tribal sovereignty, illustrate the difficulty of the legal struggle to restore the sovereign authority of tribal governments.

The following three examples reveal different aspects of the issue of native sovereignty. Like many Indian tribes, but perhaps more than most, the Quinault Indian Nation is administratively a complicated entity. Thanks to the history of allotment, it comprises not only "ethnic" Quinault but members of various tribes. Moreover, a group of people who actually own considerably more of the reservation than does the tribal government claims the right to govern the community alongside, or perhaps instead of, the elected government. The Quinault are currently participating in a Bureau of Indian Affairs (BIA)–sponsored self-governance project that some tribal members fear is actually a ploy to undermine tribal sovereignty. Unlike the Onondaga (discussed next), intratribal opposition remains generally peaceful.

Sovereignty issues take a very different form among the members of the Onondaga Nation. Unlike many Indian groups, the Onondaga are a tribe whose complete sovereignty has been formally recognized by European and U.S. governments for centuries. Yet, issues related to sovereignty, especially those of taxation and law enforcement, have caused friction between the Indians and state authorities and, in fact, have riven the tribe itself. Although the tribe's status vis-à-vis state and federal authorities is linked to and has helped exacerbate other intratribal divisions (in this there are similarities with the Quinault Nation), it also exists as a highly contentious issue in and of itself.

The case of the Inuit people of northeastern Canada differs in surface details but not in underlying issues. Unlike either the Quinault or the Onondaga, the various Inuit groups never signed treaties with the federal authorities. However, on April 1, 1999, they became the rulers of an administrative entity called Nunavut, the newest Canadian territory and one that is 85 percent Inuit. The people have gained a great deal in terms of land ownership, self-government, and economic assistance, but in exchange they ceded their aboriginal land title, something the Onondaga never did.

Recently, the Royal Commission on Aboriginal Peoples has affirmed that First Nation sovereignty exists in law even without constitutional guarantees, but many Indians continue to mistrust the Canadian parliament's approach to native sovereignty. While supporters of recent legislative proposals speak of a step toward meaningful self-government, many Indians have labeled them "White Paper 2," a reference to the Canadian-style termination legislation of a generation ago. Despite the clause in Section 35(2) stating that "the existing aboriginal and treaty rights of the aboriginal peoples of Canada are hereby recognized and confirmed," the practical exercise of tribal sovereignty is highly charged and remains very much a matter of ongoing legal argument and negotiation. This is true in both Canada and the United States.

QUINAULT

Eighteen years after the Quinault Tribe signed the 1855 Quinault River Treaty, President Ulysses S. Grant signed an executive order recognizing its sovereignty over the Quinault Reservation. Nevertheless, the government in 1907 moved to break up the reservation in accordance with the General Allotment Act. This process was suspended seven years later, largely because Quinault land, consisting mainly of beaches and forests, was considered unsuitable for individual allotments.

However, allotment soon resumed thanks to a successful legal challenge to Quinault sovereignty on the basis of wording in the 1873 executive order referring to the Quinault reservation as existing for the benefit of the "fish-eating Indians on the Pacific Coast." In 1931 the U.S. Supreme Court ruled that members of other tribes (including the Chehalis, Chinook, and Cowlitz) could own allotments on the Quinault Reservation, even if they did not live there.

Two years later, the Quinault Reservation had been allotted in its entirety. Not everyone who received an allotment was a Quinault or even an Indian. In fact, the Chinook soon became the largest landowners on the Quinault Reservation. Over the years, many allotments have been removed from trust status, resulting in a net loss of reservation land. In 1990, the Quinault Indian Nation owned less than 10 percent of its reservation lands. Individual Indians (of various tribes) owned about two-thirds of the reservation, timber corporations about one-quarter, and individual non-Indians and the tribe the rest.

Complicating the question of land ownership is the issue of identity. Tribal membership is open to anyone who can prove at least one-quarter combined descent from any of seven tribes—Quinault, Queets, Quileute, Hoh, Chehalis, Cowlitz, and Chinook—and who is not already a member of another tribe. Furthermore, people not meeting this standard may apply for adoption into the tribe. Though legal, these requirements make for an inclusive definition of the term "Quinault Indian" that has resulted in some conflict. However, the question of sovereignty remains far more difficult for the people to resolve: How is a nation to control its territory when 90 percent of that territory is owned by someone else?

In fact, there is a long history of friction between the nation per se and a group called the Quinault Allottees Association (QAA). The members of this group have often perceived their interests as different from that of the nation. Sometimes the two groups' interests have jibed, as when they both argued successfully in the case of *U.S.* v. *Mitchell* that the United States was accountable for mismanaging forests on the Quinault reservation. However, the QAA and the Quinault Nation have often battled over land and other rights. The fact that the reservation is largely owned by one group (QAA), but governed by another (Quinault Indian Nation), guarantees that issues of sovereignty over the land base will continue to be a thorny problem.

This situation raises other issues of sovereignty as well. For instance, the Chinook Indian Tribe was denied federal recognition in 1997. While the BIA held that the Chinook were not in fact a splinter group of the Quinault Nation, it did raise this as an issue by observing that Chinook actively participate in the political process of the Quinault in order to further their own perceived interests. Furthermore, the Quinault, citing potential jurisdictional issues, have angered the Cowlitz Indian Tribe by opposing its petition, provisionally granted as of July 1999, for federal recognition. Conflicts with neighbors over actual and potential threats to sovereignty are just one of the legacies of the allotment process.

Perhaps because of the exceptional degree of external influence in their internal matters, the Quinault have been especially protective of their sovereign rights. Their own school board approves curricula that highlight Quinault culture and feature instruction in the Salishan language. Quinault government policies have discouraged the location of non-Indian businesses within the reservation. To preserve habitat, and in the face of a rigorous state challenge, they closed all beaches to nontribal members in 1969. Strict zoning laws, designed to preserve beach lands, soon followed. The tribe also stopped a state road from going through the reservation when the state would not agree to let the tribe control access within the reservation.

Years of extensive clear-cutting and poor forest management practices had engendered widespread environmental destruction on the reservation. After 20 years of logging under BIA oversight, for instance, less than 1 percent of the clear-cut land had been replanted, and much of the reservation faced the danger of slash fires. When in 1971 the BIA allowed a lumber company to reduce its payments to allottees, the tribe protested this action and the general state of reservation logging by blocking a key bridge to logging trucks. This action proved to be a major step in the tribe's reclaiming responsibility for its own natural resources.

Early activities of the Quinault Resource Development Project (QRDP), created about the same time as the bridge blockade, focused on rehabilitating forest and fisheries resources on the reservation. In 1976 this organization was renamed the Quinault Department of Natural Resources and Economic Development. The Quinault now reforest their land and own three major fish propagation facilities. They also have full control over a major reforestation program that operates under the principles of the nation's own Forest Practices Act. One purpose of their careful land stewardship is to provide employment for their people indefinitely.

The Quinault Indian Nation helped develop the federal program known as the Tribal Self-Governance Demonstration Project (TSDP). Passed as the Self-Government Act of 1988 and amended in 1991 and again in 1994, the TSDP is essentially a supplement to the Indian Self-Determination and Education Assistance Act of 1975. The overall aim is to facilitate the complete transition to an effective government-to-government relationship between the tribes and the U.S. government.

Although some people believe that the TSDP is a stealth plan that leads toward termination (of the U.S. trust responsibility to the tribes), participants such as the Quinault claim that the project actually reaffirms the trust responsibility and that it really increases tribal authority. Participation in the TSDP allows the tribes to develop and manage their own affairs without going through the U.S. government bureaucracy. In fact, while acknowledging that self-governance is not for every tribe, and in any case that it will not dissolve the need for the BIA, Quinault maintain that the project's ultimate goal is to transform the BIA's role to one of support and assistance rather than a service provider.

Today, Quinault sovereignty coexists with contradictions and explicit challenges. Jurisdictional issues with the QAA remain to be resolved. Problems of fragmented land ownership continue to stymie efforts at economic development (because of heirship, each trust allotment in 1990 had an average of 15 owners of undivided interest; some 80-acre allotments actually had over 300 owners). The Nation is presently trying to acquire the reservation properties of timber companies in order to rebuild its land base and its economy. Although hampered by these obstacles and by limited financial resources, the Quinault Nation exercises virtually complete sovereignty over its territory, reserving the right to deal with other tribes and nations, including the United States, on a government-to-government basis.

ONONDAGA

The issue of sovereignty takes on a different cast when talking about the Onondaga Iroquois.[1] Not only did the Onondaga enjoy unquestioned and absolute sovereignty before the creation of the United States, as did most native groups, but from roughly the fifteenth or sixteenth century on Onondaga was also the seat of the Iroquois Confederacy, a powerful confederation of five (later six) Iroquois nations whose sovereignty was recognized even by colonial officials and by the British and early U.S. governments. Today's Onondaga base their claims to sovereignty on both of these pillars: their inherent and unceded identity as a native nation and treaties such as Fort Stanwix (1784), Jay (1794), and Canandaigua (1794).

Like many Indian groups, the Onondaga during the 1960s and early 1970s became involved in the movement for Indian rights and identity. Drawing upon their historic position as the capital of the Iroquois Confederacy, the Onondaga used both religious and cultural symbols to support their emerging role as leading Iroquois activists. Conflicts developed between the Onondaga and non-native entities as Indian groups began to place a renewed emphasis on the importance of sovereignty. One such conflict (which still has not been fully resolved) centered on the repatriation of wampum belts from the New York State Museum. Others have involved control of Indian education at a non-native school and the widening of Interstate 81.

Tribal sovereignty has had a particularly strong impact on the issue of commercial sales tax exemption. Selling cigarettes and fuel without having to pay state tax has been very profitable for the Onondaga Nation. The Council of Chiefs decided in 1983 to license certain businesses to sell cigarettes on the reservation and in turn collected a dividend on sales. Almost

---

1. Members of the Iroquois Confederacy—Cayuga, Mohawk, Oneida, Onondaga, Seneca, and Tuscarora—refer to themselves as Haudenosaunee, or People of the Longhouse.

Tax-free cigarette sales at the Oneida Nation's Sav On Market in Canastota, New York, May 1999. Issues relating to tribal sales of tax-free cigarettes have caused controversy in Oneida and Onondaga communities, among others. (AP Photo/Michael Okoniewski)

since the beginning, however, conflict arose between the council and shop owners over sales figures, profit, and regulation of the shops. Some shops refused to pay the dividends on the grounds that the council did not account for the revenue and may have distributed those funds directly to individuals. Both sides demanded that profits be used in the service of the nation and called for a formal accounting of profits and payments, but neither side agreed to these actions for itself.

In 1994, a move by the Council of Chiefs to enforce its authority resulted in clashes between council members and determined shop owners. Most Onondaga condemned the violence but recognized that ongoing resistance on the part of the shop owners to the legitimate Nation government could only bring trouble. For this reason, the withholding and redistribution of dividend payments were also condemned. People reasoned that although this action might be seen positively as an end run around a nonfunctioning and possibly corrupt bureaucracy, it could also be seen as mere bribery with the goal of undermining legitimate authority.

In 1994, the U.S. Supreme Court ruled that New York could collect taxes on reservation sales to non-natives. The state then maintained that the Indian nations were keeping up to $300 million a year in uncollected taxes, money that properly belonged to it. The Indians countered that, because of their sovereign status, the state had no authority to collect the taxes in the first place.

Several Iroquois nations, including the Onondaga, worked out a compromise with the state of New York that became effective on April 1, 1997. This temporary accord called for the elimination of the nations' gasoline sales; the institution by the nations of a detailed licensing, record-keeping, and tax stamp system; and the decrease of cigarette sales through increased prices. In return, the state agreed not to collect taxes on goods sold to non-Indians.

With this agreement, the nations were seen by many of their members as having given in to state pressure. After the deal was announced, individual Onondaga Indians continued to hold protests, saying that nobody—not even their own government—was going to take away their or their childrens' sovereign rights. Independent (unlicensed) smoke shops vowed to remain open in violation of the council's directives. On March 2, 1998, the Onondaga Council of Chiefs and Clanmothers (OCCC) again took action to enforce its authority, physically destroying four unlicensed Onondaga smoke shops. Some nation members were physically assaulted during the operation.

Onondaga County sheriff's deputies remained outside the nation's borders, keeping the curious away but refusing to stop the violence. This response was in keeping with a long-standing agreement between the sheriff and the Onondaga government, under which the former, out of respect for the nation's sovereignty, always asked permission to enter the reservation. That permission was rarely denied.

For its part, the OCCC claims that the smoke shops were operating illegally and that no one was seriously injured as a result of their action. They maintain that since they are charged with regulating commerce within the nation, they have the authority to enforce their rules. Furthermore, they link the existence of unlicensed shops to mysterious acts of violence that have occurred on the reservation in recent years. The OCCC claims to have used violence as a last resort, only after their diplomatic efforts had been repeatedly rebuffed. Even then, the chiefs claimed, the enforcers were unarmed.

Many Onondaga people opposed this action, primarily on the grounds that it was contrary to the Great Law of Peace and its emphasis on inclusion, consensus decision making, and nonviolence within the Iroquois Confederacy. Some also believe that the chiefs' actions were contrary to basic civil rights. In fact, many people became afraid that the OCCC, under Oren Lyons, would continue on the path of destruction, aiming next at the homes of supporters of independent smoke shops.

Equally controversial is the position of the non-native authorities in the matter. Some Onondaga business owners took the sheriff to court, charging discrimination by not providing proper police protection; their (ultimately unsuccessful) suit placed Onondaga sovereignty in direct jeopardy. Others condemned the lack of action by non-native forces on the grounds that in a civilized society "terrorism" should be halted if possible, sovereignty notwithstanding. These people called for worldwide attention to stop the forces of violence within the Nation, seeing the matter not as an internal one but as an issue of international human rights. On the other hand, many argue that a sovereign nation should not rely on outside forces when trouble arises. They call for the nation to get its own house in order, not to invite outside authorities to do it for them.

Viewing the issue as one of fundamental sovereignty, many Onondaga remain opposed to the tax agreement. They certainly reject its enforcement by violent means on the part of the OCCC and are determined to reopen the destroyed businesses. This position has led them to question the very legitimacy of the OCCC. Others respect the authority of the traditional government as well as its authority to negotiate with the state of New York. Unfortunately, the action of the chiefs has divided the tribe, a situation that has always boded ill for Indian people.

INUIT

In partnership with the governments of Canada and the Northwest Territories (NWT), the eastern Arctic Inuit have taken a major step in reacquiring their status as a sovereign people. Short of secession from the provincial or national entity and the establishment of a fully independent authority, this step—the creation of what is essentially a self-governing Inuit territory—allows the people more or less complete self-determination, albeit within a Canadian context. No other North American native group has moved closer to achieving full sovereignty, at least in the eyes of the Canadian or U.S. governments. (Many native nations, of course, consider themselves fully sovereign, either by unceded aboriginal right or by virtue of one or more treaties.)

The political division of Canada proceeded essentially without native input from the founding of Quebec in 1608, through the establishment of the nation in 1867, until the 1970s. Unlike Canada's Indian population, the Inuit signed no treaties with the federal government. In the late 1960s, many Inuit began to think about creating a pan-Inuit organization that would work for Inuit rights. The people formed the Inuit Tapirisat of Canada (ITC) in 1971 to look at a number of issues concerning self-government, the environment, and land claims. Among these issues was the establishment of a separate territory for Inuit people, an idea that had been floated by federal authorities as early as the 1960s. The idea was dropped at that time in part because there were no effective mechanisms in place for large-scale aboriginal self-government.

Negotiations between Inuit groups (such as the ITC and, later, the Tungavik Federation of Nunavut [TFN]) and federal and provincial authorities continued throughout the 1980s. In 1982, residents voted to divide the NWT. The boundary question was settled in 1992, after negotiations on a parallel issue, the formation in the western NWT of a Dene/Métis political entity, broke down. The final accord—known as the Nunavut Land Claims Agreement (NLCA)—was signed in October 1992 and ratified (by 85 percent of those Inuit who voted) in May 1993. The framework called for the Inuit to cede aboriginal title to the central and eastern Arctic, including off-shore waters, in exchange for certain constitutionally protected rights and benefits. In 1995, Canada's Department of Indian Affairs and Northern Development (DIAND), Nunavut Arctic College, and the territorial government instituted training programs to assist Inuit in developing appropriate management and administrative skills.

In fact, the main "right and privilege" was nothing less than the creation of Nunavut ("our land" in Inuktitut), a new, mostly Inuit territory in the eastern Arctic. Nunavut comprises roughly 770,000 square miles—roughly one-fifth of the total land area of Canada and larger than Alaska and California combined. The people negotiated (or reacquired) direct legal title to 210,000 square miles of land. The territorial capital of Nunavut is Iqaluit, its largest community (population 3,600[2]). The total Nunavut population of about 27,000 is roughly 85 percent Inuit. Among the larger communities are Coppermine (1,200), Rankin Inlet (1,800), and Resolute Bay (175). There were 28 towns and hamlets in all in 1999, most accessible only by air for most of the year.

Nunavut is composed of three distinct regions: Qikiqtaaluk, Kivalliq, and Kitikmeot. Its jurisdictional authority compares to that of other territorial governments. A popularly elected legislative assembly, a cabinet, and a territorial court are the primary institutions of public government. While the new Territory of Nunavut came into being on April 1, 1999, final transfer of all governmental functions currently held by the government of the Northwest Territories will be completed by 2009. There are three official languages: Inuktitut, English, and French.

Other aspects of the agreement call for the Inuit to retain mineral rights to roughly 10 percent of the total land area of Nunavut; equal representation of Inuit with the federal government on a new set of wildlife management, resource management, and environmental boards; the right to harvest wildlife on lands and waters of the Nunavut Settlement Area; over $1 billion in compensation; a share of federal government royalties for Nunavut Inuit for gas and mineral development on crown lands; a determination of where Inuit own surface title to land; the right to negotiate with industry for economic and social benefits from nonrenewable resource development; the right of first refusal on sport and commercial development of renewable resources in the Nunavut Settlement Area; and the creation of three new federally funded national parks.

Among the new co-management institutions created as a result of the land claims agreement is the Nunavut Planning Commission (NPC). The NPC is in charge of implementing the land claim agreement. Other responsibilities include land use and development planning in the region. Accountable to the people of Nunavut, members are nominated by the governments

---

2. All statistics 1998 unless otherwise noted.

of Canada and the Northwest Territories as well as Inuit organizations. Ongoing projects include the cleanup of abandoned waste sites (such as mining camps and Distant Early Warning sites) and the study of the potential impact of mineral development on people and caribou.

An organization related to the NPC is the Nunavut Implementation Commission (NIC). The NIC is primarily concerned with the establishment of the Nunavut government and related issues. For instance, the ideal is to create a decentralized government structure whereby many government jobs will be available outside the capital. The NIC welcomes public input and believes that this is a historic opportunity for citizens of the northeast Arctic to determine the structure and operation of their own governmental mechanisms. One result of this process was the vote in 1997 to reject a proposal that would have mandated equal gender representation in the Nunavut legislature. The idea was originally meant to ensure a decision-making process based on traditional values of balance.

All parties to the NLCA expect that the creation of Nunavut will facilitate the growth of native development corporations along with businesses such as shrimping, trucking, and tourism. Economic stability should also be assisted by the wise investment of the land claim capital transfer payments of over $1 billion. Each region is expected to create a five-year development plan, all of which will presumably include further development of mineral deposits. The new national parks are also expected to assist the Nunavut economy. For the time being, the territory will rely on federal dollars for 90 percent of its budget. With only 12 miles of highway and considering its distance from other national population centers, the cost of living in Nunavut is relatively high (a loaf of bread costs $3 Canadian [about U.S.$2]). The average Nunavut household income currently stands at $31,472 Canadian, just about two-thirds of the total national figure.

If the people are to make a success of Nunavut, they must overcome an array of problems. Years of poor treatment by non-native officials such as the Royal Canadian Mounted Police have left a legacy among some Inuit of bitterness and shame. A money economy is still very new to the people, and not all are comfortable with it. Money, in fact, often has a divisive effect on families, as older people's more traditional values conflict with the more mainstream orientation of the younger generation. Welfare payments had begun to foster dependency and hopelessness. There are few Inuit professionals in Nunavut. Nunavut's rates of suicide, poverty, crime, and substance abuse are well above the national average. Economic development and prosperity are far from certain. Still, with the creation of Nunavut, the people of the eastern Arctic are reacquiring something extremely precious—the right to make decisions for themselves. With this come the hope and the energy to revitalize a culture.

CONTEMPORARY
PROFILES OF TRIBES
AND GROUPS

Anishinabe (Leech Lake Ojibwe Nation)

By the end of the nineteenth century, most Anishinabe groups living in Michigan and Minnesota had lost up to 90 percent or more of their land to allotment, fraud, and other irregularities. Many southwestern Ojibwe worked as lumberjacks. In the east the people concentrated more on farming, although whenever possible they continued other traditional subsistence activities as well. Significant culture loss had occurred prior to the twentieth century, mainly owing to government policies encouraging forced assimilation.

Many Plains Ojibwa were not settled on reservations until the late nineteenth and early twentieth centuries. The Turtle Mountain Chippewa, led by Chief Little Shell, worked to regain lost land and to reenroll thousands of Métis whom the United States had unilaterally excluded from the tribal rolls. In 1884, the United States took most of their land, causing the people to scatter across the Dakotas and Montana. In 1904, the tribe received 10 cents an acre for a 10-million-acre land claim. Many western Chippewa groups remain landless today.

With their acceptance in the mid-1930s of the Indian Reorganization Act (IRA), Michigan Chippewa bands reclaimed their federal trust status and began an economic recovery. After World War II, many reservations lost significant population to the industrial cities of the Midwest. Many people who left for economic reasons nevertheless retained close ties with the reservation communities. Northern Ojibwa bands had made treaties with the Canadian government since the mid-nineteenth century.

Leech Lake Reservation (Mississippi and Pilanger Bands) in Beltrami, Cass, Hubbard, and Itasca Counties, Minnesota, established 1855–1874, consists of roughly 600,000 acres, of which about 3.5 percent is tribally owned. Most of this land is the Chippewa National Forest. The 1999 enrolled Indian population exceeded 7,100. Scattered communities are united by 15 tribal centers. Headquarters is in Cass Lake. The Bug-O-Nay-Ge-Shig school serves grades K–12.

The Leech Lake Tribal Council consists of five members elected to four-year staggered terms by the General Assembly. There is also a Leech Lake

Reservation Business Committee and a Tribal Executive Committee. There are four municipal tribal community centers and 11 other tribal centers that unite the reservation's scattered communities.

For years, the tribe has been beset by corruption and a serious power struggle. The former chairman of the Leech Lake Reservation Business Committee, Alfred (Tig) Pemberton; the former tribal attorney; former state senator Harold (Skip) Finn; and council member Dan Brown were convicted in 1996 of conspiring to steal money from the tribe in an insurance scam. Another council member, Myron Ellis, pleaded guilty in a related charge. Pemberton was later replaced by Eli O. Hunt, who was chairman in 1999.

Supporters of the discredited leaders, including Ellis, constitute a majority of the Tribal Council. This faction has blocked Hunt to a significant degree from exercising his leadership powers. Specifically, it has refused to recognize Martin Jennings, Hunt's appointed head of the tribe's gaming operations, and has ordered Jennings not to cooperate with the grand jury investigating those operations. Hunt and Jennings have vowed to cooperate with the investigation. The old guard also continues to meet in secret sessions and to pass legislation that may or may not be binding on the tribe. Furthermore, the confusion over tribal leadership resulted in severe financial disruption when the First National Bank of Cass Lake refused to recognize the authority of Chairman Hunt.

In response, Hunt and his supporters declared a state of emergency and enacted a new provisional government; as of July 1999 the constitution was awaiting further review. Specifically, they voted to form a General Council, consisting of the heads of the 12 local councils that represent the reservations' communities, to assume legislative authority over the band. The Tribal Council would still have financial authority as well as the power to enforce legislation.

Along with the Bois Forte Reservation, the Fond du Lac Reservation, the Grand Portage Reservation, the Mille Lacs Reservation, and the White Earth Reservation, the Leech Lake Reservation is a member of the Minnesota Chippewa Tribe (MCT). The tribe's constitution provides for a two-part executive branch consisting of a tribal executive committee and six reservation business committees. In general, the business committees administer their respective reservations insofar as they do not conflict with the tribal government. In lieu of a formal bill of rights, the constitution states that no member may be denied the usual rights of U.S. citizens.

The executive committee, which selects its own officers from within, is composed of the chairman and the secretary-treasurer of each of the six reservations. Each reservation also elects a business committee of between three and five members consisting of a chairman, a secretary-treasurer, and between one and three other members. The terms of office are four years. Regular meetings of the executive committee are held quarterly. In 1997 the president of the MCT Executive Committee was Norman DesChamps.

In 1997, the executive committee of the MCT met to give tentative approval to a controversial settlement of the tribe's $20 million land claim against the U.S. government. The basis of the claim is the 1889 Nelson Act, which led to the appropriation of over 800,000 acres of MCT land, including more than one-half of Leech Lake territory. The group proceeded despite the fact that several communities, including Leech Lake, explicitly rejected the settlement.

The U.S. population of enrolled Anishinabe stood at roughly 125,000 in the mid-1990s, including about 48,000 in Minnesota, at least 30,000 in Michigan, 25,000 members of the Turtle Mountain Band (North Dakota), 16,500 in Wisconsin, 3,100 at Rocky Boy Reservation (Montana), plus other communities in Montana and elsewhere in the United States. Canada recognizes over 130 Indian communities that are wholly or in part Anishinabe. They are located in Alberta, Manitoba, Ontario, and Saskatchewan. There were about 60,000 Anishinabe in Canada in the mid-1990s, excluding Métis.

Casinos are the key economic activity in Michigan, Minnesota, and Wisconsin, although those in Wisconsin are threatened by a proposed antigambling amendment to the state constitution. A women's cooperative produces and sells wild rice and crafts at White Earth (Minnesota), and there is a fisheries cooperative at Red Lake (Minnesota). Forestry is also an important industry, and some people are able to find work off-reservation. Turtle Mountain (North Dakota) operates a casino, a manufacturing company, and a shopping center. Many northern Ojibwa work seasonally or part-time in industries such as construction, logging, and tourism. There are also some jobs as firefighters and tree planters. Unemployment among contemporary Anishinabe often reaches or exceeds 50 percent.

At Leech Lake, a large regional sport fishing industry employs almost no Indians. Very little of the roughly $750 million in annual income generated by the industry benefits Indian businesses or individuals. Community-owned businesses include the Oningum Marina, LL Construction Building, the Che-Wa-E-Gon gift store and restaurant, Northern Lights Gaming Emporium, and Leech Lake Bingo Palace Casino and Hotel. There are also several hundred jobs with the tribal government itself. Some Leech Lake export products, such as wild rice in birchbark trays and baskets, are marketed electronically.

The Rocky Boy Chippewa-Cree Development Company (Montana) manages that tribe's economy. In addition to beadwork, which is in great demand, important economic activities include a propane company, a casino, cattle grazing, wheat and barley farming, some logging and mining, and recreation and tourism. The tribal government and Stone Child Community College are among the largest employers on the reservation.

Contemporary Anishinabe people retain their Indian identity in a number of important ways. Community Colleges, such as those at Leech Lake, Fond du Lac, Turtle Mountain, and Rocky Boy, provide crucial services and emphasize tribal culture. Land reacquisition projects and subsistence rights cases remain ongoing. There are a number of powwows and other traditional and semitraditional activities, including, in some locations, the Midewiwin Society. Many people continue to speak the Ojibwa

Ashinabe harvesters unload wild rice from their canoes before bagging it at the Leech Lake Indian Reservation in Minnesota, 1995. (Corbis/Phil Schermeister)

language. Artists and craftspeople continue to produce items such as moccasins, clothing, and baskets.

Many of those Anishinabe who live in mostly non-native cities and towns retain close ties to their home communities. Various lower court cases in the 1980s and early 1990s reaffirmed their subsistence rights on ceded land, and the people have worked especially hard to defend those rights, especially in the face of ongoing legal and even extralegal challenges. They have established a number of organizations, such as the Great Lakes Indian Fish and Wildlife Commission, to manage their natural resources and provide related enforcement and public relations services. In 1998, the U.S. Supreme Court, in a review of *Minnesota et al.* v. *Mille Lacs Band of Chippewa Indians et al.*, firmly and finally upheld native subsistence rights in Wisconsin and Minnesota pursuant to an 1837 treaty.

Northern Ojibwas have enjoyed adequate health care facilities and educational opportunities since the 1950s. Trapping and kinship ties remain important, although considerably less so than in the past. As in the United States, many of these people are Christians.

Most of the following unrecognized or partially recognized groups are working to achieve full federal recognition: the Burt Lake Band of Ottawa and Chippewa Indians, the Lake Superior Chippewa of Marquette Tribal Council (Michigan), the Consolidated Bahwetig Ojibwa and Mackinac Tribe (Michigan), the Kah-Bay Kah-Nong (Warroad) Chippewa (Minnesota), and the Little Shell Tribe of Chippewa Indians (North Dakota and Montana) as well as some of the "landless Chippewa" in Montana, the Christian Pembina Chippewa Indians, the NI-MI-WIN Ojibwey (Minnesota), the Sandy Lake Band of Ojibwe (Minnesota), and the Swan Creek and Black River Chippewa (Kansas and Montana).

APACHE (SAN CARLOS)

The San Carlos Reservation in Arizona (founded as Fort Apache in 1872; 1.87 million acres) was divided administratively from Fort Apache in 1897. In the early twentieth century, most Western Apaches lived peacefully on the reservations while corrupt agents and settlers stole their best land. There was virtually no local economy during that period, the only jobs being located off of the reservation. As U.S. policymakers lumped the various bands together, group distinctions as well as traditional identity began to blur.

Government officials also dictated the reservations' economic activities: In 1918 cattle were issued to the Apache, and lumbering began in the 1920s. Apache also worked as laborers constructing dams. Subsistence agriculture ended for the people of old San Carlos when the Coolidge Dam was constructed in the 1930s. Residents were relocated and began new work as stockmen. San Carlos accepted reorganization under the Indian Reorganization Act (1934).

San Carlos elects a nine-member council according to district voting. The tribe also elects a chairman and a vice chairman on an at-large basis. The council is charged with electing, either from among its own members or not, officers that include a secretary and a treasurer. Council members must be at least 25 years old and meet other requirements. The tribal chairman in July 1999 was Raymond Stanley. The vice chairman was Velasquez W. Sneezy Sr.

Popularly elected officials hold office for two or four years, according to a specific formula. The council enjoys customary powers and responsibilities, including negotiating with other governments; governing and representing the tribe; managing and controlling land, economic ventures, and other assets; levying taxes; and controlling natural resources. There is also a specific provision for the cultivation of Indian arts, crafts, and cultures. There are also provisions for acceptance or rejection of council actions by the superintendent and the secretary of the interior as well as popular referenda. The constitution further spells out the relationship of the tribe to the federal government, which is "similar to that which a town or a county has to state and federal governments."

In 1998, tribal members coalescing around a group called Call to Action voted to remove the vice chairman and all nine council members. The action

Interior Secretary Bruce Babbitt receives an Apache "burden basket" from San Carlos Apache Tribe vice-chairman Velasquez W. Sneezy Sr. during a water-rights signing ceremony in Phoenix, March 30, 1999. The ceremony took place after years of negotiation between the federal government, the state of Arizona, and the tribe. Sneezy gave Babbitt the basket to symbolize the burden he carried on behalf of the Apaches in their battle for water rights. (AP Photo/Jack Smith)

stemmed from a long-festering situation in which the tribal council had turned to what some residents saw as police-state tactics to maintain their power against allegations of fraud, embezzlement, and harassment. When Call to Action took over the tribal administration building, the council responded by removing tribal chair Raymond Stanley, ordering the arrest of dozens of his supporters, and suspending two tribal judges whom they regarded as sympathetic to Stanley. In elections held in November 1998, Stanley won an overwhelming victory, and four council members were defeated. As of mid-1999 the conflict had subsided, but the financial problems, as well as the structural instability, remained ongoing.

In the mid-1990s, the San Carlos Reservation had a population of about 10,000, roughly three-quarters of whom were enrolled tribal members (another 3,000 or so tribal members lived away from the reservation). Owing primarily to a lack of resources and infrastructure, combined with a particularly stubborn legacy of dependency, the community remains very poor. Economic activities at San Carlos include cattle ranching, farming, logging, mining (asbestos and other minerals) leases, basket making, and off-reservation wage work. A casino opened in 1994. San Carlos Lake has long provided the tribe with an income based on sales of fishing permits. However, the lake is drying up, in part because water is being released downstream. The tribe is currently trying to address this situation.

Given the choice between economic improvement and keeping their traditions, however, many San Carlos Apaches would choose the latter. For these people, the meaning of life still revolves around associations with family and friends. Many residents of San Carlos still speak Apache, and many still observe the old ceremonies and other traditions. Increasingly, however, contact with the outside world has opened the door to serious social problems.

In early 1999, a long-standing conflict with Phelps Dodge Corporation flared up as the tribe shut down the Black River Pump Station. The facility supplies water to Phelps Dodge's Morenci open-pit copper mine—one of the world's largest—as well as to two local communities. The dispute centers on a 1997 agreement regulating the operation of the station, which is located on reservation property. According to the tribe, it has a 50-year policy of not taking any water from the Salt River if it would decrease the flow below 20 cubic feet per second. Phelps Dodge angered the tribe by refusing to sign a lease agreement that would respect that policy. There are also disagreements about a World War II–era agreement that allowed Phelps Dodge onto the reservation in the first place.

CATAWBA

A land cession by King George III formed the basis of the Catawba land claims in South Carolina in the nineteenth and twentieth centuries. For most of the interim period the people were kept on the move by unfriendly non-native neighbors who refused to honor their treaties. The Catawba dispersed as far away as Colorado and Utah. By 1900, many had returned to ancestral land in South Carolina, where, as farmers, they maintained aspects of their traditional culture. Education was largely under the control of Mormon missionaries.

Many Catawbas worked in textile mills following World War I. The federal trust relationship was formally begun only in 1943, as a result of Catawba legal pressure. At that time, the state acquired more than 3,000 acres of land for a federal reservation, and the Catawba adopted an Indian Reorganization Act (IRA) constitution. Political pressures, however, led to the tribe's being officially terminated from its relationship with the federal government in 1962. Individuals took over possession of the recently purchased tribal lands, while the state retained over 600 acres in trust. The tribe pressed on with its land claims; the legal impasse was to last another generation.

Today, most members of the Catawba Indian Nation live near Rock Hill, South Carolina. There were roughly 1,400 people enrolled in the mid-1990s. The tribe receives income from pottery manufacture, which occurs approximately in the ancient way. Other crafts include hide tanning, blowgun making, and beadwork. There is also individual and tribal income from a 1993 land claims settlement that restored federal tribal status and resulted in a payment of $50 million, among other provisions. As of 1999, the tribe had opened a controversial high-stakes bingo facility. The people are relatively well educated and enjoy a range of economic opportunities.

The tribe gained nonprofit corporate status in 1973 and elected an eight-member tribal council and executive committee at that time. The enrolled population in 1997 had increased dramatically to about 3,000 from about 65 families just a few years before. According to the tribal constitution, the tribe is governed by the General Tribal Council, which consists of all enrolled tribal members over the age of 21. The membership meets annually to elect an executive committee consisting of a chief, an assistant chief, a secretary-treasurer, and two trustees.

Red Thunder Cloud, also known as Carlos Westez, who died in 1996 at the age of seventy-six, had learned some parts of the Catawba language (though not Catawba himself) and was an active promoter of Native American traditions and culture. Indian groups across North America are fighting for the survival of their Indian languages. (AP Photo/HO)

The responsibilities of the General Council, which meets twice a year, include negotiating with other governments, managing tribal assets, passing and enforcing ordinances, and other similar duties. The chief, who in 1999 was Gilbert Billy Blue, presides at all meetings of the General Council and supervises the executive committee. Chief Blue has been at the center of a power struggle in which some tribal members call for the release of tribal audits and salary figures and claim that they are effectively frozen out of the electoral process.

Gilbert Billy Blue has been chief of the Catawba Nation for 25 years. He was born in 1933 on the Catawba Indian Reservation and attended the Catawba Indian School and Rock Hill High School. He spent most of the 1950s in the U.S. Navy. He currently serves on the board of directors of the Native American Rights Fund and is vice chair of that organization's executive committee. He also serves as alternate vice president of the southeast area of the National Congress of American Indians. He enjoys singing, dancing, and playing the guitar.

Catawbas in Colorado and other western states, though not formally enrolled, communicate regularly with their relatives in the Carolinas. Most Catawbas are Mormons. The tribe sponsors an annual cultural festival and is involved with numerous local and regional museums. Led by a team of archivists, historians, and archaeologists, the people are engaged in a project to revive their long-lost cultural identity. They are battling the fact that most of the old knowledge and ceremonies has long since disappeared and the last native speaker died in 1959.

COLORADO RIVER
INDIAN TRIBES

In 1865, Congress created the Colorado River Indian Reservation (CRIR) in Arizona and California for "all the tribes of the Colorado River drainage," of which the Mojave and Chemehuevi were the largest. The reservation's first government boarding school, dedicated to the destruction of Indian culture, opened in 1879. Land allotments began in 1904. In the 1930s, when the great dams were built on the Colorado River, the people who had farmed the river floodplain for centuries were forced to cease growing food. During World War II, the United States summarily appropriated 25,000 acres of the CRIR in order to build the camps that housed many U.S. citizens of Japanese heritage. The Japanese provided much of the initial agricultural labor there.

After the war, the Bureau of Indian Affairs opened the CRIR to Hopis and Navajos, ostensibly because their lands were incapable of supporting so many people. In 1964 the Indians received the deed to the reservation. Now members of all four tribes are members of the Colorado River Indian Tribes (CRIT), a difficult development for the remaining Mojave elders who worry about the decline of Mojave identity. A 1963 court case guaranteed the CRIT title to federal water rights, although the issue of water rights remains a difficult one.

In 1992, roughly 1,250 members of the CRIT Indians lived on the CRIR. A majority of these people identified themselves as Mojave. Total tribal enrollment just topped 3,000. In contrast to Fort Mojave, large-scale farming is a key activity at CRIR, where unemployment stood at just 9 percent in 1997. Farming is possible because the CRIT own senior water rights to 171,000 acre-feet of the Colorado River. Roughly 85,000 acres of land are now under cultivation. An 11,000-acre cooperative produces mainly cotton, alfalfa, wheat, melons, and lettuce. The tribe also owns land within Parker, Arizona, and in 1989 successfully challenged the town's authority to regulate building activities on that land.

Tourist facilities at CRIR include a marina, casino and resort, gift shop, and restaurant. The tribe hosts motorboat races in the spring and a rodeo in November. Some people herd sheep or work in federal government jobs.

Other sources of income include long-term leases and numerous large and small businesses, such as a 10-acre recycling plant that opened in 1992. Despite the existence of a hospital, adequate health care is hard to find at CRIR, and diabetes has become a severe health problem. Children attend public schools. CRIT provides scholarship funds to their students interested in obtaining higher education.

The CRIT constitution vests all political power in the members and denotes a tribal council as the governing body. The council consists of nine popularly elected members, including a chairman and vice chairman. This group in turn elects officers, including a secretary and a treasurer. As of the late 1990s, the chair of the Colorado River Tribal Council was Daniel Eddy Jr.

Councilors serve for four-year terms and meet at least monthly. All tribal members over the age of 17 may vote in tribal elections. The tribal council reserves the usual rights of such bodies, including negotiating with other governments; representing the tribe; managing and regulating land, economic affairs, and all tribal assets; levying taxes; governing the community; and creating and enforcing civil and criminal codes.

The constitution also provides for removal, recall, referenda, and a judicial system. The latter consists of a trial court and an appeals court whose jurisdiction extends to all matters covered by the constitution except where limited by U.S. law. Accused criminals are entitled to a trial before no fewer than three jurors, unless conviction could result in a prison term, in which case they are entitled to a trial before no fewer than six jurors.

COSTANOAN/OHLONE

Costanoan/Ohlone groups, commonly known as tribelets[1] and still largely intact in 1770, declined sharply during the mission period (1770–1832). Almost all remaining communities broke up following California's failure in the 1850s to ratify 18 treaties guaranteeing native groups 85 million acres of their former land. By 1900, only small groups of people, particularly in communities such as Alisal, retained a clear Costanoan identity. The existence of these groups was ignored, however, by mainstream society, largely because most non-natives wanted to believe that Indians, especially in California, had disappeared.

In the 1920s, the prominent anthropologist Alfred Kroeber declared the Costanoan to be "ethnologically extinct." His pronouncement led other academics to follow suit. His assessment of the Ohlone people, at least partially responsible for the government's disenfranchisement of several Ohlone bands, has influenced policymakers to this day. In 1928 the United States offered to compensate any Indian who could prove that he or she was descended from Indians who lived in the state in 1852. The rate was determined to be 41¢ per acre, or $17 million. For many reasons, including illiteracy, lack of information, and relocation out of state, a great many eligible Indians were ultimately excluded from the process.

Resolution of a land claims case in the 1920s provided a ray of hope, but it was not until the 1960s that the Costanoan/Ohlone people began to think about a cultural revival. Two key events occurred during that decade: They won another land claims case, and Ohlone descendants of Mission San José

---

1. The term "tribelet," while almost universally accepted, is considered ill advised and historically inaccurate by some California Indians. They believe that an understanding of the aboriginal people of California as having belonged to small-scale, fragmented cultures severely inhibits a clear and sophisticated appraisal of their societies. The new perspective encompasses regional linkages, created largely through the process of intermarriage, in place of small, discrete "tribelets." The dynamic of regional linkages also includes special trade "friendships," which might last a lifetime and through which relationships and networks were established throughout the region and beyond.

were able to prevent the destruction of a burial ground that lay in the proposed path of a freeway. This victory sparked the group to organize as the Ohlone Indian tribe. A similar situation in 1975 gave birth to the Pajaro Valley Ohlone Indian Council.

In 1911 and again in 1988, individuals received trust allotments that became the Costanoan refuge of Indian Canyon. Today, the Amah Band of Ohlone/Costanoan Indians, the Costanoan Band of Carmel Mission Indians, the Costanoan/Ohlone Indian Families of the San Francisco Bay, the Indian Canyon Band of Costanoan/Mutsun Indians, the Muwekma Indian Tribe, the Costanoan Ohlone Rumsen-Mutsun Tribe, and the Ohlone/Costanoan-Esselen Nation all have acknowledgment petitions pending before the federal government.

The principles of government at Indian Canyon are to be truthful, to rise above negativity, and to take responsibility for your own actions. Decisions are taken by consensus. As with the other groups, there is also a formal governing structure that the U.S. government requires of all tribes petitioning for acknowledgment. The tribal chair of the Muwekma Nation in mid-1998 was Rosemary Cambra.

In mid-1999, Ann Marie Sayers was the tribal chair of the Indian Canyon Nation of Costanoan People. Sayers was raised in Indian Canyon by her mother, Elena Sayers. In 1988, she successfully claimed 128 acres of public domain land (Bureau of Land Management) after fulfilling all the requirements of the 1887 Allotment (Dawes) Act. She has built her home near where her great-grandfather, Sebastian Garcia, built his home. A tireless woman in the service of her people, she has taken on countless projects and responsibilities, including battling to protect Indian remains and artifacts, reestablishing sacred ceremonial ground at Indian Canyon, hosting meetings and conferences, and educating people about the past and present of California's Indians. She derives much of her energy from honoring the lives of her ancestors.

Patrick Orozco, of Watsonville, California, is a Rumsen Ohlone leader. Descended from Indians who lived on the San Jose, Santa Clara, and Carmel missions, Orozco maintains a full schedule of speaking engagements and educational activities, mainly on the subjects of cultural and environmental issues. In 1999 he was a leader in the fight to save the San Bruno Shell Mound. This 5,000-year-old Slipskin Ohlone site is currently threatened by a proposed $100 million commercial development. The goal is to preserve the shell mound at the base of San Bruno Mountain as a cultural and historical landmark. Orozco is also a major force in the effort to obtain federal recognition of the Rumsen Ohlone people.

The process of documenting and publicizing their cultural and historical continuity—in other words, of rejecting extinction—remains ongoing. The Muwekma Tribe, for instance, has established its own archaeological consulting firm as a means to taking control of its past, its present, and its future. Some Costanoans engage in Indian-related activities such as crafts and the recognition struggles of tribes and local sacred sites. *Noso-n* (Mutsun for "in breath so it is in spirit") is a newsletter for the contemporary community of Costanoan and neighboring peoples. In 1989, Stanford University agreed to return all of its Native American skeletal remains to local Ohlone/Costanoan people for reburial. Costanoan descendants established the Carmel Valley Indian Center to promote cultural programs and exhibits about local Indians.

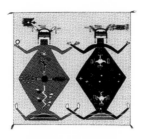

CREE

In 1800, a great diversity of Cree cultures stretched from Labrador in the east to Lubicon Lake, Alberta, in the west and from almost the Great Slave Lake in the Northwest Territories in the north to North Dakota and Montana in the south. Disease epidemics, made worse by a more settled lifestyle adopted after the fur trade declined, took a heavy toll on the Cree through the mid-twentieth century. By 1900, many Cree had been converted to Christianity, and almost all groups had signed "numbered" treaties with Canada, ceding their vast aboriginal land for a number of far smaller reserves.

Despite a general loss of their land, resources, and health, many Cree were able to live in at least a semitraditional way well into the twentieth century. That is, people lived primarily by hunting and, in some areas, fishing, and traditional technologies and customs remained more or less intact. The population of the Lubicon Lake people was about 3,000 in 1900, but a post–World War I flu epidemic killed about 90 percent of the people. In the 1920s, Canada officially required Cree and other Indian chiefs to be selected by election rather than by consensus, as was traditional.

The Cree entered a period of major change after World War II. In the east, many people began working in local cities and towns such as Moosonee and Churchill. Even Woodland (western) Cree began attending school, using non-native medicine, and accepting government financial assistance. Roads and air links connected many communities to the outside world for the first time. The 1950s and '60s were marked by extensive road building and a dramatic increase in logging, two trends that combined to increase pollution levels and reduce the numbers of game animals significantly. In 1975, eastern Cree and Inuit groups turned over 400,000 square miles of land to the James Bay Hydroelectric Project, in exchange for promises of hundreds of millions of dollars and various other provisions.

In 1999 there were roughly 140 Cree or mixed Cree reserves located in Alberta, Manitoba, the Northwest Territories, Ontario, Quebec, and Saskatchewan. This number does not include Métis and the many "unofficial" bands or groups. There are also Cree or Iroquois/Cree communities near Edmonton, Alberta, and in the Rocky Mountain foothills. In the United States, Cree live on the Rocky Boy Chippewa-Cree Reservation, Chouteau and Hill Counties, Montana. The estimated number of Cree in North America is 60,000.

Each Cree community of James Bay and Northern Quebec is a separate nation with a distinct council and government. The chief or executive officer of each council as of early 1999 is given in parentheses in the following listing. The communities are Chisasibi (Charles Bobbish), Eastmain (Kenneth Gilpin), Mistissini (Kenny Loon), Nemaska (George Wapachee), Ouje-Bougoumou (Abel Bosum), Waskaganish (Billy Diamond), Waswanipi (John Kitchen), Wemindji (Walter Hughboy), and Whapmagoostui (Mathew Mukash). The combined Cree population of the nine communities in 1999 exceeded 12,000.

An example of one such community is the Cree Nation of Mistissini. It is governed by an elected council, which is the nation's highest elected body. The council derives its powers from the consent of the people as well as from the 1984 Cree/Naskapi Act of Quebec. Its primary responsibilities include administering and promoting the welfare of the nation. Regular and special meetings require a majority of members to be present. The council's chief executive officer, the chief, is directly elected by the nation's membership. The nation also elects a deputy chief and eight councilors. There is also a five-member appointed Management Committee.

In addition to their individual governments, the communities in 1974 formed the Grand Council of the Crees (Eeyou Istchee, or "People's Land"). The council's 20 members include a grand chief, a deputy grand chief, and chiefs and representatives from each of the nine communities. Headquarters of the Grand Council is in the Nemaska Nation. The executive director of the Cree in early 1999 was Bill Namagoose.

The grand chief of the Council of the Cree of Northern Quebec is Matthew Coon Come (Mistissini). Born in 1956, Coon Come was taken by force as a child to a government school. He began serving on the Grand Council of the Crees in 1981, accepting the position of chief in 1987. At that time, his most pressing concern was opposition to James Bay II, otherwise known as the Great Whale project. Coon Come brought together a diverse coalition of environmental, human rights, and aboriginal organizations. One of their most successful tactics was targeting the state of New York, a move that resulted in that state's cancellation of its plans to purchase James Bay II power. As of 1999, the Cree appear to have stopped Great Whale. In so doing, they have also gained a stronger voice in regional affairs.

The Chippewa Cree Tribe of the Rocky Boy Reservation is governed according to a constitution by which tribal governing power is vested in an eight-member business committee and a chairman, all elected at large. The committee, which meets at least monthly, elects a vice chairman and other officers as needed from among its own members. Its powers include the usual ones of negotiating with other governments, managing tribal lands and other assets, developing and administering a budget, levying taxes, and governing the tribe. The committee is also charged with encouraging the culture and traditions of the tribe. The terms of all offices are four years. The constitution provides for referendum and recall and contains a U.S.-style bill of rights. A judicial branch of government was established in 1972.

There are relatively few job opportunities for Cree Indians. Hunting and fishing are still important economic activities for many people. Some jobs may be found in the mining, transportation, logging, and commercial fishing industries. The James Bay Project provides some income, as does sales of bark baskets and other crafts. People also work in administrative services and programs and receive government assistance. In the mid-1990s, the Meadow Lake Cree of northern Saskatchewan were considering an extremely controversial plan to allow U.S. energy companies and the state-owned Atomic Energy of Canada Limited (AECL) to build a nuclear waste repository on their land.

A growing political sophistication on the part of Cree leaders, combined with changes in Canada's laws, have given the Cree a greater voice in national affairs as well as control over local services and resources. In perhaps the most celebrated instance, a Cree man, Elijah Harper, voted by raising an eagle feather in the Manitoba legislature to kill the 1990 Meech Lake Accord (which would have given Quebec more constitutional autonomy) because of native concerns about their own exclusion. In Quebec, the people control their own schools. In 1999, Crees were considering legal action against the government of Quebec over the issue of forestry development.

There is no imminent danger of the Cree language dying out. However, Cree have yet to make significant progress on many of their most daunting challenges, including the destruction of natural resources, the need for appropriate economic development, and the need to forge a viable relationship with provincial and national governments. Severe problems linger from over a century of chronic disease, discrimination and abuse, and environmental degradation.

In early 1999, Bernard Ominayak was in his twenty-first year as chief of the Lubicon Lake Nation. Ominayak was born and grew up along Lubicon Lake, hunting, trapping, and fishing. Always close to his grandmothers, Ominayak left a mission school and started a family around the age of 16. At age 23 he began attending meetings of Isolated Communities, or Indian groups excluded from Canada's treaties with native people. He was elected to his nation's council in 1976 and became chief two years later, at the age of 28.

As chief, Ominayak has created an 11-member council of community leaders. He also engaged communications and public relations experts to help bring the plight of the Lubicon Nation to the rest of the world. These efforts have paid off handsomely, and today the nation can count on an international network of allies in its struggle with Canada. Chief Ominayak is often present when disasters strike individuals and is frequently prepared to help with medicines he creates using up to 100 or more native herbs. A true man of the people, Ominayak regularly visits the sweat lodge, takes his direction from the nation's elders, and draws his strength and sense of purpose from the traditions of his people.

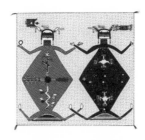

DAKOTA

The eastern Dakota people remained closer to their Woodlands origins than did their more well known western, Lakota-speaking kin. However, the eastern people too fought fiercely to retain their land and culture in the nineteenth century, notably under leaders such as Little Crow. The late nineteenth century was as disastrous for the Dakota tribes in Minnesota as it was for the Plains tribes: Congress, having unilaterally abrogated all treaties and evicted Dakota people from what remained of their lands in 1862, reestablished four small communities in 1886.

By 1900, poverty and disease was rampant. Traditional culture was actively repressed. Children were forcibly taken from their homes and sent to Indian boarding schools. Throughout the early to mid-twentieth century, Dakota communities remained poor, with few jobs and no paved roads or indoor plumbing. Dakota people sold crafts and gardened to support themselves. As the government slowly grew less interested in forcing the people to assimilate, however, they began to reclaim a pride in their Indian identity and heritage. Most Minnesota tribes received federal recognition in the 1930s.

Most of the 6,000 or more Dakota (Sisseton, Wahpeton [together known as Santee], Mdewakanton, and Wahpekute) in the United States and Canada live on reservations in the Dakotas, Nebraska, and Minnesota and in regional cities and towns. In the United States, Dakota reservations include Fort Peck (Assiniboine-Sioux [Upper Yanktonai and Sisseton-Wahpeton]), Devil's Lake (formerly Fort Totten) (Sisseton, Wahpeton, and Cuthead Yanktonai), Lake Traverse (Sisseton and Wahpeton), Santee Sioux, and Flandreau Santee Sioux. Communities in Minnesota include the Lower Sioux Community (Santee), the Prairie Island Community (Santee), the Upper Sioux Community (Sisseton, Wahpeton, Flandreau Santee, Santee, Yankton), and the Prior Lake (Shakopee) Community (Santee). Predominantly Dakota reserves in Canada include Portage la Prairie, Sioux Valley, Pipestone, and Bird Tail in Manitoba and Fort Qu'appelle, Moose Wood, and Round Plain in Saskatchewan.

The Shakopee Mdewakanton Dakota Reservation is located in Prior Lake, Minnesota. The reservation population was about 230 of a total enrollment of roughly 300 people (1998). The total area was 1,500 acres, all of which was tribally owned. The Shakopee Mdewakanton Sioux Community of Minnesota is governed under a constitution amended in 1980. It calls for a general council to exercise powers such as negotiating with other governments; managing community land, other assets, and economic activities; levying taxes; creating and enforcing a civil and criminal code; and encouraging and fostering the culture of the community. The tribal chair in March 1999 was Stanley Crooks.

The membership clauses of the tribe's constitution are at the heart of a crisis over enrollment. In the mid-1990s, the tribe, overlooking its one-quarter blood quantum membership standard, enacted an ordinance that allowed far looser qualifications. About 200 people were quickly adopted, more than doubling the size of the tribe and raising objections from tribal members as well as from the Bureau of Indian Affairs (BIA). The new ordinance has pitted neighbor against neighbor and fueled a bitter factional fight, with some—including the former head of the tribe's casino management company, who is currently facing corruption charges—labeling the move nothing more than a ploy by the tribal chair to pad the rolls of his supporters (see the "Gaming" entry in the Contemporary Issues section).

The Shakopee band is a major player in state and national politics, contributing tens of thousands of dollars to political committees and candidates and retaining a lobbyist in Washington, D.C. (In 1998, U.S. Attorney General Janet Reno launched an investigation of Interior Secretary Bruce Babbitt for allegations that he rejected an Indian casino in Wisconsin because of a promised $500,000 contribution by the Shakopee and two other Indian groups.) In 1997, the community attempted to diversify its economy by developing a 600-acre parcel of land it owns. This plan was vigorously opposed by local and state officials because the wealthy tribe would not have to pay taxes on the land.

The most important economic activity on most reservations is gaming. However, other industries include nonviolent armaments (Devil's Lake), plastic bags (Lake Traverse), and minerals, especially oil (Fort Peck). Other income is derived by leasing land to non-natives and, where possible, working in nearby cities and towns. The Wahpeton and Sisseton people remain closely related, in part as a result of a long period of intermarriage. Sisseton-Wahpeton Community College and Tiospa Zina High School, both at Lake Traverse, serve the educational needs of their communities.

Devil's Lake remains a relatively traditional community in which many people speak Dakota. Religious activity is varied among the Dakota people and includes Native American Church ceremonies, the Sacred Pipe ceremony, and Christianity. In the late 1990s, the Santee Reservation declined to open a casino, asserting that such an activity would harm important elements of their culture and values. In early 1999, the Mdewakanton Dakota community was engaged in a bitter struggle with the state government over the latter's proposal to built a road through land the Indians consider sacred. State authorities attacked a nonviolent Indian camp on the site.

INUIT

The Inuit are neither a tribe nor a nation. The word refers to the native people of the Arctic. Inuit (plural of Inuk) means "people" in the native language, Inuktitut. In recent years, especially in Canada and Greenland, "Inuit" has replaced the word "Eskimo," which is Algonquian for "eaters of raw meat" and a word that many Inuit find offensive.

Contemporary Canadian Inuit (that is, those not living in Greenland or Alaska) had traditionally been divided by anthropologists into several groups, such as Baffinland Inuit, Caribou Inuit, Copper Inuit, Iglulik, Netsilik, Inuvialuit (Mackenzie Delta Inuit), and Labrador or Ungava Inuit. Parts of the homelands of all groups except the latter are included within the territory of Nunavut. In any case, the old classifications have generally been replaced with reference to village names.

While some Inuit living in the extreme east encountered non-natives as early as 500 years ago, some living east and north of the Mackenzie delta remained isolated until as recently as the early twentieth century. In general, traditional life remained relatively unchanged until the introduction of trapping foxes for their fur in the late nineteenth century, when Inuit settlements began grouping around trading posts. The extension of credit as well as the slow increase in wage labor bound the people more and more to nontraditional routines. Missionaries arrived, as did the Royal Canadian Mounted Police.

The growing strategic importance of the far north following World War II ushered in the modern period. The Canadian government took a firm interest in the region. Roads, schools, and hospitals began to appear. Inuit were officially encouraged to settle down in fixed communities. Still, at that point the region was characterized by poor employment possibilities and high disease rates. The period of political activism, which culminated in the creation of Nunavut, began in the 1960s.

In so many ways, residents of Nunavut are meeting the challenge of reconciling the old and the new. The people of Igloolik, for instance, have revived the ancient sun ceremony that celebrated the return of the sun before outsiders arrived to negate the meaning of the old rhythms with their minutes, hours, and days. Roughly four weeks after the solstice, elders rekindle a soapstone lamp filled with seal blubber. Old and new: The people accept the fact that a cigarette lighter is used to light the wick instead of a piece of flint. They are comfortable holding the ceremony in the school gym rather than an igloo, just as they understand that seal blood may be drunk on the ice floes while soda pop is acceptable to drink in town. For many people, the collision between old and new is too jarring and contributes to problems such as substance abuse. However, with the help of leaders who can see forward as well as backward, the people are determined to prosper as Inuit in twenty-first century Nunavut.

While Nunavut represents perhaps the most successful of the Canadian-Inuit negotiations, there are many outstanding issues between the two groups. The 5,000 or so Labrador Inuit, for instance, have been negotiating for years with the provincial and national governments over land claims and development projects, most recently a mining development at Voiseys Bay. In late 1998, a tentative agreement was reached that would give the Inuit outright ownership of 9,420 square miles of Labrador and control of even more territory. The people would also be entitled to 25 percent of Newfoundland's mining revenues, and they would co-manage, with the government of Newfoundland, an additional 36,600 square miles, in which they would have preferential hunting and fishing rights.

The "Sovereignty" entry in the Contemporary Issues section provides information about Nunavut government. Paul Okalik is Nunavut's first premier. Okalik is 34 years old and comes from the Baffin Island community of

An Inuit man on a snowmobile in the middle of summer, 1996. Many Inuit survive through a combination of traditional subsistence activities and some involvement with the cash economy. (Corbis/Roger Tidman)

Iqaluit. He overcame teenage drinking problems to earn a law degree—in early 1999 he was Nunavut's only Inuit lawyer. He won election to Nunavut's legislature in 1999 and shortly thereafter was chosen premier by his colleagues. This is his first elective office.

Other Inuit leaders are found both in and out of the new Nunavut government. Rosemarie Kuptana was born in Bank's Harbour, Northwest Territories, and attended school in Inuvik. An early worker with Inuit groups, she began her career as a journalist, hosting radio shows for the Canadian Broadcasting Corporation on which local social, cultural, and political issues were discussed. She went on to work for the all-Inuktitut Inuit Broadcasting Corporation, eventually serving as president during the mid-1980s. A tireless worker on behalf of her people, Kuptana served in numerous other organizations, including the Inuit Circumpolar Conference (Canadian vice chair), the Inuit Tapirisat of Canada (president), and Television of Northern Canada. She has also published a book about child sexual abuse in Inuit communities.

Mary Sillett is another Inuit leader. Born and raised in Labrador, she has represented Inuit and other native people in various organizations, such as the Labrador Resources Advisory Council, the Labrador Inuit Association, and the Royal Commission on Aboriginal Peoples. She was one of the native leaders responsible for the inclusion of native rights in the Canadian Constitution. In 1983, she helped to found Pauktuutit, the National Inuit Women's Association, of which she served as president into the 1990s.

Charlie Watt, born in the Inuit town of Fort Chimo, realized while working for the federal Department of Indian Affairs and Northern Development (DIAND) that the Inuit people were insufficiently organized. In 1972 he therefore helped to found, and became the first president of, the Northern Québec Inuit Association. Almost immediately, the group entered into alliance with Cree organizations to fight the government's James Bay hydroelectric project. While they lost that battle, they did participate in a comprehensive land claims agreement with the Quebec government under which several Inuit government agencies were created. Watt continued his work on behalf of Inuit people in the Canadian senate, to which he was appointed in 1983. Among his business ventures was the country's first native-owned airline.

INUPIAT

Inupiat ("the people") is an Inuit name referring to groups formerly known to anthropologists as North Alaska, Bering Strait, Kotzebue, and sometimes West Alaska Eskimos. Non-native whalers entered the region in the mid-nineteenth century, bringing a host of disasters, including disease and moral corruption. Severe epidemics and even starvation plagued the region throughout the late nineteenth and early twentieth centuries. The first shore-based commercial whaling operation was established at Barrow in 1884. Commercial whaling lasted until 1914.

Mining began around the Bering Strait in the 1880s, about the same time that reindeer herding (based on imported herds, this activity was ultimately unsuccessful), missionaries, and schools began to attract people to local settlements. Many Inupiat flocked to Nome during the gold rush of 1898 to sell crafts and, eventually, to work and to attend school. Fur traders arrived around 1900, about the time of the near-depletion of the caribou herds. Along with federal responsibility for native education came sharply increased pressure to acculturate, including humiliating punishments for speaking the native language.

Several factors led to a general population increase after World War II, including the return of the caribou, the introduction of moose into the region, and government health programs. The far north became increasingly militarized with the advent of the Cold War and the growing strategic importance of the region. Although vast mineral reserves, including oil, were discovered and huge mining operations launched, most jobs that native people were able to obtain were unskilled and low paying. Radical diet changes, the adoption of a sedentary life, severe social disruption, frequent contact with non-natives who felt ambivalent at best toward their native neighbors, and the appearance of drugs and alcohol had a strongly negative effect on overall Inupiat health.

In the late 1950s, bird hunting restrictions, followed by the U.S. government's threat to use nuclear weapons in the construction of a deep-water port, galvanized the Inupiat people politically. They quickly formed groups like the Seward Peninsula Native Association, the Alaska Federation of Natives, the Inupiat Paitot, the Northwest Alaska Native Association, and the North Slope Native Association. In 1971, the Alaska Native Claims Settlement Act (ANCSA) formalized the exchange of aboriginal title to most of what is now the state of Alaska for millions of acres of land and shares in corporations worth millions of dollars. ANCSA was followed in 1980 by the enactment of major land conservation laws.

The North Slope Borough (NSB) was incorporated in 1972 under the leadership of Eben Hopson Sr. It encompasses 89,000 square miles between the Brooks Range and the Arctic Ocean. Despite its size, there are only eight villages and 6,300 residents (73 percent Inupiat Eskimo) within the borough. Villages range in size from about 140 people to 3,500. Boroughs provide education, health, housing, search and rescue, and municipal services. In 1999, the NSB was led by Benjamin P. Nageak. The president of the Native Village of Point Hope was Jack Schaefer.

The Northwest Arctic Borough was incorporated in 1986. There are 11 permanent native villages of the Kotzebue region, all of which have electricity and telephone service. Government is by elected mayors and city councils. There is also a northern interior village of Anaktuvuk Pass, which has been settled mainly since the early 1950s.

The regional corporations under ANCSA are Arctic Slope, Bering Straits, and NANA. In 1999, Jacob Adams was the president of the Arctic Slope Regional Corporation (ASRC), a multinational business with extensive and diversified interests. Headquartered in Barrow, ASRC owns nearly five million acres of land, on which it exploits oil and gas, coal, gravel, and other hard rock minerals, with the intention of respecting its shareholders' concern for their ancestral territory. Other activities include tourism, telecommunications, construction, and manufacturing.

Other ANCSA entities include the Maniilaq and Inupiat Community Nonprofit Corporations of the Arctic Slope Regional Corporation. There are also village corporations under ANCSA. The Inupiat Community of Arctic Slope (1971) is a federally recognized tribal entity under the Indian Reorganization Act. Its president in 1999 was George Edwardsen.

Today, there are roughly 7,000 Inupiat living in 150 widely scattered villages. Important sources of income in the northwest Arctic include the school system, the oil and minerals industries, and government. Employment opportunities also exist in Kotzebue, Barrow, and other population centers. Still, unemployment rates often rise to well over 50 percent, especially in the villages, and many people rely on government assistance. Severe radioactive pollution around Cape Thompson is caused by the government's use of the area as a nuclear dump, its conduct of nuclear experiments using local plant and animal life, and Soviet nuclear waste dumping.

Most Inupiat people have access to modern transportation and communication, although ancient technologies like the umiak, or old-style whaling boat, are still in use. Adults generally speak English and Inupiaq, and there are programs to help young people learn and use the native language. School curricula and the control of education began shifting to local authorities in the 1970s. Despite the successes, many people feel profound intercultural

An Inupiat hunter on a snowmobile. Among the native inhabitants of the far north, life is a challenging mixture of old and new. (Mike Swanson/Ken Graham Agency)

tensions, such as that between a cooperative ethic and one that values competition and private ownership.

Due to the seasonal nature of both employment opportunities (summer) and subsistence activities (winter), many Inupiat have been able (or have chosen) to adapt to the new economy while maintaining semitraditional patterns. However, for various reasons, including a lack of access (due to legal restrictions), a decline of skills, and growing dependence on a modern economy, the number of people who engage in traditional subsistence activities is declining. Substance abuse remains a problem, with some communities having banned the sale of alcohol and others employing other strategies to turn the situation around. The native trade fair in Kotzebue follows the Fourth of July celebration, and people hold a January Messenger Feast in Barrow. The traditional fall religious observances have largely been adapted and moved to Christmas time. These include Christmas itself as well as Kakummisaag, the winter dance and feast.

LAKOTA

The massacre of up to 300 Lakotas (Teton, or Western Dakotas) at Wounded Knee in 1890 marked the symbolic end to Indian military resistance in the United States. Well into the 1950s, the U.S. government compelled most Lakota children, often by means of direct force, to attend mission or Bureau of Indian Affairs (BIA) schools. The goals of these schools were to teach menial skills and repress traditional culture. Tipis slowly gave way to government-issue tents and then log cabins and mobile homes. Many Lakota became Catholics or Episcopalians, although many also retained traditional customs and religious practices, including the officially banned Sun Dance.

With the decline of their cultural and political structures, as well as the loss of their traditional leadership, their land, and their way of life, Lakota society underwent a profound demoralization. Despite some success at raising cattle in the early twentieth century, many Lakota sold their herds and leased their lands to non-Indians at the urging of U.S. agents. However, a financial panic in 1921 caused many of the lessees to default, at which point agents counseled the Indians to sell their allotments for cash. By the 1930s the people were bereft of both cattle and land, and general destitution began to set in.

Rising expectations, fueled in part by antipoverty programs, as well as a general postwar Indian political resurgence and Native American involvement in the ethnic pride movement of the 1960s, led to the Red Power movement of the 1970s. In 1972, many Lakota participated in a march to Washington, D.C., called the Trail of Broken Treaties. The following January, under the leadership of the American Indian Movement (AIM), several hundred Pine Ridge Lakota attempted to reverse decades of U.S.-sponsored corruption at Pine Ridge. Particularly egregious, they felt, were the strong-arm tactics of the tribal chair at that time and the numerous unsolved and uninvestigated murders of Indian people. The government responded with a full-fledged military operation. During the 71-day siege, known as Wounded Knee II, federal agents killed two Indians. The event ended inconclusively, with little fundamental change on the reservation.

Ongoing violence led in 1975 to an incident in which a Lakota man and two Federal Bureau of Investigation (FBI) agents were killed near Wounded Knee, South Dakota. In an extremely controversial trial, an Anishinabe/

Dakota Indian named Leonard Peltier was convicted of the crime and sentenced to consecutive life sentences in federal prison. Many people, Indians and non-natives alike, consider Peltier to be a political prisoner, and his case emblematic of the continuing mistreatment of Indians by the U.S. government.

Today, Lakotas live primarily on reservations governed by tribal councils. A National Sioux Council serves as a nationwide, or federal, governmental body. Composed of delegates from the constituent reservations, it meets annually to discuss and act on issues of national importance. The Great Sioux Nation Treaty Council represents the signatories of the 1851 and 1868 Fort Laramie Treaties.

The following are the names of Lakota council chairs or presidents of Lakota reservations in early 1999 (primary bands are given in parentheses): Charles W. Murphy, Standing Rock (Hunkpapa, Sihasapa, Minneconjou, O'ohenunpa and Yanktonai); Gregg Bourland, Cheyenne River (Itazipco and Sihasapa); Michael B. Jandreau, Lower Brulé (Sicangu and others); Harold "Curley" Miller, Crow Creek (Hunkpatina and others); Harold D. Salway, Oglala [Pine Ridge] (Oglala); and Norman G. Wilson, Rosebud (Sicangu and O'ohenonpa). Lakotas also live on the Standing Buffalo and the Wood Mountain Reserves in Saskatchewan, Canada.

According to its constitution, the Standing Rock Sioux Tribe is governed by a tribal council consisting of a chairman, vice chairman, secretary, and fourteen additional councilors, all elected at large. Of the latter, seven are elected in the even-numbered years, of whom four must be residents of the North Dakota part of the reservation, two must be residents of the South Dakota part of the reservation, and one must be from a particular subdistrict. Of those councilors elected in odd-numbered years, each must be from the district or subdistrict in which he or she resides. The officers are elected for four-year terms.

Tribal council members must be at least 25 years old and meet certain residence and other requirements. They are elected for two-years terms. Elections are held every other year. Members of the tribal council must swear to uphold the constitutions of both the tribe and the United States *as well as* the 1868 Fort Laramie Treaty. The council's responsibilities include negotiating with other governments, promoting the general welfare of the community, encouraging the traditions and culture of the Sioux people, levying taxes, and managing the tribe's assets.

The constitution also provides for membership requirements and contains a U.S.-style bill of rights as well as provisions for a tribal judiciary, consisting of a tribal court and a supreme court. Judges in both courts are appointed by the tribal council, although after their initial terms they are subject to continuing approval from the voters. Judicial powers are extended to all matters directly affecting the tribe or tribal members.

The Cheyenne River Reservation is governed by an elected council. Its 18 members include a chair, secretary, treasurer, and 15 representatives. The three officers are elected at large, while the representatives are elected from each of six districts, according to their size. The council members elect a vice chair from among themselves. Each local district is represented by its delegate to the national body. In addition, each elects a president, secretary, treasurer, and council.

The council enjoys the usual duties of governing bodies, such as negotiating with other governments, managing assets, regulating membership and property, and administering a budget. The chair also appoints members to 14 committees. Absolute sovereignty is compromised, however, by the requirement that some actions of the tribal council must be approved by the secretary of the interior. Judicial authority is vested in a lower court system and, along with the Sisseton, Lower Brulé, Fort Thompson, and Standing Rock Reservations, an intertribal appeals court. Located on the Crow Creek Reservation, this is the court of last resort for people of the member reservations.

Many Lakotas work off of the reservation but return for summer visits and, often, to retire. Some Indians at Pine Ridge manufacture moccasins, and a casino generates some jobs and income. In 1997, several reservations, including Pine Ridge (where it was very controversial) and Rocky Boy, were involved in American Indian Beef Products, a venture to develop and market special-genetic beef. The Cheyenne River tribe owns cattle and bison herds as well as a telephone company and an industrial park.

Indians own a few gas stations, convenience stores, and arts and crafts stores on the reservations, but most retail businesses are owned by non-Indians. Land leasing is a key economic activity, although the BIA traditionally arranged exploitative leases. Unemployment commonly exceeds 50 percent and often reaches 80 percent. There are colleges at Pine Ridge, Rosebud, Cheyenne River, and Standing Rock.

Poverty, including relatively poor health related in part to malnutrition and substance abuse, remains a major problem on Lakota reservations. Many Lakotas live isolated in poorly heated houses with poor or no plumbing. Roads are often impassable in poor weather. Still, the Cheyenne River and other reservations make a special effort to see that their elders are warm, are properly fed, get exercise, and remain part of the community.

On the Pine Ridge Reservation, the alcohol-related death rate of 61.9 per 100,000 people is twice the average for reservations and nine times the national average. There are many reasons for this situation. Some of them, such as a legacy of despair, are highly complex, and some are as simple as the location, 400 yards off the reservation, of a town of 22 people and four liquor stores. (The town—Whiteclay, Nebraska—was the focus in the summer of 1999 of a protest by Lakota people demanding a halt to this exploitative situation.) On the other hand, the community-controlled health care facility at Porcupine includes a full-service dialysis unit, a bilingual outreach program, parenting classes, and a nutritional program called Project Grow, in which elders guide younger people in traditional food preparation.

The link, or the blurring, between Christianity and traditional religion has never been stronger. Christian churches have become associated with many traditional ceremonies and now serve as the site of much *tiyospaye* (kin group) activity. Furthermore, Christian Lakotas continue to follow many traditional ceremonies and customs, such as the Sun Dance and giveaways. The Cheyenne River people guard the Lakota Nation's original sacred pipe. KILI, the Voice of the Lakota Nation, provides entertainment and information, in English and Lakota, to many remote communities. Many events in Lakota history, such as the Battle of the Greasy Grass ("Custer's Last Stand") and the Wounded Knee massacre, remain very much in the hearts and minds of the people.

Gregg Bourland, or Eagles Watch over Him, is the chairman of the Cheyenne River Sioux Tribal Council. He was born in 1956 and raised by his grandparents near Ash Butte, a remote region of South Dakota. Bourland married in 1978 and went on to study business at Black Hills State University. Around 1980, Bourland undertook a vision quest and began dancing in Sun Dances. He was first elected chair of the Cheyenne River Sioux Tribe in 1990 and reelected in 1994 and 1998. He serves on many local, state, and national organizations, has testified before Congress, and has authored several congressional bills. He and his wife have two children and own a video business as well as a ranch.

Another prominent Lakota leader and activist is Russell Means. Born in Porcupine, South Dakota, in 1940, Means was raised in and around Oakland, California. After working in various jobs he became active in Indian politics, especially AIM. Means participated in AIM's most celebrated actions, such as the call for accountability in the death of Raymond Yellow Thunder and the 1973 episode at Wounded Knee. In 1974, in a campaign marked by violence and intimidation on the part of the incumbent, Means almost wrested the Oglala tribal chairmanship from the corrupt Dick Wilson. Surviving numerous shootings and stabbings, not to mention arrests, Means continues to champion various native causes. He has also enjoyed some success as an actor.

Vine Deloria Jr., a Standing Rock Lakota, was born on the Pine Ridge Reservation in 1933 to a prominent family. He served as executive director of the National Congress of American Indians in the mid-1960s, took a law degree in 1970, and has published a number of highly influential books, including *God Is Red* (1983), *Custer Died for Your Sins* (1969), and *The Nations Within* (1984). As a teacher at the University of Colorado and as an activist he has continued to speak in favor of Indian dignity, integrity, and self-determination.

Beatrice Medicine is a well-known Standing Rock educator, author, and anthropologist. One of her main areas of specialization is the role of women in Plains Indian culture. She has also done extensive work in the area of mental health, including substance abuse; in this connection she has helped establish urban Indian social centers. After her retirement from teaching at the University of California–Northridge, she served as research coordinator for women's perspectives for Canada's Royal Commission on Aboriginal People.

Mary Brave Bird (Mary Crow Dog, Ohitika Win) is a Lakota writer and activist. Born on the Rosebud Reservation to a distinguished family on her mother's side, she quit school in her mid-teens and spent a period of time drinking and wandering. In 1970, at the age of 17, she joined AIM, sobering

Russell Means, a prominent Lakota activist, testifies in 1989 that the Bureau of Indian Affairs should be abolished. This position is controversial among Indians in the United States; many believe the bureau still has an important role to play in the government's trust relationship with the tribes. (AP Photo)

up and working for the just treatment of her people. She was involved with the 1972 Trail of Broken Treaties march to Washington and the takeover of the BIA as well as the incident at Wounded Knee the following year, during which she gave birth to her first child. Shortly thereafter she married the holy man Leonard Crow Dog, who was promptly arrested and sentenced to a prison term. Moving to New York to be near her husband, Brave Bird began to write her autobiography *(Lakota Woman)*, a best seller and American Book Award winner when it was released in 1990. In 1993 she wrote a sequel, *Ohitika Woman*.

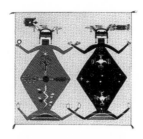

LUMBEE

The Lumbee people are a historical Indian tribe who probably descended from local Siouan Indians, African Americans, and Anglos. They named themselves after the Lumber (formerly Lumbee) River. Since at least the seventeenth century, the Lumbee have inhabited a region that includes Robeson County, North Carolina, and counties in northeastern South Carolina. Lumbees in the Carolinas and in Baltimore, Philadelphia, and Detroit numbered roughly 48,000 in the mid-1990s.

Today, the state-recognized Lumbee make up about one-third of the population of Robeson County, North Carolina. Lumbee economic activities include day care centers and a poultry farm. Some tribal members also produce a variety of arts and crafts. Despite Robeson County's scenic environment and tourist facilities, poverty and unemployment are pervasive in and around the county.

Lumbee Indians maintain a Native American identity primarily through their kinship networks and, in Robeson County, by their membership in all-Indian Protestant churches. They have long held political offices, including that of mayor, in the town of Pembroke. A July homecoming and parade bring Lumbees together from all over the country. Annual powwows are held in the spring and fall. With other members of the Eastern Seaboard Coalition of Native Americans (an association of un- or incompletely recognized tribes), the Lumbee continue to push for federal benefits.

The Lumbee Regional Development Association (LRDA; 1968), a nonprofit corporation, is recognized by state and federal authorities as the representative governing body of the tribe. Twenty directors elected by members of the Lumbee tribe represent Lumbee communities located in Robeson, Lake, and Scotland Counties. Directors serve staggered five-year terms. The LRDA manages the tribe's affairs, provides services to tribal members, and serves as the tribe's principal advocates. In early 1999, the chairman of the board of directors of the LRDA was Adolph Blue. The tribal manager/executive director was James Hardin.

Leadership of the tribe is in dispute, however, as the Tribal Council of the Lumbee Tribe of Cheraw Indians also claims to be the legitimate governing body. This split in part reflects the politics of federal recognition (see "Identity" entry in Contemporary Issues section). In late 1998, the council's coordinator was Ruth Locklear.

Lumbee leaders include Arlinda Faye Locklear, who graduated from the Duke University School of Law and began her legal career with the Native American Rights Fund. A recognized expert on tribal issues, especially land claims and recognition, she has twice argued cases (successfully) before the U.S. Supreme Court, in 1983 becoming the first Native American woman ever to do so. She has also provided expert testimony before Congress on numerous occasions. In 1987 she worked as Lumbee tribal attorney and went into private practice. She remains active in the Lumbee fight for federal recognition.

Ruth Woods is another prominent Lumbee. In addition to her work as director of Indian education in the Robeson County public school system, Woods has worked for several decades on behalf of the shared interests of urban and rural nonreservation Indians. She served as a board member of the Lumbee Regional Development Association in 1979, for which, in part, the association granted her its Henry Berry Lowry award the following year. Woods has also served in prominent positions in various women's organizations throughout her career.

MENOMINEE

By the early twentieth century, the Menominee had been forced to cede much of their 10 million acres of traditional territory in present-day Wisconsin. Under pressure from outsiders, a great deal of tension had developed between those people who wished to retain traditional cultural and religious practices ("traditionalists") and those more willing to abandon them in favor of what they perceived as progress ("progressives"). When farming failed as a viable economic activity, the tribe began harvesting its prime timber resources for sustained yield in the early twentieth century. Its sawmill soon became the reservation's most important employer.

Despite government mismanagement of the tribe's timber resources (for which the latter subsequently collected over $7.5 million in compensation), the Menominee were among the country's most economically stable and prosperous tribes by the early 1950s. However, the combination of local special interests coveting their land and evolving anti-Indian sentiment in Congress soon led to disaster. The tribe was officially terminated (removed from its treaty relationship with the federal government) in 1961. The reservation became a county and the tribe a corporation.

All of the tribe's cash reserves were soon depleted on termination-related expenses. Lack of operating finds forced the hospital to close, which led to a sharp rise in tuberculosis and other health problems. The low tax base was insufficient to finance needed services, and the tribe, once self-sufficient and prosperous, sank into poverty. Faced with total financial collapse, it was forced in the late 1960s to do what many suspected was the ulterior purpose of termination: begin selling prime waterfront real estate to non-natives. In response to the disaster, an organization called the Determination of Rights and Unity for Menominee Shareholders (DRUMS) called for a new federal trust relationship for the tribe as well as tribal self-determination. Although the government rerecognized the Menominee in 1973, and most of the former reservation has been restored, the tribe has yet to fully recover from the termination fiasco.

The Menominee Reservation, located in Menominee and Shawano Counties, Wisconsin, consists of roughly 230,000 acres of land. The tribal enrollment in 1999 was about 8,000. The constitution of the Menominee Indian Tribe of Wisconsin contains a preamble that specifically refers to the

This powwow at the Menominee Indian Reservation, Wisconsin, has been held annually since 1977. The Menominee people are still recovering from the devastating effects of the government's 1950s- and '60s-era termination policies. (Michael Shedlock)

need to "govern ourselves under our laws and customs," "to protect our homeland and conserve our natural resources," and "to insure our rights guaranteed by treaty with the federal government." Its provisions recognize a wide jurisdiction, consistent with applicable federal law. It also enumerates many specific policies and powers, some of which are described below.

A tribal legislature has the authority to make and enforce laws, including "such powers as may in the future be restored or granted to the tribe by any law of the United States, or other authority." This legislature, which meets at least four times a year, is composed of nine tribal members, seven of whom must be residents, elected at large by tribal members over the age of 17. The term of office is set at three years; terms are staggered to ensure continuity. Candidates for election to the legislature must be at least 25 years old and meet certain other requirements. The number of consecutive terms is limited to three. Furthermore, the bylaws speak to the election and duties of three legislative officers as well as numerous other matters.

The constitution also establishes a tribal judiciary, equal and separate from the legislative branch, consisting of a supreme (appellate) court and various lower courts. Lower courts may be established for specific subject areas. Tribal judges, who must be at least 35 years old and meet various other requirements, are appointed by members of the legislature for a term of three (lower court) or four (supreme court) years.

The tribal constitution contains provisions governing recall and popular referenda; hunting, fishing, trapping, and gathering rights; enumeration of civil liberties; use and disposal of land; management of tribal enterprises; and sovereign immunity. It also specifies the nature of the trust agreement between the tribe and the United States, noting that "the United States should expressly acknowledge that the Menominee Indian tribe has the right to be self-determining to the maximum possible extent."

There is a further provision calling upon the United States to acknowledge that tribal forest lands should be managed on a sustained yield basis. Finally, with regard to sovereignty, the constitution specifically states that "any long-term agreement [regarding the trust relationship] shall be effective only if such agreement is approved by a vote of a majority of tribal voters voting."

While forestry remains very important, gaming has largely taken over as the reservation's most important economic activity. Its profits underwrite a host of social and health services as well as the construction of many new buildings, including a whole new village. Nevertheless, gaming-related jobs (550 in 1998) are relatively low paying, and the tribe has recognized the need for more meaningful forms of economic development. It also offers white water rafting on the Wolf River (a federally designated wild river), operates a logging camp museum, and hosts a number of powwows and similar activities.

The Big Drum religion, the Ojibwa-based Warrior's Dance, the Native American Church, and Medicine Lodge ceremonies coexist among many people with Christianity. The Menominee have also reinvigorated their clan structure and both teach and use their language in school. The College of the Menominee Nation has pioneered many initiatives of particular interest to Indian education. In 1995, the Menominee Tribe sued the state of Wisconsin in an effort to assert its treaty-protected (1831) rights to hunt, fish, gather, and trap in a large part of the state. While substance abuse and other social ills associated with poverty remain a daunting challenge, the tribe is determined to maintain its sovereignty and its Indian identity.

The chair of the Menominee Tribal Council, serving his fourth term in 1999, is Apesanahkwat ("Black Cloud"), commonly known as "A. P." Apesanahkwat is a colorful man and an effective leader. Once jailed on drug charges, he has acted in *Northern Exposure* and other television shows as well as in movies such as *Baghdad Cafe*. He owns a home in Oceanside, California, but also lives on the Menominee Reservation. He drives a red Jaguar purchased with money earned from his acting career. Struck by the disparity between his own wealth and the income of many reservation residents, Apesanahkwat went through a period of handing out money to tribal members.

Ada Deer, another Menominee leader and activist, was the first woman to head the Bureau of Indian Affairs (BIA). With an M.S.W. degree from Columbia University, Deer was employed as a social worker (and also worked with the Peace Corps) before entering law school in the early 1970s. She left, however, in order to help her people recover from the devastating effects of termination. Deer served as tribal chair in the mid-1970s, resigning when the tribe was restored to federal recognition. She then taught at the University of Wisconsin, and she increased her political activities, narrowly losing a race for Congress. She served as assistant secretary for Indian affairs (head of the BIA) in the Department of the Interior from 1993 to 1997.

MÉTIS

Most Métis ("mixed") live in Canada (although there are also Métis living in the United States). They are people of mixed aboriginal and nonaboriginal descent. The precise definition of the word is a matter of fierce debate because of the many legal, cultural, and economic implications that rest on its resolution. Many southern Métis, centered around the Red River Valley, are descended from Ojibwa and Cree women and French *coureurs de bois* and *voyageurs*, while the ancestry of some northern groups, located near the Saskatchewan River, combines Scottish and English with Athapaskan parentage. Métis is a French word for the people the English commonly called halfbreeds.

Today's largest Métis communities originated in the old Northwest fur trade, as did the very notion of a Métis nation. In 1816, under the leadership of Cuthbert Grant Jr., the Métis defeated a force of Scottish settlers seeking to restrict their hunting and trading practices. It was then, at their victory at the Battle of Seven Oaks, that the flag of the Métis Nation was first unfurled. Métis political consciousness continued to grow throughout the mid-nineteenth century. Free trade ("La Commerce est Libre!") became the rallying cry of Métis nationalism.

Twice—around 1870 and again in 1884—the Métis people declared a provisional government that emphasized land rights, freedom of language and religion, and representation in the Canadian government. In both cases their most important leader was Louis David Riel Jr. The second instance also involved an unsuccessful armed rebellion, following which Riel was hanged and the Métis cause was dealt a severe setback. Following the failure of Riel's efforts, some Métis people, along with some Chippewa and Cree, moved into Montana. Although the U.S. government expelled these "Canadian Indians," many later returned to settle in the state.

In the United States today, there are Métis communities in Montana, specifically on the Rocky Boy Reservation and near Lewiston, Havre, Great Falls, and Helena. Intermarriage on the Rocky Boy Reservation has tended to blur the distinctions between Chippewa, Cree, and Métis, although all three languages are still in use. Many people are Christian, but other religious practices, such as the Native American Church and the Sun Dance, remain popular. Economic activities include a propane company, beadwork production, a casino, tourist facilities, and Stone Child Community College. Métis people also live among the many Anishinabe communities in the Great Lakes region.

There are also Métis communities in North Dakota, among the Turtle Mountain, Little Shell, and Pembina Bands of Chippewa. Many of these people are victims of severe policies of the late nineteenth and twentieth centuries designed to disenfranchise them and sharply reduce and fragment their land. Most lost whatever land they were able to acquire in individual allotments through nonpayment of taxes. Saved from termination in the 1950s, the Turtle Mountain Band has since developed several business ventures. Turtle Mountain Community College is a key resource, as is a casino. The band, consisting of over 25,000 enrollees in the early 1990s (about 10,000 are resident), now controls more than two-thirds of its 45,000-acre reservation. The Métis, or Mitchif, language is still commonly spoken.

The Métis National Council (MNC; Ralliement National des Métis) was formed in 1983 to ensure that the Métis people were represented at the First Ministers conference on constitutional and aboriginal affairs. It is administered by a board of governors made up of the presidents of the provincial organizations (see below) as well as the national president. The board meets bimonthly, while general assemblies are held annually.

The MNC is composed of five provincial organizations: Métis Provincial Council of British Columbia (MPCBC), the Métis Nation of Alberta (MNA), the Métis Nation of Saskatchewan (MNS), the Manitoba Métis Federation (MMF), and the Métis Nation of Ontario (MNO). Each is represented by a board or a council in province-wide elections in which every adult Métis has the right to vote. Each provincial council, in turn, is composed of regional councils made up of local and community councils. Each regional council has its own constitution. Executives of the Métis organizations listed above are as follows: MNC, Gerald Morin; MNO, Tony Belcourt; MMF, David Chartrand; MNS, Clem Chartier; MNA, Audrey Poitras; and MPCBC, Jody Pierce.

Not all Métis Nations are affiliated with the MNC. Some, such as the Métis Nation of the North West Territories (MNNWT), are affiliated with other umbrella organizations, such as (in the case of the MNNWT) the Congress of Aboriginal People. Some are unaffiliated. Métis nations other than those listed above include the MNNWT, the Fort Providence Northwest Territories Métis Nation, the British Columbia Métis Nation, the South Island Métis Nation (Victoria, British Columbia), the Hay River Métis Nation, the Labrador Métis Association/Nation, and the emerging Métis Nation of New England. The president of the South Island Métis Nation in early 1999 was Mary Collins. There is also a Métis Nation in the Province of Quebec, which is less interested in the number of enrolled members than in the conviction and dedication of its citizens. Citizenship requirements include being at least 18 years of age, being a resident of or having been born in the Province of Quebec, and having aboriginal and nonaboriginal ancestry.

The Chippewa Cree Tribe of the Rocky Boy Reservation is governed according to a constitution. According to that document, tribal governing power is vested in an eight-member business committee and a chairman, all elected at large. The committee, which meets at least monthly, elects a vice chairman and other officers as needed from among its own members. Its powers include the usual ones of negotiating with other governments, managing tribal lands and other assets, developing and administering a budget, levying taxes, and governing the tribe. The committee is also charged with encouraging the culture and traditions of the tribe. The terms of all offices are four years. The constitution provides for referendum and recall and contains a U.S.-style bill of rights. A judicial branch of government was established in 1972. As of early 1999, Bert Corcoran was chair of the reservation's Business Committee.

The 1982 constitution refers to the Métis as aboriginal people. However, the word "Métis" is not defined, and its use has historically been vague. Although most people today use it to refer to the Red River community, it was used possibly as early as the late eighteenth century in New Brunswick. In fact, contemporary Métis emphasize the existence of diverse and distinct Métis populations in Canada that both predate and postdate the Red River populations.

Today, there is a wide range of people and populations who call themselves Métis. These include traditional hunter-gatherers in northern Canada as well as urbanized populations in the south, prairie dwellers as well as those who live in the Maritime Provinces, and people with greatly varying "blood mixtures." There is a general agreement that the three fundamental factors in Métis identity are: (1) aboriginal and nonaboriginal ancestry, (2) self-declaration, and (3) community validation or acceptance. The last criterion would only come into play when an individual wished to qualify for a right or benefit that applied to a specific community.

As an indication of how charged the issue of Métis identity remains, in 1996 the president of the (Sheshatshiu) Innu Nation took the Labrador Métis Association to task as "so-called Métis" who "are trying to muscle in on scarce funding that is allocated to people of truly Aboriginal ancestry." However, recent court decisions in Saskatchewan, Manitoba, and Ontario have found that Métis enjoy the same hunting and fishing rights as do other aboriginals. These decisions may yet be appealed to the Supreme Court.

In early 1999, Ottawa angered Canadian Métis by proposing to meet its legal obligations to them (and other off-reservation natives) in the form of a $9 million payment over three years with no provision for renewal. The federal government and the provinces are currently in a battle over the legal responsibility for Métis and other off-reservation peoples. The legal situation of Canadian Métis remains precarious and very much in flux.

Most of the roughly 500,000 to 800,000 contemporary Métis people have one or more parents who are themselves Métis. Every Canadian province has a Métis population. Métis consider their core issues as the resolution of their legal status and the creation of a Métis land base. Other ongoing issues include Métis people's ignorance of and exclusion from their heritage, the question of self-government for Métis communities, a long-term campaign to educate Canadians about the diversity of Métis populations in Canada, and the creation of a national forum to address the above and other issues.

Gerald Morin has been president of the MNC since 1994. Morin was born in Green Lake, a Métis community in northwestern Saskatchewan. After receiving his law degree, he went on to serve as provincial secretary (1989–1992) and then president (1992–1995) of the Métis Nation of Saskatchewan, during which time he initiated a major land claim court action. He is a strong advocate of Métis self-determination within the context of Canadian unity. As such, he helped negotiate both the Charlottetown Accord and the 1992 Métis Nation Accord.

Audrey Dumont Poitras is the current (1999) president of the MNA. Having grown up in Elk Point, she married at the age of 16 and worked in a dry cleaning business. She and her husband opened their own dry cleaning business in 1979 and ran it successfully until 1990, after which time Poitras studied accounting and went to work for the MNA, becoming director of finance in 1993. She was elected president in 1996, the first woman to be elected to the presidency in the history of the Métis Nation. Her great great grandfather was a cousin of the Métis hero Gabriel Dumont.

W. Yvon Dumont was elected president of the MMF in 1984, at the age of 33. He has been active in Métis politics since the age of 16. At age 21, he was elected vice president of the Native Council of Canada. Dumont has succeeded in managing the Federation's finances such that it has been able to undertake new housing projects and other such activities. He is also involved with other organizations, including the University of Manitoba and the Canadian Aboriginal Economic Development Strategy.

Maria Campbell is a Métis writer and activist. Growing up in central Saskatchewan and ostracized by both non-natives and "status" Indians, she learned from her grandmother to value her own self-identity. When her mother died and her father disappeared, she was forced to assume responsibility for her seven siblings at the age of 12. After a disastrous marriage, she moved with her daughter to Vancouver, British Columbia, only to sink into degradation and despair. A therapeutic letter to herself became the best-selling book *Halfbreed*. Campbell recovered her mental and physical health and went on to write other works, including several children's books about Métis history.

MI'KMAQ

The Mi'kmaq people, having emerged from the fur trade period much diminished by war, disease, and land incursions, came under increased regulation by non-native governments in the early twentieth century. Traditional subsistence activities gradually gave way to low-wage work in the lumber, construction, and shipping industries as well as to migrant farm labor. The transition was extremely difficult, however, and starvation and disease were a constant presence.

In Canada, the federal government unilaterally appropriated most Mi'kmaq reserves. Those that remained were the target of an administrative centralization in the 1950s, a development that led to increased factionalism and population flight. When they were not logging, selling splint baskets, raking blueberries, picking potatoes, or otherwise engaged, the people enjoyed playing hockey and baseball.

In the 1960s, some Mi'kmaq men began working on "high steel" construction projects in Boston. Increasingly active in band politics, women also trained in growing numbers as nurses, teachers, and social workers. In 1969, Canadian Mi'kmaqs formed two organizations, the Union of New Brunswick Indians and the Union of Nova Scotia Indians, to coordinate programs and document land claims. The following year, Mi'kmaqs in Maine formed the Association of Aroostook Indians in an effort to raise their standard of living and fight discrimination.

In the mid-1990s there were 15,000 registered Mi'kmaqs living in the Canadian Maritime Provinces, 4,000 in Quebec, and several thousand more Mi'kmaqs in the United States. Among the roughly 28 Canadian reserves that had a Mi'kmaq population were Pictou Landing, Eskasoni, and Shubenacadie (Nova Scotia) and Burnt Church, Eel River Bar, Pabineau, Red Bank, Eel Ground, Indian Island, Bouctouche, Fort Folly, and Big Cove (New Brunswick). The three Mi'kmaq communities in Quebec are Listuguj, Gesgapegiag, and Gaspé. The following are Mi'kmaq communities on Cape Breton Island (Unama'ki), with their chiefs' names, as of 1996, given in parentheses: Chapel Island (Lindsay Marshall), Eskasoni (Allison Bernard), Membertou (Terrance Paul), Wagmatcook (Mary Louise Bernard), and Waycobah (Morley Googoo).

The Aroostook Micmac Council was established in 1982. The Aroostook Band of Micmacs is governed by an elected board of directors. Headquarters for the tribal council is in Presque Isle, Maine. Band membership was slightly less than 500 in 1991. The interim chair in early 1999 was Roy Silliboy.

Elected chiefs and councils, whose members hold office for two years, represent the officially sponsored form of government on Mi'kmaq reserves. The Grand Council, traditional government of the Mi'kmaq Nation, continues to unite the districts of Mi'kmaq territory (Quebec's Gaspé Peninsula, northern and eastern New Brunswick, Nova Scotia, Newfoundland, and Prince Edward Island. The Grand Council is particularly strong in Nova Scotia.

The Native Council of Nova Scotia advocates for Mi'kmaqs (and other native people) living off of reserves. In 1997, officers of this group were as follows: Lorraine Cook, president; Grace Conrad, vice president; Heather Joudrie, financial comptroller; Lee Paul, administrator; and Donna Hannaford, citizenship officer. Lorraine Cook was once officially considered nonnative because of the infamous Bill C-31 of Canada's Indian Act. Involved in native organizations her whole adult life, Ms. Cook believes that fair and equal treatment for native people will only be achieved through self-government, along with its attendant responsibilities. She would like to see native groups speak with one voice but, in any case, plans to move the council along toward fulfilling its goals.

Viola Robinson, of the Mi'kmaq Reserve in Shubenacadie, Nova Scotia, is another well-known Mi'kmaq leader. She began her life as an activist in 1974 when, as a 22-year-old mother of four, she began to think about the discrimination she suffered as a "non-status" Indian. Robinson began attending meetings of a group that eventually became the Non-Status Indian and Métis Association of Nova Scotia (later the Native Council of Nova Scotia). As president of the group for 15 years, she worked tirelessly to improve both the legal and the socioeconomic position of native people living in Canada. In 1991, Robinson was appointed to the Royal Commission on Aboriginal Peoples.

Mi'kmaqs continue to catch salmon and other fish. As the discussion of the Mi'kmaq in the "Natural Resource Control" entry in the Contemporary Issues section indicates, they are also asserting their logging and other prerogatives on their vast unceded forest resources. The community in Maine operates a mail-order crafts cooperative. A $35 million settlement to the Mi'kmaq of Pictou Landing reserve has been the most important Canadian land claims victory.

Mi'kmaqs tend to be active in pan-Indian organizations. Perhaps one-third of the people, especially those living in Canada, still speak (and also write) their ancestral language. There is growing interest in the traditional game of *waltes* as well as traditional skills such as basket making, working with hides, and decoration with beads and quills. The people continue to face severe problems such as substance abuse, discrimination, and high suicide and unemployment rates. Mi'kmaq chiefs in Nova Scotia are on record as opposing a proposed natural gas pipeline as a potential threat to their sovereignty and land claims. The chiefs are asking for project proponents to deal in good faith with their concerns.

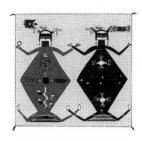

MOHAWK

One of the original members of the Iroquois Confederacy and a major player in the colonial wars of the eighteenth century, the Mohawk Nation was divided and scattered in 1900. As hunting became less important to the people, farming, dependence on annuities received for the sale of land, and some wage labor gradually became the key economic activities. Fishing and trapping retained a diminished importance. Mohawks also worked as oarsmen with shipping companies and began working in construction, particularly on high scaffolding. Pressure from non-natives to adopt Christianity and sell more land grew in intensity, and in fact, the ancient religion declined during the early twentieth century.

In Canada, several developments combined to further weaken traditional structures. Reserve lands had been allotted in the 1840s; descent was legally required to come from the male line after 1869 (Iroquois are traditionally matrilineal), and political structures were subsumed into a municipal government structure. In 1924, Canada unilaterally replaced the Iroquois Confederacy with a system of (all male) elected band governments on the reserves. These changes were opposed by traditional Mohawks but had their intended effect nevertheless.

All Iroquois people, or Haudenosaunee ("People of the Longhouse"), but perhaps especially the Mohawk, continue to resist these and other federal and state actions that they consider to be intrusions on their sovereignty. In 1968, Akwesasne Mohawks blocked the Cornwall International Bridge to protest the imposition of customs duties levied on Mohawk people crossing to another part of Akwesasne territory. The same year, a Mohawk school boycott resulted in greater Indian control over local education.

In 1974, Mohawk and other Indians established a territory called Ganienkeh on a parcel of disputed land. The same year, Mohawks formed Determined Residents United for Mohawk Sovereignty (DRUMS), which opposed speakeasies and casinos on reservation territory. In 1990, an incident sparked by the expansion of a golf course resulted in an armed standoff involving local non-natives and the communities of Oka, Kahnawake, and Kanesatake. The Mohawk (Kahniakehaka) Nation recognizes neither the United States–Canada border nor their own status as U.S. or Canadian citizens.

Mohawks at work on New York skyscrapers, 1995. Many Mohawk and Iroquois men have worked on high-steel construction projects across the country. Their ability to excel at this kind of work is a source of pride and self-esteem. (Corbis)

The Mohawk Nation Council of Chiefs oversees the social, cultural, and political health of the Mohawk people. The council's projects include various land claims negotiations, treaty obligations, social and cultural issues, education, communications, and government services, such as issuing passports and other formal documents. The Mohawk Nation includes Kahnawake, Oka/Kanesatake, Gibson Reserve (Watha Mohawk Nation), Six Nations (Grand River) Reserve, Tyendinega Reserve, Ganienke, St. Regis Reservation/Akwesasne Reserve, and Kanatsiohareke, a community of Mohawks living in the Mohawk Valley for the first time in 200 years that was established in 1993 by a small group from Akwesasne.

Kahnawake/Caughnawaga and Doncaster Reserves, Quebec, Canada, were established in 1667 as a Jesuit mission for mostly Oneida and Mohawk Indians. The mid-1990s population was about 6,500, of a total population of almost 8,000.

Oka/Kanesatake/Lake of Two Mountains, Quebec, Canada, established in 1676 by residents of Kahnawake, is populated mainly by Algonquians and several Iroquois tribes. It is roughly 6 square miles in size and is governed by a band council. The mid-1990s Mohawk population was about 1,800.

Gibson Reserve (Watha Mohawk Nation), Ontario, Canada, was established in 1881 at Georgian Bay by people from Oka/Kanesatake who resented resistance offered by the Sulpician Catholics to their cutting timber from the home reserve. The mid-1990s population was about 800.

Six Nations (Grand River), Ontario, Canada, was established in 1784. It is governed by both an elected and a hereditary council, although only the first is officially recognized by Canada (the band councils, instituted by Canada, are the only federally recognized Indian governments).

Tyendinega Reserve (Deseronto), Hastings County, Ontario, Canada, is mainly a Mohawk reserve. The mid-1990s population was around 3,000.

St. Regis Reservation/Akwesasne Reserve, Franklin County, New York, and Quebec and Ontario, Canada (1755), was formerly a mission established on the St. Lawrence River in the mid-eighteenth century for Mohawks and other groups. The resident Indian population in 1990 was 1,923, but the enrolled population approached 13,000. The 14,600 acres of this community straddle the international border. In 1999, the chief executive officer of the St. Regis Band of Mohawks was Edward D. Smoke.

The constitution of the St. Regis Mohawk Tribe (Akwesasne) was ratified in 1996. The tribe claims jurisdiction over all persons on the reservation as well as all resources of any kind within its borders. The constitution gives members of the Mohawk community the right to Mohawk culture and language and specifically notes the supremacy of the Great Law of Peace. It also contains a U.S.-style bill of rights and provides for referendum, initiative, and recall. The relationship of the tribal government to all other governments is specifically designated as "government-to-government." The principle of tribal sovereign immunity is also enshrined in the constitution.

The tribal government is divided into three branches. Executive authority is vested in the tribal chief, who, along with the vice chief, is elected for a term of four years. A tribal council exercises legislative authority. The council normally has five members but may contain up to seven members. Councilors serve three-year terms and meet monthly. There is also a tribal judiciary that consists of a tribal court, a court of appeals, and a peacemaker court. The community elects a chief judge and two associate judges to the tribal court for a term of seven years.

These communities also recognize the authority of the Grand Council of the Haudenosaunee Confederacy. The confederacy, divided since the late eighteenth century, conducts grand councils at both Six Nations and Onondaga. Their relationship to each other remains controversial. In general, however, the Grand Council at Six Nations tends to represent Iroquois people living in Canada and the Onondaga council has primary jurisdiction in the United States. The two councils meet as one when discussing matters of national importance.

Akwesasne Mohawks publish an important journal, *Akwesasne Notes*. The Mohawk have had difficulty uniting around divisive issues like state sales and cigarette taxes, pollution, land claims, and, perhaps especially, gaming. In 1980, the New York State Police assumed the responsibilities of the tribal police after averting a bloody factional showdown. The Six Nations Reserve is also marked by the existence of "progressive" and "traditional" factions, with the former generally supporting the elected band council and following the Christian faith and the latter supporting the confederacy and the Longhouse religion.

Traditional Iroquois Indians continue to observe the midwinter, green corn, condolence, and strawberry ceremonies and other traditional or semi-traditional celebrations. The Code of Handsome Lake and the Longhouse religion, based on traditional thanksgiving ceremonies, remain vital on most Iroquois communities. Roughly 15 percent of Canadian Mohawks speak their native language, which remains the people's official language. Traditional social (clan) structures remain more or less intact.

As a result of Mohawk people's having worked in high steel for generations, Mohawk communities exist in several northeastern cities of the United States, such as Brooklyn, New York. Many of these people frequently return to the reserves, however, to partake of traditional activities. Important economic activities at Kahnawake/Caughnawaga include small-scale farming, high-steel work, factory work, and reservation government. Four schools, a radio station, a newspaper, a hospital, and a credit union provide additional jobs and community identity. People at St. Regis/Akwesasne work mainly in high steel; small businesses, including bingo halls; and tribal government.

James Ransom, an Akwesasne Mohawk, served as a subchief of the Akwesasne tribe. His primary work was as an environmentalist. Akwesasne has suffered a series of environmental disasters throughout the years, especially soil and water contamination from heavy metals and other toxic materials as a result of dumping by nearby industries. Ransom would like to hold the industries legally responsible for the pollution. Another goal is to restore the suitability of the St. Lawrence River for fishing and swimming.

In 1999, Joseph Tokwiro was grand chief at Kahnawake. He has served as grand chief for 20 years, having previously worked as an ironworker for 10 years. One of 12 children, he is 50 years old and is married with two children. He was born in Kahnawake.

MOJAVE

The Mojave, already divided into communities living in the Mojave Valley and the Colorado River Valley of California and Arizona, suffered terribly from influenza epidemics and land encroachment in the early twentieth century. The first local government boarding school, dedicated to the destruction of Indian culture, had opened at the Colorado River Indian Reservation (CRIR) in 1879. Land allotments began in 1904. In the 1930s, with the construction of great dams on the Colorado River, the people who had farmed the river floodplain for centuries were forced to cease growing food.

During World War II, the United States summarily appropriated 25,000 acres of the CRIR in order to build the camps that housed many U.S. citizens of Japanese heritage. The Japanese provided much of the initial agricultural labor there. After the war, the Bureau of Indian Affairs opened the CRIR to Hopis and Navajos, ostensibly because their lands were incapable of supporting so many people. In 1964 the Indians received the deed to the reservation. Now members of all four tribes are members of the Colorado River Indian Tribes (CRIT), a difficult development for the remaining Mojave elders, who worry about the decline of Mojave identity. A 1963 court case guaranteed CRIT title to federal water rights, although the issue of water rights remains a difficult one.

Both the Colorado River Indian Reservation in Arizona and California (1865; roughly 270,000 acres) and Fort Mojave in Arizona (1870; roughly 33,000 acres) have active tribal councils. The Fort Mojave Council consists of a chair, a vice chair, and five councilors. Other officers include a secretary and a treasurer. In addition to the usual powers of such a body, the council also has the express power to protect and preserve the tribe's wildlife and natural resources and to cultivate Indian arts, crafts, and cultures. The council is also required to review the constitution not less than every five years with the purpose of proposing amendments to bring it up to date.

A provision in the constitution notes the supremacy of the tribe's inherent attributes of sovereignty. Another provision further enjoins interference in the tribe's cultural and religious practices. Referendum and recall are also provided for. Both tribal governments operate civil and criminal courts whose jurisdiction includes the reservations. Nora Helton is the chair of the Fort Mojave Indian Tribe.

The Colorado River Indian Tribes revised their constitution in 1975. Under its provisions, the tribal council directs an executive structure consisting of a chair, vice chair, secretary, and treasurer to govern the tribe on a day-to-day basis. The tribal administration also includes 28 departments as well as a committee system, a tribal police department, and a modern judicial system.

The Fort Mojave reservation is located within sight of Spirit Mountain, the ancestral homeland of all Yuman people. Of a Mojave tribal enrollment of just under 1,000, roughly 500 Indians lived at Fort Mojave (1990 figures). Agriculture has recently emerged as a major economic activity, with about 25,000 acres under tribal cultivation. A huge residential and commercial development, including a casino, is being constructed on the Nevada part of the reservation. In an unusual move for an Indian group, the tribal government has financed an associated water and sewer project by issuing bonds. Other sources of income include land leasing, another casino, some tourism, a housing development, and some job opportunities in and around the reservation. The community has recently signed a lease for the development of a 500-megawatt power plant. Unemployment on the reservation regularly reaches 50 percent.

In 1992, roughly 1,250 members of the CRIT Indians lived on the CRIR. A majority of these people identified themselves as Mojave. Total tribal enrollment just topped 3,000. In contrast to Fort Mojave, farming is the key activity at CRIR, where unemployment stood at 9 percent in 1997. Large-scale farming is largely possible because CRIT owns senior water rights to 171,000 acre-feet of the Colorado River. Roughly 85,000 acres of land are now under cultivation. An 11,000-acre cooperative produces mainly cotton, alfalfa, wheat, melons, and lettuce. The tribe also owns land within Parker, Arizona, and in 1989 successfully challenged the town's authority to regulate building activities on that land.

Tourist facilities at CRIR include a marina, casino and resort, gift shop, and restaurant. The tribe hosts motorboat races in the spring and a rodeo in November. Some people herd sheep or work in federal government jobs. Other sources of income include long-term leases and numerous large and small businesses, such as a 10-acre recycling plant that opened in 1992.

Mojaves still cremate their dead. Apart from traditional mourning ceremonies, however, few other song cycles are remembered. The last traditional chief died in 1947. Over half of the people speak their native language. Despite the existence of a hospital, adequate health care is hard to find at CRIR, and diabetes has become a severe health problem. Children attend public schools. Both tribes provide scholarship funds to their students interested in obtaining higher education.

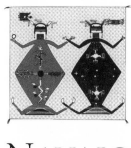

Navajo

The Navajo people recovered only slowly from their brutal military defeat and forced relocation in the mid-1860s. By 1900, commercial herding had largely replaced subsistence activities. The people remained largely band oriented well into the twentieth century. In 1915, the Bureau of Indian Affairs (BIA) divided the reservation into six superintendent-led districts. Eight years later, the secretary of the interior appointed a tribal commissioner and a tribal council. Henry Chee Dodge, who had assumed the position of head chief after the death of the great chief Manuelito, became the first tribal chair, serving until his death in 1947.

A BIA-mandated stock reduction in the 1930s led to dramatically lower standards of living. It was also largely responsible for the tribe's defeat of the Indian Reorganization Act (IRA). Navajos traveled off the reservation in large numbers for the first time during World War II. Those who returned came home with both money and honor, having distinguished themselves both as soldiers and as "code-talkers."

The 1950s brought large-scale coal, oil, and uranium development. The tribal council increased its power and range of activities dramatically. This was especially true in the following decade, when money from government antipoverty programs began to flow as well. The Office of Navajo Economic Opportunity (ONEO), created in 1965 and led by Peter MacDonald, funneled tens of millions of dollars into social programs. MacDonald later served as tribal chairman in 1970, 1974, 1978, and 1986. Navajos helped to found the Council of Energy Resource Tribes (CERT) in 1976 to help tribes exert control over their mineral resources. Despite their corps of lawyers, however, the tribes have found it difficult to resist pressure from the major energy companies to sign exploitative leases.

Today, the Navajo Reservation, established in 1868, consists of almost 14 million acres (28,803 square miles) in a patchwork of land in northern Arizona and New Mexico and southern Utah and Colorado. There are several nearby satellite communities. One such satellite is Cañoncito Reservation (1868; 76,813 acres), near Laguna Pueblo. There roughly 1,700 people (1990) are descended from generally pro-assimilation, Christian Navajo who moved south in the early nineteenth century under Spanish pressure. Other satellite communities include Utah (6,000 people), Ramah (1868; 146,953

Former Navajo Nation president Albert Hale (center) along with former Santa Ana governor Leonard Garcia and U.S. President Bill Clinton, October 1996. Indian leaders continue to work with U.S. government officials on improving relations between federal and Indian governments. (AP Photo/Jake Schoellkopf)

acres; 1,500 people), and Puertocito, or Alamo (1868; 63,109 acres; 2,000 people). Thirty thousand Navajo also live on the "checkerboard" in New Mexico, a region in which each alternate square mile is Indian owned. Navajo are also represented among the Colorado River Indian Tribes (see the Mojave entry).

Elections for the tribal council are held every four years. In 1936 the council adopted a code that serves in lieu of a constitution (they rejected organization under the IRA). The Navajo Nation was formally proclaimed in 1969. In 1990, the government was reorganized to coincide with the U.S. model, and the offices of chair and vice chair were replaced by those of president and vice president. There are also well over 100 chapters of local business councils.

The president of the Navajo Nation in 1999 was Kelsey Begaye. Born in 1951, Begaye grew up in the reservation town of Kaibito and was educated in reservation and public schools. His maternal clan is *todichiini,i* and his paternal clan is *tabaha*. He wanted to be an evangelist but fell victim to alcoholism in Vietnam. By 1975, Begaye was living on the streets of Los Angeles. He soon found his way to a substance abuse treatment center in Page, Arizona, however, where he turned his life around.

Begaye became a counselor himself and later ran for the Navajo Tribal Council, where he eventually became speaker. Although he embraced Pentecostal Christianity, Begaye maintains that he is "Navajo first, Christian second." He is generally seen as dependable and deliberate, as opposed to flashy or charismatic. His watchword on the campaign trail was "family values." Among other priorities, he plans to focus on the tribe's scholarship program and to encourage more young people to become involved in tribal politics.

In 1999, 172,000 Indians lived on the Navajo Reservation. Many thousands more live off reservation. The total population of the Navajo Nation in the late 1990s approached 225,000 people.

Mining companies, particularly Peabody Coal, remain the largest employers of Navajos. About 75 percent of the tribal operating budget comes from royalties from coal sales. Still, in 1999 the tribe filed a $600 million lawsuit against Peabody Coal, charging that years of corruption and influence peddling had cost the tribe at least that sum in lost royalties. Navajo Agricultural Products Industries and Navajo Forests Products Industries are also important employers. There is also some retail business as well as some off-reservation employment. Farmers and herders often depend upon a wage-earning family member. Many Navajos make arts and crafts such as weavings, jewelry, baskets, pottery, and commercial sandpaintings. The tribe plans to develop various tourist-related industries, such as a controversial development at the Antelope Point Marina on Lake Powell. One-third or more of the tribal workforce is regularly un- or underemployed.

Furthermore, substance abuse and related problems, including gang violence, have grown in seriousness. Massive strip mining has ruined the land, and coal and uranium mining have caused major health problems. Severe pollution has led to strong sentiment against further development; the Nation is very much divided over this issue, as it is about long-term leases of questionable legality signed by former Nation officials. MacDonald was jailed in the 1990s over felony corruption-related crimes, and corruption has continued to dog tribal politics. In 1999, the Nation had its fifth president within a year, not all of whom were legally elected.

The Navajo Reservation is a complex place, where the twenty-first century coexists uneasily with the nineteenth. Perhaps as many as 25,000 people

Smokestacks from the Four Corners coal-processing plant on the Navajo reservation in New Mexico can be seen in the background. Coal and uranium mining have been poisoning Indian people and lands for years, though virtually all of the power generated by those resources is transmitted to Los Angeles. (Woodfin Camp & Associates, Inc.)

Navajo jewelry on display in Arizona. Navajo Indians are world famous for their silver and turquoise jewelry. (Photophile)

speak only or mostly Navajo. Native healers practice alongside modern doctors. The reservation has yet to receive complete telephone service, and about half of all homes lack indoor plumbing. Most people live in trailers or frame homes, but the hogan is the spiritual center and the only place for ceremonies. Matriarchal kinship systems remain strong, as does traditional religious practice, although some ceremonials can be prohibitively expensive. Many Navajos are also Christians and/or adherents of the Native American Church. Community schools (including Navajo Community College), which many people attend, feature a Navajo-based curriculum. Ties between urban Navajos and the reservation remain generally close.

ONEIDA

The Oneida Nation is a founding member of the Iroquois Confederacy. Long a power in the eastern Great Lakes and, with their fellow confederacy members, the Ohio Valley, the Oneida emerged much weakened from the colonial wars of the eighteenth century. By early in the next century they were scattered into communities in New York, Wisconsin, the Indian Territory, and several locations in Canada.

In the early twentieth century, most Wisconsin Oneida were practicing Christians who retained little of their aboriginal religion. Traditional political structures had been replaced by a municipal form of government. Most of their land, which was allotted in 1908, had been lost to tax default and foreclosure. In Canada, the economic focus shifted from farming and some seasonal lumbering to wage labor in white communities. Unfortunately, the communities were poorly equipped to withstand change. Factionalism, strongly encouraged by the creation of band councils, consumed much of the people's energy. In 1924, the Canadian government unilaterally proclaimed an elective system.

Today, there are roughly 11,000 members of the Wisconsin Oneida Tribe, most of whom live in the Green Bay area. Another 4,600 Oneida live in Ontario, Canada, and about 700 live in New York. "Progressive" and "traditional" factions still battle over power on the Six Nations Reserve in Ontario. The former faction generally supports the elected band council and the latter the Iroquois, or Haudenosaunee, Confederacy. Most "progressives" are Christian, while "traditionalists" favor the Handsome Lake and/or the Longhouse religion. Traditional Iroquois Indians also observe the midwinter, green corn, condolence, and strawberry ceremonies and other traditional or semitraditional celebrations. In part because Canadian law mandates patrilineal descent, clan identification has lost much of its significance.

New York Iroquois in the later twentieth century have taken strong stands on issues such as Indian burial sites, sovereignty, gambling casinos, and land claims. Regarding the latter, the nation is involved in a lawsuit (supported by the federal government as of early 1999) that contends that the treaties by which state and local governments took 270,000 acres of their land were illegal, even though signed by both sides, because they were not ap-

Oneida women take advantage of a campaign visit by First Lady Hillary Clinton in 1998 to publicize their land-claim issues. (AP Photo/Ron Frehm)

proved by Congress. In a controversial tactic, the tribe has named local property owners in the suit.

The New York Oneida community owns 32 acres of land in Madison County, near Oneida. The land, acquired in 1794, is not recognized as a reservation by either the state or federal governments. The Indian population of the reservation in 1990 was 37, but membership in the Oneida Nation in

1999 was around 1,100 people. Some Oneidas also live on the Onondaga Reservation, New York.

Sachems and clan mothers now hold the leadership positions. Specifically, leadership is vested in the Men's Council and Clan Mothers. Members come from the three clans: Wolf, Turtle, and Bear. In 1999, members included Ray Halbritter, Keller George, and Chuck Fougnier (Wolf Clan); Clint Hill, Kenneth Phillips, Dale Rood, Richard Lynch, Beulah Green (Clan Mother), Iva Rodgers (Clan Mother), and Ruth Burr (Clan Mother) (Turtle Clan); and Brian Patterson and Marilyn John (Clan Mother) (Bear Clan).

In 1999, Ray Halbritter was the Oneida Nation representative and chief executive officer of Oneida Nation Enterprises and the Men's Council and Clan Mothers. A member of the Wolf Clan, Halbritter has led the tribe since 1987 and has been a driving force behind the Turning Stone Casino. During the mid-1990s he was opposed by a traditionalist group that opposed gaming.

The checkerboard Oneida Reservation (1838) is located in Brown and Outagamie Counties, Wisconsin. In the mid-1990s it contained roughly 2,500 acres, most of which had been repurchased since the 1930s by the federal government. The 1990 Indian population was 2,447. The community is governed under an Indian Reorganization Act (IRA) constitution by an elected business committee, which itself is subject to the general assembly.

Other Oneidas live in Ontario on the Six Nations (Grand River) Reserve (1,800 Indian residents in the mid-1990s) and Oneida of the Thames, near London (2,800 Indian residents in the mid-1990s). The Six Nations (Grand River) Reserve was established in 1784. It is governed by both an elected and a hereditary council, although only the first is federally recognized. In 1934, Canada mandated a political system consisting of elected councilors and an elected chief, although adherents of the Longhouse religion maintain their own hereditary council. Many Iroquois continue to see their relationship with the Canadian and U.S. governments as one between independent nations and allies, as opposed to one marked by paternalism and dependence.

Each of the Six Nations is also a member of the Grand Council of the Haudenosaunee Confederacy. The confederacy, divided since the late eighteenth century, conducts grand councils at both Six Nations and Onondaga. Their relationship to each other remains controversial. In general, however, the Grand Council at Six Nations tends to represent Iroquois people living in Canada and the Onondaga Council has primary jurisdiction in the United States. The two councils meet as one when discussing matters of national importance.

Some New York Oneidas still speak Oneida Iroquoian. Most are Christians, although many also participate in Longhouse ceremonies. A newsletter helps maintain community identity. The Oneida Nation operates a health center, a pool and recreation center, a museum/cultural center, youth and elderly programs, and a housing development. Furthermore, ownership of 15 business enterprises in addition to the Turning Stone Casino Resort makes the Nation the largest employer in Oneida and Madison Counties. The Nation also aids the local region through such activities as compensating school districts for lost tax revenue when it reacquires land. In late 1998, the Oneida Nation bought the well-known newspaper *Indian Country Today*. In an effort to prevent editorial influence from the tribal council, the tribe plans to run the paper through an independent corporation.

Matriarchal structures have given way to bilateral descent in Wisconsin, where, despite some interest in the Longhouse religion, most Oneidas are either Episcopalian or Methodist. Although the tribal school teaches classes in the native language, few people can speak it fluently. People display their beadwork, wood carving, and silver work at the annual powwow and at other venues as well. In the late 1990s, the tribe was considering a highly controversial move to establish a government on the Oneida Indian Nation reservation in New York.

ONONDAGA

The Onondaga, one of the founding members of the Iroquois (Haudenosaunee) Confederacy, have lived primarily in upstate New York and at the Six Nations (Grand River) Reserve in Canada since the late eighteenth century. They are known as perhaps the most conservative of the Haudenosaunee Nations. Many Haudenosaunee adopted the Handsome Lake religion in the nineteenth century. This doctrine, while centered on traditional native beliefs, incorporates some elements of Christianity and served somewhat to bridge the cultural gap of the period. As traditional structures weakened during the nineteenth century, the hereditary council came increasingly to resemble a town government. In 1924, Canada unilaterally imposed an elected political system, officially terminating council rule entirely.

Today, like most Haudenosaunee, the Onondaga do not recognize the international border between the United States and Canada. They have fought consistently for their independence and sovereignty, rejecting the 1924 Indian Citizenship Act, the 1934 Indian Reorganization Act, the Selective Service Act (although many serve voluntarily in the armed forces), and other attempts of the U.S. and Canadian governments to exercise political authority over them. Since 1994, leaders of the Onondaga Nation have even refused all federal and state grants on these grounds. Unemployment often reached high levels on the Onondaga Reservation. Those who can find work tend to do so in Syracuse. The people continue to pursue extensive land claims.

Onondagas live on the Six Nations reserve as well as on a 6,100-acre reservation near Syracuse, New York. Their population in 1990 was about 1,600 in the United States and another 500 or so in Canada. The people continue to maintain a traditional governmental structure. Members of the hereditary council of chiefs are still selected by women clan leaders. One additional requirement of Onondaga chiefs is that they must be followers of the teachings of Handsome Lake. Thus, linked to the Longhouses on other Iroquois reservations, they are in a position to maintain the continuity and the vitality of the roughly 500-year-old Iroquois League. Leon Shenendoah, Tadodaho ("firekeeper") of the Six Nations Confederacy for almost 30 years, died in 1996. In early 1999, Irving Powless Jr. was chief of the Onondaga Nation.

In 1999 Oren Lyons was faithkeeper, or subchief, of the Onondaga Nation. He is a member of the Turtle clan. Born in 1930, Lyons grew up on the

Seneca and Onondaga reservations. He hunted as a boy in order to feed his mother, sister, and six brothers. After serving in the army, he attended Syracuse University, graduating with a degree in fine arts. While in college he was an All-American lacrosse player (he later entered the Lacrosse National Hall of Fame and helped to create an Iroquois national lacrosse team).

Lyons worked in New York City as a commercial artist but returned to Onondaga in 1970. He is well known as an advocate for Native Americans and sought after as a speaker. Among his many awards and honors is an honorary law degree from Syracuse University and the Ellis Island Congressional Medal of Honor. He has served and continues to serve as a member of numerous human rights and native organizations and has mediated between Indian groups and non-native governments, notably during the 1990 Oka crisis between Mohawks and the state of New York. In addition to his many other activities, he directs the Native American studies program at the State University of New York (SUNY) at Buffalo. In 1992 he published, along with John Mohawk, his colleague at SUNY, a book entitled *Exiled in the Land of the Free*.

The Haudenosaunee (Iroquois) Confederacy, divided since the late eighteenth century, conducts Grand Councils at both Six Nations and Onondaga. Their relationship to each other remains controversial. In general, however, the Grand Council at Six Nations tends to represent Iroquois people living in Canada and the Onondaga Council has primary jurisdiction in the United States. The two councils meet as one when discussing matters of national importance. Matters of pressing importance to the confederacy at the turn of the century include protecting Indian burial sites, sovereignty, gaming, and land claims.

Despite the various laws designed to undermine traditional patterns, political and social (clan) structures remain generally intact. There is a K–8 school on the reservation, and English is the official tribal language, although many people speak Onondaga. Traditional Onondagas still celebrate the midwinter, green corn, and strawberry festivals as well as other traditional or semitraditional events. Onondaga artists and athletes—especially lacrosse players—have achieved special distinction.

OSAGE

Having ceded most of their land in the early nineteenth century and sold what remained in 1870, the Osage had resettled in the Indian Territory (Oklahoma) in the 1870s. There they created five villages and retained a structure of 24 clans and two divisions. In 1897, large oil deposits were discovered on Osage land. In 1906, the people implemented a voluntary allotment plan, dividing the tribal land individually but retaining collective mineral rights.

Oil made the Osage very wealthy during the 1920s. In addition to its many benefits, however, oil wealth also brought a large measure of corruption. Many people were cheated out of land and money. Many also fell victim to substance abuse. By the 1960s, despite the continuation of considerable oil income, half of the individual allotments had been lost, mainly to tax authorities and swindlers.

In 1993, most of the roughly 11,000 enrolled members of the Osage tribe lived in Osage County, Oklahoma. Despite, or perhaps because of, oil's uncertain future as an income producer, it remains at the center of Osage economic and political life. Many individuals not employed by the oil industry work in tribal administration or for the tribal bingo parlor. Other Osages maintain farms or ranches. The Native American Church, Protestant sects, and especially Catholicism are the most popular religious affiliations. Probably fewer than 3 percent of the people spoke Osage fluently in 1993. The Osage hold traditional dances in June and are active in the national pow-wow circuit.

The administrative center of the Osage Nation is in Pawhuska, Oklahoma. Only those people who have inherited land from the original (1906) allottees may vote in tribal elections. In the mid-1990s only about one-third of the parcels allotted in 1906 were still owned by Osage Indians. There are also three 160-acre community-held village sites (Pawhuska, Hominy, and Grayhorse) and a larger site for tribal administration and facilities. Any Osage can live free of charge in one of the villages.

Article II of the 1994 constitution explicitly gives the secretary of the interior control over aspects of mineral estate. Article III, which refers to membership, explicitly disassociates tribal membership from mineral estate income. Article IV of the constitution provides for a tripartite governmental structure. Article V provides that any tribal member who attends the annual meeting on the last Saturday in April shall be considered part of the general council.

Legislative power is vested in a nine-member national council elected at large every other year for staggered four-year terms. Officers include a president, vice president, speaker, and second speaker. The national council meets monthly. Among its other responsibilities, it is empowered to govern the nation (aspects of the mineral estate excepted), negotiate with other governments, levy taxes (with certain exceptions relating to mineral extraction and the mineral estate), manage land and other assets and enterprises (partially excluding the mineral estate), and pass and enforce laws.

The constitution also establishes a national judiciary consisting of a supreme court and lower courts. Judges are elected and hold office for four-year terms. There are also provisions for recall, removal, referenda, and initiative; a U.S.-style bill of rights; and a formal elders council, meant to advise the national council on matters of national culture, history, and tradition. As of the June 1998 elections, the members of the Osage Tribal Council were as follows: Camille Pangburn, Kenny Bighorse, Charles Tallchief, Rosemary Wood, Everett Waller, Joe Trumbly, Ralph Adkisson, and John Essley. Charles Tillman served as chief.

Osage people tend to work in the oil industry, in tribal administration, or for the local bingo parlor. Others farm or ranch for a living. Most Osages are Catholic, although Protestantism and the Native American Church are also well represented by tribal members. Fewer than 300 people spoke Osage fluently in the mid-1990s. Osages hold their own traditional dances in June; many also attend various pan-Indian gatherings across the country.

PEQUOT

Well into the twentieth century it was widely believed that the Pequot Indians, losers in the devastating Pequot War of 1637, had disappeared. Some survivors joined the Pequot-derived Mohegan people, and others scattered throughout New England, perhaps joining other tribes. The Mohegan were among the founders of the Brotherton (or Brothertown) tribe in the late eighteenth century. This group acquired land in Wisconsin in the nineteenth century, but by the early twentieth century, most Brotherton Indians had been dispossessed.

Although their traditional culture is gone, identity within the Brotherton community remains vital, and those living away return regularly for gatherings and reunions. Brotherton Indians, who include Pequot descendants and numbered roughly 1,650 in 1990, now live primarily in Milwaukee, Racine, and Green Bay, Wisconsin. The tribe maintains a headquarters in Fond du Lac, Wisconsin, although its spiritual center is in Gresham. The Brotherton tribe is governed by an elected, nine-member tribal council.

Mohegan Indians began a political revival in the early twentieth century, forming the Mohegan Indian Council and becoming involved with the Algonquin Indian Council of New England. The roughly 1,000-member Mohegan Tribe has a land claim pending against the state of Connecticut for approximately 600 acres of land alienated in the seventeenth century. The Golden Hill Reservation (Paugussett Tribe [Pequot and Mohegan]), New London and Fairfield Counties, Connecticut, was established in 1886. Important centers of Mohegan tribal life include the Tantaquidgeon museum, the Mohegan church (1831), and the Fort Shantok burial ground. The contemporary wigwam festival or powwow has its origins in the green corn festival of ancient times.

From a low of about 10 in 1910, and a reservation population of only one in the early 1970s, the Mashantucket (western) Pequot population rebounded to about 530 in the late 1990s. New tribal members must trace their descent from a person on the tribal roles in either 1900 or 1910. Almost half of Mashantucket Pequots have some African ancestry, a fact that surprised even them when members began returning to the reservation in the 1980s.

The constitution of the Mashantucket (western) Pequot Tribe calls for an elected, five-member tribal council. The tribal membership elects a tribal

Terry Bell, director of the Mashantucket Pequot Museum and Research Center, poses on the museum's construction site, March 22, 1996. According to Bell, Mashantucket Pequots had a project such as this in mind when they first voted to become involved in gaming. (AP Photo/Bob Child)

chair from among the five councilors. The council itself then chooses a vice chair and, from within or without, a secretary and treasurer (the offices may be combined) and other officers as needed. The term of office is three years with no limit on the number of terms one person can serve. The tribal council manages tens of millions of dollars in investments. Council meetings take place monthly. Tribal officers in 1998 included Kenneth Reels, chairman; Ruth Thomas, treasurer-secretary; and Robert Smith, finance officer.

Richard "Skip" Hayward was chair of the Mashantucket Pequot Tribal Council from 1975 until 1999. Born in 1947, Haywood is the grandson of Elizabeth George Plouffe, who at one time was the last remaining Pequot living on reservation land. He grew up with his mother and grandmother while his father was away at sea. Heeding his grandmother's admonition to hold onto the land, Haywood became the driving force behind the Pequots' spectacular recovery.

The Mashantucket Pequot were formally recognized in 1983. They own about 1,800 acres of land in Ledyard, Connecticut, which they acquired in 1667. They would like to expand their reservation lands by 165 acres and are currently locked in a legal battle with the state of Connecticut over this issue. The fabulously successful casino dominates their economy. They have also built a large museum and research/cultural center. Casino revenues have

Former Mashantucket Pequot Indian tribal Chairman Skip Hayward welds his initials into the keel of Sassacus, *a high-speed ferry, during keel-laying ceremonies at the Pequot River Shipworks in New London, Connecticut, Tuesday, July 30, 1996. The Mashantucket Pequots have exclusive rights to build this type of ferry for North America, South America, the Caribbean, and Hawaii. (AP Photo/Bob Child)*

made the people enormously wealthy. Pequot descendants also live among the small Schaghticoke tribe in northwestern Connecticut.

The Paucatuck (eastern) Pequot claim the approximately 226-acre Lantern Hill State Reservation in New London County (North Stonington), Connecticut (established 1623). There were about 600 Paucatuck Pequot in the mid-1990s. These people continue to fight for land claims and full federal recognition as well as full recognition by the state of Connecticut. Building tribal cohesiveness is high on their agenda. Only a few people, mainly tribal elders, understand elements of the Pequot language.

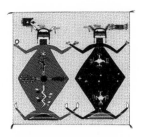

PIMA

An agricultural people who had enjoyed considerable success as late as the late nineteenth century, the Pima were an impoverished tribe by 1900. They waited in vain for the federal government to address the key issue of Pima water rights. Meanwhile, government-supported Presbyterian missionaries replaced the Pima religious structure with one of their own creation. Church- and government-run schools opened on the Arizona reservation. Beginning in 1914, allotment further broke up tribal land patterns and disrupted community life.

Although its political structure had fallen almost completely apart, the Gila River Pima and Maricopa community adopted a constitution and tribal council in 1934. Also in the 1930s, the San Carlos Project began returning irrigation water to the Pima. By this time, however, the people were reluctant to return to subsistence farming, in part because they had become used to working in the wage economy. Prospective farmers would also have had to deal with a water-management bureaucracy that mandated required crops as well as chronic ongoing water shortages. In any case, allotments (heirship) had effectively destroyed their land base.

The Gila River reservation was established in 1859. Today, it consists of roughly 370,000 acres. The community's constitution provides for government by a community council consisting of 17 members elected on a district-wide basis. All terms of elected office are three years. It also contains a U.S.-style bill of rights. Officers—governor, lieutenant governor, and the chief judge—as well as associate judges and councilors must be at least 25 years old and meet certain other requirements. A secretary and treasurer are appointed by the council, but the governor appoints standing committees and boards. As of the late 1990s, the governor of the Gila River Indian Community was Mary V. Thomas.

The community council has a range of responsibilities, such as negotiating with other governments; regulating and managing land and other tribal assets; creating, adopting, and executing a budget; and representing the community. The constitution enumerates two lists of council powers, those subject to review by the secretary of the interior and those not subject to such review. Other constitutional provisions address removal from office, referendum and initiative, and land ownership.

The Salt River Pima-Maricopa Indian Community near Phoenix, Arizona, was established by executive order in 1879, in Maricopa County, and contains roughly 52,600 acres. The enrollment topped 5,700 people in 1999. As of the late 1990s, the president of the Salt River Pima-Maricopa Indian Community Council was Ivan Makil.

The community's constitution and by-laws were adopted in 1940 and most recently revised in 1989. According to their provisions, officers who are also voting members of the community council include a president and vice president. There are other officers as well, some of whom are determined on an ad hoc basis. Legislative authority is vested in a community council that consists of seven members, in addition to the president and vice president, elected on a district basis. The term of office is four years. Elected officials may not be employed by either the community government or the U.S. government. The constitution also provides for a police force; a court system; initiative, referendum, and recall; and a U.S.-style bill of rights. The constitution also explicitly forbids the alienation of land outside of the community and mandates the acquisition of land within the reservation not currently owned by the community.

Arizona governor Jane Hull, right, signs one of the copies of the standard-form gaming compact as Salt River Pima–Maricopa Indian Community (SRPMIC) president Ivan Makil looks on during a ceremony at the Executive Office in Phoenix, 1998. Members of the SRPMIC stand in the background. The compact allows tribal casinos to offer limited gaming. (AP Photo/Ken LeVine)

In 1999 the Salt River Community had an enrolled population of 7,500, while the Gila River Reservation was home to around 11,550 Pima and Maricopa Indians. There are also at least several hundred Pima living among the Tohono O'odham on the Ak-chin reservation in southern Arizona as well as off-reservation locations. A slowly growing economy has allowed contemporary Pima once again to assume a degree of control over their own resources and lives. Although most reservation land is leased to non-Indians, Gila River Farms produces a number of crops, and the Salt River reservation cultivates roughly 12,000 acres. Community businesses include a large retail center, industrial parks, a motor racing park, sand and gravel sales, and the issuing of apiary and traders' licenses. Tourists buy baskets and other items at the Gila River Arts and Crafts Center, which includes a restaurant and a museum. Some Indians are able to find work in nearby cities and with the tribe.

Most contemporary Pimas are Presbyterians and are assimilated, more or less comfortably, into mainstream U.S. life. Gatherings such as the *mul-chu-tha* festival, a rodeo, and parades are highlights of the year. The fall Fiesta de Magdalena, held in Sonora, Mexico, remains a powerful connection between the Arizona and Mexican O'odham. Students attend Bureau of Indian Affairs schools (at Gila River) as well as public schools. In addition to health, issues of pressing concern include water rights—the local water table has been lowered some 300 feet over the years—and creeping urban and suburban sprawl. In late 1998, parts of the Salt River reservation received an experimental communications technology that uses small dish antennae to provide telephone service to remote areas.

POMO

Pomo-speaking people, devastated by centuries of abuse by Spanish missionaries, Russian traders, Mexican soldiers, and Anglo thieves and mass murderers, were generally homeless, landless, and relatively few in number by the late-nineteenth century. Around that time, however, survivors instituted a project to buy back a land base in their traditional territory north-northeast of San Francisco Bay. Establishing a number of rancherias (settlements), they worked as agricultural laborers in summer and returned to their own land in winter to keep their cultures alive. However, the period of recovery had not yet arrived: The Pomo lost almost all their land to foreclosure and debt, and local non-natives practiced severe social and economic discrimination against them.

The early twentieth century saw small legal gains for the Pomo. After World War I, Indian and white advocacy groups proliferated, and reforms were instituted in the areas of health, education, and welfare. Increasing contact with outsiders brought new ideas about industry and labor organization to the Pomo. Women gained more independence and began to assume a greater role in religious and political affairs. Treaties that had been concluded between native groups and the state of California in 1851–1852, which guaranteed the former over 8 million acres of land but had been "lost" before they could be ratified, reemerged, leading to the purchase of small, isolated, barren reservations or rancherias.

After World War II, several rancherias were terminated, and services declined drastically, leading to a period of general impoverishment. Since the 1960s, however, some California state agencies have stepped in to provide services, and the Pomo have become more politically and economically savvy. The Clear Lake Pomo were involved in the takeover of Alcatraz Island in 1969–1971, reflecting their involvement in pan-Indian politics. Beginning in the 1970s, many Pomo bands successfully sued the government for rerecognition, although many of these lost most or all of what little land they had in the process.

Today there are roughly 20 Pomo rancherias in northern California, especially in Lake, Mendocino, and Sonoma Counties. In addition to cities and towns in and around northern California, Pomos live at the following locations: the Big Valley Rancheria, the Cloverdale Rancheria, the Dry Creek

Rancheria, the Coyote Valley Rancheria, the Elem/Sulphur Bank Rancheria, the Grindstone Rancheria, the Guidiville Rancheria, the Hopland Rancheria, the Laytonville Rancheria, the Lytton Rancheria, the Stewart's Point Rancheria (Kashia Band), the Manchester–Point Arena Rancheria, the Middletown Rancheria, the Pinoleville Reservation, the Potter Valley Rancheria, the Redding Valley Rancheria, the Redwood Valley Rancheria, the Robinson Rancheria, the Round Valley Reservation (Little Lake Band), the Sherwood Valley Rancheria, the Sugar Bowl Rancheria, and the Upper Lake Rancheria. The Pomo population stood at roughly 4,900 in 1990, roughly one-third of whom lived on tribal land.

Rancherias and reservations are generally governed by elected councils. According to the constitution of the Elem Indian Colony, for example, a general council, consisting of all voting-age tribal members, governs the tribe. However, the general council elects an executive committee consisting of a chairman, vice chairman, secretary-treasurer, and two members, for two-year terms. The committee is empowered with customary responsibilities, including control over membership, negotiating with other governments, managing tribal land and other assets, overseeing a budget, and governing the tribe.

Executive officers of Pomo rancherias and reservations in 1999 include Valentino Jack, Big Valley; Thomas Brown, Elem; Patricia Hermosillo, Cloverdale; Priscilla Hunter, Coyote Valley; Gregg Cordova, Dry Creek; Eliza Swearinger, Grindstone; Merlene Sanchez, Guidiville; Sandra Sigala, Hopland; Marjorie Mejia, Lytton; Genevieve Campbell, Laytonville; Jose Orapeza, Manchester–Point Arena; Bradford Knight, Middletown; Leona Williams, Pinoleville; Shirlee Smith, Potter Valley; Gayle Zepeda, Redwood Valley; Edward Foreman, Redding; Norman Whipple, Round Valley; Robin Phillips, Sherwood; and Lynn Silva, Stewart's Point.

Pomo country is still relatively poor and continues to be under attack by development interests and local non-native governments. Lingering effects of the infamous Bureau of Indian Affairs Relocation Program of the 1960s—in which Pomo (and members of other tribes) were separated from their homelands—include irreparable losses in the areas of language, culture, and government. The local economy includes seasonal farmwork as well as some nonagricultural and government jobs. Some people continue to hunt and gather their food.

The extended family is still key in Pomo life. Pomo languages are still spoken, and some traditional customs, including ritual restrictions, traditional food feasts, ceremonies, ceremonial exchange, singing and dancing, and seasonal trips to the coast, are still performed. Pomo doctors are still called in to cure certain kinds of illnesses.

Many Christian Pomos practice a mixture of Christian and traditional ritual. Some Pomos would like to unite politically, but the lack of such a tradition makes this a difficult goal to achieve. However, various organizations do exist to bring the Pomo people together and advance their common interests. The struggle continues to reacquire a land base and to win recognition (or rerecognition) for some bands. Pinoleville must deal with environmentally hazardous industries established within its borders. The pan-Pomo Ya-Ka-Ama Indian Center features a plant nursery among other economic development, educational, and cultural projects. The intertribal Sinkyone Wilderness Council works to restore heavily logged areas using modern native techniques.

In recent years the small (about 80 people in 1996) Elem Indian Colony, already reeling from ecological problems caused by a non-native mining company, has experienced a gambling-related disaster. The context is a long-running feud between two factions located within a single family. The catalyst was a casino that opened in 1994. Gambling money lifted the once-destitute tribe into brief and somewhat illusory prosperity, as big-ticket consumer goods, such as expensive cars, appeared like a veneer over a community still dealing with poor housing and inadequate services. It also caused a 20-year-old political rivalry to explode, to the point where within two years of the casino's opening it was shut down by the National Indian Gaming Commission amid several gun battles and a rash of arson. Perhaps the worst result of this episode is that the tribe, riven and apparently no longer able to resolve its differences, may have been driven permanently from this last vestige of its ancestral homeland.

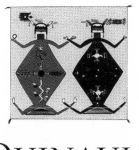

QUINAULT

In 1873, having ceded the bulk of their land eighteen years earlier, most Quinault people moved to a reservation at Taholah, Washington, established for them by the U.S. government. The Quinault managed to resist the allotment process around 1910, when the government agreed that the reservation, with its beaches and extensive forests, was unsuitable to be broken up into individual farming plots. However, when a federal court ruled that Quinault lands could be allotted to allow timber cutting and that members of other tribes, as signatories of the 1855 treaty, were entitled to receive such allotments, the reservation soon became virtually taken over by non-Quinault, particularly Chinook, people. As a result of the allotment process and the clear-cutting and environmental destruction that followed, many Quinaults were forced off of the reservation entirely.

The population of the Quinault Reservation in 1990 was 942, but in addition to Quinault people that number included members of tribes such as the Hoh, Quileute, Chinook, Chehalis, Queets, and Cowliss. The government of the Quinault Indian Nation is based on a constitution approved in 1975. In Article I, the nation claims sovereignty over several different categories of resources and groups of people, including all usual and accustomed fishing grounds, all open and unclaimed lands necessary for subsistence activities, and all tribal members. The constitution further sets enrollment qualifications at one-quarter blood Quinault, Queets, Quileute, Hoh, Chinook, Chehalis, or Cowlitz if that person is not already a member of another Indian tribe or nation. There are also provisions for adoption into the tribe.

All members of the Quinault Indian Nation over the age of 17 are considered voting members of the General Council, which meets annually to hold elections (and/or recall votes), accept new members, allocate fishing grounds, and take action on other business. The Quinault Business Committee, which consists of four executive officers and seven council members, is charged with day-to-day responsibility for the nation's business and legislative affairs. Officers are elected for three-year staggered terms. The Business Committee must obtain the consent of the General Council before certain actions, such as relinquishing any jurisdiction or rights and adoptions, may be considered binding. The constitution expressly limits the review power of the secretary of the interior to the greatest extent allowable by law.

Quinault Indians gillnet for salmon at the mouth of the Quinault River. Fishing and its associated industries remain a key part of the Quinault economy. The people have worked hard to maintain the integrity of the natural environment in part so that fish would continue to thrive. (Corbis/Natalie Fobes)

Administrative departments include finance, human resources, natural resources, community development, social and health services, facilities management, information services, public safety, judicial, and education. The Nation also maintains a separate judiciary. Modern leaders include Harry Shale, Horton Capoeman, Pearl Capoeman-Baller, James (Jug) Jackson, and Joe DeLaCruz.

In 1999, the president of the Quinault Indian Nation was Pearl Capoeman-Baller. Now in her second term as tribal chair, Capoeman-Baller was first elected to the tribal council in the early 1970s. One of her most significant victories was persuading tribal members not to take per capita payments from the tribe's first casino. Her reasoning, and that which ultimately convinced a majority of tribal members, was that it is unwise to foster any dependency on Indian gaming, an industry with an uncertain future. She prefers to invest any casino profits in ways that will benefit the tribe as a whole.

Joseph DeLaCruz led the Quinault Nation for 22 years. DeLaCruz's stature as a leader and his political and business acumen gave him influence far beyond the Quinault Nation. For instance, he was president of the National Tribal Chairmen Association, and he helped to organize the Conference of Tribal Governments, the Northwest Indian Fish Commission, and the National Commission on American Indian, Alaska Native, and Hawaiian Housing. DeLaCruz also served as president of the National Congress of American Indians in the mid-1980s. His major policy initiatives as tribal president included the Quinault Forest Management Program, Quinault land restoration, the Quinault Housing Program, the Quinault Seafood Plant, and the Quinault Land and Timber Enterprises.

Tribal members who work on the Quinault Reservation do so for the tribal government. The most important economic activities are forest products, salmon fishing, and seafood processing. Few Quinaults own businesses on the reservation, however, and most work in the mainstream economy off of the reservation. In 1984, for the first time in almost 60 years, the Quinault held a traditional potlatch ceremony to mark the ascension as chief of Oliver Mason, the great-great-grandson of the legendary Chief Taholah, after whom the main Quinault village is named.

The Quinault economy was poised to make a big leap with the opening, planned for New Year's Eve 1999, of its new seaside resort. The $40 million complex will feature 12,000 square feet of gaming, 160 hotel rooms, two restaurants, a swimming pool, a spa, a children's center, and up to 13,000 square feet of convention or other space. Located on 220 acres near the reservation, the Quinault Beach Resort is completely financed by, and will be managed by, the nation itself.

SALISH (FLATHEAD)

Although the 1855 Hellgate Treaty reserved the Bitterroot Valley of Montana as the Salish homeland, the U.S. government soon moved them to a new location. In 1905, the people lost much of their remaining land when the government unilaterally opened the reservation to non-native settlement. In 1926, members of several Salish, Kootenai, and Kalispel (Pend d'Oreilles) bands formally organized as the Confederated Salish and Kootenai Tribes (CSKT) of the Flathead Reservation. Tribal leaders were able to stave off termination in the 1950s. In 1960, the tribe won roughly $4.4 million in land claims settlements.

More recently, the tribes have taken over nearly all of the programs formerly administered by the Bureau of Indian Affairs and the Indian Health Service. Farmers grow potatoes, cherries, and other crops, despite the fact that non-natives own much of the best farmland. The tribes have leased the Kerr Dam to Montana Power but will become the sole operators in 2015. They also manage and operate the Mission Valley Power Company. Timber, another valuable resource, is harvested on a sustained-yield basis. Key parts of the reservation economy also include ranching and tourism (especially the KwaTaqNuk resort on Flathead Lake). There are jobs with tribal industries such as S&K Electronics (a contractor for the National Aeronautics and Space Administration) and gravel sales.

The Flathead Reservation (established 1855; CSKT) is located in Flathead, Lake, Missoula, and Sanders Counties, Montana. It contains roughly 1,244,000 acres. There were approximately 7,000 enrolled tribal members in the late 1990s, of whom slightly more than half lived on or near the reservation. Only about 20 percent of the reservation population of over 21,000 is Native American. The tribe currently owns slightly more than 60 percent of its preallotment land base and would like to reacquire the full amount.

Tribal headquarters is located in Pablo, Montana. In 1999, Michael T. "Mickey" Pablo was serving his twelfth year as chair of the Salish and Kootenai Tribal Council. Other council members included Donald "Frederick" Matt (vice chair), Carole Lankford (secretary), Henry Baylor (treasurer), Donald Dupuis, Michael Durglo Jr., Mary Lefthand, Jamie Hamel, Elmer "Sonny" Morigeau, and Lloyd Irvine.

According to the tribal constitution, the CSKT are governed by a 10-member tribal council (one member elected from each of 10 districts), which in turn elects its own officers and committees. The term for council members is four years. Half of the council is up for reelection every other year. Any tribal member over the age of 21 may vote for representatives to the tribal council. Among the duties of the tribal council are regulating the use and disposition of tribal property, negotiating with other governments, regulating the tribal roll, and managing the tribe's economic affairs. All duties and responsibilities are subject to federal, state, and local laws, and some are subject to Interior Department approval as well. The constitution also contains a bill of rights similar to that of the U.S. Constitution.

Michael T. "Mickey" Pablo, the current tribal chairman of the CSKT, was born in St. Ignatius, Montana, in 1948. He was elected to his present position in 1988. His great-great-grandfather, Michel Pablo, developed ranching practices that revived the shrinking western bison herds. Mickey carries on the family tradition of ranching. His father, Thomas E. Pablo, served 13 years on the Tribal Council with five years as chairman.

As chairman, Mickey Pablo believes in the paramount importance of asserting tribal jurisdiction. Toward this end, CSKT in 1993 increased its legal authority on the Flathead Reservation. He expects to continue the battle over jurisdiction into the indefinite future.

While he believes strongly in tribes' becoming involved in the local, state, and national political process, he also believes that this must be carried out within the context of a strong tribal identity. His ongoing goal is to achieve full sovereignty and self-sufficiency for his people. His most important methods are restoring self-esteem and balancing traditional cultural values with economic development.

Despite their various economic activities, however, the CSKT still suffer from occasionally high unemployment, which is only one of several factors that threaten the tribe's cultural integrity. The per capita income in the late 1990s was roughly $6,400. Many people cope with social ills that often accompany poverty, such as violence and substance abuse.

The tribes maintain a strong commitment to retaining their culture and transmitting it to the young. Classes are offered in the old languages (fewer than 100 people speak either Salish or Kootenai fluently). Other traditional knowledge is kept alive as well, such as certain crafts and clothing manufacture and decoration. In connection with a cultural heritage project, the tribes maintain a tribal museum called the People's Center. The tribes hold two large powwows in July and sponsor various other cultural activities.

Education is one of the community's strong points. The tribes operate a national Job Corps training center for Indian youth as well as Two Eagle River School for high-risk students. Salish Kootenai College, established in 1976, provides motivated, college-oriented students with the means to succeed in the contemporary economy while grounding them in their Indian heritage. The college offers two- and four-year degrees in a number of subjects; its many resources include a 55,000-volume library and an excellent media-telecommunications center. With the help and encouragement of community members, the public schools are adding and transforming curricula to reflect the history and culture of local Indians. Almost three-quarters of tribal members had graduated from high school but just over 5 percent had completed a college degree in the late 1990s.

One example of the community's proactive and contemporary orientation is its new forest management plan. Through the use of spatial analysis, computer modeling, and satellite photography, a team of experts has developed a plan to restore tribal forests to a condition more closely resembling the diverse structure that obtained before non-natives arrived in North America. The new plan, which recognizes other forest values besides resource production, hopes to create a forest ecology that is both stable and sustainable. As of early 1999, the tribal forest management team was still in the process of determining the preferred degree of forest restoration.

Another example of the tribes' leadership in natural resource management is their fishery management. Beginning in 1985, resource managers inventoried all waters and fish populations on the reservation. They then used a combination of strategies, such as habitat improvement, stocking, possession limits, and access restriction, to set and meet population goals for specific locations. Tribal leaders note that when they assume control of the Kerr Dam they will operate it so that it does not damage the fisheries. They further note that the main purpose of this entire approach is to provide for a sizable pristine region for the practical (subsistence fishing) and spiritual enjoyment of tribal members.

SEMINOLE

The Seminole tribe formed in the eighteenth century from groups of local Creek, Oconee, Yamasee, Chiaha, Hitichi, and other tribes as well as escaped slaves. In the nineteenth century, the Seminole fought a series of wars with the United States that had at least three results: The people retreated farther south and deeper into the swamps, they were divided and many were removed (force-marched) to the Indian Territory (Oklahoma), and they emerged from the final war, in 1858, undefeated.

By the 1890s the western Seminole had formed 14 self-governing bands, including two composed of freedmen, or Black Seminoles. Most of their reservation was allotted in the early twentieth century. Through fraud and other such means, non-natives by 1920 had acquired about 80 percent of the land originally deeded to Indians. Tribal governments were unilaterally dissolved when Oklahoma became a state in 1907. Many Oklahoma Seminoles left the community to look for work during and after World War II.

Florida Seminoles largely resisted Christianity until pressured by Indian Baptists from Oklahoma in the early twentieth century. Most of the people lived by subsistence activities, as well as by trading, until non-natives overhunted and outtrapped the region. At the time of World War I, subsisting on the land became even more difficult as Florida began to drain the swamps and promote agriculture. By the 1920s, the new land boom, combined with the drainage projects, led to significant Indian impoverishment and displacement. Most Seminoles relocated to reservations during the 1930s and '40s, where they quickly adopted cattle herding, wage labor, and mainstream schooling.

The tribe avoided termination in the 1950s with the help of Florida's congressional delegation. Formal federal recognition came in 1957, around the time that the tribe replaced government by a council of elders associated with corn dance groups with an Indian Reorganization Act–style corporate charter. Also about the same time, a group of more traditional Mikasuki-speaking Indians, many still living deep in the Everglades, moved to separate themselves from the Seminole. After a great deal of struggle, the Miccosukee won official permission to form their own political entity, the Miccosukee Tribe, which they did in 1962.

Today there are roughly 500 enrolled Miccosukees and 2,700 enrolled Florida Seminoles. Constituent reservations of the Seminole Tribe of Florida

A Miccosukee father teaches his son how to clean bark from a tree for use in a traditional chickee building. The intergenerational transmission of culture is as important for Indians as it is for non-natives. (Michal Heron/Woodfin Camp & Associates, Inc.)

are as follows: Big Cypress Reservation (Seminole), Broward and Hendry Counties, 42,700 acres, 447 Indian population; Brighton Reservation (Seminole), Glades County, 35,805 acres, 402 Indian population; and Hollywood (formerly Dania) Reservation (Seminole), Broward County, 480 acres, 481 Indian population. All populations are as of 1990. The Florida State Reservation (Miccosukee and Seminole) is located in Broward County. It consists of 104,000 acres, and there are no residents. There is also a Seminole community in Tampa, Florida.

The Miccosukee Reservation is located in Broward and Dade Counties. It consists of 333 acres and had a 1990 Indian population of 94. Its leadership is elected but is traditionally dominated by certain families and clans.

Under a charter and constitution adopted in 1957, and later amended, the Seminole Tribe of Florida elects a five-member tribal council with representation from all reservations. It also elects a board of directors to supervise business affairs. Council officers include a chairman and vice chairman; the latter is also the president of the board of directors, while the chairman is also vice president of the board of directors. Councilors serve for two-year terms, except that the term of the chairman is four years. Council meetings are held bimonthly.

The powers of the tribal council are similar to those of other tribal councils and include negotiating with other governments, managing and regulating land and other assets, creating and overseeing a tribal budget, and gov-

Fourteen-year-old Seminole William Osceola dances as protestors who want the mysterious stone circle at the mouth of the Miami River to be preserved hold a vigil in downtown Miami, February 2, 1999. (AP Photo/Alan Diaz)

erning the tribe. The tribe may also constitutionally remove or exclude non-Seminoles from its lands upon cause. The manner of review by the secretary of the interior is specifically addressed. There are also provisions for referenda and, with a bill of rights, strict protections of religious practice.

The tribal government administers the tribal gaming concerns, its citrus groves, the Billie Swamp Safari, and the Ah-Tah-Thi-Ki Museum as well as the tribal police department, human resources programs, and most cigarette sales. Its legal services department oversees a public defender's office, water resources management, and tribal utilities. A trial and appellate court system, created in 1982, consists of a chief judge and two associate judges. Both are appointed positions subject to confirmation by the tribal council.

The officers of the Seminole Tribe of Florida, as of 1999, were James E. Billie, chair, and Mitchell Cypress, vice chair. The following members represented the reservations shown in parentheses: David Cypress (Big Cypress), Jack Smith (Brighton), Elaine Aguilar (Immokalee [non-voting]), and Max Osceola (Hollywood). Betty Mae Tiger Jumper, the first Seminole to graduate from high school, was the first woman elected Seminole tribal chair (1967). She worked for decades on behalf of her people and now serves as role model and elder.

Jim Billie was elected chairman and chief of the Seminole Nation of Florida in 1979. A member of the Bird clan and a Vietnam veteran, he was raised in both Indian and non-native families. Billie drew on his long experience as an airplane and helicopter pilot to involve the tribe in Micco Aircraft. In addition to his tribal responsibilities, Billie is also a songwriter and musician with several tapes and compact discs to his credit. Billie's music demonstrates both folk and country influences, but the heart of his style is his own identity as a Seminole living in the swamps of south Florida. Comfortable in boardrooms as well as in airboats, Billie has played a large part in the tremendous financial expansion and success of his people.

Most Oklahoma Seminoles live in Seminole County, Oklahoma. Tribal headquarters is located near Wewoka. Other tribal buildings are south of Seminole, Oklahoma. Roughly 35,000 acres remain in Seminole hands. A 1970 constitution calls for an elected chief, assistant chief, and tribal council that represents all 14 bands.

Unemployment among the roughly 10,500 Oklahoma Seminoles is chronically high. Most jobs that exist are in the oil industry, small business, and agriculture. Although most Oklahoma Seminoles are Christians, many also retain many traditional religious and cultural practices, such as fluency in the Muskogee language. The three stomp grounds (religious centers) plus several more located among the Creek serve as the focus of traditional religious activities, especially the Green Corn Dance. The clan structure survives in a much weakened condition.

The Miccosukee tribe operates a restaurant–service station, a cultural center, and gaming facilities. Tribal members live in modern housing near Miami. The tribe offers classes, provides health and recreation services, maintains its own police and court system, and controls about 200,000 acres of wetlands. It also hold an annual arts festival. The allure of Miami and modern life is finally making inroads into traditional Miccosukee culture, which remained very strong until at least the 1950s. The severe pollution and reduction in area of the Everglades have also had a negative effect on the traditional life of the Miccosukees and Seminoles.

Seminole reservations feature modern amenities such as recreation facilities and community centers. Most children attend public school or the tribal elementary school at Big Cypress. While both Florida tribes have largely retained their traditional languages of Muskogee and Mikasuki and although clan and kinship structures remain in place, other aspects of traditional culture are in danger of being lost.

TLINGIT

Tlingit—a people of mariners, fishers, and artists—protested in vain when, in 1867, the United States purchased Alaska from Russia. They argued that if anyone "owned" Alaska it was the native people who lived there. Non-natives passed laws denying Indians the right to file legal claims, therefore keeping virtually all of the gold rush wealth of the late nineteenth century out of Indian hands. By 1900, many—but not all—Tlingit had abandoned village life with its subsistence economy in favor of work (when they could get it) in the commercial fishing and caning industries.

The Klondike gold rush (1898–1899) brought an influx of non-natives, including missionaries, into Tlingit country. Religious ceremonialism, such as the potlatch, came under wholesale attack. As traditional culture declined, many ceremonial objects were sold to museums. Despite the 1915 enfranchisement of all "civilized" Alaska natives, the Tlingit remained in the grip of a virtual apartheid system during the first half of the twentieth century. In a bid to attract economic activity, some villages incorporated in the 1930s under the Indian Reorganization Act. After World War II, the issue of land led to the formation of the Central Council of the Tlingit and Haida Nations of Alaska, which in 1968 won a land claims settlement of $7.5 million (43¢ an acre).

In 1912, a group of Presbyterian Indians formed the Alaska Native Brotherhood (ANB) to push for rapid acculturation; economic opportunity, including land rights; and the abolition of political discrimination. The Alaska Native Sisterhood (ANS) was founded four years later. Both organizations condemned the continuation of traditional cultural practices until they reversed their positions in the late 1960s, when the modern political and cultural revival of Tlingit culture began in earnest. After the 1968 land claim settlement and formation of the Central Council, the Tlingit in 1971 agreed to give up aboriginal title to their Alaska lands in exchange for various goods and services as part of the Alaska Native Claims Settlement Act (ANCSA).

The Central Council of the Tlingit and Haida Nations of Alaska established a constitution, according to the preamble, in part to "preserve their identity as Indian tribes and the identity and culture of their members and their descendants as Indian people [and to] provide for the exercise of their tribal sovereignty." The constitution calls for a council composed of delegates

Tlingit Indians attend a celebration in Juneau, Alaska, 1998. The Tlingit have reestablished a healthy economy, in part through the workings of the Sealaska Corporation. (Ken Graham Agency)

elected from the prescribed communities (21 in 1987, of which all but two—San Francisco and Seattle—are in Alaska) on a proportional basis. Elections take place in every even-numbered year. The council must meet at least annually. Terms of office are two years.

The council elects from its members an executive committee composed of a president and six vice presidents. When the full council is not in session, the executive committee may act with full council powers except that it may not negate any action of the previous full council. Unlike the majority of oaths of office enshrined in tribal constitutions, this one calls for officers to swear allegiance only to the Tlingit and Haida tribes and people (as opposed to the United States as well).

The council reserves for itself various rights and powers, including government and management of the affairs of the tribe, management and regulation of land and other assets, oversight of community councils, establishment of a judicial system, and tax assessment. A section details strict restrictions on waiving the tribe's sovereign immunity. There is also a U.S.-style bill of rights. The tribal court consists of an appointed chief judge and other associate judges. Their terms are at least four years and two years respectively.

In 1993, the Central Council was removed from the list of federally recognized tribes, only to be reinstated the following year on the grounds that removal would require an act of Congress. Central Council officers in 1999 were as follows: Edward K. Thomas, president; Bill Martin, first vice president; Connie Simpson, second vice president; Mark Jacobs Jr., third vice president; Herbert Hope, fourth vice president; Liv Gray, fifth vice president; Millie Stevens, sixth vice president; and Raymond Paddock III, youth.

Under the leadership of Richard Stitt, the Central Council is currently involved in a Bureau of Indian Affairs–sponsored self-governance demonstration project. The project's purpose is to provide tribal governments with the ability, control, and authority for decision making regarding the management of federal funds. Self-governance is not tantamount to termination but rather a means of accountability for resource management, service delivery, and development. In addition to administration and tribal government, other council services include enrollment, trust services, cultural preservation, education, employment and training, housing and transportation, business enterprise, human services, and health and safety.

Inland Tlingits—those Tlingit-speaking groups originally from the upper Taku River region—form a part of the Carcross Tagish First Nation (Da Ka Nation Tribal Council) in Canada. The Teslin Tlingit Council Band (part of the Da Ka Nation) controls three reserves on roughly 450 acres of land in the southwest part of Teslin. The 1993 population was 482 (119 houses). Elections have been mandatory (imposed by Canada's Department of Indian Affairs) since the late 1940s. The clan leadership is composed of a chief and five councilors.

Many contemporary Interior Tlingits live in Teslin Village (Yukon Territory) and Atlin (British Columbia). Some also live in Whitehorse (Yukon) and Juneau (Alaska) as well as in traditional villages. Most villages now have full electric service as well as amenities such as satellite television. Every village has a grade school, some have high schools, and all have at least one church. Inland regular communications with the "outside" began when the Alaska Highway opened in the 1940s. Contact increased in the 1960s when radio and television became generally available and boomed in the 1980s and '90s with the availability of satellite and Internet communications.

In the early 1990s there were roughly 14,000 Tlingits living in the United States and another 1,200 living in Canada. Most Coastal Tlingits live in Alaska and in cities of the greater Northwest. Relatively few people speak the Tlingit language (despite a concerted preservation effort in the schools), and most Tlingits are Christian. Still, potlatching, singing and dancing, crest arts (especially woodworking and carving), and other aspects of traditional culture and ceremonialism, including the clan system, have undergone a revival in recent years. In 1993, the U.S. government ruled that Alaska native communities have the same government status as other federally acknowledged Indian tribes.

Rosita Worl (Yeidiklatsokw) is a prominent Tlingit leader. She has made her mark primarily as an educator, helping to implement a higher education program for the state of Alaska. She has been associated with numerous organizations, including the International Whaling Commission, the Chilkat Institute, the Alaska Native Education Association, and the Alaska State Arts Council. Worl was also a representative to the Tlingit-Haida Central Council. She was cofounder and publisher of *Alaska Native News* in the mid-1980s. In conjunction with her extensive work promoting awareness of Tlingit culture, she has served on the board of trustees of both the Sealaska Heritage Foundation and the Sealaska Corporation. She currently works as a research anthropologist with her own company and with the Smithsonian Institution.

WAMPANOAG

The Wampanoag or, more properly, Pokanoket people were a local power-house in the early seventeenth century, but their defeat in King Philip's War (1675) proved disastrous. Survivors died of disease or were displaced until few remained in southeastern New England. In 1869–1870, the Massachusetts state legislature unilaterally made two Wampanoag communities, Mashpee and Gay Head, towns, a move that did much to undermine the people's traditional culture. One hundred years later the people of Mashpee had lost control of their town government to a growing number of non-natives. When they sued to recover the lands they had lost as a result of the state's action, a federal court ruled that they were not legally a tribe.

Indians living in Fall River continued to govern themselves until Massachusetts unilaterally assumed this privilege in the early nineteenth century. The state had imposed a reservation of 160 acres in 1709 but reclaimed possession of the land 200 years later. Of the three nineteenth-century reservations on Martha's Vineyard—Chappaquiddick, Christiantown, and Gay Head—only the latter remained by 1900. Partly because of their isolation, the Gay Head people never completely lost their identity and cohesion. Although this community lost control of its local government to non-natives, it did receive federal tribal status, in 1987.

In 1928, in response to the pan-Indian movement of the times, the Wampanoag Nation was founded. Today, there are roughly 3,500 Wampanoag people in the United States, most of whom live in southeastern New England. The Wampanoag Nation is divided into five groups: Gay Head (Aquinnah), Mashpee, Assonet, Herring Pond, and Nemasket, all in Massachusetts, each with a written constitution, a chief, and an elected tribal council. There is also a council of chiefs, and the mainland groups recognize a supreme medicine man. Issues of importance to contemporary Wampanoag communities include federal recognition, hunting and fishing rights, and a Gay Head gaming initiative. The Pokanoket tribe, led by descendants of Massasoit, seeks federal recognition as well as stewardship of 267 acres of land in Bristol, Rhode Island.

The roughly 900-member Wampanoag Tribe (Aquinnah) owns and/or has in trust several parcels of land totaling about 150 acres. Roughly 300 members of this tribe live on Martha's Vineyard, with about half living in the

Wampanoag Milton Hendricks, a character interpreter at the Hobbamocks' (Wampanaog Indian) homesite at the Plymouth Plantation living history museum village in Plymouth, Massachusetts, talks with visitors at the 1627 Pilgrim village, 1995. (AP Photo/Dan Loh)

town of Gay Head. The constitution of the Wampanoag Tribe of Gay Head (Aquinnah) dates from 1990. It vests governing authority in a tribal council that consists of a chairman, a vice chairman, a secretary, a treasurer, and seven members. Officers are elected for two-year terms, while members are elected to terms that vary between one and three years. Decisions of the council may be overridden by the general membership according to a prescribed formula. There are also two ceremonial positions, a chief and a medicine man, both of which are lifetime appointments.

The Aquinnah Tribal Council oversees a number of advisory committees, including constitution/election, gaming, economic development, education, investment, health, human services, land use, and cultural enrichment. It enjoys a government-to-government relationship with the United States. The council meets twice monthly, and the general membership meets four times a year. Council meetings are open to the general membership, which may override any action of the tribal council. Since 1995, the tribe and the town of Gay Head have agreed to provide joint medical and emergency services on tribal lands.

The constitution also guarantees many of the same freedoms contained in the U.S. Bill of Rights. Also included are the right to free access to the clay in the cliffs (provided the resource is preserved) and to virtually all tribal records and meetings. Recall and referendum are also provided for, as is the right to establish a judiciary.

In 1999, Beverly M. Wright was the chair of the Aquinnah Tribal Council (Wampanoag Tribe of Gay Head). Other members included Frank Gonsalves (vice chair), Jenie Fortes (secretary), Stephanie White (treasurer), Sharon Araujo, Naomi Carney, Lewis Colby Jr., Eleanor Herbert, Bertha Robinson, Alfred Vanderhoop, and Elmer Vanderhoop. Donald Malonson served as tribal chief. The medicine man was Luther Madison.

Aquinnah Wampanoags celebrate Cranberry Day, the Moshup Pageant, and the annual spring social. Some of these festivals have both sacred and secular or public components. There is a small local economy based on tourism and small Indian-owned businesses. While the people there hope to make remaining on the island a viable option, many Aquinnah Indians are forced, at least temporarily, to leave the island in search of employment. The tribe is planning a tribal museum and archive, a fine arts-cultural center, and a family entertainment center. Its members hope some day to regain sovereignty over all of Gay Head.

More than half of the 1,500 Mashpee Wampanoags live in Mashpee, Massachusetts. The people hold a powwow on the Fourth of July. Negotiations continue with representatives of the town's increasingly non-native population regarding fair land use. In late 1998 the tribe was second on the government's "ready list" for federal recognition. Its members expected "active consideration" to follow in 1999. They hope that federal recognition will help them to gain a land base as well as other important benefits. In April 1999, the state supreme court overturned the convictions of several Mashpee Wampanoag men who had been charged with illegally harvesting shellfish. Although the court ruled that the law in question does not properly account for native fishing rights, it did not directly address the issue of fishing rights in its decision.

WESTERN SHOSHONE

Despite disruptions of their lives that included disease epidemics, degradation of the natural environment and thus their subsistence activities, and starvation, most Western Shoshone—decentralized bands with a common language—remained unconfined by reservations into the twentieth century. In fact, the percentage of Western Shoshone living on reservations actually began to decline after peaking at 50 in 1927. At that time the people combined semitraditional subsistence activities with seasonal or other wage work in mines and on ranches and farms. Finally acknowledging the rejection of the Western Shoshone reservation (Duck Valley) in Nevada, the government created a series of Western Shoshone "colonies" during the first half of the century.

In 1936, Western Shoshone Chief Temoak led some Paiute and most Shoshone groups in creating the Paiute-Shoshone Business Council. The U.S. government rejected this traditional council, however, and instead organized its own Te-Moak Bands Council. In 1974, the traditionalist-backed United Western Shoshone Legal Defense and Education Association argued that the government entity did not represent Western Shoshone interests and, further, that the Western Shoshone retained title to 24 million acres of unceded land. The courts rejected their claim in 1979 and ordered a compensation payment of $26 million. In 1985, the Supreme Court ruled that the 1979 payment legally extinguished their land claim. Negotiations remain in progress.

In 1990, 3,815 Paiute-Shoshone, Goshute Shoshone, and Shoshone lived on Indian land. This figure does not include 2,078 Te-moak Shoshone (1992). Ely Shoshone Tribe, White Pine County, Nevada (1931; Shoshone; 111 acres; 274 enrollment in 1990), is governed by a tribal council under a constitution and by-laws approved in 1966 and revised in 1990. According to that constitution, a five-member tribal council is the governing body of the community. Council members must be at least 21 years of age, although anyone over 18 years old may vote in tribal elections. Terms are three years. The chair of the tribal council in 1999 was Christine Stones.

Among the powers of the tribal council are negotiating with other governments and organizations, managing land and other tribal assets, regulating all tribal economic enterprises, levying taxes, enacting a civil and criminal code, and governing the community. Some powers are expressly limited by or subject to U.S. law. The constitution also provides for initiative, referendum, and recall and contains a U.S.-style bill of rights. A tribal judiciary consists of a tribal court, a juvenile court, and an appellate court. Judges of the first two courts are elected for six-year terms. A tribal member may not win a judgment against the tribe itself for more than $10,000.

Yomba Shoshone Tribe, Nye County, Nevada (1937; 4,718.49 acres; 192 Indians in 1992), is governed under a 1939 constitution. Three members each are elected to the tribal council from two residential districts. The council in turn elects officers, including a chairman, vice chairman, secretary, and treasurer. The term of office is three years. Council powers are very similar to those of the Ely Shoshone Tribal Council. Like many tribal constitutions, this one provides for referendum and recall. The chairman of the Yomba tribal council in 1999 was Kevin Brady.

Duckwater Reservation, Nye County, Nevada (1940; Duckwater Shoshone Tribe; 3,815 acres, 288 enrollment in 1990), is governed by a five-member tribal council under a 1940 constitution. A detailed section speaks to land use policy in which individual allotment is specifically proscribed. Other constitutional provisions are nearly identical to those of the Ely and Yomba constitutions. The chairman of the tribal council in 1999 was Tim Thompson.

Constituent communities of the Te-Moak Bands of Western Shoshone Indians include the following: Battle Mountain Reservation (1917; 700 acres), Elko Band (1918; 193 acres), South Fork Band (1941; 15,600 acres), and Wells Band (1980; 80 acres). The Te-Moak Bands adopted a constitution in 1938. The governing body is the Te-Moak Western Shoshone Council, to which members are elected based on overall membership of the Te-Moak Bands. The council itself elects a tribal chief and subchief as well as officers, including a secretary and treasurer. Its powers are similar to those of other tribal constitutions and include negotiating with other governments, regulating and managing land and other assets, managing the tribe's economic affairs, and making and enforcing a civil and criminal code.

The constitution allows for each group of 100 resident members to be recognized as a distinct community entitled to representation on both the Te-Moak Western Shoshone Council and a community council. The constitution further provides for recall and referendum and the specific duties of officers. A number of constitutional provisions are specifically subject to review or restriction by the secretary of the interior. Executive officers in 1999 were as follows: Lydia Sam, chair of the Battle Mountain Band Council; Wilbur Woods, chairman of the Elko Band Council; Nevada P. Penoli, chair of the Wells Indian Colony Band Council; and Marvin McDade, chair of the South Fork Band Council. Elwood Mose was chairman of the Te-Moak Tribe of Western Shoshone in 1999.

There are several other Western Shoshone communities. Duck Valley Reservation, Owyhee County, Idaho, and Elko County, Nevada (1877, Shoshone and Paiute; 289,819 acres; 1,701 enrollment in 1990), is governed by a business council under a constitution and by-laws approved in 1936. Fallon Reservation and Colony, Churchill County, Nevada (1887; Paiute and Shoshone; 69 [colony] plus 3,480 [tribal, plus 4,640 allotted] acres; 506 Indians in 1990), is governed by a business council. Fort McDermitt Reservation, Humboldt County, Nevada, and Malheur County, Oregon (1892; Shoshone and Paiute; 16,354 tribal acres in Nevada plus almost 19,000 acres of tribal land in Oregon; 387 Indians in 1990), is governed by a tribal council. The chair in 1999 was Helen Snapp. Big Pine Reservation, Inyo County, California (1939; Paiute and Shoshone; 279 acres; 331 Indians in 1990), is governed by a tribal council whose chair in 1999 was Roseanne Moose. Bishop Indian Colony, Inyo County, California (1912; Paiute-Shoshone; 877 acres; 934 Indians in (1990), is governed by a tribal council. Death Valley Indian Community, Inyo County, California (1982, Timbi-sha Shoshone; 40 acres; 199 Indians in 1992), is governed by a tribal council whose chair in 1999 was Pauline Esteves. Fort Independence Reservation, Inyo County, California (1915; Paiute and Shoshone; 234 acres; 38 Indians in 1990), is governed by a tribal council. Lone Pine Reservation, Inyo County, California (1939; Paiute-Shoshone; 237 acres; 168 Indians in 1990), is governed by a tribal council. Goshute Reservation, White Pine County, Nevada, and Juab and Tooele Counties, Utah (1863; 7,489 acres; 98 Indians in 1990; 413 enrolled members in 1993), is governed by a business council under a 1940 constitution and by-laws. The chair of the business council in 1999 was David Pete. Skull Valley Reservation, Tooele County, Utah (1917; Goshute Tribe; 17,444 acres; 32 Indians in 1990; 111 enrolled members in1993), has no constitu-

Shoshone children work on traditional Indian crafts at a summer workshop in Ethete, Wyoming. (John Easdtcott/YVA Momatiuk/Woodfin Camp & Associates, Inc.)

tion. The chair of the executive committee of the Skull Valley Band of Goshutes in 1999 was Leon D. Bear.

There were roughly 10,000 Western Shoshone people in 1998. A limited number of jobs are available with federal and tribal entities, smoke shops, motels, gas stations, and other small businesses. Several reservations and colonies operate cattle and farming business. There is also some income from leases and land claims funds. Traditional round dances, prayers, and games form the core of tribal gatherings ("fandangos"). Most groups are actively trying to preserve their native language. In 1998, the Western Shoshone National Council (WSNC) was led by Chief Raymond Yowell.

Few employment opportunities exist on the Goshute Reservation outside of limited cattle and hay ranching. Some Skull Valley residents work at Hercules (aerospace) or at a convenience store and with a seasonal water project. Communications remain difficult on these remote reservations. Goshute day students are bused 60 miles to high school; the ride is 16 miles at Skull Valley. Most Goshute attend Native American Church and/or Mormon ceremonies. Craftspeople create beadwork, basketry, and buckskin items.

In 1999, the Timbi-sha Shoshone, exiled from their homes in Death Valley for generations, struck a deal with the federal government regarding management of that 3.2 million-acre resource. In a precedent-setting agreement, the tribe will gain ownership of roughly 6,000 acres of land outside Death Valley National Park, will have exclusive use of 1,000 acres, and will manage about 300,000 acres to be known as the Timbi-sha Natural and Cultural Preservation Area. The tribe will also acquire 300 acres in the heart of the park to use for housing and other facilities. The deal still must be approved by Congress.

WYANDOTTE

The Wyandotte people are successors to the Huron and other members of the Huron Confederacy, which was destroyed in the mid-seventeenth century. Adopting the name Wyandotte in the early eighteenth century, the people had been forced into the Indian Territory (Kansas) by the 1840s. An 1855 treaty ended their tribal status and allowed them to become citizens by taking their lands in severalty.

While most agreed, those who did not removed themselves from the group, eventually settling in the new Indian Territory (Oklahoma). There they regained tribal status and disassociated themselves from the Kansas Wyandots. They acquired land from the Seneca people, most of which was allotted before 1900. The Wyandotte Tribe of Oklahoma, established in 1937, lost federal recognition in the 1950s but regained it in 1978. The "citizen" (or "absentee") group remained in Kansas, incorporating in 1959 as the Wyandot Nation of Kansas. Located near Kansas City, Kansas, its chief in 1999 was Jan English. This state-recognized group was under consideration for federal acknowledgment as of mid-1999.

In the mid-1990s, the combined population of Wyandot and Wyandotte people in the United States was roughly 4,000. In the early 1990s, about 3,600 members of the Wyandotte Tribe of Oklahoma lived in Ottawa County, Oklahoma. The land base consists of 192 acres of land in addition to individual allotments. The tribe offers services such as student scholarships and meals for the elderly. In addition to the existing houses, tribal center, and preschool, the tribe is planning a museum and cultural center.

The tribe recently purchased Collegiate Systems, Inc., which operates an accredited four-year college with six locations in five states. There are plans to place profits from this venture into a trust fund designed to provide educational services to young people. The tribe also plans to expand its health services, develop retirement and nursing home facilities, and construct new tribal headquarters. The people are currently engaged in identifying and preserving aspects of their cultural traditions.

The Wyandotte Tribe of Oklahoma is governed by a constitutionally authorized council consisting of all tribal members who live in Oklahoma. Male members must be at least 21 years old, but women may become members at age 18. The council elects its officers—chief, second chief, secretary-treasurer, and two councilors—by majority vote. These officers, who must be at least 25 years old, constitute the membership of the tribe's business committee, whose powers are enumerated in a corporate charter. Officers are elected for two-year terms at odd-numbered annual meetings, which are held on the first Tuesday in September. The constitution also provides for certain standing committees, such as grievance, credit, welfare, and education. In 1999, Leaford Bearskin was serving his fifteenth year as chief.

Some Hurons who remained after their general destruction in the mid-seventeenth century settled near Lorette, Quebec. Today, the land of their descendants, known as Huron Village (Wendake), Quebec, Canada, consists of 167.5 acres of land. There were about 1,000 residents in the mid-1990s, of a total population of about 2,650. The community is governed by a band council. The healthy reserve economy provides jobs for Indians as well as non-natives. The manufacture and sale of crafts such as snowshoes, moccasins, and canoes remains important. A museum draws tourists in summer and fall, as does an Indian-owned bed and breakfast. Children attend school on the reserve, which is similar to those in neighboring towns in Quebec, through grade four. The people are trying to revive the Huron language.

YAKAMA

The Klickitat, Wanapam, Wishram, Paluse (Palouse), and Wenatchi, as well as the Yakama, became part of the Yakama tribe (eventually the Confederated Tribes and Bands of the Yakama Indian Nation) established in eastern Washington after the wars of the late 1850s. Unlike most tribes, the Yakama, under Chief Shawaway Lotiahkan, were able to retain the "surplus" land usually sold to non-Indians after qualified individuals received their allotments. Still, in a pattern that was typical, most allotments, including some of the best irrigated land, were lost, leased, or sold for a fraction of their value. As much as 80 percent of the reservation was in non-Indian hands in the early twentieth century. However, some Indians were able to establish homesteads on original village sites off of the reservation. Also, many people retained their Wáashat (Longhouse) religion in the face of government and missionary repression.

From time immemorial, the Yakama people had depended on fish, which were also closely connected to their religious practices, but during the course of the twentieth century they saw the number of salmon and steelheads that returned to spawn in the Yakima River decline by about 99 percent. Dams on the Columbia River (Bonneville, 1938; Grand Coulee, 1941; Dalles, 1956) were the main culprit, as was water diversion for non-native farms. There were other environmental and political disasters, such as destruction of plant and animal habitats due to non-native plowing and development. Confinement to the reservation contributed to skyrocketing death and infant mortality rates prior to World War II.

Despite these profound losses, however, Yakama continued much of their traditional subsistence and ceremonial activities well into the twentieth century. In fact, a tribal renaissance began after World War II. The renewed spirit of the Yakama people gave rise to several tribal industries, such as a furniture factory, clothing manufactures, and a ceramic center. The Yakama all-Indian rodeo dates from that time as well.

The Yakima Reservation and Trust Lands, located in Klickitat, Lewis, and Yakima Counties, Washington, contain almost 1.4 million acres, and the Nation continues to buy back portions of its former territory. The 1999 membership was almost 9,100. Yakama also live off reservation and in regional cities and towns, and some are members of the Columbia River Indians.

Owing primarily to allotment, however, only about one-quarter of reservation residents are Indian.

The formal government of the Yakama Nation consists of a continuing series of resolutions by the general council, or adult members of the tribe. The council exists, in part, to "safeguard, protect and secure rights, privileges and benefits, guaranteed to the members of the Yakima Indian nation by the treaty of June 9, 1855." This body votes on all matters of importance to the tribe and retains all governmental authority except that which it expressly delegates. During the late-November meetings of the general council, anyone may speak for as long as he or she feels is necessary. Council meetings are presided over by four officers: a chair, vice chair, secretary-treasurer, and sergeant at arms. Officers hold their positions for life. In early 1999 the chair of the Yakama Nation Tribal Council was Bill Yallup.

There are three levels of Yakama government—legislative, administrative, and operational. The tribal council (the legislative level), created in 1944, meets monthly to carry out the general council's directives. It consists of 14 members elected at large. Half of the tribal council members are elected every two years for four-year terms. The tribal council itself elects three people from within to serve as an executive committee. There are also seven standing committees. Tribal headquarters is located in Toppenish, Washington. The administrative and operational levels of government are coordinated by an administrative director, an assistant administrative director, and a comptroller.

The spiritual and economic role of fish notwithstanding, it is timber and its associated industries that produce roughly 90 percent of all tribal revenue. Timber is harvested on a sustained-yield basis. In late 1998 the nation opened its first sawmill. Instead of selling its logs to other mills, as it has in the past, this resource will enable the people to convert small logs into boards and keep more timber money at home. It is expected to generate about $2 million in profit. The nation maintains extensive range and farmland, including fruit orchards, although 80 percent of irrigated land remains leased by non-Indians.

Fishing does play a significant role in the Yakama economy (see the "Natural Resource Control" entry in the Contemporary Issues section). Both Indian and non-native interests are represented in a tribal industrial park. Despite the existence of additional jobs provided by the federal government, the nation, and small business enterprises, unemployment regularly approaches and even exceeds 50 percent, and up to 75 percent of the people live below the poverty level. Nuclear pollution, most of it originating from the highly contaminated Handford Nuclear Reservation, remains a threat to people's health as well as their economic activities.

Despite the diversity of its economy, the Yakama Nation remains relatively traditional in many ways. Customs regarding family, service, and leadership remain strong. Yakama basketry is still an important activity. Many people speak the native language, especially as part of religious ceremonies that include the Longhouse (Seven Drums) religion as well as sweathouse customs and first foods feasts. In many ways, the four reservation longhouses serve as the locus of Indian identity, linking the Yakama with other Longhouse families throughout the Plateau region. Yakamas also attend Indian Shaker as well as various Christian services.

A full-service cultural center, museum, and restaurant are on the Yakima Reservation, in addition to two community centers; a retirement center; a tribally run school; a private, accredited, four-year liberal arts college; tribal newspapers; and a radio station. The nation provides education incentives such as scholarships and summer programs. Community activities include an annual all-Indian rodeo, a powwow, a huckleberry festival, and several basketball tournaments.

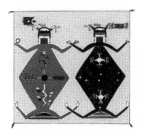

ZUNI

In many ways, ancient Zuni in 1900 had changed very little from its first encounter with non-natives in the early 1500s. The pueblo remained self-sufficient until the mid-nineteenth century: In 1877, the United States recognized a reservation that was too small to support traditional subsistence farming. Tribal opposition effectively blocked the implementation of allotment at Zuni. Still, agriculture continued to decline in the early twentieth century, hurt now by erosion and a series of spectacularly unsuccessful government-mandated irrigation projects. By the 1930s, the government was actively encouraging the Zuni to abandon agriculture in favor of raising livestock. The continuing shift in political power from priests to politicians after World War II led to the growth of political parties and the increased importance of the tribal council.

Notwithstanding the return of their most sacred site, Katsina Village, or Ko/lhu/wa/a la:walts, in 1984, the reservation's 636 square miles is less than 3 percent of the tribe's original holdings. Of the roughly 10,000 Zunis in 1997, almost 90 percent lived on the reservation. Most live in the old pueblo, now consisting of single-story houses and trailers. Zuni has been relatively successful in bridging the old and the new, as evidenced by the peaceful coexistence of modern and traditional associations such as the Lions Club, American Legion, clans, kiva groups, priesthoods and medicine societies, school boards, and cattle, farm, and irrigation associations.

Zuni accepted the Indian Reorganization Act and an elected tribal council in 1934. The people ratified a constitution in 1970. The preamble to that constitution states that the document was established, among other reasons, to exercise the right of self-government and to maintain tribal customs and traditions. The constitution, which contains a U.S.-style bill of rights, sets membership requirements, empowers a tribal council, and allows for popular referenda.

The tribal council consists of eight members, including the governor and lieutenant governor, all elected at large. All must be at least 25 years of age and meet certain other requirements. Elected officials generally serve four-year terms. The council is given customary powers, such as making tribal policy, representing the tribe, negotiating with other governments, and man-

Zuni Pueblo governor Donald Eriacho asks the New Mexico congressional delegation to help the Zunis oppose a proposed coal mine 15 miles northwest of Quemado, New Mexico, during the 1996 Pueblo-Congressional Government-to-Government Summit at Acoma Pueblo. (AP Photo/Jake Schorllkopf)

aging and regulating tribal assets. The council meets at least monthly. In February 1999, the governor of Zuni Pueblo was Malcolm Bowekaty.

The governor, as chief executive, presides over council meetings, makes nonelective appointments, serves as the tribe's contracting and budgetary officer, directs the tribal police, and, according to constitutional provisions, may veto tribal council actions. The constitution also provides for a tribal court system. A chief judge and two associate judges are appointed by the governor, subject to confirmation by the council, for a term of six years. There is also an appellate level.

While the Zuni elect their own governors and tribal councils, traditional religious leaders remain powerful. Real societal organization is provided not by imported or imposed structures but by family, extended family, and clan. Everyone is part of a network so that no one is excluded from the overall structure of the community.

Modern though it is, Zuni remains a close and cohesive community in which heritage remains intact and vital. In many ways, Zuni remains an oral society, one in which communication by action, speech, and sometimes silence is more important than the written word. Gossip—or, more properly,

Zuni Pueblo, New Mexico. Lake many Indian groups, the Zuni people are committed to succeeding as Indians in the twenty-first century. (Nicholas DeVore III)

awareness of one's place in society as seen by one's fellow citizens—is probably the most effective means of social control. Radio programs in the Zuni language help maintain a sense of community. Native language and culture figure prominently in the Zuni schools, which the people control. Shalako, celebrating the continuity of the Zuni people, remains a major ceremony. In fact, most people maintain their cultural identity by devoting a considerable amount of time, money, and energy to religious commitments.

The Zuni economy is dominated by craft manufacture and tribal employment. A few people still farm and raise livestock, and several individuals operate small businesses. Zuni Cultural Resources Enterprise provides local archaeological services. There are some jobs in Gallup, the nearest city, and other off-reservation sites. In 1990, the tribe settled its land claims for $50 million. Important ongoing issues include water rights and planning for economic development.

DOCUMENTS:
ACTS OF CONGRESS,
EXECUTIVE ORDERS,
COURT DECISIONS,
LAWS, AND
RESOLUTIONS

NATIVE AMERICAN GRAVES PROTECTION AND REPATRIATION ACT (1990)

INTRODUCTION

It is a measure of the way non-natives have generally regarded native people that a law like the Native American Graves Protection and Repatriation Act (NAGPRA) was needed in the first place. For centuries, non-natives generally considered Indian graves simply as places to loot. Even more indicative of this attitude of profound disrespect was the behavior of the nation's museums. There will always be unscrupulous people who desecrate sacred places or are willing to sell items illegally pilfered from graves, but one expects better behavior from scholars and museum curators.

Unfortunately, it is just this last group of people who have traditionally been the most egregious offenders of Indian sensibilities in this regard. Hundreds of museums across the country, including some of the most prestigious, such as the Smithsonian Institution, include in their collections hundreds of thousands of Indian skeletons and various funerary objects. Like other "exotic" objects that may be found in museums' anthropology collections, such items are considered to have scientific value: They were weighed, measured, dated, and studied in various ways before being put on public display. It is easy to forget, perhaps, that these items are the bones of real people, in most cases with living descendants, and that the objects, like any funerary objects, properly belong in the grave.

For years, native groups have been lobbying, filing legislation, demonstrating, writing letters, pleading, and otherwise trying to encourage non-natives to treat the native dead with proper respect. In general, this has been a steeply uphill battle. Businesses did not want to be bothered with regulations, scholars saw an affront to science (they often pointed out that their study of such items helped native people to reconstruct their own histories), and individuals fought for the "right" to buy curios. Most non-natives wondered what the fuss was all about, never stopping to think how they would feel if the graves of their ancestors were similarly violated.

NAGPRA is the culmination of a long series of half-hearted and incomplete attempts by state and federal officials to do the right thing vis-à-vis native grave sites and remains. This act followed a similar one (PL 101-185) and targets both federal agencies and institutions that receive federal support. It calls for the inventory and repatriation of native remains and funerary objects to culturally affiliated native groups, criminalizes the traffic in such items, increases the protection of native graves on federal and tribal land, and provides for the establishment of a committee to review and monitor the act's mandates.

Since the enactment of NAGPRA in 1990, tens of thousands of items have been returned to native groups. In addition to skeletons, artifacts have included wampum belts, medicine bundles, and the Sacred Pole of the Omaha people. On the other hand, NAGPRA is full of loopholes and exceptions. For instance, the seven-member review and monitoring committee may be composed of a majority of non-natives. Cultural items may be retained if they are "indispensable for completion of a specific scientific study." Furthermore, as with any law, enforcement largely determines compliance, and the scientific community, in particular, has resisted complying with NAGPRA to a significant extent. NAGPRA is an important law, but native groups continue to fight many battles, both legal and otherwise, in their effort to win proper respect for and treatment of their ancestors.

NATIVE AMERICAN GRAVES PROTECTION AND REPATRIATION ACT
Public Law 101-601 [H.R. 5237]
November 16, 1990
Native American Graves Protection and Repatriation Act
An Act
To provide for the protection of Native American graves, and for other purposes.
Be it enacted by the Senate and House of Representatives of the United States of
America in Congress assembled,

Section 1. <25 USC 3001 note> Short Title.

This Act may be cited as the "Native American Graves Protection and Repatriation Act".

Sec. 2. <25 USC 3001> Definitions.

For purposes of this Act, the term—

(1) "burial site" means any natural or prepared physical location, whether originally below, on, or above the surface of the earth, into which as a part of the death rite or ceremony of a culture, individual human remains are deposited.

(2) "cultural affiliation" means that there is a relationship of shared group identity which can be reasonably traced historically or prehistorically between a present day Indian tribe or Native Hawaiian organization and an identifiable earlier group.

(3) "cultural items" means human remains and—

  (A) "associated funerary objects" which shall mean objects that, as a part of the death rite or ceremony of a culture, are reasonably believed to have been placed with individual human remains either at the time of death or later, and both the human remains and associated objects are presently in the possession or control of a Federal agency or museum, except that other items exclusively made for burial purposes or to contain human remains shall be considered as associated funerary objects.

  (B) "associated funerary objects" which shall mean objects that, as a part of the death rite or ceremony of a culture, are reasonably believed to have been placed with individual human remains either at the time of death or later, where the remains are not in the possession or control of the Federal agency or museum and the objects can be identified by a preponderance of the evidence as related to specific individuals or families or to known human remains or, by a preponderance of the evidence, as having been removed from a specific burial site of an individual culturally affiliated with a particular Indian tribe,

(C)   "sacred objects" which shall mean specific ceremonial objects which are needed by traditional Native American religious leaders for the practice of traditional Native American religions by their present day adherents, and

(D)   "cultural patrimony" which shall mean an object having ongoing historical, traditional, or cultural importance central to the Native American group or culture itself, rather than property owned by an individual Native American, and which, therefore, cannot be alienated, appropriated, or conveyed by any individual regardless of whether or not the individual is a member of the Indian tribe or Native Hawaiian organization and such object shall have been considered inalienable by such Native American group at the time the object was separated from such group.

(4)   "Federal agency" means any department, agency, or instrumentality of the United States. Such term does not include the Smithsonian Institution.

(5)   "Federal lands" means any land other than tribal lands which are controlled or owned by the United States, including lands selected by but not yet conveyed to Alaska Native Corporations and groups organized pursuant to the Alaska Native Claims Settlement Act of 1971.

(6)   "Hui Malama I Na Kupuna O Hawai'i Nei" means the nonprofit, Native Hawaiian organization incorporated under the laws of the State of Hawaii by that name on April 17, 1989, for the purpose of providing guidance and expertise in decisions dealing with Native Hawaiian cultural issues, particularly burial issues.

(7)   "Indian tribe" means any tribe, band, nation, or other organized group or community of Indians, including any Alaska Native village (as defined in, or established pursuant to, the Alaska Native Claims Settlement Act), which is recognized as eligible for the special programs and services provided by the United States to Indians because of their status as Indians.

(8)   "museum" means any institution or State or local government agency (including any institution of higher learning) that receives Federal funds and has possession of, or control over, Native American cultural items. Such term does not include the Smithsonian Institution or any other Federal agency.

(9)   "Native American" means of, or relating to, a tribe, people, or culture that is indigenous to the United States.

(10)   "Native Hawaiian" means any individual who is a descendant of the aboriginal people who, prior to 1778, occupied and exercised sovereignty in the area that now constitutes the State of Hawaii.

(11)   "Native Hawaiian organization" means any organization which—

(A)   serves and represents the interests of Native Hawaiians,

(B)   has as a primary and stated purpose the provision of services to Native Hawaiians, and

(C)   has expertise in Native Hawaiian Affairs, and shall include the Office of Hawaiian Affairs and Hui Malama I Na Kupuna O Hawai'i Nei.

(12) "Office of Hawaiian Affairs" means the Office of Hawaiian Affairs established by the constitution of the State of Hawaii.

(13) "right of possession" means possession obtained with the voluntary consent of an individual or group that had authority of alienation. The original acquisition of a Native American unassociated funerary object, sacred object or object of cultural patrimony from an Indian tribe or Native Hawaiian organization with the voluntary consent of an individual or group with authority to alienate such object is deemed to give right of possession of that object, unless the phrase so defined would, as applied in section 7(c), result in a Fifth Amendment taking by the United States as determined by the United States Claims Court pursuant to 28 U.S.C. 1491 in which event the "right of possession" shall be as provided under otherwise applicable property law. The original acquisition of Native American human remains and associated funerary objects which were excavated, exhumed, or otherwise obtained with full knowledge and consent of the next of kin or the official governing body of the appropriate culturally affiliated Indian tribe or Native Hawaiian organization is deemed to give right of possession to those remains.

(14) "Secretary" means the Secretary of the Interior.

(15) "tribal land" means—

   (A) all lands within the exterior boundaries of any Indian reservation;

   (B) all dependent Indian communities;

   (C) any lands administered for the benefit of Native Hawaiians pursuant to the Hawaiian Homes Commission Act, 1920, and section 4 of Public Law 86-3.

Sec. 3. <25 USC 3002> Ownership.

(a) Native American Human Remains and Objects.—The ownership or control of Native American cultural items which are excavated or discovered on Federal or tribal lands after the date of enactment of this Act shall be (with priority given in the order listed)—

   (1) in the case of Native American human remains and associated funerary objects, in the lineal descendants of the Native American; or

   (2) in any case in which such lineal descendants cannot be ascertained, and in the case of unassociated funerary objects, sacred objects, and objects of cultural patrimony—

      (A) in the Indian tribe or Native Hawaiian organization on whose tribal land such objects or remains were discovered;

      (B) in the Indian tribe or Native Hawaiian organization which has the closest cultural affiliation with such remains or objects and which, upon notice, states a claim for such remains or objects; or

      (C) if the cultural affiliation of the objects cannot be reasonably ascertained and if the objects were discovered on Federal land that is recognized by a final judgment of the Indian Claims Commission or the United States Court of Claims as the aboriginal land of some Indian tribe—

         (1) in the Indian tribe that is recognized as aboriginally occupying the area in which the objects were discovered, if upon notice, such tribe states a claim for such remains or objects, or

(2) if it can be shown by a preponderance of the evidence that a different tribe has a stronger cultural relationship with the remains or objects than the tribe or organization specified in paragraph (1), in the Indian tribe that has the strongest demonstrated relationship, if upon notice, such tribe states a claim for such remains or objects.

(b) Unclaimed Native American Human Remains and Objects.—Native American cultural items not claimed under subsection (a) shall be disposed of in accordance with regulations promulgated by the Secretary in consultation with the review committee established under section 8, Native American groups, representatives of museums and the scientific community.

(c) Intentional Excavation and Removal of Native American Human Remains and Objects.—The intentional removal from or excavation of Native American cultural items from Federal or tribal lands for purposes of discovery, study, or removal of such items is permitted only if—

(1) such items are excavated or removed pursuant to a permit issued under section 4 of the Archaeological Resources Protection Act of 1979 (93 Stat. 721; 16 U.S.C. 470aa et seq.) which shall be consistent with this Act;

(2) such items are excavated or removed after consultation with or, in the case of tribal lands, consent of the appropriate (if any) Indian tribe or Native Hawaiian organization;

(3) the ownership and right of control of the disposition of such items shall be as provided in subsections (a) and (b); and

(4) proof of consultation or consent under paragraph (2) is shown.

(d) Inadvertent Discovery of Native American Remains and Objects.—

(1) Any person who knows, or has reason to know, that such person has discovered Native American cultural items on Federal or tribal lands after the date of enactment of this Act shall notify, in writing, the Secretary of the Department, or head of any other agency or instrumentality of the United States, having primary management authority with respect to Federal lands and the appropriate Indian tribe or Native Hawaiian organization with respect to tribal lands, if known or readily ascertainable, and, in the case of lands that have been selected by an Alaska Native Corporation or group organized pursuant to the Alaska Native Claims Settlement Act of 1971, the appropriate corporation or group. If the discovery occurred in connection with an activity, including (but not limited to) construction, mining, logging, and agriculture, the person shall cease the activity in the area of the discovery, make a reasonable effort to protect the items discovered before resuming such activity, and provide notice under this subsection. Following the notification under this subsection, and upon certification by the Secretary of the department or the head of any agency or instrumentality of the United States or the appropriate Indian tribe or Native Hawaiian organization that notification has been received, the activity may resume after 30 days of such certification.

(2) The disposition of and control over any cultural items excavated or removed under this subsection shall be determined as provided for in this section.

(3) If the Secretary of the Interior consents, the responsibilities (in whole or in part) under paragraphs (1) and (2) of the Secretary of any department (other than the Department of the Interior) or the head of any other agency or instrumentality may be delegated to the Secretary with respect to any land managed by such other Secretary or agency head.

(e) Relinquishment.—Nothing in this section shall prevent the governing body of an Indian tribe or Native Hawaiian organization from expressly relinquishing control over any Native American human remains, or title to or control over any funerary object, or sacred object.

Sec. 4. Illegal Trafficking.

(a) Illegal Trafficking.—Chapter 53 of title 18, United States Code, is amended by adding at the end thereof the following new section:

"1170. Illegal Trafficking in Native American Human Remains and Cultural Items

"(a)   Whoever knowingly sells, purchases, uses for profit, or transports for sale or profit, the human remains of a Native American without the right of possession to those remains as provided in the Native American Graves Protection and Repatriation Act shall be fined in accordance with this title, or imprisoned not more than 12 months, or both, and in the case of a second or subsequent violation, be fined in accordance with this title, or imprisoned not more than 5 years, or both.

"(b)   Whoever knowingly sells, purchases, uses for profit, or transports for sale or profit any Native American cultural items obtained in violation of the Native American Graves Protection and Repatriation Act shall be fined in accordance with this title, imprisoned not more than one year, or both, and in the case of a second or subsequent violation, be fined in accordance with this title, imprisoned not more than 5 years, or both."

(b) Table of Contents.—The table of contents for chapter 58 of title 18, United States Code, is amended by adding at the end thereof the following new item:

"1170. Illegal Trafficking in Native American Human Remains and Cultural Items".

Sec. 5. <25 USC 3003> Inventory for Human Remains and Associated Funerary Objects.

(a)   In General.—Each Federal agency and each museum which has possession or control over holdings or collections of Native American human remains and associated funerary objects shall compile an inventory of such items and, to the extent possible based on information possessed by such museum or Federal agency, identify the geographical and cultural affiliation of such item.

(b)   Requirements.

(1)   The Inventories and Identifications Required under Subsection (a) Shall Be—

(A)   completed in consultation with tribal government and Native Hawaiian organization officials and traditional religious leaders;

      (B)   completed by not later than the date that is 5 years after the date of enactment of this Act, and

      (C)   made available both during the time they are being conducted and afterward to a review committee established under section 8.

  (2)   Upon request by an Indian tribe or Native Hawaiian organization which receives or should have received notice, a museum or Federal agency shall supply additional available documentation to supplement the information required by subsection (a) of this section. The term "documentation" means a summary of existing museum or Federal agency records, including inventories or catalogues, relevant studies, or other pertinent data for the limited purpose of determining the geographical origin, cultural affiliation, and basic facts surrounding acquisition and accession of Native American human remains and associated funerary objects subject to this section. Such term does not mean, and this Act shall not be construed to be an authorization for, the initiation of new scientific studies of such remains and associated funerary objects or other means of acquiring or preserving additional scientific information from such remains and objects.

(c) Extension of Time for Inventory.—Any museum which has made a good faith effort to carry out an inventory and identification under this section, but which has been unable to complete the process, may appeal to the Secretary for an extension of the time requirements set forth in subsection (b)(1)(B). The Secretary may extend such time requirements for any such museum upon a finding of good faith effort. An indication of good faith shall include the development of a plan to carry out the inventory and identification process.

(d) Notification.—

  (1)   If the cultural affiliation of any particular Native American human remains or associated funerary objects is determined pursuant to this section, the Federal agency or museum concerned shall, not later than 6 months after the completion of the inventory, notify the affected Indian tribes or Native Hawaiian organizations.

  (2)   The notice required by paragraph (1) shall include information—

      (A)   which identifies each Native American human remains or associated funerary objects and the circumstances surrounding its acquisition;

      (B)   which lists the human remains or associated funerary objects that are clearly identifiable as to tribal origin; and

      (C)   which lists the Native American human remains and associated funerary objects that are not clearly identifiable as being culturally affiliated with that Indian tribe or Native Hawaiian organization, but which, given the totality of circumstances surrounding acquisition of the remains or objects, are determined by a reasonable belief to be remains or objects culturally affiliated with the Indian tribe or Native Hawaiian organization.

  (3)   A copy of each notice provided under paragraph (1) shall be sent to the Secretary who shall publish each notice in the Federal Register.

(e) Inventory.—For the purposes of this section, the term "inventory" means a simple itemized list that summarizes the information called for by this section.

Sec. 6. <25 USC 3004> Summary for Unassociated Funerary Objects, Sacred Objects, and Cultural Patrimony.

(a) In General.—Each Federal agency or museum which has possession or control over holdings or collections of Native American unassociated funerary objects, sacred objects or objects of cultural patrimony shall provide a written summary of such objects based upon available information held by such agency or museum. The summary shall describe the scope of the collection, kinds of objects included, reference to geographical location, means and period of acquisition and cultural affiliation, where readily ascertainable.

(b) Requirements.—(1) The summary required under subsection (a) shall be—

    (A) in lieu of an object-by-object inventory;

    (B) followed by consultation with tribal government and Native Hawaiian organization officials and traditional religious leaders; and

    (C) completed by not later than the date that is 3 years after the date of enactment of this Act.

(2) Upon request, Indian Tribes and Native Hawaiian organizations shall have access to records, catalogues, relevant studies or other pertinent data for the limited purposes of determining the geographic origin, cultural affiliation, and basic facts surrounding acquisition and accession of Native American objects subject to this section. Such information shall be provided in a reasonable manner to be agreed upon by all parties.

Sec. 7. <25 USC 3005> Repatriation.

(a) Repatriation of Native American Human Remains and Objects Possessed or Controlled by Federal Agencies and Museums.—

    (1) If, pursuant to section 5, the cultural affiliation of Native American human remains and associated funerary, objects with a particular Indian tribe or Native Hawaiian organization is established, then the Federal agency or museum, upon the request of a known lineal descendant of the Native American or of the tribe or organization and pursuant to subsections (b) and (e) of this section, shall expeditiously return such remains and associated funerary objects.

    (2) If, pursuant to section 6, the cultural affiliation with a particular Indian tribe or Native Hawaiian organization is shown with respect to unassociated funerary objects, sacred objects or objects of cultural patrimony, then the Federal agency or museum, upon the request of the Indian tribe or Native Hawaiian organization and pursuant to subsections (b), (c) and (e) of this section, shall expeditiously return such objects.

    (3) The return of cultural items covered by this Act shall be in consultation with the requesting lineal descendant or tribe or organization to determine the place and manner of delivery of such items.

    (4) Where cultural affiliation of Native American human remains and funerary objects has not been established in an inventory prepared pursuant to section 5, or the summary pursuant to section 6, or where Native American human remains and funerary objects are not included upon any such inventory, then, upon request and pursuant to subsections (b) and (e) and, in the case of unassociated funerary objects, subsection (c), such Native American human remains and funerary objects shall be

expeditiously returned where the requesting Indian tribe or Native Hawaiian organization can show cultural affiliation by a preponderance of the evidence based upon geographical, kinship, biological, archaeological, anthropological, linguistic, folkloric, oral traditional, historical, or other relevant information or expert opinion.

(5) Upon request and pursuant to subsections (b), (c) and (e), sacred objects and objects of cultural patrimony shall be expeditiously returned where—

(A) the requesting party is the direct lineal descendant of an individual who owned the sacred object;

(B) the requesting Indian tribe or Native Hawaiian organization can show that the object was owned or controlled by the tribe or organization; or

(C) the requesting Indian tribe or Native Hawaiian organization can show that the sacred object was owned or controlled by a member thereof, provided that in the case where a sacred object was owned by a member thereof, there are no identifiable lineal descendants of said member or the lineal descendants, upon notice, have failed to make a claim for the object under this Act.

(b) Scientific Study.—If the lineal descendant, Indian tribe, or Native Hawaiian organization requests the return of culturally affiliated Native American cultural items, the Federal agency or museum shall expeditiously return such items unless such items are indispensable for completion of a specific scientific study, the outcome of which would be of major benefit to the United States. Such items shall be returned by no later than 90 days after the date on which the scientific study is completed.

(c) Standard of Repatriation.—If a known lineal descendant of an Indian tribe or Native Hawaiian organization requests the return of Native American unassociated funerary objects, sacred objects or objects of cultural patrimony pursuant to this Act and presents evidence which, if standing alone before the introduction of evidence to the contrary, would support a finding that the Federal agency or museum did not have the right of possession, then such agency or museum shall return such objects unless it can overcome such inference and prove that it has a right of possession to the objects.

(d) Sharing of Information by Federal Agencies and Museums.—Any Federal agency or museum shall share what information it does possess regarding the object in question with the known lineal descendant, Indian tribe, or Native Hawaiian organization to assist in making a claim under this section.

(e) Competing Claims.—Where there are multiple requests for repatriation of any cultural item and, after complying with the requirements of this Act, the Federal agency or museum cannot clearly determine which requesting party is the most appropriate claimant, the agency or museum may retain such item until the requesting parties agree upon its disposition or the dispute is otherwise resolved pursuant to the provisions of this Act or by a court of competent jurisdiction.

(f) Museum Obligation.—Any museum which repatriates any item in good faith pursuant to this Act shall not be liable for claims by an aggrieved party or for claims of breach of fiduciary duty, public trust, or violations of state law that are inconsistent with the provisions of this Act.

Sec. 8. <25 USC 3006> Review Committee.

(a) Establishment.—Within 120 days after the date of enactment of this Act, the Secretary shall establish a committee to monitor and review the implementation of the inventory and identification process and repatriation activities required under sections 5, 6 and 7.

(b) Membership.—(1) The Committee established under subsection (a) shall be composed of 7 members,

    (A) 3 of whom shall be appointed by the Secretary from nominations submitted by Indian tribes, Native Hawaiian organizations, and traditional Native American religious leaders with at least 2 of such persons being traditional Indian religious leaders;

    (B) 3 of whom shall be appointed by the Secretary from nominations submitted by national museum organizations and scientific organizations; and

    (C) 1 who shall be appointed by the Secretary from a list of persons developed and consented to by all of the members appointed pursuant to subparagraphs (A) and (B).

  (2) The Secretary may not appoint Federal officers or employees to the committee.

  (3) In the event vacancies shall occur, such vacancies shall be filled by the Secretary in the same manner as the original appointment within 90 days of the occurrence of such vacancy.

  (4) Members of the committee established under subsection (a) shall serve without pay, but shall be reimbursed at a rate equal to the daily rate for GS-18 of the General Schedule for each day (including travel time) for which the member is actually engaged in committee business. Each member shall receive travel expenses, including per diem in lieu of subsistence, in accordance with sections 5702 and 5703 of title 5, United States Code.

(c) Responsibilities.—The committee established under subsection (a) shall be responsible for—

  (1) designating one of the members of the committee as chairman;

  (2) monitoring the inventory and identification process conducted under sections 5 and 6 to ensure a fair, objective consideration and assessment of all available relevant information and evidence;

  (3) upon the request of any affected party, reviewing and making findings related to—

    (A) the identity or cultural affiliation of cultural items, or

    (B) the return of such items;

  (4) facilitating the resolution of any disputes among Indian tribes, Native Hawaiian organizations, or lineal descendants and Federal agencies or museums relating to the return of such items including convening the parties to the dispute if deemed desirable;

  (5) compiling an inventory of culturally unidentifiable human remains that are in the possession or control of each Federal agency and museum and recommending specific actions for developing a process for such remains;

  (6) consulting with Indian tribes and Native Hawaiian organizations and museums on matters within the scope of the work of the committee affecting such tribes or organizations;

    (7)   consulting with the Secretary in the development of regulations to carry out this Act;

    (8)   performing such other related functions as the Secretary may assign to the committee; and

    (9)   making recommendations, if appropriate, regarding future care of cultural items which are to be repatriated.

(d)   Any records and findings made by the review committee pursuant to this Act relating to the identity or cultural affiliation of any cultural items and the return of such items may be admissible in any action brought under section 15 of this Act.

(e)   Recommendations and Report.—The committee shall make the recommendations under paragraph (c)(5) in consultation with Indian tribes and Native Hawaiian organizations and appropriate scientific and museum groups.

(f)   Access.—The Secretary shall ensure that the committee established under subsection (a) and the members of the committee have reasonable access to Native American cultural items under review and to associated scientific and historical documents.

(g)   Duties of Secretary.—The Secretary shall—

    (1)   establish such rules and regulations for the committee as may be necessary, and

    (2)   provide reasonable administrative and staff support necessary for the deliberations of the committee.

(h)   Annual Report.—The committee established under subsection (a) shall submit an annual report to the Congress on the progress made, and any barriers encountered, in implementing this section during the previous year.

(i)   Termination.—The committee established under subsection (a) shall terminate at the end of the 120-day period beginning on the day the Secretary certifies, in a report submitted to Congress, that the work of the committee has been completed.

Sec. 9. <25 USC 3007> Penalty.

(a)   Penalty.—Any museum that fails to comply with the requirements of this Act may be assessed a civil penalty by the Secretary of the Interior pursuant to procedures established by the Secretary through regulation. A penalty assessed under this subsection shall be determined on the record after opportunity for an agency hearing. Each violation under this subsection shall be a separate offense.

(b)   Amount of Penalty.—The amount of a penalty assessed under subsection (a) shall be determined under regulations promulgated pursuant to this Act, taking into account, in addition to other factors—

    (1)   the archaeological, historical, or commercial value of the item involved;

    (2)   the damages suffered, both economic and noneconomic, by an aggrieved party, and

    (3)   the number of violations that have occurred.

(c)   Actions to Recover Penalties.—If any museum fails to pay an assessment of a civil penalty pursuant to a final order of the Secretary that has been issued under subsection (a) and not appealed or after a final judgment has been rendered on appeal of such order, the Attorney General may institute a civil action in an appropriate district court of the United States to collect the penalty. In such action, the validity and amount of such penalty shall not be subject to review.

(d) Subpoenas.—In hearings held pursuant to subsection (a), subpoenas may be issued for the attendance and testimony of witnesses and the production of relevant papers, books, and documents. Witnesses so summoned shall be paid the same fees and mileage that are paid to witnesses in the courts of the United States.

Sec. 10. <25 USC 3008> Grants.

(a) Indian Tribes and Native Hawaiian Organizations.—The Secretary is authorized to make grants to Indian tribes and Native Hawaiian organizations for the purpose of assisting such tribes and organizations in the repatriation of Native American cultural items.

(b) Museums.—The Secretary is authorized to make grants to museums for the purpose of assisting the museums in conducting the inventories and identification required under sections 5 and 6.

Sec. 11. <25 USC 3009> Savings Provisions.

Nothing in this Act shall be construed to—

(1) limit the authority of any Federal agency or museum to—
    (A) return or repatriate Native American cultural items to Indian tribes, Native Hawaiian organizations, or individuals, and
    (B) enter into any other agreement with the consent of the culturally affiliated tribe or organization as to the disposition of, or control over, items covered by this Act;
(2) delay actions on repatriation requests that are pending on the date of enactment of this Act;
(3) deny or otherwise affect access to any court;
(4) limit any procedural or substantive right which may otherwise be secured to individuals or Indian tribes or Native Hawaiian organizations; or
(5) limit the application of any State or Federal law pertaining to theft or stolen property.

Sec. 12. <25 USC 3010> Special Relationship Between Federal Government and Indian Tribes.

This Act reflects the unique relationship between the Federal Government and Indian tribes and Native Hawaiian organizations and should not be construed to establish a precedent with respect to any other individual, organization or foreign government.

Sec. 13. <25 USC 3011> Regulations.

The Secretary shall promulgate regulations to carry out this Act within 12 months of enactment.

Sec. 14. <25 USC 3012> Authorization of Appropriations.

There is authorized to be appropriated such sums as may be necessary to carry out this Act.

Sec. 15. <25 USC 3013> Enforcement.

The United States district courts shall have jurisdiction over any action brought by any person alleging a violation of this Act and shall have the authority to issue such orders as may be necessary to enforce the provisions of this Act.

Speaker of the House of Representatives.
Vice President of the United States and President of the Senate.

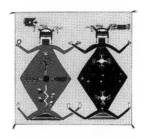

EXECUTIVE ORDER ON CONSULTATION AND COORDINATION WITH TRIBAL GOVERNMENTS (1998), MEMORANDUM REGARDING GOVERNMENT-TO-GOVERNMENT RELATIONS (1994), AND DEPARTMENT OF JUSTICE POLICY ON INDIAN SOVEREIGNTY (1995)

INTRODUCTION

The documents presented here bear directly on the question of tribal sovereignty (see the "Sovereignty" entry in the Contemporary Issues section for extended discussion). This highly complex issue, with deep roots in law and custom, has been a point of contention between native and non-native nations for centuries. European governments, especially France and England, historically made treaties with native groups in North America as with nations fully as sovereign as themselves. Even the United States recognized the complete sovereignty of, for example, Iroquois and Lakota Nations, enshrining this acknowledgment in treaties such as the 1794 Jay Treaty and the Fort Laramie Treaty of 1868.

However, at the same time that it acknowledged the sovereignty of some Indian nations, the U.S. government officially viewed others, such as the Cherokee, as "domestic dependent nations." In fact, U.S. Indian policy has always been marked by a fundamental and profound inconsistency, recognizing sovereignty and concluding treaties on the one hand and undermining that sovereignty and acting unilaterally on the other hand. Policy has undergone many shifts, abrupt changes, and reversals over the years. However, few—if any—of the results have suited most native tribes and nations, who have consistently called for the United States simply to honor treaty rights and, within that context, to let them alone to live as Indians.

Following the disastrous termination policies of the 1950s and early 1960s, Indian groups in general become more educated and politically sophisticated and pressured the government to begin a period of partnership (largely on the government's terms, of course) with them that lasts to this day. The "government-to-government" relationship was first defined in 1983 (a date, it is important to note, that is well after federal agencies had forced most tribes to adopt tribal councils and other nontraditional political and legal institutions). The documents presented here indicate the current status of the official relationship between the United States and the tribes. At about the same time these policies were adopted in the 1990s, the Department of Justice also created an office of Tribal Justice (OTJ) to foster improved communication between the department and Indian tribes.

The policies outlined in these documents are based on the premise, considered retrograde and paternalistic by some Indian tribes, that the tribes remain dependent upon and under the protection of the United States. The May 14, 1998, executive order specifically states (first paragraph) that the right of Indian tribes to self-government is "guaranteed" by the United States, as though sovereign nations do not have an inherent right to self-government. In practice, on the principle that tribal governments have the authority to direct the actions of their tribes (within limits set by U.S. law), the federal government must defer to tribal governments with respect to tribal resolutions, laws, or regulations if they were duly enacted. Also, the federal government is bound to determine the tribal position on any particular issue and to adopt that position if possible. In cases where the tribe is divided, federal authorities defer to the tribal council if it is the governing body of the tribe.

U.S. courts have not gone so far as to uphold many important treaty rights as Indian groups view those rights, but they have tended to affirm the principle of tribal sovereignty as defined by documents such as the ones presented here. Especially in matters such as taxation, subsistence rights, and legal jurisdiction (see, for instance, *Kiowa Tribe of Oklahoma v. Manufacturing Technologies, Inc.* [USSC 1998]), courts regularly side with Indian tribes over state and federal governments, as well as the private sector, based on the principle of tribal sovereignty. It is important to note that it is the tribes themselves, through their (increasingly Indian) legal representatives, who have more or less forced the government to accept them as sovereign entities. As the relationship between native and non-native governments continues to evolve, Indian groups will try to defeat threats (such as the recent neotermination efforts of Senator Slade Gorton of Washington) to the gains they have made and build on the government-to-government relationship toward a general acceptance of their view of themselves as nations with sovereignty fully equal to that of the U.S. government.

Executive Order on Consultation and Coordination with Indian Tribal Governments

The United States has a unique legal relationship with Indian tribal governments as set forth in the Constitution of the United States, treaties, statutes, Executive orders, and court decisions. Since the formation of the Union, the United States has recognized Indian tribes as domestic dependent nations under its protection. In treaties, our Nation has guaranteed the right of Indian tribes to self-government. As domestic dependent nations, Indian tribes exercise inherent sovereign powers over their members and territory. The United States continues to work with Indian tribes on a government-to-government basis to address issues concerning Indian tribal self-government, trust resources, and Indian tribal treaty and other rights.

Therefore, by the authority vested in me as President by the Constitution and the laws of the United States of America, and in order to establish regular and meaningful consultation and collaboration with Indian tribal governments in the development of regulatory practices on Federal matters that significantly or uniquely affect their communities; to reduce the imposition of unfunded mandates upon Indian tribal governments; and to streamline the application process for and increase the availability of waivers to Indian tribal governments; it is hereby ordered as follows:

Section 1. Definitions. For purposes of this order:

(a) "State" or "States" refer to the States of the United States of America, individually or collectively, and, where relevant, to State governments, including units of local government and other political subdivisions established by the States.
(b) "Indian tribe" means an Indian or Alaska Native tribe, band, nation, pueblo, village, or community that the Secretary of the Interior acknowledges to exist as an Indian tribe pursuant to the Federally Recognized Indian Tribe List Act of 1994, 25 U.S.C. 479a.
(c) "Agency" means any authority of the United States that is an "agency" under 44 U.S.C. 3502(1), other than those considered to be independent regulatory agencies, as defined in 44 U.S.C. 3502(5).

Sec. 2. Policy making Criteria. In formulating policies significantly or uniquely affecting Indian tribal governments, agencies shall be guided, to the extent permitted by law, by principles of respect for Indian tribal self-government and sovereignty, for tribal treaty and other rights, and for responsibilities that arise from the unique legal relationship between the Federal Government and Indian tribal governments.

Sec. 3. Consultation.

(a) Each agency shall have an effective process to permit elected officials and other representatives of Indian tribal governments to provide meaningful and timely input in the development of regulatory policies on matters that significantly or uniquely affect their communities.
(b) To the extent practicable and permitted by law, no agency shall promulgate any regulation that is not required by statute, that significantly or uniquely affects the communities of the Indian tribal governments, and that imposes substantial direct compliance costs on such communities, unless:
   (1) funds necessary to pay the direct costs incurred by the Indian tribal government in complying with the regulation are provided by the Federal Government; or
   (2) the agency, prior to the formal promulgation of the regulation,
      (A) in a separately identified portion of the preamble to the regulation as it is to be issued in the Federal Register, provides to the Director

of the Office of Management and Budget a description of the extent of the agency's prior consultation with representatives of affected Indian tribal governments, a summary of the nature of their concerns, and the agency's position supporting the need to issue the regulation; and

(B) makes available to the Director of the Office of Management and Budget any written communications submitted to the agency by such Indian tribal governments.

Sec. 4. Increasing Flexibility for Indian Tribal Waivers.

(a) Agencies shall review the processes under which Indian tribal governments apply for waivers of statutory and regulatory requirements and take appropriate steps to streamline those processes.

(b) Each agency shall, to the extent practicable and permitted by law, consider any application by an Indian tribal government for a waiver of statutory or regulatory requirements in connection with any program administered by that agency with a general view toward increasing opportunities for utilizing flexible policy approaches at the Indian tribal level in cases in which the proposed waiver is consistent with the applicable Federal policy objectives and is otherwise appropriate.

(c) Each agency shall, to the extent practicable and permitted by law, render a decision upon a complete application for a waiver within 120 days of receipt of such application by the agency. The agency shall provide the applicant with timely written notice of the decision and, if the application for a waiver is not granted, the reasons for such denial.

(d) This section applies only to statutory or regulatory requirements that are discretionary and subject to waiver by the agency.

Sec. 5. Cooperation in developing regulations. On issues relating to tribal self-government, trust resources, or treaty and other rights, each agency should explore and, where appropriate, use consensual mechanisms for developing regulations, including negotiated rulemaking.

Sec. 6. Independent agencies. Independent regulatory agencies are encouraged to comply with the provisions of this order.

Sec. 7. General provisions.

(a) This order is intended only to improve the internal management of the executive branch and is not intended to, and does not, create any right, benefit, or trust responsibility, substantive or procedural, enforceable at law or equity by a party against the United States, its agencies or instrumentalities, its officers or employees, or any other person.

(b) This order shall supplement but not supersede the requirements contained in Executive Order 12866 ("Regulatory Planning and Review"), Executive Order 12988 ("Civil Justice Reform"), OMB Circular A-19, and the Executive Memorandum of April 29, 1994, on Government-to-Government Relations with Native American Tribal Governments.

(c) This order shall complement the consultation and waiver provisions in sections 4 and 5 of the Executive order, entitled "Federalism," being issued on this day.

(d) This order shall be effective 90 days after the date of this order.

William J. Clinton
The White House, May 14, 1998.

MEMORANDUM FOR THE HEADS OF
EXECUTIVE DEPARTMENTS AND AGENCIES
The White House
Office of the Press Secretary
For Immediate Release April 29, 1994
Subject: Government-to-Government Relations with Native American Tribal Governments

The United States Government has a unique legal relationship with Native American tribal governments as set forth in the Constitution of the United States, treaties, statutes, and court decisions. As executive departments and agencies undertake activities affecting Native American tribal rights or trust resources, such activities should be implemented in a knowledgeable, sensitive manner respectful of tribal sovereignty. Today, as part of an historic meeting, I am outlining principles that executive departments and agencies, including every component bureau and office, are to follow in their interactions with Native American tribal governments. The purpose of these principles is to clarify our responsibility to ensure that the Federal Government operates within a government-to-government relationship with federally recognized Native American tribes. I am strongly committed to building a more effective day-to-day working relationship reflecting respect for the rights of self-government due the sovereign tribal governments. In order to ensure that the rights of sovereign tribal governments are fully respected, executive branch activities shall be guided by the following:

(a) The head of each executive department and agency shall be responsible for ensuring that the department or agency operates within a government-to-government relationship with federally recognized tribal governments.

(b) Each executive department and agency shall consult, to the greatest extent practicable and to the extent permitted by law, with tribal governments prior to taking actions that affect federally recognized tribal governments. All such consultations are to be open and candid so that all interested parties may evaluate for themselves the potential impact of relevant proposals.

(c) Each executive department and agency shall assess the impact of Federal Government plans, projects, programs, and activities on tribal trust resources and assure that tribal government rights and concerns are considered during the development of such plans, projects, programs, and activities.

(d) Each executive department and agency shall take appropriate steps to remove any procedural impediments to working directly and effectively with tribal governments on activities that affect the trust property and/or governmental rights of the tribes.

273

(e) Each executive department and agency shall work cooperatively with other Federal departments and agencies to enlist their interest and support in cooperative efforts, where appropriate, to accomplish the goals of this memorandum.

(f) Each executive department and agency shall apply the requirements of Executive Orders Nos. 12875 ("Enhancing the Intergovernmental Partnership") and 12866 ("Regulatory Planning and Review") to design solutions and tailor Federal programs, in appropriate circumstances, to address specific or unique needs of tribal communities.

The head of each executive department and agency shall ensure that the department or agency's bureaus and components are fully aware of this memorandum, through publication or other means, and that they are in compliance with its requirements.

This memorandum is intended only to improve the internal management of the executive branch and is not intended to, and does not, create any right to administrative or judicial review, or any other right or benefit or trust responsibility, substantive or procedural, enforceable by a party against the United States, its agencies or instrumentalities, its officers or employees, or any other person.

The Director of the Office of Management and Budget is authorized and directed to publish this memorandum in the Federal Register.

William J. Clinton

Department of Justice Policy on Indian Sovereignty and Government-to-Government Relations with Indian Tribes

Purpose: To reaffirm the Department's recognition of the sovereign status of federally recognized Indian tribes as domestic dependent nations and to reaffirm adherence to the principles of government-to-government relations; to inform Department personnel, other federal agencies, federally recognized Indian tribes, and the public of the Department's working relationships with federally recognized Indian tribes; and to guide the Department in its work in the field of Indian affairs.

I. Introduction

From its earliest days, the United States has recognized the sovereign status of Indian tribes as "domestic dependent nations." *Cherokee Nation v. Georgia*, 30 U.S. (5 Pet.) 1, 17 (1831). Our Constitution recognizes Indian sovereignty by classing Indian treaties among the "supreme Law of the land," and establishes Indian affairs as a unique area of federal concern. In early Indian treaties, the United States pledged to "protect" Indian tribes, thereby establishing one of the bases for the federal trust responsibility in our government-to-government relations with Indian tribes. These principles continue to guide our national policy towards Indian tribes.

A. *The Executive Memorandum on Government-to-Government Relations Between the United States and Indian Tribes*

On April 29, 1994, at a historic meeting with the heads of tribal governments, President Clinton reaffirmed the United States' "unique legal relationship with Native

American tribal governments" and issued a directive to all executive departments and agencies of the Federal Government that:

As executive departments and agencies undertake activities affecting Native American tribal rights or trust resources, such activities should be implemented in a knowledgeable, sensitive manner respectful of tribal sovereignty.

President Clinton's directive requires that in all activities relating to or affecting the government or treaty rights of Indian tribes, the executive branch shall:

1) operate within a government-to-government relationship with federally recognized Indian tribes;
2) consult, to the greatest extent practicable and permitted by law, with Indian tribal governments before taking actions that affect federally recognized Indian tribes;
3) assess the impact of agency activities on tribal trust resources and assure that tribal interests are considered before the activities are undertaken;
4) remove procedural impediments to working directly with tribal governments on activities that affect trust property or governmental rights of the tribes; and
5) work cooperatively with other agencies to accomplish these goals established by the President.

The Department of Justice is reviewing programs and procedures to ensure that we adhere to principles of respect for Indian tribal governments and honor our Nation's trust responsibility to Indian tribes. Within the Department, the Office of Tribal Justice has been formed to coordinate policy towards Indian tribes both within the Department and with other agencies of the Federal Government, and to assist Indian tribes as domestic dependent nations within the federal system.

B. *Federal Indian Self-Determination Policy*

President Clinton's executive memorandum builds on the firmly established federal policy of self-determination for Indian tribes. Working together with Congress, previous Presidents affirmed the fundamental policy of federal respect for tribal self-government. President Johnson recognized "the right of the first Americans . . . to freedom of choice and self-determination." President Nixon strongly encouraged "self-determination" among the Indian people. President Reagan pledged "to pursue the policy of self-government" for Indian tribes and reaffirmed "the government-to-government basis" for dealing with Indian tribes. President Bush recognized that the Federal Government's "efforts to increase tribal self-governance have brought a renewed sense of pride and empowerment to this country's native peoples."

II. Principles of Indian Sovereignty and the Trust Responsibility

Though generalizations are difficult, a few basic principles provide important guidance in the field of Indian affairs: 1) the Constitution vests Congress with plenary power over Indian affairs; 2) Indian tribes retain important sovereign powers over "their members and their territory," subject to the plenary power of Congress; and 3) the United States has a trust responsibility to Indian tribes, which guides and limits the Federal Government in dealings with Indian tribes. Thus, federal and tribal law generally have primacy over Indian affairs in Indian country, except where Congress has provided otherwise.

III. Department of Justice Recognition of Indian Sovereignty and the Federal Trust Responsibility

The Department resolves that the following principles will guide its interactions with the Indian tribes.

A. *The Sovereignty of Indian Tribes*

The Department recognizes that Indian tribes as domestic dependent nations retain sovereign powers, except as divested by the United States, and further recognizes that the United States has the authority to restore federal recognition of Indian sovereignty in order to strengthen tribal self-governance.

The Department shall be guided by principles of respect for Indian tribes and their sovereign authority and the United States' trust responsibility in the many ways in which the Department takes action on matters affecting Indian tribes. For example, the Department reviews proposed legislation, administers funds that are available to tribes to build their capacity to address crime and crime-related problems in Indian country, and in conjunction with the Bureau of Indian Affairs and tribal police, provides essential law enforcement in Indian country. The Department represents the United States, in coordination with other federal agencies, in litigation brought for the benefit of Indian tribes and individuals, as well as in litigation by Indian tribes or individuals against the United States or its agencies. In litigation as in other matters, the Department may take actions and positions affecting Indian tribes with which one or more tribes may disagree. In all situations, the Department will carry out its responsibilities consistent with the law and this policy statement.

B. *Government-to-Government Relationships with Indian Tribes*

In accord with the status of Indian tribes as domestic dependent nations, the Department is committed to operating on the basis of government-to-government relations with Indian tribes.

Consistent with federal law and other Departmental duties, the Department will consult with tribal leaders in its decisions that relate to or affect the sovereignty, rights, resources or lands of Indian tribes. Each component will conduct such consultation in light of its mission. In addition, the Department has initiated national and regional listening conferences and has created the Office of Tribal Justice to improve communications with Indian tribes. In the Offices of the United States Attorneys with substantial areas of Indian country within their purview, the Department encourages designation of Assistant U.S. Attorneys to serve as tribal liaisons.

In order to fulfill its mission, the Department of Justice endeavors to forge strong partnerships between the Indian tribal governments and the Department. These partnerships will enable the Department to better serve the needs of Indian tribes, Indian people, and the public at large.

C. *Self-Determination and Self-Governance*

The Department is committed to strengthening and assisting Indian tribal governments in their development and to promoting Indian self-governance. Consistent with federal law and Departmental responsibilities, the Department will consult with tribal governments concerning law enforcement priorities in Indian country, support duly recognized tribal governments, defend the lawful exercise of tribal governmental powers in coordination with the Department of the Interior and other federal agencies, investigate government corruption when necessary, and support and assist Indian tribes in the development of their law enforcement systems, tribal courts, and traditional justice systems.

D. Trust Responsibility

The Department acknowledges the federal trust responsibility arising from Indian treaties, statutes, executive orders, and the historical relations between the United States and Indian tribes. In a broad sense, the trust responsibility relates to the United States' unique legal and political relationship with Indian tribes. Congress, with plenary power over Indian affairs, plays a primary role in defining the trust responsibility, and Congress recently declared that the trust responsibility "includes the protection of the sovereignty of each tribal government." 25 U.S.C. § 3601.

The term "trust responsibility" is also used in a narrower sense to define the precise legal duties of the United States in managing property and resources of Indian tribes and, at times, of individual Indians.

The trust responsibility, in both senses, will guide the Department in litigation, enforcement, policymaking and proposals for legislation affecting Indian country, when appropriate to the circumstances. As used in its narrower sense, the federal trust responsibility may be justiciable in some circumstances, while in its broader sense the definition and implementation of the trust responsibility is committed to Congress and the Executive Branch.

E. Protection of Civil Rights

Federal law prohibits discrimination based on race or national origin by the federal, state and local governments, or individuals against American Indians in such areas as voting, education, housing, credit, public accommodations and facilities, employment, and in certain federally funded programs and facilities. Various federal criminal civil rights statutes also preserve personal liberties and safety. The existence of the federal trust responsibility towards Indian tribes does not diminish the obligation of state and local governments to respect the civil rights of Indian people.

Through the Indian Civil Rights Act, Congress selectively has derived essential civil rights protections from the Bill of Rights and applied them to Indian tribes. 25 U.S.C. § 1301. The Indian Civil Rights Act is to be interpreted with respect for Indian sovereignty. The primary responsibility for enforcement of the Act is invested in the tribal courts and other tribal fora. In the criminal law context, federal courts have authority to decide habeas corpus petitions after tribal remedies are exhausted.

The Department of Justice is fully committed to safeguarding the constitutional and statutory rights of American Indians, as well as all other Americans.

F. Protection of Tribal Religion and Culture

The mandate to protect religious liberty is deeply rooted in this Nation's constitutional heritage. The Department seeks to ensure that American Indians are protected in the observance of their faiths. Decisions regarding the activities of the Department that have the potential to substantially interfere with the exercise of Indian religions will be guided by the First Amendment of the United States Constitution, as well as by statutes which protect the exercise of religion such as the Religious Freedom Restoration Act, the American Indian Religious Freedom Act, the Native American Graves Protection and Repatriation Act, and the National Historic Preservation Act.

The Department also recognizes the significant federal interest in aiding tribes in the preservation of their tribal customs and traditions. In performing its duties in Indian country, the Department will respect and seek to preserve tribal cultures.

IV. Directive to All Components of the Department of Justice

The principles set out here must be interpreted by each component of the Department of Justice in light of its respective mission. Therefore, each component head shall make all reasonable efforts to ensure that the component's activities are consistent with the above sovereignty and trust principles. The component heads shall circulate this policy to all attorneys in the Department to inform them of their responsibilities. Where the activities and internal procedures of the components can be reformed to ensure greater consistency with this policy, the component head shall undertake to do so. If tensions arise between these principles and other principles which guide the component in carrying out its mission, components will develop, as necessary, a mechanism for resolving such tensions to ensure that tribal interests are given due consideration. Finally, component heads will appoint a contact person to work with the Office of Tribal Justice in addressing Indian issues within the component.

V. Disclaimer

This policy is intended only to improve the internal management of the Department and is not intended to create any right enforceable in any cause of action by any party against the United States, its agencies, officers, or any person.

June 1, 1995

Janet Reno
Attorney General

NATIVE AMERICAN CHURCH AND PEYOTE: *UNITED STATES OF AMERICA V. ROBERT LAWRENCE BOYLL* (1991)

INTRODUCTION

United States of America v. *Robert Lawrence Boyll* involves the sacramental use of peyote by a member of the Native American Church. Peyote is a small, spineless cactus that has psychotropic properties. One often vomits after eating peyote, after which one experiences euphoria, relaxation, mild hallucinations, and a sense of timelessness. The use of peyote is not habit forming.

Peyote has been used medicinally and ceremonially by the native people of Mexico for millennia. In the last part of the nineteenth century, when Plains tribes were herded onto reservations in Oklahoma, a religious institution developed among them that became known around 1920 as the Native American Church. Mainly of native origin, the church has some elements of Christianity and was probably introduced into the Indian Territory (Oklahoma) by the tribes of southern Texas and New Mexico. Within a short period of time, the "peyote religion" had spread throughout the Plains and beyond.

Needless to say, practitioners of the peyote religion were persecuted by Christian missionaries and government officials. Opponents claimed that peyote was immoral and addictive and that it made Indians lazy or crazy. Efforts began in the early twentieth century to outlaw the use of the plant. Early legislation of that kind was defeated, mainly because non-native anthropologists testified that not only were none of the claims against the plant's use true but that users actually tended to demonstrate sobriety and other manifestations of psychological strength. Still, antipeyote efforts continued, among both native governments (such as those of Taos Pueblo and the Navajo tribe) and non-native governments. Today there are probably more than 200,000 members of the Native American Church.

The American Indian Religious Freedom Act (1978) has generally protected members of the Native American Church from legal persecution. There have been some important exceptions to this trend, however, and church members, as well as defenders of religious freedom and other civil rights, have had to be on their guard. The most egregious court case to undermine church members' rights was *Employment*

Division Department of Human Resources of Oregon v. *Smith* (1990), in which the U.S. Supreme Court held that a state may enforce its criminal laws even if they conflict with recognized religious practice.

In *United States of America* v. *Robert Lawrence Boyll,* a U.S. District Court ruled in the case of a non-native man arrested for unlawfully importing peyote through the U.S. mail and possessing peyote with an intent to distribute. The defendant pleaded not guilty on the grounds that he was exercising his religious freedom as a member of the Native American Church. In terms of the facts of the case, the court rejected what it called a "racially restrictive reading" of [the law] that denied that the defendant could be a church member because he was not an Indian. Finding that he was, in fact, a church member, the court upheld his religious rights under the constitution and denied the prosecutor an indictment in the case.

Significantly, however, the court went even further than a narrow ruling on the merits of the case. It specifically repudiated *Oregon* v. *Smith* by stating that the Supreme Court made its decision "without the benefit of any constitutional scrutiny at all." It found that there was no "compelling interest" for the state to deny the defendant his religious rights. Finally, it seriously questioned the entire basis of the law in question as a manifestation of a seriously misguided "war on drugs" that "threatens to consume those fundamental rights of the individual deliberately enshrined in our constitution."

UNITED STATES OF AMERICA V. ROBERT LAWRENCE BOYLL

In the United States District Court for the District of New Mexico
United States of America,
Plaintiff,
v. Criminal No. 90-207-JB
Robert Lawrence Boyll,
Defendant.
Memorandum Opinion and Order

There is a genius to our Constitution. Its genius is that it speaks to the freedoms of the individual. It is this genius that brings the present matter before the Court. More specifically, this matter concerns a freedom that was a natural idea whose genesis was in the Plymouth Charter, and finds its present form in the First Amendment to the United States Constitution—the freedom of religion.

The Government's "war on drugs" has become a wildfire that threatens to consume those fundamental rights of the individual deliberately enshrined in our Constitution. Ironically, as we celebrate the 200th anniversary of the Bill of Rights, the tattered Fourth Amendment right to be free from unreasonable searches and seizures and the now frail Fifth Amendment right against self-incrimination or deprivation of liberty without due process have fallen as casualties in this "war on drugs." It was naive of this Court to hope that this erosion of constitutional protections would stop at the Fourth and Fifth Amendments. But today, the "war" targets one of the most deeply held fundamental rights—the First Amendment right to freely exercise one's religion.

To us in the Southwest, this freedom of religion has singular significance because it affects diverse cultures. It is as much of us as the rain on our hair, the wind on the grass, and the sun on our faces. It is so naturally a part of us that when the joy of this beautiful freedom sings in our souls, we find it hard to conceive that it could ever be imperilled. Yet, today, in this land of bright blue skies and yellow grass, of dusty prairies and beautiful mesas, and vistas of red earth with walls of weathered rock, eroded by oceans of time, the free spirit of the individual once again is threatened by the arrogance of Government.

The issue presented is the recurring conflict between the Native American Church members' right to freely exercise their religion through the ceremonial use of peyote and the Government's efforts to eradicate illegal drugs. To the Government, peyote is a dangerous hallucinogen. To Robert Boyll, peyote is both a sacrament and a deity essential to his religion. But this matter concerns competing interests far greater than those relating to this small, spineless cactus having psychedelic properties. It draws forth a troublesome constitutional conflict which arises from fundamentally different perspectives of peyote.

In its "war" to free our society of the devastating effects of drugs, the Government slights its duty to observe the fundamental freedom of individuals to practice the religion of their choice, regardless of race. Simply put, the Court is faced with the quintessential constitutional conflict between an inalienable right upon which this country was founded and the response by the Government to the swelling political passions of the day. In this fray, the Court is compelled to halt this menacing attack on our constitutional freedoms.

On May 10, 1990, the Federal Grand Jury indicted Robert Lawrence Boyll, a non–Native American, for unlawfully importing peyote through the United States mail and possessing peyote with the intent to distribute it, in violation of 21 U.S.C. §§ 952(a), 960(b)(3), 843(b) & (c), & 841(a)(1) (1981). The three-count indictment arose out of Mr. Boyll mailing himself a quantity of peyote from Mexico to his home in San Cristobal, New Mexico.

In his motions to dismiss, Mr. Boyll argues that the indictment violates his First Amendment right to freely exercise his religion. Mr. Boyll also claims that, pursuant to 21 C.F.R. § 1307.31 (1990), the listing of peyote as a controlled substance does not apply to him because he is a member of the Native American Church and he imported and possessed peyote for use in bona fide religious ceremonies of the Native American Church.

The United States adopts a racially restrictive reading of 21 C.F.R. § 1307.31, arguing that the protection contained therein applies only to members of the Native America Church who are American Indians. It claims that Mr. Boyll cannot be a member of the Native American Church because "membership is limited to 'Persons who [sic] ethnic descent is at least twenty-five percent derived from American Indian stock, and to the spouses of such persons"; that, therefore, Mr. Boyll cannot be a member of the Native American Church since neither he nor his spouse is twenty-five percent American Indian.

The Court held an evidentiary hearing in this matter on October 18, 1990. It immediately became apparent that an examination and understanding of the history and present structure of the Peyote Religion and the Native American Church, as well as of 21 C.F.R. § 1307.31, is essential to a faithful resolution of the issues presented by Mr. Boyll's motions.

The following will constitute the Court's findings of fact and conclusions of law.

The peyote plant is a small, spineless cactus having psychedelic properties and the experience of eating it is central to the Peyote Religion. Unlike traditional religions which have sacramental symbols such as bread and wine, peyote is more than a sacrament to members of the Native American Church. Peyote is, itself, considered a deity which cannot be owned by any individual. Peyote is worshiped and eaten at a religious ceremony called a peyote meeting. "Peyote is a sacred medicine; peyote protects; peyote allows one to see the future, or to find lost objects; peyote gives power to the user that may be manifest in various ways; peyote teaches; peyote may be used by Christians or may be incorporated with Christian ideas; a pilgrimage to gather peyote plants is viewed as an act of piety to be undertaken if possible. . . ." Omer C. Stewart Peyote Religion 41 (1987). It is considered sacrilegious to use peyote for nonreligious purposes.

The peyote ceremony is unique and the very cornerstone of the Peyote Religion. It is always conducted by individuals who hold honored posts which have specially assigned duties. The leader of the ceremony is called a "roadman." The roadman is responsible for inviting the participants, although worshipers who are not personally invited are usually welcomed as well. Other officials present at a peyote meeting include the chief drummer, who sits on the right of the roadman; the cedarman, who sits on the left of the roadman and sprinkles sagebrush "incense" on the fire; and the fireman or doorman, who tends the fire and sits near the opening of the tepee. Each meeting also has a sponsor who is responsible for securing a site, the roadman, the tepee and other materials necessary for the service. Although not all ceremonies of the Native American Church are identical, the general concepts have been so well defined, so established in traditional practice, that they have not changed significantly for nearly a hundred years. Peyote Religion at 36, 339-75. At these peyote meetings, the worshipers usually gather in a tepee at dusk and the ceremony passes through a series of ritualistic stages. During these rituals, a staff and a rattle are passed around and the person who receives them leads in singing peyote hymns and prayer. Around midnight, peyote is ingested by the worshipers and the singing, praying and drumming continues throughout the night until dawn. When the "buttons" of the plant are eaten, or brewed into tea and imbibed, the user experiences hallucinations. The peyote plant produces "a warm and pleasant euphoria, an agreeable point of view, relaxation, colorful visual distortions, and a sense of timelessness that are conducive to the all-night ceremony of the Native American Church." Peyote Religion at 3. Finally, at noon of the following day, all worshipers share in a ceremonial feast. See generally Peyote Religion at 327-336 (description of peyote ritual); T. Hillerman, *People of Darkness* 153 (1980) (description of Navajo peyote ritual).

The Native American Church combines elements of Christianity with traditional Native American beliefs and the sacramental use of peyote. Peyote Religion at 33; Toledo v. Nobel-Sysco, Inc., 892 F.2d 1481, 1485 (10th Cir. 1989), cert. denied, 110 S. Ct. 2208 (1990). Although the religious use of peyote has existed for centuries, the Peyote Religion's corporate form, the Native American Church, was established in Oklahoma in 1918. At that time, the leaders of the Peyote Religion reasoned that an "incorporated" church would provide greater protection from early attempts to suppress the use of peyote for religious purposes.

While the Oklahoma Chapter of the Native American Church is sentimentally referred to as the Mother Church, no single branch speaks for the numerous brances throughout the United States. Unlike more traditional churches, the Native American Church is a non-hierarchical church and has no central organization which ditates church policy. The Native American Church consists of a number of loosely affiliated local chapters. Each chapter is responsible for establishing its own charter, if it so chooses. "Each congregation makes its own rules, just as each meeting is conducted by its own roadman." Peyote Religion at 334. Nevertheless, the teachings of all the Native American Church chapters are essentially the same.

"Church" refers to a body of believers and their shared practices, rather than the existence of a formal structure or a membership roll. Membership in the Native American Church derives from the sincerity of one's beliefs and participation in its ceremonies. Historically, the church has been hospitable to and, in fact, has proselytized non-Indians. The vast majority of Native American Church congregations, like most conventional congregations, maintain an "open door" policy and do not exclude persons on the basis of their race. Racial restrictions to membership have never been a general part of Peyote Religion or of the Native American Church. See Peyote Religion at 333-34; *State v. Whittingham*, 504 P.2d 950, 951 (Ariz. Ct. App. 1973) (membership to non-Indians is usually not refused), review denied, 517 P.2d 1275, cert. denied, 417 U.S. 946 (1974). Although one branch of the Native American Church, the Native American Church of North America, is known to restrict membership to Native Americans, most other branches of the Native American Church do not. As a result, non-Indian members are accepted within the Native American Church.

Since attending his first ceremony of the Native American Church at Taos, New Mexico, in 1981, Mr. Boyll has been, and continues to be, an active member of the Native American Church. In fact, while living in Mill Valley, California, from 1981 until 1989, Mr. Boyll participated in ceremonies of the Native American Church an average of once every two to three weeks. Mr. Boyll often sponsored these meetings or participated as a drummer, cedarman or fireman. He sincerely believes in the teachings and practices of the Native American Church. He has only used peyote in connection with bona fide religious purposes and has never been excluded from the Native American Church because of his non-Indian race.

In 1989, motivated in part by his commitment to the Native American Church, Mr. Boyll moved to New Mexico. He continues his active participation in meetings of Native American Church congregations in northern New Mexico and southern Colorado. During one specific peyote meeting, Mr. Boyll was explicitly recognized as a member of the Native American Church by Rutherford Loneman, a well-known roadman who is also a former Vice-Chairman of the Native American Church in Oklahoma. Yet, Mr. Boyll has always considered himself a member of the Native American Church rather than of a specific branch.

The act of traveling to the place where peyote is harvested is considered an act of piety which has its own rewards. The long, sacred pilgrimage to harvest peyote is considered to be one of the most important aboriginal traditions of the Peyote Religion. Peyote Religion at 31-32 ("When the [peyote]-seekers arrive [back] at their homes, the people turn out to welcome the plants with music, and a festival . . . ."). Peyote is grown only in northern Mexico and the Rio Grande Valley of southern Texas. Peyote is not grown anywhere else and its growth area, especially in the United States, is being considerably depleted. Peyote Religion at 334-35.

Because the peyote fields in Texas are depleted, Mr. Boyll went on a "pilgrimage" to Mexico to obtain peyote for himself and members of the congregations with whom he worships. From Mexico, Mr. Boyll mailed the peyote to his post office box in San Cristobal, New Mexico, to avoid violating Texas law, which restricts religious possession and use of peyote only to Native Americans. See Tex. Health & Safety Code Anno. § 481.111 (Vernon 1989). On April 27, 1990, Mr. Boyll picked up the parcel of peyote from the post office in San Cristobal, New Mexico. He was on his way to deliver the peyote to Tellus Goodmorning, an elder of the Taos Pueblo and nationally respected roadman, when he was arrested.

The Court will first address whether 21 C.F.R. § 1307.21 applies to all sincere members of the Native American Church, including Mr. Boyll, or whether it excludes non-Indian members. Stated differently, does the federal exemption place a racial restriction on membership in the Native American Church?

As far back as the late 18th century, efforts were being made to restrict the ceremonial use of peyote. See Peyote Religion at 128-147. However, not until the popularity of psychedelic drugs in the 1960's did Congress restrict the possession, consumption and sale of peyote. See Drug Abuse Control Amendments of 1965, 79 Stat. 226 §3(a). Thereafter, for the first time, peyote was classified as a Schedule I controlled substance. See Controlled Substance Act of 1970, 21 U.S.C. § 812(c), Schedule I (c) (12). But Congress never intended to prohibit the ceremonial use of peyote. See *Kennedy v. Bureau of Narcotics & Dangerous Drugs*, 459 F.2d 415, 719 (9th Cir. 1972), cert. denied, 409 U.S. 1115 (1973); *Peyote Way Church of God, Inc. v. Meese*, 698 F. Supp. 1342, 1346 (N.D. Tex. 1988); *Native American Church of New York v. United States*, 468 F. Supp. 1247, 1449-51 (S.D.N.Y. 1979), aff'd, 633 F.2d 205 (2d Cir. 1980); *People v. Woody*, 394 p.2d 813, 817-18 (Cal. 1964). In implementing regulations, Congress exempted the religious use of peyote by members of the Native American Church. Sec 11 Cong. Rec. 14608, 15977 (1965); see also Native American Church, 468 F. Supp. at 1249-50; *Peyote Way Church of God, Inc. v. Smith*, 742 F.2d 193,197 n.15 (5th Cir. 1984). The Drug Enforcement Administration regulation relating to the listing of peyote as a controlled substance provides:

Special Exempt Persons § 1307.31 Native American Church.
The listing of peyote as a controlled substance [under federal law] does not apply to the nondrug use of peyote in bona fide ceremonies of the Native American Church, and members of the Native American Church so using peyote are exempt from registration. 21 C.F.R. § 1307.31.

As many as twenty-three states have similar statutory or judicially crafted exemptions in their drug laws for the religious use of peyote. See, e.g., N.M. Stat. Ann. § 30-31-6(D) (Supp. 1989); Colo. Rev. Stat. § 12-22-317(3) (1990); Ariz. Rev. Stat. Ann. § 13-3402(b) (1)-(3) (1989); Kan. Stat. Ann. § 65-4116(c)(8) (1985); Utah Code Ann. § 58-37-3(3) (1986).

"The language of a regulation or statute is the starting point for its interpretation," *Dyer v. United States*, 832 F.2d 1062,1066 (9th Cir. 1987) (citing *Consumer Product Safety Comm'n v. GTE Sylvania, Inc.*, 447 U.S. 102, 108 (1980)). "The plain meaning governs unless a clearly expressed legislative intent is to the contrary." Id. "When we find the terms of a statute unambiguous, judicial inquiry is complete." *Rubin v. United States*, 449 U.S. 424, 430 (1981); see also, e.g., *Wilson v. Stocker*, 819 F.2d 943, 948 (10th Cir. 1987).

The language of 21. C.F.R. § 1307.31 is clear, unambiguous and wholly consistent with the regulation's history and purpose. The plain language of 21 C.F.R. § 1307.31 exempts all worshipers engaged "in bona fide religious ceremonies of the Native American Church. "The regulation plainly declares Congress' purpose to exempt Native American Church members. Nowhere is it even suggested that the exemption applies only to Indian members of the Native American Church. Had the intention been to exclude non-Indian members, as the United States argues, the language of the exemption would have so clearly provided. Indeed, the federal peyote exemption makes no reference whatsoever to a racial exclusion. Compare 21 C.F.R. § 1307.31 & N.M. Stat. Ann. 30-31-6(D) (Supp. 1989) with Tex. Health

& Safety Code Anno. § 481.111 (Vernon 1989) (including the language "[t]he exemption granted to members of the Native American Church under this section does not apply to a member with less than 25 percent Indian Blood"). The plain language of the federal peyote exemption applies to all members of the Native American Church, regardless of race. Cf. Native American Church, 468 F. Supp. at 1251 (rejecting the argument that the exemption should apply to "Indian" churches alone); Kennedy, 459 F.2d at 416-17 (rejecting the Government's proposed racial reading of the exemption: "[w]e cannot say that the Government has a lesser or different interest in protecting the health of Indians than it has in protecting the health of non-Indians").

A racially neutral reading of the exemption is consistent not only with the racially neutral language of the exemption but also with its legislative history. During hearings on the Controlled Substances Act of 1970, a representative of the Bureau of Narcotics and Dangerous Drugs, presently the Drug Enforcement Agency, explained the rationale for the special exemption and assured Congress that the exemption would not be affected by the new legislation:

> We consider the Native American Church to be sui generis. The history and tradition of the church is such that there is no question but that they regard peyote as a deity as it were, and we will continue the exemption.

Native American Church, 468 F. Supp. at 1251 (quoting Drug Abuse Control Amendments of 1970, Hearing before the Subcommittee on Public Health & Welfare of the Committee on Interstate and Foreign Commerce, House of Representatives, 91 Cong., 2d Sess. 117-18(1970)). Clearly, the nature and history of the Native American Church played a significant role in the promulgation of 21 C.F.R. § 1307.31. As the uncontradicted evidence in this case shows, the history of the Native American Church attests to the fact that non-Indian worshipers have always been, and continue to be, active and sincere members of the Native American Church.

The Government's racially restrictive reading and application of the exemption reveals a fundamental misunderstanding of the history and present structure of the Native American Church. Indeed, the Drug Enforcement Administration's own rationale acknowledges that the exemption is not based on the racial makeup of the Native American Church membership. See Olsen v. Drug Enforcement Admin., 878 F.2d 1458, 1465-1468 (D.C. Cir. 1989) (final order of the Drug Enforcement Administration in connection with the exemption makes no mention of any distinction between Indian and non-Indian members of the Native American Church). While there may exist some legitimate support for the argument that Congress never intended to extend the exemption to non-Native American Church members, see Peyote Way Church of God, Inc. v. Thornburgh, 922 F.2d 1210 (5th Cir. 1991); but see Native American Church, 468 F. Supp. at 1249-51, the plain language of the exemption and the legislative history clearly support this Court's finding that Congress intended the exemption to apply to all members of the Native American Church, Indian and non-Indian alike.

The Court also finds persuasive Mr. Boyll's argument that to construe the racially neutral language of the exemption "to provide only racially discriminatory protection would place the exemption unnecessarily in direct conflict with the first amendment." Such a consequence would, at the very least, violate the canon of statutory construction that "[f]ederal statutes are to be construed as to avoid serious doubts of their constitutionality." Int'l Ass'n of Machinists v. Street, 367 U.S. 740, 749 (1961); see also Hooper v. California, 155 U.S. 648, 657 (1895); United States v. Security In-

dustrial Bank, 459 U.S. 70, 78 (1982). "[T]his principle is fully applicable to cases such as the instant one, in which a . . . constitutionally suspect statutory interpretation is embodied in an administrative regulation." *Rust* v. *Sullivan,* 111 S. Ct. 1759, 1778 (1991) (Blackman, J., dissenting).

The Court will next address tile constitutional question of whether the indictment violates Mr. Boyll's First Amendment right to freely exercise his religion. It is disingenuous for the Government to contend that its racially restrictive reading of 21 C.F.R. § 1307.31—which would restrict religious freedom through the imposition of a racial exclusion—does not give rise to valid constitutional concerns. Since the use of peyote by Native American Church members is the very essence of their religious beliefs, the proposed racially restrictive reading of 21 C.F.R. § 1307.31 would have the sure effect of imposing a racial exclusion to membership in the Native American Church itself. To exclude individuals of a particular race from being members of a recognized religious faith is offensive to the very heart of the First Amendment. See *Waltz* v. *Tax Comm'n of New York,* 397 U.S. 664, 668-69 (1970) (the First Amendment's Establishment Clause ensures that governmental interference with religion will be not tolerated). In fact, there can be no more excessive entanglement of Government with religion than the Government's attempt to impose a racial restriction to membership in a religious organization. The decision as to who can and who cannot be members of the Native American Church is an internal church judgment which the First Amendment shields from governmental interference. Cf. *Paul* v. *Watchtower Bible & Tract Society,* 819 F.2d 875, 878, n.l. (9th Cir.) (constitutionally improper for government to resolve a dispute about religious doctrine or practices), cert. denied, 484 U.S. 926 (1987). It is one thing for a local branch of the Native American Church to adopt its own restrictions on membership, but it is entirely another for the Government to restrict membership in a religious organization on the basis of race. Any such attempt to restrict religious liberties along racial lines would not only be a contemptuous affront to the First Amendment guarantee of freedom of religion but also to the Fourteenth Amendment right to equal justice under the law.

Applying the above-mentioned canon of statutory construction, we find that the United States' racially restrictive reading of 21 C.F.R. § 1307.31 does raise the sort of "grave and doubtful constitutional questions," *United States* v. *Delaware & Hudson Co.,* 213 U.S. 366, 408 (1909), that would lead this Court to assume Congress did not intend such an interpretation. *Federal Trade Comm'n* v. *American Tobacco Co.,* 264 U.S. 298, 305-307 (1924)(assuming Congress legislates in the light of constitutional limitations).

The Free Exercise Clause of the First Amendment provides that "Congress shall make no law respecting an establishment of religion, or prohibiting the free exercise thereof; or abridging of freedom, . . . or the right of the people to assemble . . . ." U.S. Const. Amend. I. While the freedom to act upon religious beliefs is not absolute, "only those interests of the highest order and those not otherwise served can overbalance legitimate claims to the free exercise of religion." *Wisconsin* v. *Yoder,* 406 U.S. 205, 215 (1972). Traditional free exercise jurisprudence has long held that in order for government to substantially burden religiously motivated conduct, the Government must justify such restriction by a compelling state interest and use, means narrowly tailored to achieve that interest. See *Hernandez* v. *Commissioner,* 490 U.S. 680, 699 (1989); *United States* v. *Lee,* 455 U.S. 252, 257-58 (1982); *Thomas* v. *Review Bd. of Indiana Employment Secur. Div.,* 450 U.S. 707, 717-19 (1981); *Sherbert* v. *Verner,* 374 U.S. 398, 403 (1963).

In order for government action to withstand a challenge under the Free Exercise Clause, the action must satisfy the two-step analysis of the "compelling interest" test. The Court must first "determine whether the Government's action "imposes any burden on the free exercise of [defendant]'s religion." *Sherbert*, 374 U.S. at 403. Then, if such a burden exists, the Court must "consider whether some compelling state interest . . . justifies the substantial' infringement of [defendant]'s First Amendment right." Id. at 406. "The compelling interest test reflects the First Amendment's mandate of preserving religious liberty to the fullest extent possible in a pluralistic society." *Employment Division, Dept. of Human Resources of Oregon v. Smith*, 110 S. Ct. 1595, 1613 (1990) (O'Connor, J., concurring).

Recently, the Supreme Court in *Employment Division, Dept. of Human Resources of Oregon v. Smith*, 110 S. Ct. 1595, 1603 (1990) ["Smith"], elected to abandon the compelling interest test in cases involving a "neutral, generally applicable [criminal] law," reasoning that the application of such a statute does not implicate First Amendment concerns. Accordingly—without the benefit of any constitutional scrutiny at all—the Court held that Oregon's across-the-board prohibition against peyote was constitutional.

This Court is convinced that 21 C.F.R. § 1307.31 is "specifically directed to religious practices and therefore not within the ambit of *Smith*." *Salvation Army v. Dept. of Community Affairs of State of New Jersey*, 919 F.2d 183, 194, 204 (3d Cir. 1990) (Becker, J., concurring). The Drug Enforcement Agency regulation in the present case, unlike the statute in *Smith*, is neither neutral nor generally applicable. Indeed, the plain language of the exemption speaks directly to "bona fide religious ceremonies of the Native American Church." Therefore, this Court will proceed to apply the traditional compelling interest test. See Cf. Id. at 1603 ("where the [Government] has in place a system of individual exemptions, it may not refuse to extend that system to cases of 'religious hardships' without compelling reason").

With respect to the first step of the analysis, it is uncontradicted that the racially restrictive interpretation of 21 C.F.R. § 1307.31 would impose a substantial burden on Mr. Boyll's free exercise of religion. On this issue, the Court's findings of fact and conclusions of law are not very different from those in *Woody*, 394 P.2d at 816, 818, which concluded:

> An examination of the record as to the nature of peyote and its role in the religion practiced by defendants as [Indian and non-Indian] members of the Native American Church ... compels the conclusion that the [racially restrictive] prohibition most seriously infringes upon the observance of the religion. . . .

The record thus establishes that the [indictment for] ... the use of peyote results in a virtual inhibition of the practice of defendants' religion. Id. Indian and non-Indian "believers who worship at the Native American Church cannot freely exercise their religious beliefs absent the use of peyote." *Whittingham*, 504 P.2d at 952. "Thereis no dispute that [the] criminal prohibition of peyote places a severe burden on the ability of [Defendant] to freely exercise [his] religion." *Smith* at 1613 (O'Connor, J., concurring); *Peyote Way Church of God*, 742 F.2d at 200-01. Additionally, the Court finds that Mr. Boyll's trip to Mexico to obtain peyote is an integral part of the Peyote Religion practiced by the Native American Church. Such a substantial infringement necessarily triggers further First Amendment scrutiny.

The Court must next "consider whether some compelling [governmental] interest ... justifies the substantial infringement of [defendant]'s First Amendment right." *Sher-*

bert, 374 U.S. at 406. While the Court is well aware that drug abuse is "one of the greatest problems affecting the health and welfare of our population" and, thus, "one of the most serious problems confronting our society today," *National Treasury Employees Union v. Van Raab*, 489 U.S. 656, 668, 674 (1989), this amorphorous problem, without more, cannot justify the serious infringement on "the observance of religion."

First, the United States has failed to present any evidence of a compelling interest to justify its actions in the present case. "In the absence of evidence, we cannot simply assume that the psychedelic is so baneful that its use must be prohibited to a group of [non-Indian] members but poses no equal threat when used by [Indian] members of the Native American Church." *Peyote Way Church of God*, 742 F.2d at 201. In fact, in light of the absence of factual support and the scarcity of legal support for the United States' opposition to Defendant's motions to dismiss, this Court cannot help but believe that the present prosecution is, at best, an overreaction driven by political passions or, at worst, influenced by religious and racial insensitivity, if not outright hostility.

Finally, the existence of 21 C.F.R. § 1307.31 itself, negates the existence of a compelling governmental interest in prosecuting non-Indian members of the Native American Church for their religious use of peyote. Id. ("The exemption granted both by federal and [state] law to the ritual use of peyote by the Native American Church tends . . . to negate the existence of a compelling [governmental] interest in the same use of it"). Indeed, the federal exemption explicitly establishes a governmental interest in preserving the exemption of peyote as a controlled substance for its ritual use by Indian and non-Indian members of the Native American Church. The only compelling interest in the present case is Congress' considered and continued conviction that the use of peyote in the Native American Church is the kind of free exercise of religion the First Amendment protects. See, e.g., *Native American Church*, 468 F. Supp. at 1249-50; Peyote Religion, 128-147. Finding no compelling interest to justify the constitutional infringement at issue, the Court need not reach the often critical question of balancing two competing interests.

Congress has articulated an unequivocal federal policy protecting the right of the Native American Church and its members to worship, possess and use peyote in bona fide religious ceremonies. This policy arises out of our country's recognition of the importance of individual freedom. For,

> the right to free religious expression embodies a precious heritage of our history. In a mass society, which presses at every point toward conformity, the protection of a self-expression, however unique, of the individual and the group become ever more important.
>
> The varying currents of the subcultures that flow into the mainstream of our national life give it depth and beauty.

Woody, 394 P.2d at 821-22; see also 111 Cong. Rec. 15977 (1965). The court in *Woody* eloquently speaks to the freedom of the individual.

Individual freedom, whether it be freedom of religion, expression or association, has been particularly important to maintaining the cultrually diverse character of New Mexico. Here, we celebrate the right of the individual to revel in the passions of the spirit. The survival of this right owes much to the protection afforded by the First Amendment, which has allowed New Mexico's distinct cultures to learn mutual respect for each other's jealously-guarded customs and traditions. Diversity is New Mexico's enchantment.

For the reasons set out in this Memorandum Opinion and Order, the Court holds that, pursuant to 21 C.F.R. § 1307.31 (1990), the classification of peyote as a Schedule I controlled substance, see 21 U.S.C. §812(c), Schedule I (c)(12), does not apply to the importation, possession or use of peyote for bona fide ceremonial use by members of the Native American Church, regardless of race.

Wherefore,

It is ordered, adjudged and decreed that Defendant Robert Boyll's motions to dismiss the indictment be and hereby are granted.

Dated at Albuquerque the — of September, 1991.

Chief Judge

Indian Fishing Rights in Canada: *Ronald Edward Sparrow v. Her Majesty The Queen* (1990)

Introduction

Ronald Edward Sparrow v. *Her Majesty The Queen* may be compared to *United States* v. *State of Washington* (1974), the famous Boldt decision, which more or less resolved the highly contentious issue of native fishing rights in the northwestern United States. Sparrow, a member of the Musqueam Indian Band, was arrested under the Fisheries Act for using a drift net longer than that allowed by the license granted to his band. In his defense, the man charged that the net length restriction was invalid because it conflicted with his rights under section 35(1) of the Constitution Act of 1982 (see Constitution Act, 1982 entry). Sparrow was convicted; his appeal eventually reached the Canadian Supreme Court.

In the first major judicial scrutiny of the 1982 Constitution Act as it applies to native fishing rights, the Canadian Supreme Court specifically noted that "the Crown failed to discharge its burden of proving extinguishment [of aboriginal rights]." It held that "an aboriginal right is not extinguished merely by its being controlled in great detail by regulations under the Fisheries Act." Acknowledging that Indian rights had been virtually ignored in the past, the court, in referring to the words "recognition and affirmation" in section 35(1), put a strict onus on the Crown to justify regulations that infringed upon native fishing rights.

Of course, implicit in this argument is the premise that Canadian institutions (such as courts) have the sole authority to interpret the nature of aboriginal rights. Specifically, the court found that "an existing aboriginal right cannot be read so as to incorporate the specific manner in which it was regulated before 1982. The phrase 'existing aboriginal rights' must be interpreted flexibly so as to permit their [the rights'] evolution over time." The court affirmed the Crown's fiduciary responsibility toward native people only in the context of calling for "some restraint on [its] exercise of sovereign power." In other words, the court recognized definite aboriginal rights but only as it defined those rights, and then only as "some restraint" on unbridled state authority.

To summarize, the court clarified and affirmed the existence of aboriginal fishing rights as a further expression of the fiduciary relationship between the Crown and aboriginal peoples. At the same time, it ruled that such rights could be regulated. The standard it adopted differed from the U.S. approach in *United States* v. *Washington State*. Rather than acknowledging a one-half interest in the resource to be aboriginal, the court established a priority allocation approach with aboriginal rights coming first after conservation. This standard, the court hoped, would ensure that the rights of aboriginal peoples are taken seriously. The specific issue involving the length of drift nets was referred back to a lower court to be decided based on these principles.

RONALD EDWARD SPARROW V. *HER MAJESTY THE QUEEN*
R. v. Sparrow, [1990] 1 S.C.R. 1075
Ronald Edward Sparrow   Appellant
v.
Her Majesty The Queen   Respondent
and
The National Indian Brotherhood/Assembly of First Nations, the B.C. Wildlife Federation, the Steelhead Society of British Columbia, the Pacific Fishermen's Defence Alliance, Northern Trollers' Association, the Pacific Gillnetters' Association, the Gulf Trollers' Association, the Pacific Trollers' Association, the Prince Rupert Fishing Vessel Owners' Association, the Fishing Vessel Owners' Association of British Columbia, the Pacific Coast Fishing Vessel Owners' Guild, the Prince Rupert Fishermen's Cooperative Association, the Co-op Fishermen's Guild, Deep Sea Trawlers' Association of B.C., the Fisheries Council of British Columbia, the United Fishermen and Allied Workers' Union, the Attorney General for Ontario, the Attorney General of Quebec, the Attorney General of British Columbia, the Attorney General for Saskatchewan, the Attorney General for Alberta and the Attorney General of Newfoundland
indexed as: r. v. sparrow

Appellant was charged in 1984 under the Fisheries Act with fishing with a drift net longer than that permitted by the terms of his Band's Indian food fishing licence. He admitted that the facts alleged constitute the offence, but defended the charge on the basis that he was exercising an existing aboriginal right to fish and that the net length restriction contained in the Band's licence was invalid in that it was inconsistent with s. 35(1) of the Constitution Act, 1982.

Appellant was convicted. The trial judge found that an aboriginal right could not be claimed unless it was supported by a special treaty and that s. 35(1) of the Constitution Act, 1982 accordingly had no application. An appeal to County Court was dismissed for similar reasons. The Court of Appeal found that the trial judge's findings of facts were insufficient to lead to an acquittal. Its decision was appealed and cross-appealed. The constitutional question before this Court queried whether the net length restriction contained in the Band's fishing licence was inconsistent with s. 35(1) of the Constitution Act, 1982.

Held: The appeal and cross-appeal should be dismissed. The constitutional question should be sent back to trial to be answered according to the analysis set out in these reasons.

Section 35(1) applies to rights in existence when the Constitution Act, 1982 came into effect; it does not revive extinguished rights. An existing aboriginal right cannot be read so as to incorporate the specific manner in which it was regulated before 1982. The phrase "existing aboriginal rights" must be interpreted flexibly so as to permit their evolution over time.

The Crown failed to discharge its burden of proving extinguishment. An aboriginal right is not extinguished merely by its being controlled in great detail by the regulations under the Fisheries Act. Nothing in the Fisheries Act or its detailed regulations demonstrated a clear and plain intention to extinguish the Indian aboriginal right to fish. These fishing permits were simply a manner of controlling the fisheries, not of defining underlying rights. Historical policy on the part of the Crown can neither extinguish the existing aboriginal right without clear intention nor, in itself, delineate that right. The nature of government regulations cannot be determinative of the content and scope of an existing aboriginal right. Government policy can, however, regulate the exercise of that right but such regulation must be in keeping with s. 35(1).

Section 35(1) of the Constitution Act, 1982, at the least, provides a solid constitutional base upon which subsequent negotiations can take place and affords aboriginal peoples constitutional protection against provincial legislative power. Its significance, however, extends beyond these fundamental effects. The approach to its interpretation is derived from general principles of constitutional interpretation, principles relating to aboriginal rights, and the purposes behind the constitutional provision itself.

Section 35(1) is to be construed in a purposive way. A generous, liberal interpretation is demanded given that the provision is to affirm aboriginal rights. The provision is not subject to s. 1 of the Canadian Charter of Rights and Freedoms. Any law or regulation affecting aboriginal rights, however, will not automatically be of no force or effect by the operation of s. 52 of the Constitution Act, 1982. Legislation that affects the exercise of aboriginal rights will be valid if it meets the test for justifying an interference with a right recognized and affirmed under s. 35(1).

Section 35(1) does not explicitly authorize the courts to assess the legitimacy of any government legislation that restricts aboriginal rights. The words "recognition and affirmation", however, incorporate the government's responsibility to act in a fiduciary capacity with respect to aboriginal peoples and so import some restraint on the exercise of sovereign power. Federal legislative powers continue, including the right to legislate with respect to Indians pursuant to s. 91(24) of the Constitution Act, 1867, but must be read together with s. 35(1). Federal power must be reconciled with federal duty and the best way to achieve that reconciliation is to demand the justification of any government regulation that infringes upon or denies aboriginal rights.

The test for justification requires that a legislative objective must be attained in such a way as to uphold the honour of the Crown and be in keeping with the unique contemporary relationship, grounded in history and policy, between the Crown and Canada's aboriginal peoples. The extent of legislative or regulatory impact on an existing aboriginal right may be scrutinized so as to ensure recognition and affirmation. Section 35(1) does not promise immunity from government regulation in contemporary society but it does hold the Crown to a substantive promise. The government is required to bear the burden of justifying any legislation that has some negative effect on any aboriginal right protected under s. 35(1).

The first question to be asked is whether the legislation in question has the effect of interfering with an existing aboriginal right. The inquiry begins with a reference to the characteristics or incidents of the right at stake. Fishing rights are not traditional property rights. They are rights held by a collective and are in keeping with the culture and existence of that group. Courts must be careful to avoid the application of traditional common law concepts of property as they develop their understanding of the "sui generis" nature of aboriginal rights. While it is impossible to give an easy definition of fishing rights, it is crucial to be sensitive to the aboriginal perspective itself on the meaning of the rights at stake.

To determine whether the fishing rights have been interfered with such as to constitute a prima facie infringement of s. 35(1), certain questions must be asked. Is the limitation unreasonable? Does the regulation impose undue hardship? Does the regulation deny to the holders of the right their preferred means of exercising that right? The onus of proving a prima facie infringement lies on the individual or group challenging the legislation.

Here, the regulation would be found to be a prima facie interference if it were found to be an adverse restriction on the exercise of the natives' right to fish for food. The issue does not merely require looking at whether the fish catch has been reduced below that needed for the reasonable food and ceremonial needs. Rather the test involves asking whether either the purpose or the effect of the restriction on net length unnecessarily infringes the interests protected by the fishing right.

If a prima facie interference is found, the analysis moves to the issue of justification. This test involves two steps. First, is there a valid legislative objective? Here the court would inquire into whether the objective of Parliament in authorizing the department to enact regulations regarding fisheries is valid. The objective of the department in setting out the particular regulations would also be scrutinized. The "public interest" justification is so vague as to provide no meaningful guidance and so broad as to be unworkable as a test for the justification of a limitation on constitutional rights. The justification of conservation and resource management, however, is uncontroversial.

If a valid legislative objective is found, the analysis proceeds to the second part of the justification issue: the honour of the Crown in dealings with aboriginal peoples. The special trust relationship and the responsibility of the government vis-à-vis aboriginal people must be the first consideration in determining whether the legislation or action in question can be justified. There must be a link between the question of justification and the allocation of priorities in the fishery. The constitutional recognition and affirmation of aboriginal rights may give rise to conflict with the interests of others given the limited nature of the resource.

Guidelines are necessary to resolve the allocational problems that arise regarding the fisheries. Any allocation of priorities after valid conservation measures have been implemented must give top priority to Indian food fishing.

The justificatory standard to be met may place a heavy burden on the Crown. However, government policy with respect to the British Columbia fishery, regardless of s. 35(1), already dictates that, in allocating the right to take fish, Indian food fishing is to be given priority over the interests of other user groups. Section 35(1) requires the Crown to ensure that its regulations are in keeping with that allocation of priority and guarantees that those plans treat aboriginal peoples in a way ensuring that their rights are taken seriously.

Within the analysis of justification, there are further questions to be addressed, depending on the circumstances of the inquiry. These include: whether there has been as little infringement as possible in order to effect the desired result; whether, in a situation of expropriation, fair compensation is available; and whether the aboriginal group in question has been consulted with respect to the conservation measures being implemented. This list is not exhaustive.

(Deletions)

"Recognized and Affirmed"

We now turn to the impact of s. 35(1) of the Constitution Act, 1982 on the regulatory power of Parliament and on the outcome of this appeal specifically.

Counsel for the appellant argued that the effect of s. 35(1) is to deny Parliament's power to restrictively regulate aboriginal fishing rights under s. 91(24) ("Indians and Lands Reserved for the Indians"), and s. 91(12) ("Sea Coast and Inland Fisheries"). The essence of this submission, supported by the intervener, the National Indian Brotherhood / Assembly of First Nations, is that the right to regulate is part of the right to use the resource in the Band's discretion. Section 35(1) is not subject to s. 1 of the Canadian Charter of Rights and Freedoms nor to legislative override under s. 33. The appellant submitted that, if the regulatory power continued, the limits on its extent are set by the word "inconsistent" in s. 52(1) of the Constitution Act, 1982 and the protective and remedial purposes of s. 35(1). This means that aboriginal title entails a right to fish by any non-dangerous method chosen by the aboriginals engaged in fishing. Any continuing governmental power of regulation would have to be exceptional and strictly limited to regulation that is clearly not inconsistent with the protective and remedial purposes of s. 35(1). Thus, counsel for the appellant speculated, "in certain circumstances, necessary and reasonable conservation measures *might* qualify" (emphasis added)—where for example such measures were necessary to prevent serious impairment of the aboriginal rights of present and future generations, where conservation could only be achieved by restricting the right and not by restricting fishing by other users, and where the aboriginal group concerned was unwilling to implement necessary conservation measures. The onus of proving a justification for restrictive regulations would lie with the government by analogy with s. 1 of the Charter.

In response to these submissions and in finding the appropriate interpretive framework for s. 35(1), we start by looking at the background of s. 35(1).

It is worth recalling that while British policy towards the native population was based on respect for their right to occupy their traditional lands, a proposition to which the Royal Proclamation of 1763 bears witness, there was from the outset never any doubt that sovereignty and legislative power, and indeed the underlying title, to such lands vested in the Crown; see *Johnson* v. *M'Intosh* (1823), 8 Wheaton 543 (U.S.S.C.); see also the Royal Proclamation itself (R.S.C., 1985, App. II, No. 1, pp. 4-6); *Calder*, supra, per Judson J., at p. 328, Hall J., at pp. 383 and 402. And there can be no doubt that over the years the rights of the Indians were often honoured in the breach (for one instance in a recent case in this Court, see *Canadian Pacific Ltd.* v. *Paul*, [1988] 2 S.C.R. 654. As MacDonald J. stated in *Pasco* v. *Canadian National Railway Co.*, [1986] 1 C.N.L.R. 35 (B.C.S.C.), at p. 37: "We cannot recount with much pride the treatment accorded to the native people of this country."

For many years, the rights of the Indians to their aboriginal lands—certainly as *legal* rights—were virtually ignored. The leading cases defining Indian rights in the early part of the century were directed at claims supported by the Royal Proclamation or other legal instruments, and even these cases were essentially concerned with settling legislative jurisdiction or the rights of commercial enterprises. For fifty years after the publication of Clement's *The Law of the Canadian Constitution* (3rd ed. 1916), there was a virtual absence of discussion of any kind of Indian rights to land even in academic literature. By the late 1960s, aboriginal claims were not even recognized by the federal government as having any legal status. Thus the Statement of the Government of Canada on Indian Policy (1969), although well meaning, contained the assertion (at p. 11) that "aboriginal claims to land ... are so general and undefined that it is not realistic to think of them as specific claims capable of remedy except through a policy and program that will end injustice to the Indians as members of the Canadian community". In the same general period, the James Bay development by Quebec Hydro was originally initiated without regard to the rights of the Indians who lived there, even though these were expressly protected by a constitutional instrument; see The Quebec Boundaries Extension Act, 1912, S.C. 1912, c. 45. It took a number of judicial decisions and notably the *Calder* case in this Court (1973) to prompt a reassessment of the position being taken by government.

In the light of its reassessment of Indian claims following *Calder*, the federal Government on August 8, 1973 issued "a statement of policy" regarding Indian lands. By it, it sought to "signify the Government's *recognition and acceptance* of its continuing responsibility under the British North America Act for Indians and lands reserved for Indians", which it regarded "as an historic evolution dating back to the Royal Proclamation of 1763, which, whatever differences there may be about its judicial interpretation, stands as a basic declaration of the Indian people's interests in land in this country". (Emphasis added.) See Statement made by the Honourable Jean Chrétien, Minister of Indian Affairs and Northern Development on Claims of Indian and Inuit People, August 8, 1973. The remarks about these lands were intended "as an expression of acknowledged responsibility". But the statement went on to express, for the first time, the government's willingness to negotiate regarding claims of aboriginal title, specifically in British Columbia, Northern Quebec, and the Territories, and this without regard to formal supporting documents. "The Government", it stated, "is now ready to negotiate with authorized representatives of these native peoples on the basis that where their traditional interest in the lands concerned can be established, an agreed form of compensation or benefit will be provided to native peoples in return for their interest."

It is obvious from its terms that the approach taken towards aboriginal claims in the 1973 statement constituted an expression of a policy, rather than a legal position; see also *In All Fairness: A Native Claims Policy—Comprehensive Claims* (1981), pp. 11-12; Slattery, "Understanding Aboriginal Rights" op. cit., at p. 730. As recently as *Guerin v. The Queen*, [1984] 2 S.C.R. 335, the federal government argued in this Court that any federal obligation was of a political character.

It is clear, then, that s. 35(1) of the Constitution Act, 1982, represents the culmination of a long and difficult struggle in both the political forum and the courts for the constitutional recognition of aboriginal rights. The strong representations of native associations and other groups concerned with the welfare of Canada's aboriginal peoples made the adoption of s. 35(1) possible and it is important to note that the provision applies to the Indians, the Inuit and the Métis. Section 35(1), at the least, provides a solid constitutional base upon which subsequent negotiations can take place. It also affords aboriginal peoples constitutional protection against provincial legislative power. We are, of course, aware that this would, in any event, flow from the *Guerin* case, supra, but for a proper understanding of the situation, it is essential to remember that the *Guerin* case was decided after the commencement of the Constitution Act, 1982. In addition to its effect on aboriginal rights, s. 35(1) clarified other issues regarding the enforcement of treaty rights (see Sanders, "Pre-existing Rights: The Aboriginal Peoples of Canada," in Beaudoin and Ratushny, eds., *The Canadian Charter of Rights and Freedoms*, 2nd ed., especially at p. 730).

In our opinion, the significance of s. 35(1) extends beyond these fundamental effects. Professor Lyon in "An Essay on Constitutional Interpretation" (1988), 26 Osgoode Hall L.J. 95, says the following about s. 35(1), at p. 100:

> ... the context of 1982 is surely enough to tell us that this is not just a codification of the case law on aboriginal rights that had accumulated by 1982. Section 35 calls for a just settlement for aboriginal peoples. It renounces the old rules of the game under which the Crown established courts of law and denied those courts the authority to question sovereign claims made by the Crown.

The approach to be taken with respect to interpreting the meaning of s. 35(1) is derived from general principles of constitutional interpretation, principles relating to aboriginal rights, and the purposes behind the constitutional provision itself. Here, we will sketch the framework for an interpretation of "recognized and affirmed" that, in our opinion, gives appropriate weight to the constitutional nature of these words.

In *Reference re Manitoba Language Rights*, [1985] 1 S.C.R. 721, this Court said the following about the perspective to be adopted when interpreting a constitution, at p. 745:

> The Constitution of a country is a statement of the will of the people to be governed in accordance with certain principles held as fundamental and certain prescriptions restrictive of the powers of the legislature and government. It is, as s. 52 of the Constitution Act, 1982 declares, the "supreme law" of the nation, unalterable by the normal legislative process, and unsuffering of laws inconsistent with it. The duty of the judiciary is to interpret and apply the laws of Canada and each of the provinces, and it is thus our duty to ensure that the constitutional law prevails.

The nature of s. 35(1) itself suggests that it be construed in a purposive way. When the purposes of the affirmation of aboriginal rights are considered, it is clear that a generous, liberal interpretation of the words in the constitutional provision is demanded. When the Court of Appeal below was confronted with the submission that s. 35 has no effect on aboriginal or treaty rights and that it is merely a preamble to the parts of the Constitution Act, 1982, which deal with aboriginal rights, it said the following, at p. 322:

> This submission gives no meaning to s. 35. If accepted, it would result in denying its clear statement that existing rights are hereby recognized and affirmed, and would turn that into a mere promise to recognize and affirm those rights sometime in the future ... . To so construe s. 35(1) would be to ignore its language and the principle that the Constitution should be interpreted in a liberal and remedial way. We cannot accept that that principle applies less strongly to aboriginal rights than to the rights guaranteed by the Charter, particularly having regard to the history and to the approach to interpreting treaties and statutes relating to Indians required by such cases as *Nowegijick v. R.*, [1983] 1 S.C.R. 29. ...

In *Nowegijick v. The Queen*, [1983] 1 S.C.R. 29, at p. 36, the following principle that should govern the interpretation of Indian treaties and statutes was set out:

> ... treaties and statutes relating to Indians should be liberally construed and doubtful expressions resolved in favour of the Indians.

297

In *R.* v. *Agawa*, supra, Blair J.A. stated that the above principle should apply to the interpretation of s. 35(1). He added the following principle to be equally applied, at pp. 215–16:

> The second principle was enunciated by the late Associate Chief Justice MacKinnon in *R.* v. *Taylor and Williams* (1981), 34 O.R. (2d) 360. He emphasized the importance of Indian history and traditions as well as the perceived effect of a treaty at the time of its execution. He also cautioned against determining Indian rights "in a vacuum". The honour of the Crown is involved in the interpretation of Indian treaties and, as a consequence, fairness to the Indians is a governing consideration. He said at p. 367:
>
> "The principles to be applied to the interpretation of Indian treaties have been much canvassed over the years. In approaching the terms of a treaty quite apart from the other considerations already noted, the honour of the Crown is always involved and no appearance of 'sharp dealing' should be sanctioned."
>
> This view is reflected in recent judicial decisions which have emphasized the responsibility of Government to protect the rights of Indians arising from the special trust relationship created by history, treaties and legislation: see *Guerin* v. *The Queen*, [1984] 2 S.C.R. 335; 55 N.R. 161; 13 D.L.R. (4th) 321.

In *Guerin*, supra, the Musqueam Band surrendered reserve lands to the Crown for lease to a golf club. The terms obtained by the Crown were much less favourable than those approved by the Band at the surrender meeting. This Court found that the Crown owed a fiduciary obligation to the Indians with respect to the lands. The *sui generis* nature of Indian title, and the historic powers and responsibility assumed by the Crown constituted the source of such a fiduciary obligation. In our opinion, *Guerin*, together with *R.* v. *Taylor and Williams* (1981), 34 O.R. (2d) 360, ground a general guiding principle for s. 35(1). That is, the Government has the responsibility to act in a fiduciary capacity with respect to aboriginal peoples. The relationship between the Government and aboriginals is trust-like, rather than adversarial, and contemporary recognition and affirmation of aboriginal rights must be defined in light of this historic relationship.

We agree with both the British Columbia Court of Appeal below and the Ontario Court of Appeal that the principles outlined above, derived from *Nowegijick*, *Taylor and Williams* and *Guerin*, should guide the interpretation of s. 35(1). As commentators have noted, s. 35(1) is a solemn commitment that must be given meaningful content (Lyon, op. cit.; Pentney, op. cit.; Schwartz, "Unstarted Business: Two Approaches to Defining s. 35—'What's in the Box?' and 'What Kind of Box?'", Chapter XXIV, in First Principles, Second Thoughts: Aboriginal Peoples, Constitutional Reform and Canadian Statecraft; Slattery, op. cit.; and Slattery, "The Hidden Constitution: Aboriginal Rights in Canada" (1984), 32 Am. J. of Comp. Law 361).

In response to the appellant's submission that s. 35(1) rights are more securely protected than the rights guaranteed by the Charter, it is true that s. 35(1) is not subject to s. 1 of the Charter. In our opinion, this does not mean that any law or regulation affecting aboriginal rights will automatically be of no force or effect by the operation of s. 52 of the Constitution Act, 1982. Legislation that affects the exercise of aboriginal rights will nonetheless be valid, if it meets the test for justifying an interference with a right recognized and affirmed under s. 35(1).

There is no explicit language in the provision that authorizes this Court or any court to assess the legitimacy of any government legislation that restricts aboriginal rights. Yet, we find that the words "recognition and affirmation" incorporate the fiduciary relationship referred to earlier and so import some restraint on the exercise of sovereign power. Rights that are recognized and affirmed are not absolute. Federal legislative powers continue, including, of course, the right to legislate with respect to Indians pursuant to s. 91(24) of the Constitution Act, 1867. These powers must, however, now be read together with s. 35(1). In other words, federal power must be reconciled with federal duty and the best way to achieve that reconciliation is to demand the justification of any government regulation that infringes upon or denies aboriginal rights. Such scrutiny is in keeping with the liberal interpretive principle enunciated in *Nowegijick*, supra, and the concept of holding the Crown to a high standard of honourable dealing with respect to the aboriginal peoples of Canada as suggested by *Guerin* v. *The Queen*, supra.

We refer to Professor Slattery's "Understanding Aboriginal Rights", supra, with respect to the task of envisioning a s. 35(1) justificatory process. Professor Slattery, at p. 782, points out that a justificatory process is required as a compromise between a "patchwork" characterization of aboriginal rights whereby past regulations would be read into a definition of the rights, and a characterization that would guarantee aboriginal rights in their original form unrestricted by subsequent regulation. We agree with him that these two extreme positions must be rejected in favour of a justificatory scheme.

Section 35(1) suggests that while regulation affecting aboriginal rights is not precluded, such regulation must be enacted according to a valid objective. Our history has shown, unfortunately all too well, that Canada's aboriginal peoples are justified in worrying about government objectives that may be superficially neutral but which constitute de facto threats to the existence of aboriginal rights and interests. By giving aboriginal rights constitutional status and priority, Parliament and the provinces have sanctioned challenges to social and economic policy objectives embodied in legislation to the extent that aboriginal rights are affected. Implicit in this constitutional scheme is the obligation of the legislature to satisfy the test of justification. The way in which a legislative objective is to be attained must uphold the honour of the Crown and must be in keeping with the unique contemporary relationship, grounded in history and policy, between the Crown and Canada's aboriginal peoples. The extent of legislative or regulatory impact on an existing aboriginal right may be scrutinized so as to ensure recognition and affirmation.

The constitutional recognition afforded by the provision therefore gives a measure of control over government conduct and a strong check on legislative power. While it does not promise immunity from government regulation in a society that, in the twentieth century, is increasingly more complex, interdependent and sophisticated, and where exhaustible resources need protection and management, it does hold the Crown to a substantive promise. The government is required to bear the burden of justifying any legislation that has some negative effect on any aboriginal right protected under s. 35(1).

In these reasons, we will outline the appropriate analysis under s. 35(1) in the context of a regulation made pursuant to the Fisheries Act. We wish to emphasize the importance of context and a case-by-case approach to s. 35(1). Given the generality of the text of the constitutional provision, and especially in light of the complexities of aboriginal history, society and rights, the contours of a justificatory standard must be defined in the specific factual context of each case.

Section 35(1) and the Regulation of the Fisheries

Taking the above framework as guidance, we propose to set out the test for prima facie interference with an existing aboriginal right and for the justification of such an interference. With respect to the question of the regulation of the fisheries, the existence of s. 35(1) of the Constitution Act, 1982, renders the authority of *R. v. Derriksan*, supra, inapplicable. In that case, Laskin C.J., for this Court, found that there was nothing to prevent the Fisheries Act and the Regulations from subjecting the alleged aboriginal right to fish in a particular area to the controls thereby imposed. As the Court of Appeal in the case at bar noted, the *Derriksan* line of cases established that, before April 17, 1982, the aboriginal right to fish was subject to regulation by legislation and subject to extinguishment. The new *constitutional* status of that right enshrined in s. 35(1) suggests that a different approach must be taken in deciding whether regulation of the fisheries might be out of keeping with constitutional protection.

The first question to be asked is whether the legislation in question has the effect of interfering with an existing aboriginal right. If it does have such an effect, it represents a prima facie infringement of s. 35(1). Parliament is not expected to act in a manner contrary to the rights and interests of aboriginals, and, indeed, may be barred from doing so by the second stage of s. 35(1) analysis. The inquiry with respect to interference begins with a reference to the characteristics or incidents of the right at stake. Our earlier observations regarding the scope of the aboriginal right to fish are relevant here. Fishing rights are not traditional property rights. They are rights held by a collective and are in keeping with the culture and existence of that group. Courts must be careful, then, to avoid the application of traditional common law concepts of property as they develop their understanding of what the reasons for judgment in *Guerin*, supra, at p. 382, referred to as the "sui generis" nature of aboriginal rights. (See also Little Bear, "A Concept of Native Title," [1982] 5 Can. Legal Aid Bul. 99.)

While it is impossible to give an easy definition of fishing rights, it is possible, and, indeed, crucial, to be sensitive to the aboriginal perspective itself on the meaning of the rights at stake. For example, it would be artificial to try to create a hard distinction between the right to fish and the particular manner in which that right is exercised.

To determine whether the fishing rights have been interfered with such as to constitute a prima facie infringement of s. 35(1), certain questions must be asked. First, is the limitation unreasonable? Second, does the regulation impose undue hardship? Third, does the regulation deny to the holders of the right their preferred means of exercising that right? The onus of proving a prima facie infringement lies on the individual or group challenging the legislation. In relation to the facts of this appeal, the regulation would be found to be a prima facie interference if it were found to be an adverse restriction on the Musqueam exercise of their right to fish for food. We wish to note here that the issue does not merely require looking at whether the fish catch has been reduced below that needed for the reasonable food and ceremonial needs of the Musqueam Indians. Rather the test involves asking whether either the purpose or the effect of the restriction on net length unnecessarily infringes the interests protected by the fishing right. If, for example, the Musqueam were forced to spend undue time and money per fish caught or if the net length reduction resulted in a hardship to the Musqueam in catching fish, then the first branch of the s. 35(1) analysis would be met.

If a prima facie interference is found, the analysis moves to the issue of justification. This is the test that addresses the question of what constitutes legitimate regulation of a constitutional aboriginal right. The justification analysis would proceed as follows. First, is there a valid legislative objective? Here the court would inquire into whether the objective of Parliament in authorizing the department to enact regulations regarding fisheries is valid. The objective of the department in setting out the particular regulations would also be scrutinized. An objective aimed at preserving s. 35(1) rights by conserving and managing a natural resource, for example, would be valid. Also valid would be objectives purporting to prevent the exercise of s. 35(1) rights that would cause harm to the general populace or to aboriginal peoples themselves, or other objectives found to be compelling and substantial.

The Court of Appeal below held, at p. 331, that regulations could be valid if reasonably justified as "necessary for the proper management and conservation of the resource *or in the public interest*". (Emphasis added.) We find the "public interest" justification to be so vague as to provide no meaningful guidance and so broad as to be unworkable as a test for the justification of a limitation on constitutional rights.

The justification of conservation and resource management, on the other hand, is surely uncontroversial. In *Kruger* v. *The Queen*, [1978] 1 S.C.R. 104, the applicability of the B.C. Wildlife Act, S.B.C. 1966, c. 55, to the appellant members of the Penticton Indian Band was considered by this Court. In discussing that Act, the following was said about the objective of conservation (at p. 112):

> Game conservation laws have as their policy the maintenance of wildlife resources. It might be argued that without some conservation measures the ability of Indians or others to hunt for food would become a moot issue in consequence of the destruction of the resource. The presumption is for the validity of a legislative enactment and in this case the presumption has to mean that in the absence of evidence to the contrary the measures taken by the British Columbia Legislature were taken to maintain an effective resource in the Province for its citizens and not to oppose the interests of conservationists and Indians in such a way as to favour the claims of the former.

While the "presumption" of validity is now outdated in view of the constitutional status of the aboriginal rights at stake, it is clear that the value of conservation purposes for government legislation and action has long been recognized. Further, the conservation and management of our resources is consistent with aboriginal beliefs and practices, and, indeed, with the enhancement of aboriginal rights.

If a valid legislative objective is found, the analysis proceeds to the second part of the justification issue. Here, we refer back to the guiding interpretive principle derived from *Taylor and Williams* and *Guerin*, supra. That is, the honour of the Crown is at stake in dealings with aboriginal peoples. The special trust relationship and the responsibility of the government vis-à-vis aboriginals must be the first consideration in determining whether the legislation or action in question can be justified.

The problem that arises in assessing the legislation in light of its objective and the responsibility of the Crown is that the pursuit of conservation in a heavily used modern fishery inevitably blurs with the efficient allocation and management of this scarce and valued resource. The nature of the constitutional protection afforded by s. 35(1) in this context demands that there be a link between the question of justification and the allocation of priorities in the fishery. The constitutional recognition and affirmation of aboriginal rights may give rise to conflict with the interests of others given the limited nature of the resource. There is a clear need for guidelines that will resolve the allocational problems that arise regarding the fisheries. We refer to the reasons of Dickson J., as he then was, in *Jack* v. *The Queen*, supra, for such guidelines.

In *Jack*, the appellants' defence to a charge of fishing for salmon in certain rivers during a prohibited period was based on the alleged constitutional incapacity of Parliament to legislate such as to deny the Indians their right to fish for food. They argued that art. 13 of the British Columbia Terms of Union imposed a constitutional limitation on the federal power to regulate. While we recognize that the finding that such a limitation had been imposed was not adopted by the majority of this Court, we point out that this case concerns a different constitutional promise that asks this Court to give a meaningful interpretation to recognition and affirmation. That task requires equally meaningful guidelines responsive to the constitutional priority accorded aboriginal rights. We therefore repeat the following passage from *Jack*, at p. 313:

> Conservation is a valid legislative concern. The appellants concede as much. Their concern is in the allocation of the resource after reasonable and necessary conservation measures have been recognized and given effect to. They do not claim the right to pursue the last living salmon until it is caught. Their position, as I understand it, is one which would give effect to an order of priorities of this nature: (i) conservation; (ii) Indian fishing; (iii) non-Indian commercial fishing; or (iv) non-Indian sports fishing; the burden of conservation measures should not fall primarily upon the Indian fishery.
>
> I agree with the general tenor of this argument ... . With respect to whatever salmon are to be caught, then priority ought to be given to the Indian fishermen, subject to the practical difficulties occasioned by international waters and the movement of the fish themselves. But any limitation upon Indian fishing that is established for a valid conservation purpose overrides the protection afforded the Indian fishery by art. 13, just as such conservation measures override other taking of fish.

The constitutional nature of the Musqueam food fishing rights means that any allocation of priorities after valid conservation measures have been implemented must give top priority to Indian food fishing. If the objective pertained to conservation, the conservation plan would be scrutinized to assess priorities. While the detailed allocation of maritime resources is a task that must be left to those having expertise in the area, the Indians' food requirements must be met first when that allocation is established. The significance of giving the aboriginal right to fish for food top priority can be described as follows. If, in a given year, conservation needs required a reduction in the number of fish to be caught such that the number equalled the number required for food by the Indians, then all the fish available after conservation would go to the Indians according to the constitutional nature of their fishing right. If, more realistically, there were still fish after the Indian food requirements were met, then the brunt of conservation measures would be borne by the practices of sport fishing and commercial fishing.

The decision of the Nova Scotia Court of Appeal in *R. v. Denny* (1990), 9 W.C.B. (2d) 438, unreported, judgment rendered March 5, 1990, addresses the constitutionality of the Nova Scotia Micmac Indians' right to fish in the waters of Indian Brook and the Afton River, and does so in a way that accords with our understanding of the constitutional nature of aboriginal rights and the link between allocation and justification required for government regulation of the exercise of the rights. Clarke C.J.N.S., for a unanimous court, found that the Nova Scotia Fishery Regulations enacted pursuant to the federal Fisheries Act were in part inconsistent with the constitutional rights of the appellant Micmac Indians. Section 35(1) of the Constitution Act, 1982, provided the appellants with the right to a top priority allocation of any surplus of the fisheries resource which might exist after the needs of conservation had been taken into account. With respect to the issue of the Indians' priority to a food fishery, Clarke C.J.N.S. noted that the official policy of the federal government recognizes that priority. He added the following, at pp. 22-23:

> I have no hesitation in concluding that factual as well as legislative and policy recognition must be given to the existence of an Indian food fishery in the waters of Indian Brook, adjacent to the Eskasoni Reserve, and the waters of the Afton River after the needs of conservation have been taken into account. ...
>
> To afford user groups such as sports fishermen (anglers) a priority to fish over the legitimate food needs of the appellants and their families is simply not appropriate action on the part of the Federal government. It is inconsistent with the fact that the appellants have for many years, and continue to possess an aboriginal right to fish for food. The appellants have, to employ the words of their counsel, a "right to share in the available resource". This constitutional entitlement is second only to conservation measures that may be undertaken by federal legislation.

Further, Clarke C.J.N.S. found that s. 35(1) provided the constitutional recognition of the aboriginal priority with respect to the fishery, and that the regulations, in failing to guarantee that priority, were in violation of the constitutional provision. He said the following, at p. 25:

> Though it is crucial to appreciate that the rights afforded to the appellants by s. 35(1) are not absolute, the impugned regulatory scheme fails to recognize that this section provides the appellants with a priority of allocation and access to any surplus of the fisheries resource once the needs of conservation have been taken into account. Section 35(1), as applied to these appeals, provides the appellants with an entitlement to fish in the waters in issue to satisfy their food needs, where a surplus exists. To the extent that the regulatory scheme fails to recognize this, it is inconsistent with the Constitution. Section 52 mandates a finding that such regulations are of no force and effect.

In light of this approach, the argument that the cases of *R. v. Hare and Debassige*, supra, and *R. v. Eninew, R. v. Bear* (1984), 12 C.C.C. (3d) 365 (Sask. C.A.), stand for the proposition that s. 35(1) provides no basis for restricting the power to regulate must be rejected, as was done by the Court of Appeal below. In *Hare and Debassige*, which addressed the issue of whether the Ontario Fishery Regulations, C.R.C. 1978, c. 849, applied to members of an Indian Band entitled to the benefit of the Manitoulin Island Treaty which granted certain rights with respect to taking fish, Thorson J.A. emphasized the need for priority to be given to measures directed to the management and conservation of fish stocks with the following observation (at p. 17):

> Since 1867 and subject to the limitations thereon imposed by the Constitution, which of course now includes s. 35 of the Constitution Act, 1982, the constitutional authority and responsibility to make laws in relation to the fisheries has rested with Parliament. Central to Parliament's responsibility has been, and continues to be, the need to provide for the proper management and conservation of our fish stocks, and the need to ensure that they are not depleted or imperilled by deleterious practices or methods of fishing.
>
> The prohibitions found in ss. 12 and 20 of the Ontario regulations clearly serve this purpose. Accordingly, it need not be ignored by our courts that while these pro-

hibitions place limits on the rights of all persons, they are there to serve the larger interest which all persons share in the proper management and conservation of these important resources.

In *Eninew*, Hall J.A. found, at p. 368, that "the treaty rights can be limited by such regulations as are reasonable". As we have pointed out, management and conservation of resources is indeed an important and valid legislative objective. Yet, the fact that the objective is of a "reasonable" nature cannot suffice as constitutional recognition and affirmation of aboriginal rights. Rather, the regulations enforced pursuant to a conservation or management objective may be scrutinized according to the justificatory standard outlined above.

We acknowledge the fact that the justificatory standard to be met may place a heavy burden on the Crown. However, government policy with respect to the British Columbia fishery, regardless of s. 35(1), already dictates that, in allocating the right to take fish, Indian food fishing is to be given priority over the interests of other user groups. The constitutional entitlement embodied in s. 35(1) requires the Crown to ensure that its regulations are in keeping with that allocation of priority. The objective of this requirement is not to undermine Parliament's ability and responsibility with respect to creating and administering overall conservation and management plans regarding the salmon fishery. The objective is rather to guarantee that those plans treat aboriginal peoples in a way ensuring that their rights are taken seriously.

Within the analysis of justification, there are further questions to be addressed, depending on the circumstances of the inquiry. These include the questions of whether there has been as little infringement as possible in order to effect the desired result; whether, in a situation of expropriation, fair compensation is available; and, whether the aboriginal group in question has been consulted with respect to the conservation measures being implemented. The aboriginal peoples, with their history of conservation-consciousness and interdependence with natural resources, would surely be expected, at the least, to be informed regarding the determination of an appropriate scheme for the regulation of the fisheries.

We would not wish to set out an exhaustive list of the factors to be considered in the assessment of justification. Suffice it to say that recognition and affirmation requires sensitivity to and respect for the rights of aboriginal peoples on behalf of the government, courts and indeed all Canadians.

Application to this Case—Is the Net Length Restriction Valid?

The Court of Appeal below found that there was not sufficient evidence in this case to proceed with an analysis of s. 35(1) with respect to the right to fish for food. In reviewing the competing expert evidence, and recognizing that fish stock management is an uncertain science, it decided that the issues at stake in this appeal were not well adapted to being resolved at the appellate court level.

Before the trial, defence counsel advised the Crown of the intended aboriginal rights defence and that the defence would take the position that the Crown was required to prove, as part of its case, that the net length restriction was justifiable as a necessary and reasonable conservation measure. The trial judge found s. 35(1) to be inapplicable to the appellant's defence, based on his finding that no aboriginal right had been established. He therefore found it inappropriate to make findings of fact with respect to either an infringement of the aboriginal right to fish or the justification of such an infringement. He did, however, find that the evidence called by the appellant "[c]asts some doubt as to whether the restriction was necessary as a conservation measure. More particularly, it suggests that there were more appropriate measures that could have been taken if necessary; measures that would not impose such a hardship on the Indians fishing for food. That case was not fully met by the Crown."

According to the Court of Appeal, the findings of fact were insufficient to lead to an acquittal. There was no more evidence before this Court. We also would order a re-trial which would allow findings of fact according to the tests set out in these reasons.

The appellant would bear the burden of showing that the net length restriction constituted a prima facie infringement of the collective aboriginal right to fish for food. If an infringement were found, the onus would shift to the Crown which would have to demonstrate that the regulation is justifiable. To that end, the Crown would have to show that there is no underlying unconstitutional objective such as shifting more of the resource to a user group that ranks below the Musqueam. Further, it would have to show that the regulation sought to be imposed is required to accomplish the needed limitation. In trying to show that the restriction is necessary in the circumstances of the Fraser River fishery, the Crown could use facts pertaining to fishing by other Fraser River Indians.

In conclusion, we would dismiss the appeal and the cross-appeal and affirm the Court of Appeal's setting aside of the conviction. We would accordingly affirm the order for a new trial on the questions of infringement and whether any infringement is nonetheless consistent with s. 35(1), in accordance with the interpretation set out here.

For the reasons given above, the constitutional question must be answered as follows:

Question: Is the net length restriction contained in the Musqueam Indian Band Indian Food Fishing Licence dated March 30, 1984, issued pursuant to the British Columbia Fishery (General) Regulations and the Fisheries Act, R.S.C. 1970, c. F-14, inconsistent with s. 35(1) of the Constitution Act, 1982?

Answer: This question will have to be sent back to trial to be answered according to the analysis set out in these reasons.

Appeal and cross-appeal dismissed. The constitutional question should be sent back to trial to be answered according to the analysis set out in these reasons.

LANDMARK CANADIAN SUPREME COURT DECISION ON ABORIGINAL LAND TITLE: *DELGAMUUKW V. BRITISH COLUMBIA* (1997)

INTRODUCTION

In the 1980s, the Gitksan and Wet'suwet'en peoples filed suit in British Columbia over ownership and jurisdiction over their traditional lands in that province. In finding against the people, the lower court held that they might have an "aboriginal interest" in the land but nothing like ownership. A subsequent appeal, based now on aboriginal title and self-government as opposed to jurisdiction and ownership, was dismissed. Lawyers for the First Nations then took the case to the Supreme Court.

The 1997 Supreme Court of Canada decision on this case is considered by many to be the most significant statement by Canadian courts on the question of aboriginal land rights. This is ironic because the long-term effects of the decision remain largely unknown. It confirms aboriginal title to traditional lands that have not been ceded by treaty. Furthermore, it specifically states that land title is one form of "aboriginal right" referred to in the 1982 Constitution Act (see Constitution Act, 1982 entry). Finally, in sending the case back to lower courts, the judges made a strong point that cases such as this ought to be settled by negotiation rather than by litigation.

One important aspect of the decision was its acknowledgment of the legitimacy and admissibility of the oral evidence of chiefs and elders. On the other hand, however, the entire proceeding (as well as the precedent set by a previous case, *R. v. Van der Peet* [1996]) reinforced the idea that Canadian institutions, such as its courts and governments, have the authority to determine the rights of the native people who live in that country. The court ruled that, while aboriginal title is "*sui generis* and so distinguished from other proprietary interests," aboriginal lands "cannot be used in a manner that is irreconcilable with the nature of the claimant's attachment to those lands." On the grounds that "aboriginal title crystallized at the time [Canadian] sovereignty was asserted," the court reserved for itself the right to make these kinds of determinations and, finally, to determine the nature and scope of aboriginal title.

The full implications of the Delgamuukw decision are still unclear. Businesses, fearing potential legal battles over property rights, have reacted defensively. Federal and provincial authorities across the country are rethinking their entire approach to treaty negotiations. The federal government, through its Indian and Northern Affairs Canada (INAC) agency, has taken the extraordinary step of placing a two-year delay on addressing the implementation of the decision regarding aboriginal title, in effect refusing to abide by the ruling for at least two years. Some First Nations groups suspect that Canada is studying how to get around the intent of the Delgamuukw decision, possibly by implementing Self-Government Framework Agreements that recognize "inherent rights" but not "inherent powers" or by transferring or "devolving" federal responsibilities for some aboriginal people to the provinces and municipalities.

A number of First Nations have filed lawsuits seeking to expand or at least confirm their land titles based on this decision. They hope that the government will, at long last, reject policies of extinguishment and assimilation in favor of a partnership that preserves aboriginal land title, as defined in the Delgamuukw decision. However, despite the rejection of the White Paper some 25 years ago (see Constitution Act, 1982 entry), many fear that federal authorities have begun a new round of efforts to evade their responsibilities. If this is the case, the government will seek to reverse the meaning of the Delgamuukw decision and use it as another political justification for the continued dispossession of the native people who live in Canada.

Delgamuukw v. British Columbia, [1997] 3 S.C.R. 1010

Delgamuukw, also known as Earl Muldoe, suing on his own behalf and on behalf of all the members of the Houses of Delgamuukw and Haaxw (and others suing on their own behalf and on behalf of thirty-eight Gitksan Houses and twelve Wet'-suwet'en Houses as shown in Schedule 1)
Appellants/Respondents on the cross-appeal
v.
Her Majesty The Queen in Right of the Province of British Columbia
Respondent/Appellant on the cross-appeal
and
The Attorney General of Canada
Respondent
and
The First Nations Summit, the Musqueam Nation *et al.* (as shown in Schedule 2), the Westbank First Nation, the B.C. Cattlemen's Association *et al.* (as shown in Schedule 3), Skeena Cellulose Inc., Alcan Aluminum Ltd.
Interveners
Indexed as: Delgamuukw *v.* British Columbia
File No.: 23799.
1997: June 16, 17; 1997: December 11.
Present: Lamer C.J. and La Forest, L'Heureux-Dubé, Sopinka,[1] Cory, McLachlin and Major JJ.
on appeal from the court of appeal for British Columbia

The appellants, all Gitksan or Wet'suwet'en hereditary chiefs, both individually and on behalf of their "Houses", claimed separate portions of 58,000 square kilome-

---

1. Sopinka J. took no part in this judgment.

tres in British Columbia. For the purpose of the claim, this area was divided into 133 individual territories, claimed by the 71 Houses. This represents all of the Wet'-suwet'en people, and all but 12 of the Gitksan Houses. Their claim was originally for "ownership" of the territory and "jurisdiction" over it. (At this Court, this was transformed into, primarily, a claim for aboriginal title over the land in question.) British Columbia counterclaimed for a declaration that the appellants have no right or interest in and to the territory or alternatively, that the appellants' cause of action ought to be for compensation from the Government of Canada.

At trial, the appellants' claim was based on their historical use and "ownership" of one or more of the territories. In addition, the Gitksan Houses have an "adaawk" which is a collection of sacred oral tradition about their ancestors, histories and territories. The Wet'suwet'en each have a "kungax" which is a spiritual song or dance or performance which ties them to their land. Both of these were entered as evidence on behalf of the appellants. The most significant evidence of spiritual connection between the Houses and their territory was a feast hall where the Gitksan and Wet'-suwet'en people tell and retell their stories and identify their territories to remind themselves of the sacred connection that they have with their lands. The feast has a ceremonial purpose but is also used for making important decisions.

The trial judge did not accept the appellants' evidence of oral history of attachment to the land. He dismissed the action against Canada, dismissed the plaintiffs' claims for ownership and jurisdiction and for aboriginal rights in the territory, granted a declaration that the plaintiffs were entitled to use unoccupied or vacant land subject to the general law of the province, dismissed the claim for damages and dismissed the province's counterclaim. No order for costs was made. On appeal, the original claim was altered in two different ways. First, the claims for ownership and jurisdiction were replaced with claims for aboriginal title and self-government, respectively. Second, the individual claims by each House were amalgamated into two communal claims, one advanced on behalf of each nation. There were no formal amendments to the pleadings to this effect. The appeal was dismissed by a majority of the Court of Appeal.

The principal issues on the appeal, some of which raised a number of sub-issues, were as follows: (1) whether the pleadings precluded the Court from entertaining claims for aboriginal title and self-government; (2) what was the ability of this Court to interfere with the factual findings made by the trial judge; (3) what is the content of aboriginal title, how is it protected by s. 35(1) of the *Constitution Act, 1982*, and what is required for its proof; (4) whether the appellants made out a claim to self-government; and, (5) whether the province had the power to extinguish aboriginal rights after 1871, either under its own jurisdiction or through the operation of s. 88 of the *Indian Act*.

Held: The appeal should be allowed in part and the cross-appeal should be dismissed.

Whether the Claims Were Properly before the Court

Per Lamer C.J. and Cory, McLachlin, and Major JJ.: The claims were properly before the Court. Although the pleadings were not formally amended, the trial judge did allow a *de facto* amendment to permit a claim for aboriginal rights other than ownership and jurisdiction. The respondents did not appeal this *de facto* amendment and the trial judge's decision on this point must accordingly stand.

No amendment was made with respect to the amalgamation of the individual claims brought by the individual Gitksan and Wet'suwet'en Houses into two collective claims, one by each nation, for aboriginal title and self-government. The collective claims were simply not in issue at trial and to frame the case on appeal in a different manner would retroactively deny the respondents the opportunity to know the appellants' case.

A new trial is necessary. First, the defect in the pleadings prevented the Court from considering the merits of this appeal. The parties at a new trial would decide whether any amendment was necessary to make the pleadings conform with the other evidence. Then, too, appellate courts, absent a palpable and overriding error, should not substitute their own findings of fact even when the trial judge misapprehended the law which was applied to those facts. Appellate intervention is warranted, however, when the trial court fails to appreciate the evidentiary difficulties inherent in adjudicating aboriginal claims when applying the rules of evidence and interpreting the evidence before it.

Per La Forest and L'Heureux-Dubé JJ.: The amalgamation of the appellants' individual claims technically prevents a consideration of the merits. However, there is a more substantive problem with the pleadings. The appellants sought a declaration of "aboriginal title" but attempted, in essence, to prove that they had complete control over the territory. It follows that what the appellants sought by way of declaration and what they set out to prove by way of the evidence were two different matters. A new trial should be ordered.

McLachlin J. was in substantial agreement.

The Ability of the Court to Interfere with the Trial Judge's Factual Findings
Per Lamer C.J. and Cory, McLachlin and Major JJ.: The factual findings made at trial could not stand because the trial judge's treatment of the various kinds of oral histories did not satisfy the principles laid down in R. v. Van der Peet. The oral histories were used in an attempt to establish occupation and use of the disputed territory which is an essential requirement for aboriginal title. The trial judge refused to admit or gave no independent weight to these oral histories and then concluded that the appellants had not demonstrated the requisite degree of occupation for "ownership". Had the oral histories been correctly assessed, the conclusions on these issues of fact might have been very different.

The Content of Aboriginal Title, How It Is Protected by s. 35(1) of the Constitution Act, 1982, and the Requirements Necessary to Prove It
Per Lamer C.J. and Cory, McLachlin and Major JJ.: Aboriginal title encompasses the right to exclusive use and occupation of the land held pursuant to that title for a variety of purposes, which need not be aspects of those aboriginal practices, customs and traditions which are integral to distinctive aboriginal cultures. The protected uses must not be irreconcilable with the nature of the group's attachment to that land.

Aboriginal title is sui generis, and so distinguished from other proprietary interests, and characterized by several dimensions. It is inalienable and cannot be transferred, sold or surrendered to anyone other than the Crown. Another dimension of aboriginal title is its sources: its recognition by the Royal Proclamation, 1763 and the relationship between the common law which recognizes occupation as proof of possession and systems of aboriginal law pre-existing assertion of British sovereignty. Finally, aboriginal title is held communally.

The exclusive right to use the land is not restricted to the right to engage in activities which are aspects of aboriginal practices, customs and traditions integral to the claimant group's distinctive aboriginal culture. Canadian jurisprudence on aboriginal title frames the "right to occupy and possess" in broad terms and, significantly, is not qualified by the restriction that use be tied to practice, custom or tradition. The nature of the Indian interest in reserve land which has been found to be the same as the interest in tribal lands is very broad and incorporates present-day needs. Finally, aboriginal title encompasses mineral rights and lands held pursuant to aboriginal title should be capable of exploitation. Such a use is certainly not a traditional one.

The content of aboriginal title contains an inherent limit in that lands so held cannot be used in a manner that is irreconcilable with the nature of the claimants' attachment to those lands. This inherent limit arises because the relationship of an aboriginal community with its land should not be prevented from continuing into the future. Occupancy is determined by reference to the activities that have taken place on the land and the uses to which the land has been put by the particular group. If lands are so occupied, there will exist a special bond between the group and the land in question such that the land will be part of the definition of the group's distinctive culture. Land held by virtue of aboriginal title may not be alienated because the land has an inherent and unique value in itself, which is enjoyed by the community with aboriginal title to it. The community cannot put the land to uses which would destroy that value. Finally, the importance of the continuity of the relationship between an aboriginal community and its land, and the non-economic or inherent value of that land, should not be taken to detract from the possibility of surrender to the Crown in exchange for valuable consideration. On the contrary, the idea of surrender reinforces the conclusion that aboriginal title is limited. If aboriginal peoples wish to use their lands in a way that aboriginal title does not permit, then they must surrender those lands and convert them into non-title lands to do so.

Aboriginal title at common law was recognized well before 1982 and is accordingly protected in its full form by s. 35(1). The constitutionalization of common law aboriginal rights, however, does not mean that those rights exhaust the content of s. 35(1). The existence of an aboriginal right at common law is sufficient, but not necessary, for the recognition and affirmation of that right by s. 35(1).

Constitutionally recognized aboriginal rights fall along a spectrum with respect to their degree of connection with the land. At the one end are those aboriginal rights which are practices, customs and traditions integral to the distinctive aboriginal culture of the group claiming the right but where the use and occupation of the land where the activity is taking place is not sufficient to support a claim of title to the land. In the middle are activities which, out of necessity, take place on land and indeed, might be intimately related to a particular piece of land. Although an aboriginal group may not be able to demonstrate title to the land, it may nevertheless have a site-specific right to engage in a particular activity. At the other end of the spectrum is aboriginal title itself which confers more than the right to engage in site-specific activities which are aspects of the practices, customs and traditions of distinctive aboriginal cultures. Site-specific rights can be made out even if title cannot. Because aboriginal rights can vary with respect to their degree of connection with the land, some aboriginal groups may be unable to make out a claim to title, but will nevertheless possess aboriginal rights that are recognized and affirmed by s. 35(1), including site-specific rights to engage in particular activities.

Aboriginal title is a right to the land itself. That land may be used, subject to the inherent limitations of aboriginal title, for a variety of activities, none of which need be individually protected as aboriginal rights under s. 35(1). Those activities are parasitic on the underlying title. Section 35(1), since its purpose is to reconcile the prior presence of aboriginal peoples with the assertion of Crown sovereignty, must recognize and affirm both aspects of that prior presence—first, the occupation of land, and second, the prior social organization and distinctive cultures of aboriginal peoples on that land.

The test for the identification of aboriginal rights to engage in particular activities and the test for the identification of aboriginal title, although broadly similar, are distinct in two ways. First, under the test for aboriginal title, the requirement that the land be integral to the distinctive culture of the claimants is subsumed by the requirement of occupancy. Second, whereas the time for the identification of aboriginal rights is the time of first contact, the time for the identification of aboriginal title is the time at which the Crown asserted sovereignty over the land.

In order to establish a claim to aboriginal title, the aboriginal group asserting the claim must establish that it occupied the lands in question at the time at which the Crown asserted sovereignty over the land subject to the title. In the context of aboriginal title, sovereignty is the appropriate time period to consider for several reasons. First, from a theoretical standpoint, aboriginal title arises out of prior occupation of the land by aboriginal peoples and out of the relationship between the common law and pre-existing systems of aboriginal law. Aboriginal title is a burden on the Crown's underlying title. The Crown, however, did not gain this title until it asserted sovereignty and it makes no sense to speak of a burden on the underlying title before that title existed. Aboriginal title crystallized at the time sovereignty was asserted. Second, aboriginal title does not raise the problem of distinguishing between distinctive, integral aboriginal practices, customs and traditions and those influenced or introduced by European contact. Under common law, the act of occupation or possession is sufficient to ground aboriginal title and it is not necessary to prove that the land was a distinctive or integral part of the aboriginal society before the arrival of Europeans. Finally, the date of sovereignty is more certain than the date of first contact.

Both the common law and the aboriginal perspective on land should be taken into account in establishing the proof of occupancy. At common law, the fact of physical occupation is proof of possession at law, which in turn will ground title to the land. Physical occupation may be established in a variety of ways, ranging from the construction of dwellings through cultivation and enclosure of fields to regular use of definite tracts of land for hunting, fishing or otherwise exploiting its resources. In considering whether occupation sufficient to ground title is established, the group's size, manner of life, material resources, and technological abilities, and the character of the lands claimed must be taken into account. Given the occupancy requirement, it was not necessary to include as part of the test for aboriginal title whether a group demonstrated a connection with the piece of land as being of central significance to its distinctive culture. Ultimately, the question of physical occupation is one of fact to be determined at trial.

If present occupation is relied on as proof of occupation pre-sovereignty, there must be a continuity between present and pre-sovereignty occupation. Since conclusive evidence of pre-sovereignty occupation may be difficult, an aboriginal community may provide evidence of present occupation as proof of pre-sovereignty occupation in support of a claim to aboriginal title. An unbroken chain of continuity need not be established between present and prior occupation. The fact that the nature of occupation has changed would not ordinarily preclude a claim for aboriginal title, as long as a substantial connection between the people and the land is maintained. The only limitation on this principle might be that the land not be used in ways which are inconsistent with continued use by future generations of aboriginals.

At sovereignty, occupation must have been exclusive. This requirement flows from the definition of aboriginal title itself, which is defined in terms of the right to exclusive use and occupation of land. The test must take into account the context of the aboriginal society at the time of sovereignty. The requirement of exclusive occupancy and the possibility of joint title can be reconciled by recognizing that joint title can arise from shared exclusivity. As well, shared, non-exclusive aboriginal rights short of aboriginal title but tied to the land and permitting a number of uses can be established if exclusivity cannot be proved. The common law should develop to recognize aboriginal rights as they were recognized by either *de facto* practice or by aboriginal systems of governance.

Per La Forest and L'Heureux-Dubé JJ.: "Aboriginal title" is based on the continued occupation and use of the land as part of the aboriginal peoples' traditional way of life. This *sui generis* interest is not equated with fee simple ownership; nor can it be described with reference to traditional property law concepts. It is personal in that it is generally inalienable except to the Crown and, in dealing with this interest, the Crown is subject to a fiduciary obligation to treat the aboriginal peoples fairly. There is reluctance to define more precisely the right of aboriginal peoples to live on their lands as their forefathers had lived.

The approach to defining the aboriginal right of occupancy is highly contextual. A distinction must be made between (1) the recognition of a general right to occupy and possess ancestral lands and (2) the recognition of a discrete right to engage in an aboriginal activity in a particular area. The latter has been defined as the traditional use, by a tribe of Indians, that has continued from pre-contact times of a particular area for a particular purpose. By contrast, a general claim to occupy and possess vast tracts of territory is the right to use the land for a variety of activities related to the aboriginal society's habits and mode of life. As well, in defining the nature of "aboriginal title", reference need not be made to statutory provisions and regulations dealing with reserve lands.

In defining the nature of "aboriginal title", reference need not be made to statutory provisions and regulations dealing specifically with reserve lands. Though the interest of an Indian band in a reserve has been found to be derived from, and to be of the same nature as, the interest of an aboriginal society in its traditional tribal lands, it does not follow that specific statutory provisions governing reserve lands should automatically apply to traditional tribal lands.

The "key" factors for recognizing aboriginal rights under s. 35(1) are met in the present case. First, the nature of an aboriginal claim must be identified precisely with regard to particular practices, customs and traditions. When dealing with a claim of "aboriginal title", the court will focus on the occupation and use of the land as part of the aboriginal society's traditional way of life.

Second, an aboriginal society must specify the area that has been continuously used and occupied by identifying general boundaries. Exclusivity means that an aboriginal group must show that a claimed territory is indeed its ancestral territory and not the territory of an unconnected aboriginal society. It is possible that two or more aboriginal groups may have occupied the same territory and therefore a finding of joint occupancy would not be precluded.

Third, the aboriginal right of possession is based on the continued occupation and use of traditional tribal lands since the assertion of Crown sovereignty. However, the date of sovereignty may not be the only relevant time to consider. Continuity may still exist where the present occupation of one area is connected to the pre-sovereignty occupation of another area. Also, aboriginal peoples claiming a right of possession may provide evidence of present occupation as proof of prior occupation. Further, it is not necessary to establish an unbroken chain of continuity.

Fourth, if aboriginal peoples continue to occupy and use the land as part of their traditional way of life, the land is of central significance to them. Aboriginal occupancy refers not only to the presence of aboriginal peoples in villages or permanently settled areas but also to the use of adjacent lands and even remote territories used to pursue a traditional mode of life. Occupancy is part of aboriginal culture in a broad sense and is, therefore, absorbed in the notion of distinctiveness. The *Royal Proclamation, 1763* supports this approach to occupancy.

McLachlin J. was in substantial agreement.

Infringements of Aboriginal Title: The Test of Justification

Per Lamer C.J. and Cory, McLachlin and Major JJ.: Constitutionally recognized aboriginal rights are not absolute and may be infringed by the federal and provincial governments if the infringement (1) furthers a compelling and substantial legislative objective and (2) is consistent with the special fiduciary relationship between the Crown and the aboriginal peoples. The development of agriculture, forestry, mining and hydroelectric power, the general economic development of the interior of British Columbia, protection of the environment or endangered species, and the building of infrastructure and the settlement of foreign populations to support those aims, are objectives consistent with this purpose. Three aspects of aboriginal title are relevant to the second part of the test. First, the right to exclusive use and occupation of land is relevant to the degree of scrutiny of the infringing measure or action. Second, the right to choose to what uses land can be put, subject to the ultimate limit that those uses cannot destroy the ability of the land to sustain future generations of aboriginal peoples, suggests that the fiduciary relationship between the Crown and aboriginal peoples may be satisfied by the involvement of aboriginal peoples in decisions taken with respect to their lands. There is always a duty of consultation and, in most cases, the duty will be significantly deeper than mere consultation. And third, lands held pursuant to aboriginal title have an inescapable economic component which suggests that compensation is relevant to the question of justification as well. Fair compensation will ordinarily be required when aboriginal title is infringed.

Per La Forest and L'Heureux-Dubé JJ.: Rights that are recognized and affirmed are not absolute. Government regulation can therefore infringe upon aboriginal rights if it meets the test of justification under s. 35(1). The approach is highly contextual.

The general economic development of the interior of British Columbia, through agriculture, mining, forestry and hydroelectric power, as well as the related building of infrastructure and settlement of foreign populations, are valid legislative objectives that, in principle, satisfy the first part of the justification analysis. Under the second part, these legislative objectives are subject to accommodation of the aboriginal peoples' interests. This accommodation must always be in accordance with the honour and good faith of the Crown. One aspect of accommodation of "aboriginal title" entails notifying and consulting aboriginal peoples with respect to the development of the affected territory. Another aspect is fair compensation.

McLachlin J. was in substantial agreement.

Self-Government

Per The Court: The errors of fact made by the trial judge, and the resultant need for a new trial, made it impossible for this Court to determine whether the claim to self-government had been made out.

Extinguishment

Per Lamer C.J. and Cory, McLachlin and Major JJ.: Section 91(24) of the *Constitution Act, 1867* (the federal power to legislate in respect of Indians) carries with it the jurisdiction to legislate in relation to aboriginal title, and by implication, the jurisdiction to extinguish it. The ownership by the provincial Crown (under s. 109) of lands held pursuant to aboriginal title is separate from jurisdiction over those lands. Notwithstanding s. 91(24), provincial laws of general application apply *proprio vigore* to Indians and Indian lands.

A provincial law of general application cannot extinguish aboriginal rights. First, a law of general application cannot, by definition, meet the standard "of clear and plain intention" needed to extinguish aboriginal rights without being *ultra vires* the province. Second, s. 91(24) protects a core of federal jurisdiction even from provincial laws of general application through the operation of the doctrine of inter-jurisdictional immunity. That core has been described as matters touching on "Indianness" or the "core of Indianness".

Provincial laws which would otherwise not apply to Indians *proprio vigore* are allowed to do so by s. 88 of the *Indian Act* which incorporates by reference provincial laws of general application. This provision, however, does not "invigorate" provincial laws which are invalid because they are in relation to Indians and Indian lands.

Per La Forest and L'Heureux-Dubé JJ.: The province had no authority to extinguish aboriginal rights either under the *Constitution Act, 1867* or by virtue of s. 88 of the *Indian Act.*

McLachlin J. was in substantial agreement.

The Chief Justice

The judgment of Lamer C.J. and Cory and Major JJ. was delivered by

THE CHIEF JUSTICE—

I. Introduction

1. This appeal is the latest in a series of cases in which it has fallen to this Court to interpret and apply the guarantee of existing aboriginal rights found in s. 35(1) of the *Constitution Act, 1982.* Although that line of decisions, commencing with *R. v. Sparrow,* [1990] 1 S.C.R. 1075, proceeding through the *Van der Peet* trilogy (*R. v. Van der Peet,* [1996] 2 S.C.R. 507, *R. v. N.T.C. Smokehouse Ltd.,* [1996] 2 S.C.R. 672, and *R. v. Gladstone,* [1996] 2 S.C.R. 723), and ending in *R. v. Pamajewon,* [1996] 2 S.C.R. 821, *R. v. Adams,* [1996] 3 S.C.R. 101, and *R. v. Côté,* [1996] 3 S.C.R. 139, have laid down the jurisprudential framework for s. 35(1), this appeal raises a set of interrelated and novel questions which revolve around a single issue—the nature and scope of the constitutional protection afforded by s. 35(1) to common law aboriginal title.

2. In *Adams,* and in the companion decision in *Côté,* I considered and rejected the proposition that claims to aboriginal rights must also be grounded in an underlying claim to aboriginal title. But I held, nevertheless, that aboriginal title was a distinct species of aboriginal right that was recognized and affirmed by s. 35(1). Since aboriginal title was not being claimed in those earlier appeals, it was unnecessary to say more. This appeal demands, however, that the Court now explore and elucidate the implications of the constitutionalization of aboriginal title. The first is the specific content of aboriginal title, a question which this Court has not yet definitively addressed, either at common law or under s. 35(1). The second is the related question of the test for the proof of title, which, whatever its content, is a right *in land,* and its relationship to the definition of the aboriginal rights recognized and affirmed

by s. 35(1) in *Van der Peet* in terms of *activities*. The third is whether aboriginal title, as a right in land, mandates a modified approach to the test of justification first laid down in *Sparrow* and elaborated upon in *Gladstone*.

3. In addition to the relationship between aboriginal title and s. 35(1), this appeal also raises an important practical problem relevant to the proof of aboriginal title which is endemic to aboriginal rights litigation generally — the treatment of the oral histories of Canada's aboriginal peoples by the courts. In *Van der Peet*, I held that the common law rules of evidence should be adapted to take into account the *sui generis* nature of aboriginal rights. In this appeal, the Court must address what specific form those modifications must take.

4. Finally, given the existence of aboriginal title in British Columbia, this Court must address, on cross-appeal, the question of whether the province of British Columbia, from the time it joined Confederation in 1871, until the entrenchment of s. 35(1) in 1982, had jurisdiction to extinguish the rights of aboriginal peoples, including aboriginal title, in that province. Moreover, if the province was without this jurisdiction, a further question arises—whether provincial laws of general application that would otherwise be inapplicable to Indians and Indian lands could nevertheless extinguish aboriginal rights through the operation of s. 88 of the *Indian Act*, R.S.C., 1985, c. I-5.

II. Facts

5. At the British Columbia Supreme Court, McEachern C.J. heard 374 days of evidence and argument. Some of that evidence was not in a form which is familiar to common law courts, including oral histories and legends. Another significant part was the evidence of experts in genealogy, linguistics, archeology, anthropology, and geography.

6. The trial judge's decision (reported at [1991] 3 W.W.R. 97) is nearly 400 pages long, with another 100 pages of schedules. Although I am of the view that there must be a new trial, I nevertheless find it useful to summarize some of the relevant facts, so as to put the remainder of the judgment into context.

A. The Claim at Trial

7. This action was commenced by the appellants, who are all Gitksan or Wet'suwet'en hereditary chiefs, who, both individually and on behalf of their "Houses" claimed separate portions of 58,000 square kilometres in British Columbia. For the purpose of the claim, this area was divided into 133 individual territories, claimed by the 71 Houses. This represents all of the Wet'suwet'en people, and all but 12 of the Gitksan Houses. Their claim was originally for "ownership" of the territory and "jurisdiction" over it. (At this Court, this was transformed into, primarily, a claim for aboriginal title over the land in question.) The province of British Columbia counterclaimed for a declaration that the appellants have no right or interest in and to the territory or alternatively, that the appellants' cause of action ought to be for compensation from the Government of Canada.

B. The Gitksan and Wet'suwet'en Peoples
(1) Demography

8. The Gitksan consist of approximately 4,000 to 5,000 persons, most of whom now live in the territory claimed, which is generally the watersheds of the north and central Skeena, Nass and Babine Rivers and their tributaries. The Wet'suwet'en consist of approximately 1,500 to 2,000 persons, who also predominantly live in the ter-

ritory claimed. This territory is mainly in the watersheds of the Bulkley and parts of the Fraser-Nechako River systems and their tributaries. It lies immediately east and south of the Gitksan.

9. Of course, the Gitksan and Wet'suwet'en are not the only people living in the claimed territory. As noted by both McEachern C.J. at trial (at p. 440) and Lambert J.A. on appeal (at p. 243), there are other aboriginals who live in the claimed territory, notably the Carrier-Sekani and Nishga peoples. Some of these people have unsettled land claims overlapping with the territory at issue here. Moreover, there are also numerous non-aboriginals living there. McEachern C.J. found that, at the time of the trial, the non-aboriginal population in the territory was over 30,000.

(2) *History*

10. There were numerous theories of the history of the Gitksan and Wet'-suwet'en peoples before the trial judge. His conclusion from the evidence was that their ancestors migrated from Asia, probably through Alaska, and spread south and west into the areas which they found to be liveable. There was archeological evidence, which he accepted, that there was some form of human habitation in the territory and its surrounding areas from 3,500 to 6,000 years ago, and intense occupation of the Hagwilget Canyon site (near Hazelton), prior to about 4,000 to 3,500 years ago. This occupation was mainly in or near villages on the Skeena River, the Babine River or the Bulkley River, where salmon, the staple of their diet, was easily obtainable. The other parts of the territory surrounding and between their villages and rivers were used for hunting and gathering for both food and ceremonial purposes. The scope of this hunting and gathering area depended largely on the availability of the required materials in the areas around the villages. Prior to the commencement of the fur trade, there was no reason to travel far from the villages for anything other than their subsistence requirements.

(3) *North American Exploration*

11. There was little European influence in western Canada until the arrival of Capt. Cook at Nootka on Vancouver Island in 1778, which led to the sea otter hunt in the north Pacific. This influence grew with the establishment of the first Hudson's Bay trading post west of the Rockies (although east of the territories claimed) by Simon Fraser in 1805-1806. Trapping for the commercial fur trade was not an aboriginal practice, but rather one influenced by European contact. The trial judge held that the time of direct contact between the Aboriginal Peoples in the claimed territory was approximately 1820, after the trader William Brown arrived and Hudson's Bay had merged with the North West Company.

(4) *Present Social Organization*

12. McEachern C.J. set out a description of the present social organization of the appellants. In his opinion, this was necessary because "one of the ingredients of aboriginal land claims is that they arise from long-term communal rather than personal use or possession of land" (at p. 147). The fundamental premise of both the Gitksan and the Wet'suwet'en peoples is that they are divided into clans and Houses. Every person born of a Gitksan or Wet'suwet'en woman is automatically a member of his or her mother's House and clan. There are four Gitksan and four Wet'suwet'en clans, which are subdivided into Houses. Each House has one or more Hereditary Chief as its titular head, selected by the elders of their House, as well as possibly the Head Chief of the other Houses of the clan. There is no head chief for the clans, but there is a ranking order of precedence within communities or villages, where one House or clan may be more prominent than others.

13. At trial, the appellants' claim was based on their historical use and "ownership" of one or more of the territories. The trial judge held that these are marked, in some cases, by physical and tangible indicators of their association with the territories. He cited as examples totem poles with the Houses' crests carved, or distinctive regalia. In addition, the Gitksan Houses have an "adaawk" which is a collection of sacred oral tradition about their ancestors, histories and territories. The Wet'suwet'en each have a "kungax" which is a spiritual song or dance or performance which ties them to their land. Both of these were entered as evidence on behalf of the appellants (see my discussion of the trial judge's view of this evidence, *infra*).

14. The most significant evidence of spiritual connection between the Houses and their territory is a feast hall. This is where the Gitksan and Wet'suwet'en peoples tell and retell their stories and identify their territories to remind themselves of the sacred connection that they have with their lands. The feast has a ceremonial purpose, but is also used for making important decisions. The trial judge also noted the *Criminal Code* prohibition on aboriginal feast ceremonies, which existed until 1951.

(Deletions)

IV. *Issues*

15. The following are the principal issues which must be addressed in this appeal. As will become apparent in my analysis, some of these issues in turn raise a number of sub-issues which I will address as well:

A. Do the pleadings preclude the Court from entertaining claims for aboriginal title and self-government?

B. What is the ability of this Court to interfere with the factual findings made by the trial judge?

C. What is the content of aboriginal title, how is it protected by s. 35(1) of the *Constitution Act, 1982*, and what is required for its proof?

D. Has a claim to self-government been made out by the appellants?

E. Did the province have the power to extinguish aboriginal rights after 1871, either under its own jurisdiction or through the operation of s. 88 of the *Indian Act*?

(Deletions)

VI. *Conclusion and Disposition*

16. For the reasons I have given above, I would allow the appeal in part, and dismiss the cross-appeal. Reluctantly, I would also order a new trial.

17. I conclude with two observations. The first is that many aboriginal nations with territorial claims that overlap with those of the appellants did not intervene in this appeal, and do not appear to have done so at trial. This is unfortunate, because determinations of aboriginal title for the Gitksan and Wet'suwet'en will undoubtedly affect their claims as well. This is particularly so because aboriginal title encompasses an exclusive right to the use and occupation of land, i.e., to the exclusion of both non-aboriginals and members of other aboriginal nations. It may, therefore, be advisable if those aboriginal nations intervened in any new litigation.

18. Finally, this litigation has been both long and expensive, not only in economic but in human terms as well. By ordering a new trial, I do not necessarily encourage the parties to proceed to litigation and to settle their dispute through the

courts. As was said in *Sparrow*, at p. 1105, s. 35(1) "provides a solid constitutional base upon which subsequent negotiations can take place". Those negotiations should also include other aboriginal nations which have a stake in the territory claimed. Moreover, the Crown is under a moral, if not a legal, duty to enter into and conduct those negotiations in good faith. Ultimately, it is through negotiated settlements, with good faith and give and take on all sides, reinforced by the judgments of this Court, that we will achieve what I stated in *Van der Peet, supra*, at para. 31, to be a basic purpose of s. 35(1)—"the reconciliation of the pre-existence of aboriginal societies with the sovereignty of the Crown". Let us face it, we are all here to stay.

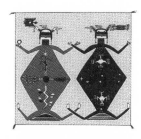

Navajo-Hopi Land Dispute Settlement Act (1996) and Navajo-Hopi Settlement Agreement (1995)

INTRODUCTION

The land dispute between the Hopi and Navajo governments is an extremely complex one. It originated in a conflict over lifestyle and cosmology between the two groups but has been infinitely exaggerated and augmented by the politics of colonialism and coal. The documents presented here are just two of many that have been crafted over the years in an effort to settle what has become a very messy and painful situation.

In 1882, President Chester A. Arthur created a Hopi reservation in the heart of territory that the Hopi considered theirs but that had been intruded upon (homesteaded) by Navajos and some Mormons. At the time, this reservation contained some Navajo families who, against Hopi wishes, refused to move. A conflict grew and intensified until in 1958 the two tribes sued each other in federal court. In the 1962 decision, known as *Healing v. Jones*, the court ruled that the Navajo who had squatted on Hopi land enjoyed "squatters rights" and were entitled to a one-half interest in most of the Hopi reservation. This ruling pleased no one, and in 1974 Congress took matters into its own hands. It passed Public Law 93-531, the Navajo-Hopi Land Settlement Act, partitioning the Hopi reservation and setting up a relocation program to pay for and otherwise assist families that chose to relocate to their own tribal lands.

Some observers at the time believed that the strongly pro-Navajo court decision and subsequent congressional action reflected the government's belief that the Navajo Tribal Council would be more favorable than the Hopi to coal mining. In fact, Peabody Coal has since set up an enormous (and enormously profitable) mining operation on Black Mesa. Black Mesa was once part of Hopi territory, but from the 1930s on it was part of a Bureau of Indian Affairs–mandated Navajo-Hopi Joint Use Area until the 1974 partition left it under Navajo control. Long-time Navajo tribal chair (and convicted felon) Peter MacDonald began his rise to power right after the court decision was announced. Today, the Navajo Nation receives $75 million a year in mining royalties, and many Indian families, mostly Navajo, work at the mines. Access to the Black Mesa mine is from roads built on Navajo territory to the north.

The partition was supposed to take five years, but 25 years later it remains a source of great bitterness on both sides. Since 1882, according to the Hopi Tribal Council, the Hopi have lost to the Navajo roughly one million acres of the original 2.5 million acre reservation. Nevertheless, all of the Hopi have left the land now designated as Navajo. However, especially at Big Mountain, where Navajo have lived for over 100 years, but which is formally Hopi territory, thousands of Navajo have refused to relocate.

The two documents presented here, along with a related Accommodation Agreement, are the latest effort to settle the issue once and for all. They feature a provision for 75-year leases to be offered by the Hopi tribe to Navajo families who insist on remaining on Hopi land. They also grant certain rights to the Navajo pertaining to subsistence activities and land acquisition. The Hopi are anxious to move the process along, in part because they fear that history will repeat itself and that, if the Navajo are allowed to remain, a court will recognize their ownership of the relatively little that remains of the Hopi reservation.

However, like previous efforts, the most recent "settlement" has so far failed to achieve its goal. The Navajo strenuously object to the clause that states that the land they would be leasing is part of the Hopi Nation. Some of these people are old, do not speak English, and live in remote places; they claim that they were left out of the negotiating process entirely. They believe that if they sign the leases they will lose their home lands, their civil rights, and their religious freedom. Many of the Navajo who did sign claim that they did so under duress. Furthermore, in light of the fact that both tribal governments receive extensive payments from Peabody Coal and that large coal beds lie under the disputed land, resisters also fear that the agreements are a prelude to more intensive environmental destruction of their sacred lands.

Ironically, traditional Navajo and Hopi elders have consistently maintained that, freed from interference by both non-native politicians and accommodationist tribal councils, they could work out a just and satisfactory solution to the dispute. These statements have generally received little attention in the press. As of mid-1999, the situation remained unresolved. The latest deadline for signing the leases and agreements is February 1, 2000. After that date, barring any new developments, Hopi and U.S. government authorities may move in at any time to evict unyielding Navajo by force.

NAVAJO-HOPI LAND DISPUTE SETTLEMENT ACT
Public Law 104-301 [S. 1973]
October 11, 1996
Navajo-Hopi Land Dispute Settlement Act of 1996
An Act
To provide for the settlement of the Navajo-Hopi land dispute, and for other purposes.
Be it enacted by the Senate and House of Representatives of the United States of America in Congress assembled,

Section 1. <25 USC 640d note> Short Title.
This Act may be cited as the "Navajo-Hopi Land Dispute Settlement Act of 1996".

Sec. 2. <25 USC 640d note> Findings.

The Congress finds that—

(1) it is in the public interest for the Tribe, Navajos residing on the Hopi Partitioned Lands, and the United States to reach a peaceful resolution of the long-standing disagreements between the parties under the Act commonly known as the "Navajo-Hopi Land Settlement Act of 1974" (Public Law 93-531; 25 U.S.C. 640d et seq.);

(2) it is in the best interest of the Tribe and the United States that there be a fair and final settlement of certain issues remaining in connection with the Navajo-Hopi Land Settlement Act of 1974, including the full and final settlement of the multiple claims that the Tribe has against the United States;

(3) this Act, together with the Settlement Agreement executed on December 14, 1995, and the Accommodation Agreement (as incorporated by the Settlement Agreement), provide the authority for the Tribe to enter agreements with eligible Navajo families in order for those families to remain residents of the Hopi Partitioned Lands for a period of 75 years, subject to the terms and conditions of the Accommodation Agreement;

(4) the United States acknowledges and respects—

    (A) the sincerity of the traditional beliefs of the members of the Tribe and the Navajo families residing on the Hopi Partitioned Lands; and

    (B) the importance that the respective traditional beliefs of the members of the Tribe and Navajo families have with respect to the culture and way of life of those members and families;

(5) this Act, the Settlement Agreement, and the Accommodation Agreement provide for the mutual respect and protection of the traditional religious beliefs and practices of the Tribe and the Navajo families residing on the Hopi Partitioned Lands;

(6) the Tribe is encouraged to work with the Navajo families residing on the Hopi Partitioned Lands to address their concerns regarding the establishment of family or individual burial plots for deceased family members who have resided on the Hopi Partitioned Lands; and

(7) neither the Navajo Nation nor the Navajo families residing upon Hopi Partitioned Lands were parties to or signers of the Settlement Agreement between the United States and the Hopi Tribe.

Sec. 3. <25 USC 640d note> Definitions.

Except as otherwise provided in this Act, for purposes of this Act, the following definitions shall apply:

(1) Accommodation.—The term "Accommodation" has the meaning provided that term under the Settlement Agreement.

(2) Hopi partitioned lands.—The term "Hopi Partitioned Lands" means lands located in the Hopi Partitioned Area, as defined in section 168.1(g) of title 25, Code of Federal Regulations (as in effect on the date of enactment of this Act).

(3) Navajo partitioned lands.—The term "Navajo Partitioned Lands" has the meaning provided that term in the proposed regulations issued on November 1, 1995, at 60 Fed. Reg. 55506.

(4) New lands.—The term "New Lands" has the meaning provided that term in section 700.701(b) of title 25, Code of Federal Regulations.

(5) Secretary.—The term "Secretary" means the Secretary of the Interior.

(6) Settlement agreement.—The term "Settlement Agreement" means the agreement between the United States and the Hopi Tribe executed on December 14, 1995.

(7) Tribe.—The term "Tribe" means the Hopi Tribe.

(8) Newly acquired trust lands.—The term "newly acquired trust lands" means lands taken into trust for the Tribe within the State of Arizona pursuant to this Act or the Settlement Agreement.

Sec. 4. <25 USC 640d note> Ratification of Settlement Agreement.

The United States approves, ratifies, and confirms the Settlement Agreement.

Sec. 5. <25 USC 640d note> Conditions for Lands Taken into Trust.

The Secretary shall take such action as may be necessary to ensure that the following conditions are met prior to taking lands into trust for the benefit of the Tribe pursuant to the Settlement Agreement:

(1) Selection of lands taken into trust.—

   (A) Primary area.—In accordance with section 7(a) of the Settlement Agreement, the primary area within which lands acquired by the Tribe may be taken into trust by the Secretary for the benefit of the Tribe under the Settlement Agreement shall be located in northern Arizona.

   (B) Requirements for lands taken into trust in the primary area.—Lands taken into trust in the primary area referred to in subparagraph (A) shall be—

      (i) land that is used substantially for ranching, agriculture, or another similar use; and

      (ii) to the extent feasible, in contiguous parcels.

(2) Acquisition of lands.—Before taking any land into trust for the benefit of the Tribe under this section, the Secretary shall ensure that—

   (A) at least 85 percent of the eligible Navajo heads of household (as determined under the Settlement Agreement) have entered into an accommodation or have chosen to relocate and are eligible for relocation assistance (as determined under the Settlement Agreement); and

   (B) the Tribe has consulted with the State of Arizona concerning the lands proposed to be placed in trust, including consulting with the State concerning the impact of placing those lands into trust on the State and political subdivisions thereof resulting from the removal of land from tax rolls in a manner consistent with the provisions of part 151 of title 25, Code of Federal Regulations.

(3) Prohibition.—The Secretary may not, pursuant to the provisions of this Act and the Settlement Agreement, place lands, any portion of which are located within or contiguous to a 5-mile radius of an incorporated town or city (as those terms are defined by the Secretary) in northern Arizona, into trust for benefit of the Tribe without specific statutory authority.

(4) Expeditious action by the secretary.—Consistent with all other provisions of this Act, the Secretary is directed to take lands into trust under this Act expeditiously and without undue delay.

Sec. 6. <25 USC 640d note> Acquisition through Condemnation of Certain Interspersed Lands.

    (a)   In General.—

        (1)   Action by the secretary.—

            (A)   In general.—The Secretary shall take action as specified in subparagraph (B), to the extent that the Tribe, in accordance with section 7(b) of the Settlement Agreement—

                (i)   acquires private lands; and

                (ii)   requests the Secretary to acquire through condemnation interspersed lands that are owned by the State of Arizona and are located within the exterior boundaries of those private lands in order to have both the private lands and the State lands taken into trust by the Secretary for the benefit of the Tribe.

            (B)   Acquisition through condemnation.—With respect to a request for an acquisition of lands through condemnation made under subparagraph (A), the Secretary shall, upon the recommendation of the Tribe, take such action as may be necessary to acquire the lands through condemnation and, with funds provided by the Tribe, pay the State of Arizona fair market value for those lands in accordance with applicable Federal law, if the conditions described in paragraph (2) are met.

        (2)   Conditions for acquisition through condemnation.—The Secretary may acquire lands through condemnation under this subsection if—

            (A)   that acquisition is consistense of obtaining not more than 500,000 acres of land to be taken into trust for the Tribe;

            (B)   the State of Arizona concurs with the United States that the acquisition is consistent with the interests of the State; and

            (C)   the Tribe pays for the land acquired through condemnation under this subsection.

    (b)   Disposition of Lands.—If the Secretary acquires lands through condemnation under subsection (a), the Secretary shall take those lands into trust for the Tribe in accordance with this Act and the Settlement Agreement.

    (c)   Private Lands.—The Secretary may not acquire private lands through condemnation for the purpose specified in subsection (a)(2)(A).

Sec. 7. <25 USC 640d note> Action to Quiet Possession.

If the United States fails to discharge the obligations specified in section 9(c) of the Settlement Agreement with respect to voluntary relocation of Navajos residing on Hopi Partitioned Lands, or section 9(d) of the Settlement Agreement, relating to the implementation of sections 700.137 through 700.139 of title 25, Code of Federal Regulations, on the New Lands, including failure for reason of insufficient funds made available by appropriations or otherwise, the Tribe may bring an action to quiet possession that relates to the use of the Hopi Partitioned Lands after February 1, 2000, by a Navajo family that is eligible for an accommodation, but fails to enter into an accommodation.

Sec. 8. <25 USC 640d note> Payment to State of Arizona.

    (a)   Authorization of Appropriations.—Subject to subsection (b), there are authorized to be appropriated to the Department of the Interior $250,000 for fiscal year 1998, to be used by the Secretary of the Interior for making a payment to the State of Arizona.

(b)   Payment.—The Secretary shall make a payment in the amount specified in subsection (a) to the State of Arizona after an initial acquisition of land from the State has been made by the Secretary pursuant to section 6.

Sec. 9. <25 USC 640d note> 75-Year Leasing Authority.

The first section of the Act of August 9, 1955 (69 Stat. 539, chapter 615; 25 U.S.C. 415) is amended by adding at the end the following new subsections:

"(c)   Leases Involving the Hopi Tribe and the Hopi Partitioned Lands Accommodation Agreement.—Notwithstanding subsection (a), a lease of land by the Hopi Tribe to Navajo Indians on the Hopi Partitioned Lands may be for a term of 75 years, and may be extended at the conclusion of the term of the lease.

"(d)   Definitions.—For purposes of this section—
   "(1)   the term 'Hopi Partitioned Lands' means lands located in the Hopi Partitioned Area, as defined in section 168.1(g) of title 25, Code of Federal Regulations (as in effect on the date of enactment of this subsection); and
   "(2)   the term 'Navajo Indians' means members of the Navajo Tribe".

Sec.10. <25 USC 640d note> Reauthorization of the Navajo-Hopi Relocation Housing Program.

Section 25(a)(8) of Public Law 93-531 (25 U.S.C. 640d-24(a)(8)) is amended by striking "1996, and 1997" and inserting "1996, 1997, 1998, 1999, and 2000".

Sec. 11. <25 USC 640d note> Effect of This Act on Cases Involving the Navajo Nation and the Hopi Tribe.

Nothing in this Act or the amendments made by this Act shall be interpreted or deemed to preclude, limit, or endorse, in any manner, actions by the Navajo Nation that seek, in court, an offset from judgments for payments received by the Hopi Tribe under the Settlement Agreement.

Sec. 12. <25 USC 640d note> Water Rights.

(a)   In General.—
   (1)   Water rights.—Subject to the other provisions of this section, newly acquired trust lands shall have only the following water rights:
      (A)   The right to the reasonable use of groundwater pumped from such lands.
      (B)   All rights to the use of surface water on such lands existing under State law on the date of acquisition, with the priority date of such right under State law.
      (C)   The right to make any further beneficial use on such lands which is unappropriated on the date each parcel of newly acquired trust lands is taken into trust. The priority date for the right shall be the date the lands are taken into trust.
   (2)   Rights not subject to forfeiture or abandonment.—The Tribe's water rights for newly acquired trust lands shall not be subject to forfeiture or abandonment arising from events occurring after the date the lands are taken into trust.

(b) Recognition as valid uses.—

 (1) Groundwater.—With respect to water rights associated with newly acquired trust lands, the Tribe, and the United States on the Tribe's behalf, shall recognize as valid all uses of groundwater which may be made from wells (or their subsequent replacements) in existence on the date each parcel of newly acquired trust land is acquired and shall not object to such groundwater uses on the basis of water rights associated with the newly acquired trust lands. The Tribe, and the United States on the Tribe's behalf, may object only to the impact of groundwater uses on newly acquired trust lands which are initiated after the date the lands affected are taken into trust and only on grounds allowed by the State law as it exists when the objection is made. The Tribe, and the United States on the Tribe's behalf, shall not object to the impact of groundwater uses on the Tribe's right to surface water established pursuant to subsection (a)(3) when those groundwater uses are initiated before the Tribe initiates its beneficial use of surface water pursuant to subsection (a)(3).

 (2) Surface water.—With respect to water rights associated with newly acquired trust lands, the Tribe, and the United States on the Tribe's behalf, shall recognize as valid all uses of surface water in existence on or prior to the date each parcel of newly acquired trust land is acquired and shall not object to such surface water uses on the basis of water rights associated with the newly acquired trust lands, but shall have the right to enforce the priority of its rights against all junior water rights the exercise of which interfere with the actual use of surface water rights.

 (3) Rule of construction.—Nothing in paragraph (1) or (2) shall preclude the Tribe, or the United States on the Tribe's behalf, from asserting objections to water rights and uses on the basis of the Tribe's water rights on its currently existing trust lands.

(c) Applicability of State Law on Lands Other Than Newly Acquired Lands.— The Tribe, and the United States on the Tribe's behalf, further recognize that State law applies to water uses on lands, including subsurface estates, that exist within the exterior boundaries of newly acquired trust lands and that are owned by any party other than the Tribe.

(d) Adjudication of Water Rights on Newly Acquired Trust Lands.—The Tribe's water rights on newly acquired trust lands shall be adjudicated with the rights of all other competing users in the court now presiding over the Little Colorado River Adjudication, or if that court no longer has jurisdiction, in the appropriate State or Federal court. Any controversies between or among users arising under Federal or State law involving the Tribe's water rights on newly acquired trust lands shall be resolved in the court now presiding over the Little Colorado River Adjudication, or, if that court no longer has jurisdiction, in the appropriate State or Federal court. Nothing in this subsection shall be construed to affect any court's jurisdiction: Provided, that the Tribe shall administer all water rights established in subsection (a).

(e) Prohibition.—Water rights for newly acquired trust lands shall not be used, leased, sold, or transported for use off of such lands or the Tribe's other trust lands: Provided, that the Tribe may agree with other persons having junior water rights to subordinate the Tribe's senior water rights. Water rights for newly acquired trust lands can only be used on those lands or other trust lands of the Tribe located within the same river basin tributary to the main stream of the Colorado River.

(f) Subsurface Interests.—On any newly acquired trust lands where the subsurface interest is owned by any party other than the Tribe, the trust status of the surface ownership shall not impair any existing right of the subsurface owner to develop the subsurface interest and to have access to the surface for the purpose of such development.

(g) Statutory Construction with Respect to Water Rights of Other Federally Recognized Indian Tribes.—Nothing in this section shall affect the water rights of any other federally recognized Indian tribe with a priority date earlier than the date of the newly acquired trust.

(h) Statutory Construction.—Nothing in this section shall be construed to determine the law applicable to water use on lands owned by the United States, other than on the newly acquired trust lands. The granting of the right to make beneficial use of unappropriated surface water on the newly acquired trust lands with a priority date such lands are taken into trust shall not be construed to imply that such right is a Federal reserved water right. Nothing in this section or any other provision of this Act shall be construed to establish any Federal reserved right to groundwater. Authority for the Secretary to take land into trust for the Tribe pursuant to the Settlement Agreement and this Act shall be construed as having been provided solely by the provisions of this Act.

NAVAJO-HOPI SETTLEMENT AGREEMENT

This Settlement Agreement ("Agreement") is made and entered into this 14th day of December, 1995, between the United States of America ("United States") and the Hopi Tribe ("Tribe"), acting by and through their designated representatives.

A. WHEREAS, it is in the public benefit for the Tribe, Navajos residing on the Hopi Partitioned Lands ("HPL"), and the United States to reach a peaceful resolution of a disagreement that has caused great acrimony and hardship and drained both the Hopi Tribe and the Navajo Nation of resources for many decades.

B. WHEREAS, the Tribe and the United States agree that it is in the best interest of the Tribe and the United States that a final settlement of certain issues remaining in connection with the Navajo-Hopi Settlement Act, Pub. L. 93-531, as amended, be reached by negotiation and voluntary agreement among the affected parties.

C. WHEREAS, the Tribe and Navajo families living on the HPL have reached by negotiation and voluntary accord an agreement on the terms pursuant to which certain Navajo families may continue to live on the HPL under a 75-year accommodation agreement. These negotiated terms are set forth in the documents included here as Attachment A, when read together, and are hereinafter referred to as the "Accommodation Terms." An accommodation provided to an eligible Navajo family in accordance with the Accommodation Terms is referred to hereinafter as an "Accommodation." The Navajos eligible for an Accommodation are Navajos on List A (a copy of which is included here as Attachment B), and, in addition, (i) those Navajos domiciled on the HPL who were temporarily away for purposes of education, employment, military service or medical need at the time List A was prepared in 1992; (ii) those Navajo legal residents who resided full-time on the HPL in 1992 who are certi-fied by the Office of Navajo Hopi Indian Relocation ("ONHIR") after October 30, 1992, as eligible for relocation assistance; and (iii) such other individuals, as agreed to by the Navajo and Hopi tribes. (In calculating the percentages discussed in Sec-tions 3, 6 and 7 of this Agreement, the head of household (as defined in 25 C.F.R. 700.69(b) (1995)) included on List A, or his/her successor head of household, is counted but other family members are not included in the calculation.)

D. WHEREAS, the United States and the Tribe wish to encourage the circumstances under which the Tribe will allow those Navajo families currently residing on the HPL who enter into an Accommodation to remain on the HPL. A Navajo family that has entered into an Accommodation with the Hopi Tribe is referred to herein as an "Ac-commodation Signatory.

E. WHEREAS, the continued occupation of the HPL by the Navajo families deprives the Tribe of certain uses of its land. The Tribe's agreement to allow Navajo families to remain on the HPL is based on the understanding that additional lands will be taken into trust for the Tribe for use by Hopi Tribal members. The Tribe and the Secretary of the Department of the Interior ("Secretary") agree that, under the unusual circum-stances of this long, historical disagreement over the Hopi Lands, the taking of addi-tional lands into trust for the Tribe, as specified in Section 7, is necessary to bring about a resolution of the litigation and the problems that underlie it and is consonant with the goals identified in 25 U.S.C. Sec. 465 and the corresponding regulations.

F. WHEREAS, to the extent the Tribe accommodates Navajo families who would other-wise have to be relocated from the HPL, the United States will save some of the ex-pense of completing the relocation program, which has already cost over $330 million.

G. WHEREAS, the Tribe currently has three actions pending against the United States and, as part of this settlement, is forgoing a fourth action against the United States. These are:

i. Hopi Tribe v. Navajo Tribe, et al., CIV 85-801 PHX-EHC, which is pending in the United States District Court in Phoenix, Arizona. In this case ("the Rental case"), the Tribe has brought an action against the United States, among other things, for the alleged failure of the Secretary of the Interior ("Secretary") to make on a timely basis the fair rental value determinations required by 25 U.S.C. Sec. 640d- 15(a). On July 5, 1985, the Tribe filed a motion for partial summary judgment on this ground against the United States. On April 2, 1990, the District Court denied as moot, without prejudice, the portion of the motion dealing with the United States. The Tribe has indicated to the United States its desire formally to renew its motion and to seek, either in the District Court or in the Court of Federal Claims, damages on a claim alleging a breach of the Secretary's duty to issue certain rental determinations in a timely manner.

ii. Secakuku v. Hale, et al., Nos. 94-17032, 95-15029, which is pending in the United States Court of Appeals for the Ninth Circuit. In this case ("the Dam-age case"), the Tribe has brought an action against the United States pursuant to 25 U.S.C. Sec. 640d-17(a)(3), alleging, among other things, that the United States is jointly and severally liable with the Navajo Nation for any post-parti-tion damage to the HPL caused by pre-partition overgrazing. On January 15,

1993, the United States District Court in Phoenix entered judgment for the United States, holding that the United States in not liable to the Tribe for any portion of the post-partition damage. The Tribe has appealed this issue and is awaiting a decision by the Ninth Circuit Court of Appeals.

iii.   Hopi Tribe v. United States of America, CIV Nos. 319-84L, 320-84L, 321-84L, and 651-89L, which are pending in the United States Court of Federal Claims. In these cases (referred to collectively as "the Court of Federal Claims cases"), the Tribe is suing the United States, inter alia, for breach of its fiduciary duty arising from its failure to collect (a) livestock trespass penalties (No. 319-84L), (b) forage consumed fees (No. 320-84L), and (c) property damage fees on behalf of the Tribe (No. 321-84L). All three claims are asserted in No. 651-89L. In these actions, the United States argued that some of the Tribe's claims were barred by the statute of limitations. The Tribe concedes that the six-year statute of limitations, 25 U.S.C. 2501, governing claims against the United States bars the Tribe's claims arising prior to June 22, 1978. For purposes of settlement, the Tribe and the United States have parsed the Court of Federal Claims cases into three parts: (1) all livestock trespass penalty claims for the period prior to and through 1982 and all other non-livestock trespass penalty claims alleged in the Court of Federal Claims cases for all periods through and including 1996; (2) all livestock trespass penalty claims for the period 1983 through and including 1988; and (3) all livestock trespass penalty claims for the period 1989 through and including 1996. The Court of Federal Claims cases are currently stayed.

iv.   Claim by the Hopi Tribe Against the United States for Failure to Give the Tribe Quiet Possession of Its Lands. During the course of the Ninth Circuit ordered mediation, which commenced in May 1991, and as part of the parties' efforts to bring about a consensual resolution of the longstanding problems concerning use of the Hopi Lands, the Tribe has refrained from bringing litigation against the United States for the alleged failure of the United States, in the past and currently, to give it quiet possession of Hopi Lands that are used and occupied by Navajo families. Such potential litigation includes, inter alia, an injunctive action seeking to have the Navajo families removed, an action for a temporary taking without compensation, and an action for breach of trust. Any such potential actions are referred to herein as the "Quiet Possession Claim."

H. WHEREAS, the United States has denied that it has any liability to the Tribe in the Rental, Damage, or Court of Federal Claims cases and denies it has any liability in the Quiet Possession Claim.

I. WHEREAS, the United States and the Tribe wish to improve their relationship and to compromise their differences in the Rental, Damage and Court of Federal Claims cases and in a Quiet Possession Claim.

J. WHEREAS, the Tribe and the United States benefit from these voluntary settlements and, to that end, the Tribe, the Secretary and the United States Attorney General will fully support this settlement.

K. NOW, THEREFORE, it is hereby agreed by the Tribe and the United States that the Rental, Damage, and Court of Federal Claims cases, and the Quiet Possession Claim be settled and compromised on the following terms and conditions.

Terms of the Agreement

1. Compromise and Settlement by the Tribe of Certain Claims against the United States in the Rental Case Regrading Certain Fair Rental Value Determinations: The Tribe agrees to refrain forever from instituting, maintaining, prosecuting or continuing to maintain or prosecute any suit or action against the United States based upon any claim, demand, action, cause of action, or liability of any nature whatsoever (including any claim for damages or compensatory interest for delay in issuance of the rental determinations), whether known or unknown, which claim, demand, action, cause of action, or liability arises from the Secretary's failure, prior to January 1, 1997, to issue initial final rental determinations on the merits for Navajo homesite, farming and grazing use of the HPL for the years 1979 through 1995. (This bar to the Tribe's claim applies even if the Secretary's initial final rental determination on the merits is subsequently set aside or remanded by a court which reviews the administrative decision.) Claims, if any, concerning a failure by the Secretary (a) after January 1, 1997, to have entered initial final rental determinations on the merits for the above-described rental periods and (b) to enter rental determinations for any rental period after 1995, are not covered by this Agreement.

2. Compromise and Settlement by the Tribe of all Claims Against the United States in the Damage Case: The Tribe agrees to refrain forever from instituting, maintaining, prosecuting, or continuing to maintain or prosecute any suit or action against the United States based upon any claim, demand, action, cause of action, or liability that was alleged, or could have been alleged, in the Damage case. The Tribe and the United States agree, pursuant to FRAP 42(b), to file a motion to dismiss the Tribe's appeal against the United States in the Damage case within one week of the date of the signing of this Agreement. If the motion is not granted and the Tribe is ultimately awarded at judgment in damages against the United States, the Tribe agrees that the obligations of the United States in the Damage case will be met by the United States' payment of $2,400,000.00 pursuant to Section 6(a) of this Agreement. If, prior to a joint filing of the United States' and Tribe's motion to dismiss the Tribe's claims against the United States, the Ninth Circuit issues a decision or enters judgment in the United States' favor, the United States shall pay nothing to the Tribe for compromise of the Damage case.

3. Compromise and Settlement by the Tribe of all Claims Against the United States in the Court of Federal Claims Cases:

    (a) The Tribe and the United States agree to file stipulations for dismissal with prejudice of all claims in the Court of Federal Claims cases, except those identified in Subsections 3(b) and 3(c). That stipulation shall be made within two weeks after the United States Congress enacts and the President signs the amendment to 25 U.S.C. Sec. 415(a) or Sec. 635 described in Section 5 below. The Tribe further agrees that after so moving for dismissal it must and will refrain forever from instituting, maintaining, prosecuting, or continuing to maintain or prosecute any suit or action against the United States based upon any claim, demand, actions, cause of action, or liability that was alleged or could have been alleged in any pleading in the Court of Federal Claims cases for any year prior to and through 1982.

    (b) The Tribe and the United States further agree to file stipulations for dismissal with predjudice, pursuant to Rule 41 of the Court of Federal

Claims Rules, of any livestock trespass penalty claims for the period 1983 through and including 1988 after 65 percent of the Navajo heads of household eligible for an Accommodation (as defined in paragraph C on pages 1-2 of this Agreement) have entered into an Accommodation or have chosen to relocate and are eligible for relocation assistance. The Tribe further agrees that after so moving for dismissal it must and will refrain forever from instituting, maintaining, prosecuting, or continuing to maintain or prosecute any suit or action against the United States based upon any claim, demand, actions, cause of action, or liability that was alleged or could have been alleged in any pleading in the Court of Federal Claims cases for any year prior to and through 1988.

(c) The Tribe and the United States further agree to file stipulations for dismissal with prejudice, pursuant to Rule 41 of the Court of Federal Claims Rules, of any livestock trespass penalty claims for the period 1989 through and including 1996 after 75 percent of the Navajo heads of household eligible for an Accommodation (as defined in paragraph C on pages 1-2 of this Agreement) have entered into an Accommodation or have chosen to relocate and are eligible for relocation assistance. The Tribe further agrees that after so moving for dismissal it must and will refrain forever from instituting, maintaining, prosecuting, or continuing to maintain or prosecute any suit or action against the United States based upon any claim, demand, actions, cause of action, or liability that was alleged or could have been alleged in any pleading in the Court of Federal Claims cases for any year prior to and through 1996.

(d) With each dismissal with prejudice of the claims described in subsection (a), (b) or (c) above, the Tribe may obtain funds from the trust account as provided in Section 6 below.

4. Compromise and Settlement of the Quiet Possession Claim and Agreement by the Tribe to Provide an Accommodation for Certain Navajo Families Pursuant to the Accommodation Terms:

(a) The Tribe agrees to accommodate Navajo residents of the HPL who, pursuant to the Accommodation Terms, are eligible to enter into an Accommodation, in the manner and according to the terms as set forth in Attachment A.

(b) The Tribe agrees to refrain forever from instituting, maintaining, prosecuting, or continuing to maintain or prosecute any suit or action in law or equity against the United States based on any claim, demand, cause of action, or liability regarding quiet possession of Hopi Partitioned Lands which action arises out of: (i) any Navajo use or occupancy that occurred prior to the date of the signing of this Agreement; and (ii) any use or occupancy of Hopi Partitioned Lands that occurs prior to February 1, 2000, by Navajos who are eligible for an Accommodation; and (iii) any use or occupancy of Hopi Partitioned Lands by Navajo Accommodation Signatories in accordance with the Accommodation Terms during the term of the Accommodation.

(c) Contingencies and Remedies.—However, in the event that the United States does not provide consideration pursuant to the terms of Section 7, the Tribe preserves pursuant to Section 7(d) any Quiet Possession Claim it may have under 28 U.S.C. Sec. 1491 and 1505 arising out of the use of the HPL after January 1, 1997, by any Navajo family who has entered into an Accommodation. In the event that the United States does not discharge the obligations set forth in Sections 9(c) and 9(d), the Tribe preserves pursuant to Section 9(e) any Quiet Possession Claim it may have arising out of the use of the HPL after February 1, 2000, by any Navajo family eligible for an Accommodation who does not enter into one.

5. Agreement by the Tribe to Seek Legislation: The Tribe agrees to seek enactment prior to December 31, 1996, by the United States Congress, of an amendment to 25 U.S.C. Sec. 415(a) or Sec. 635 that would authorize the Tribe to lease land to the Navajo families for a term of seventy-five (75) years. If such legislation is not enacted, the Tribe shall in good faith attempt to negotiate an alternative leasing arrangement, and the terms of this Agreement could be amended to meet that circumstance.

6. Agreement by the United States to Pay the Tribe: In consideration for the compromise of the Rental, Damage and Court of Federal Claims cases and for forgoing a Quiet Possession Claim as specified in Section 4(b), and for the Hopi Tribe's promise and commitment to provide an accommodation, as set forth in the Accommodation Terms, the United States agrees to pay in settlement and compromise to the Tribe a sum of $50,200,000.00, plus interest, to the extent provided below, in the following manner:

    (a) Upon filing in the Ninth Circuit Court of Appeals of a joint motion to dismiss with prejudice the Tribe's appeal of the United States' liability in the Damage case as specified in Section 2, the United States shall pay the Tribe $2,400,000.00 in settlement and compromise of those claims.

    (b) After the Tribe has obtained the enactment of legislation as described in Section 5 and upon dismissal with prejudice of the claims describe in Section 3(a), the United States shall pay $22,700,000.00 in settlement and compromise of those claims into an interest-bearing trust account in the United States Treasury for the benefit of the Tribe. Thereafter, and subject to otherwise applicable law, the Tribe may obtain from the trust account $22,700,000.00 of the funds plus any interest accrued, even if fewer than 65% of the Navajo heads of household eligible for an Accommodation have entered into an Accommodation or have chosen to relocate and are eligible for relocation assistance.

    (c) After sixty-five percent (65%) of the eligible Navajo heads of household have entered into an Accommodation or have chosen to relocate (and are eligible for relocation assistance) and upon dismissal with prejudice of the Tribe's livestock trespass penalty claim against the United States for the period 1983 through and including 1988, the United States shall pay $10,000,000 in settlement and compromise of those claims into an interest-bearing trust account in the United States Treasury for the benefit of the Tribe. Thereafter, and subject to otherwise applicable law, the Tribe may obtain from the trust account $10,000,000.00 of the funds plus any interest accrued.

    (d) After seventy-five (75%) percent of the eligible Navajo heads of household have entered into an Accommodation or have chosen to relocate (and are eligible for relocation assistance) and upon dismissal with prejudice of the Tribe's livestock trespass penalty claims for the period 1989 through and including 1996, the United States shall pay $15,100,000.00 in settlement and compromise of those claims into an interest-bearing

trust account in the United States for the benefit of the Tribe. Thereafter, and subject to otherwise applicable law, the Tribe may obtain from
the trust account $15,100,000.00 of the funds plus any interest accrued.

(e) It is a form of this Agreement that the Tribe fulfill its obligations to the
Navajo families pursuant to the Accommodation Terms, as specified in
Section 4(a). If the Tribe is not in compliance with the undertakings
specified in Section 4(a), it shall not be entitled to receive distribution of
compensation under this Agreement, including the funds described in
subsections (a) through (d) of this Section or the federal government's
action with respect to lands, described in Section 7.

(f) None of the releases described in Section 1 through 4 which are being
given to the United States by the Tribe are intended to release the
Navajo Nation from any liability it might have to the Tribe. Nor is any
of the consideration provided under this Agreement from the United
States to the Tribe intended to release the Navajo Nation from any liability it might have to the Tribe. The United States does not take a position on the effect of this Agreement, if any, on satisfaction of claims between the Hopi Tribe and the Navajo Nation; that issue is one to be
resolved between the tribes.

7. Agreement by the United States to Take Land Into Trust for the Tribe and to
Acquire State Lands with the State's Concurrence:

(a) As partial consideration for this settlement, the Secretary agrees that, if
seventy-five percent (75%) or more of the Navajo heads of household eligible for an Accommodation either have entered into an Accommodation or have chosen to relocate and are eligible for relocation assistance,
the Department of the Interior will take in trust up to five hundred thousand (500,000) acres of land for the benefit of the Tribe under the terms
set forth in this Section.

(i) It is contemplated that the Tribe will acquire lands. With respect
to any specific parcel of land acquired by the Tribe, the Secretary,
at the request of the Tribe and subject to all existing applicable
laws and regulations (including the National Environmental
Policy Act ("NEPA") and 25 CFR Part 151, and provided that any
environmental problems identified as a result of NEPA compliance are mitigated to the satisfaction of the Secretary), will take
the parcel into trust for the Tribe. Although no specific land
parcels have been identified at the time of this Agreement, it is
understood that land the Secretary agrees to take into trust is land
in northern Arizona that is used substantially for ranching, agriculture, or other similar rural uses and, to the extent feasible, is in
contiguous parcels.

(ii) Although the Secretary may, in his/her absolute discretion, take
some of this land into trust prior to seventy- five percent (75%) of
the eligible Navajo heads of household entering into an Accommodation or choosing to relocate, he/she is not committing to
take any land into trust unless the 75% condition is met. Once the
75% condition is met, however, the Secretary shall take land into
trust, in accordance with the provisions of paragraph (i).

(b) To the extent that the Tribe acquires private lands and would like to acquire the interspersed State of Arizona lands, so that both the private

and interspersed state lands may be taken into trust, and because of the State's legal restrictions on the sale and exchange of state lands, the United States agrees to acquire for the Tribe (consistent with existing law and provided the further terms set forth in this subsection are also met) for fair market value the interspersed state lands within the exterior boundaries of private lands acquired by the Tribe, under the following conditions: (i) seventy-five percent (75%) of the eligible Navajo heads of household have entered into an Accommodation or have chosen to relocate and are eligible for relocation assistance; and (ii) the United States has the State's concurrence that such acquisition is consistent with the State's interests; and (iii) the Tribe, not the United States, will pay the value of any state lands so acquired; and (iv) acquisition of the interspersed state land is consistent with the purpose of obtaining up to 500,000 acres of land in trust for the Tribe. Once the United States has acquired state lands pursuant to these conditions, the Secretary will take the land into trust pursuant to and in accordance with the provisions of subsection (a).

If the State does not concur in the United States' acquisition of state lands interspersed with the private lands acquired by the Tribe, the Secretary, instead, at the Tribe's request, will take into trust for the Tribe other private lands (as set forth in subsection (a)), to meet its commitment to take up to 500,000 acres into trust.

Contingencies and Remedies

(c) In the extraordinary event that, by a ruling of the United States Court of Appeals for the Ninth Circuit or the United States Supreme Court or other change of legal authority, the Secretary is not authorized to take land into trust or to acquire state lands at the time he/she is requested to do so by the Tribe, the Secretary and the Tribe will seek federal legislation to give effect to the Secretary's commitment pursuant to this Agreement to take land into trust and to acquire state lands.

(d) The Tribe promises to forego a claim against the United States for quiet possession of the Tribe's property occupied by Navajo families that enter into an Accommodation (as provided in Section 4), except as provided in this subsection. Without acknowledging the validity of any such claim, the Tribe and the United States agree that the Tribe will be released from its commitment to forego the portion of the Quiet Possession Claim identified in Section 4(b)(iii) in the circumstances and to the extent provided in paragraphs (i) and (ii) of this subsection. In any such claim for damages, the benefits already received by the Tribe from the United States pursuant to this Agreement will be considered in measuring damages.

(i) If, when the Tribe asks the Secretary to take land into trust: (A) the Secretary is unauthorized to take the subject lands into trust as set forth in subsection (c) of this Section; and (B) federal legislation is not enacted within two years of submission of a legislative proposal to provide the Tribe with the lands in trust described above, the Tribe will be released from its commitment to forego an action under 28 U.S.C. 1491 and 1505 based on use and occupancy by Navajo families that enter into an Accommodation, as provided in Section 4(b)(iii). This provision rests on the Tribe's assertions that it would not have chosen to allow Navajo families to remain on the HPL except for the Secretary's promise to take 500,000 acres of land into trust and that the rent provided by the Navajo Nation does not fully compensate the Tribe for its lost use of Hopi Lands occupied by Navajo families.

(ii) If, when the Tribe asks the Secretary to acquire interspersed state lands: (A) the State does not concur in the sale of state lands interspersed within the exterior boundaries of private lands acquired by the Hopi for a period of at least 5 years after the Tribe's request to acquire specific interspersed state lands; and (B) the Tribe has acquired significantly less than 500,000 acres of land into trust and does not wish to have additional private lands taken into trust, the Tribe will be released from its commitment to forgo an action under 28 U.S.C. 1491 and 1505 based on use and occupancy of the HPL by Navajo families who have entered into an Accommodation, as provided in Section 4(b)(iii). The measure of damages, if any, should consider, inter alia, the consideration already received by the Tribe, such as the value of lands taken into trust and the value of rent received from the Navajo Nation for use of the HPL. This provision rests on the Tribe's assertions that (1) it would not have chosen to allow Navajo families to remain on the HPL except for the Secretary's promise to take 500,000 acres of land into trust, (2) that the rent provided by the Navajo Nation does not fully compensate the Tribe for its lost use of Hopi Lands occupied by Navajo families, and (3) that it may not be practicable for the Tribe to acquire or manage 500,000 acres of land in trust if interspersed state lands cannot be acquired.

8. Agreement as to the Precedential Effect of the Ruling in the Damage Case: As partial consideration for this Agreement, the United States and the Tribe agree that, absent a specific request by a court, neither the United States nor the Tribe will cite or rely on the United States District Court's ruling in the Damage case for principles concerning the trust responsibility and liability of the United States in any subsequent administrative or legal proceedings between the United States and the Tribe involving the Hopi Reservation.

9. Assistance with Management of Resources and Enforcement:

   (a) The Secretary hereby agrees that, commencing within one year of the signing of this Agreement, the HPL will be included and considered in Interior's future resource allocations to the Tribe. The Secretary also agrees that, as of one year from the signing of this Agreement, to the extent enforcement program resources provided to tribes by the Department of the Interior are linked to reservation acreage and/or population, the acreage of the HPL and number of residents at the homesites of the Navajo Accommodation Signatories will be included in determining future allocations for the Tribe.

   (b) The United States agrees that it will assist the Tribe with its management of the lands taken into trust pursuant to this Agreement by providing advice on management for those lands, subject to the availability of Phoenix Area Office, Bureau of Indian Affairs, personnel (or its successor or other appropriately situated personnel, if any) to perform this function.

(c) By January 1, 2000, the Office of Navajo Hopi Indian Relocation ("ONHIR") shall have completed all of the activities with regard to voluntary relocation of Navajos residing on the HPL.

(d) By February 1, 1997, the ONHIR will begin implementing 25 C.F.R. 700.137, 700.138 and 700.139 (1992 ed.) on the New Lands for all Navajos residing on the HPL who are eligible for a replacement home from the ONHIR but who have not made timely application for relocation benefits, and have not made timely arrangements for an Accommodation on the HPL. These provisions shall be fully implemented by February 1, 2000.

(e) Assurance.—If the United States fails to discharge the obligations set forth in subsections (c) or (d), including for reason of inadequate congressional appropriations, without acknowledging the validity of any such claim the Tribe preserves any action regarding quiet possession against the United States arising out of the use of the HPL after February 1, 2000, by any Navajo family eligible for an Accommodation who does not enter into an Accommodation.

(f) The transfer of jurisdiction from the BIA to the Hopi Tribe concerning grazing on the Hopi Partitioned Lands will be effected through proceedings in Hopi v. Watt, Civ. No. 81-272 PCT-EHC (D. Ariz.). The BIA does not contemplate that grazing permits issued by the BIA when considered in conjunction with permits issued by the Tribe to Navajo residents of the HPL will exceed the total number of sheep units made available to HPL Navajos under the Accommodation Terms.

10. Enforcement of Settlement Agreement and Costs and Attorneys' Fees: The United States and the Tribe hereby agree that the provisions of this Settlement Agreement shall be enforceable in either the United States Court of Federal Claims in Washington, D.C., or in the United States District Court in Phoenix, Arizona, as appropriate. Both parties also agree that as to the cases settled by this Agreement each party will bear its own costs and attorneys' fees for these cases (except as otherwise provided in 25 U.S.C. Sec. Sec. 640d-7(e), 640d-27).

11. Settlement Agreement Not Evidence: The parties hereto agree that this is a settlement of disputed claims, that the execution of this Agreement and the passage of consideration hereunder shall not be construed as an admission of liability on the part of any party, and that no party shall assert that any party has admitted liability to any other, and that such liability is expressly denied. This Agreement shall neither be used as evidence nor construed in any way whatsoever as an admission by the United States or the Tribes as to any issue related to liability or damages, but may be used to show, inter alia, breach, or settlement or release in the Rental, Damage, Court of Federal Claims case or Quiet Possession claims.

12. Anti-Deficiency Act: Any section requiring the United States to provide government services and/or funds is subject to the limitations of the Anti-Deficiency Act, 31 U.S.C. 1341(a)(1).

13. Authority to Enter Agreement: Each of the signatories hereto hereby warrants that he/she is authorized to enter into this Agreement on behalf of the party on whose behalf he/she has executed the Agreement.

14. Counterparts: This Agreement can be executed in counterpart originals and each copy will have the same force and effect as if signed by all parties.

15. Entire Agreement: This Agreement discharges the obligations of the United States and the Tribe to each other in the Damage and Court of Federal Claims cases and the parts of the Rental case that are being compromised and settled and it bars suit by the Tribe against the United States for a Quiet Possession Claim, pursuant to the terms of Sections 4, 7 and 9. This Agreement supersedes any prior written or oral agreement.

December 1995

PROHIBITION OF RECLASSIFICATION AND TERMINATION OF TRIBES: PUBLIC LAW 103-263 (1994)

INTRODUCTION

Of all the sorry history of Indian–non-native interactions, events in California may be the grimmest of all. It was in California that the Spaniards built missions to bring the word of God to the heathen native people. Those missions were ultimately responsible, by spreading disease and instituting slave labor and culture eradication programs, for the death of thousands of native people and the near-destruction of their cultures. In the mid- to late nineteenth century, California was the scene of numerous cold-blooded massacres carried out by non-native settlers, miners, and adventurers against native populations. Most of the survivors were unilaterally dispossessed with no regard whatsoever for their rights or, in most cases, any provision for their subsistence.

In 1851 and 1852, the federal government made 18 treaties with native groups in California. However, political pressure brought to bear by citizens of the new state prevented the treaties from ever being ratified. That is, the Indians agreed to and carried out their terms, but in the end they gave up everything the treaties called for, and more, but received none of the promised benefits. Any efforts the now-landless Indians made to improve their lot, such as trying to engage in farming or raising cattle, were stymied by corrupt agents and/or local opposition.

The situation improved only very slowly for Indians in California. Small amounts of land were set aside under various provisions over the years, but many Indians remained landless and, for the most part, destitute. In the 1940s and '50s, land claims were settled for several hundred dollars per capita. Termination hit California Indians especially hard; many groups were arbitrarily removed from the federal trust relationship. Although many of these groups were restored to federal status in the 1980s, the land they lost was not restored. In the meantime, other groups, some of whom were judged to be "extinct" (see discussion of the Costanoan/Ohlone people in the "Identity" entry in the Contemporary Issues section), never received recognition in the first place.

Lacking either federal recognition or a land base, many California groups have found it impossible to qualify for various federal assistance programs. Consequently, they are fighting for both recognition and land restoration. Unfortunately, they continue to encounter opposition from both state and federal officials. In 1981, for instance, the government made a concerted effort to force tribes to reestablish their status retroactively, with the new caveat that they be required to prove that they were historically recognized tribes. In 1994, the government went on to propose that all tribes unable to pass the new and very vague litmus test be administratively terminated. Official doubt was expressed that any historic tribes existed in California.

Indian groups immediately pointed out that up to 230 tribes could be terminated in this way and that the policy would lead to disaster for Indian tribes, not to mention extensive litigation. In response, Congress enacted Public Law 103-263, which bars the Bureau of Indian Affairs from differential treatment or reclassification of Indian tribes and reverses all such instances of abuse against recognized tribes. In separate floor statements, Senators Daniel Inouye of Hawaii and John McCain of Arizona called the legislation the most important contribution to the protection of tribal sovereignty in 60 years. This may or may not be the case, but what is certain is that, in the face of actions such as the 1998 attempt to transfer their trust lands into fee simple deeds, unrecognized tribes in California must continue to fight for the basic justice that has been denied them for so long.

PUBLIC LAW 103-263 [INDIAN LAWS TECHNICAL CORRECTIONS]
United States Public Laws
103rd Congress—Second Session
Public Law 103-263 [S. 1654]
May 31, 1994
[Indian Laws Technical Corrections]
An Act to make certain technical corrections. Be it enacted by the Senate and House of Representatives of the United States of America in Congress assembled . . .

Sec. 5 Amendments
(deletions)

(f) Privileges and Immunities of Indian Tribes; Prohibition on New Regulations.— Departments or agencies of the United States shall not promulgate any regulation or make any decision or determination pursuant to the Act of June 18, 1934 (25 U.S.C. 461 et seq., 48 Stat. 984) as amended, or any other Act of Congress, with respect to a federally recognized Indian tribe that classifies, enhances, or diminishes the privileges and immunities available to the Indian tribe relative to other federally recognized tribes by virtue of their status as Indian tribes.

(g) Privileges and Immunities of Indian Tribes; Existing Regulations.—Any regulation or administrative decision or determination of a department or agency of the United States that is in existence or effect on the date of enactment of this Act and that classifies, enhances, or diminishes the privileges and immunities available to a federally recognized Indian tribe relative to the privileges and immunities available to other federally recognized tribes by virtue of their status as Indian tribes shall have no force or effect.

Speaker of the House of Representatives

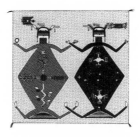

Rights of the Aboriginal Peoples of Canada: Constitution Act (1982)

Introduction

The provisions excerpted here from the Constitution Act of 1982 are the most significant—in fact, the first—constitutional guarantees of aboriginal rights in Canada's history. Their importance lies in the fact that aboriginal and treaty rights, previously subject to a variety of legislative infringements, were given formal constitutional recognition. Section 35 also defines or includes as aboriginal "the Indian, Inuit, and Metis peoples of Canada"; gives land claims the legal status of treaties; and guarantees all such rights equally to men and women (this was specifically not the case before this provision and Bill C-31 rendered sex discrimination in the Indian Act obsolete).

The native people of Canada have traditionally pointed to the Proclamation Act of 1763 as one of the fundamental guarantors of their rights under British and Canadian law. In part, that document guarantees that "the several Nations or Tribes of Indians with whom we are connected, and who live under our Protection, should not be molested or disturbed in the Possession of such parts of our Dominions and Territories as, not having been ceded to or purchased by Us, are reserved to them or any of them as their Hunting Grounds." Despite rampant and chronic violations, Canadian courts have consistently held this act to have "the force of a statute which has never been repealed." For years it was, and still in part is, the basis of aboriginal land claims.

After confederation, Canada concluded a series of "numbered treaties" with Indian groups, which made various promises, subsequently more or less ignored, in return for native land cessions. However, while Canadian courts have always recognized treaty rights to at least some extent, they have not extended even the same minimal degree of recognition to aboriginal rights. (The question of aboriginal and treaty rights for Inuit and Métis must be addressed differently, since neither group has ever signed any treaties per se with Canada and the definition of Métis people is highly controversial.) This situation is especially unstable and problematic in British Columbia, where aboriginal title still exists in much of the province, and in Quebec and the Northwest Territories, where modern land claims settlements have been negotiated on the basis of unextinguished aboriginal title.

Like the United States, Canada has tried many times over the years simply to dismiss the question of native rights. In the 1920s, federal authorities unilaterally dislodged the traditional Six Nations chiefs and instituted a system of elected representation that remains highly divisive today. About the same time, an amendment to the Indian Act made it illegal to raise funds or to retain counsel to advance an Indian claim. In 1969, Canada developed the White Paper, its own version of termination, but pressure by Indian groups forced the withdrawal of this proposal within a few years.

One of the key questions posed and left unanswered by the 1982 Constitution Act was that of what rights were "existing" (Section 35 [1]) in 1982. The Supreme Court ruled on this issue in 1990 with its Sparrow decision (see *Ronald Edward Sparrow* v. *Her Majesty The Queen* entry). The court decided that the rights protected by Section 35 were those that had not been extinguished by statute or by the consent of the Indians. At the same time, however, the court allowed federal authorities to regulate Indian rights as long as the regulations were "justified."

Despite the constitutional protections of 1982, Canada, like the United States, has its share of "unreconstructed" legislators, and native groups must be constantly on guard for threats to aboriginal and treaty rights. The conclusion of the Royal Commission on Aboriginal Peoples (1996) that the right of self-government is constitutionally protected by Section 35 has no force of law. Given the history of Indian-federal relations since 1982, and especially the government's response to the Delgamuukw decision (see *Delgamuukw* v. *British Columbia* entry), these constitutional protections may be seen as crucial on paper but of dubious value in practice.

CONSTITUTION ACT, 1982(1), SCHEDULE B

Part I: Canadian Charter of Rights and Freedoms

Whereas Canada is founded upon the principles that recognize the supremacy of God and the rule of law:

Guarantee of Rights and Freedoms
(deletions)

25. The guarantee in this Charter of certain rights and freedoms shall not be construed so as to abrogate or derogate from any aboriginal, treaty or other rights or freedoms that pertain to the aboriginal peoples of Canada including
    (a) any rights or freedoms that have been recognized by the Royal Proclamation of October 7, 1763; and
    (b) any rights or freedoms that may be acquired by the aboriginal peoples of Canada by way of land claims settlement.(15)
    (deletions)

Part II: Rights of the Aboriginal Peoples of Canada

35. (1) The existing aboriginal and treaty rights of the aboriginal peoples of Canada are hereby recognized and affirmed. (2) In this Act, "aboriginal peoples of Canada" includes the Indian, Inuit, and Metis peoples of Canada. (3) For greater certainty, in subsection (1) "treaty rights" includes rights that now exist by way of land claims agreements or may be so acquired. (4) Notwithstanding

any other provision of this Act, the aboriginal and treaty rights referred to in subsection (1) are guaranteed equally to male and female persons.(17)

35.1 The government of Canada and the provincial governments are committed to the principal that, before any amendment is made to Class 24 of section 91 of the "Constitution Act, 1867", to section 25 of this Act or to this Part,

    (a) a constitutional conference that includes in its agenda an item relating to the proposed amendment, composed of the Prime Minister of Canada and the first ministers of the provinces, will be convened by the Prime Minister of Canada; and

    (b) the Prime Minister of Canada will invite representatives of the aboriginal peoples of Canada to participate in the discussions on that item.(18)

INDIAN ARTS AND CRAFTS ACT (1990)

The Arts and Crafts entry in the "Contemporary Issues" section revealed several aspects of Indian arts and crafts. One was the financial angle: Production of crafts is a billion-dollar business and a vital source of income for some tribes and individual Indian artisans and craftspeople. Another was the cultural angle: Virtually all producers of native crafts draw on centuries-old traditions that are inseparable from the cultural identity of their people. In continuing to produce their wares, these people consciously and proudly reaffirm the traditions of, their place in, and the continued existence and growth of their particular tribe or group. In the context of contemporary native life, which includes a legacy of extreme oppression, if not genocide, these are no small matters. A third angle is, of course, the aesthetic one, which is something that concerns all reputable artisans and craftspeople.

The entry also touched on another important aspect of native crafts: their susceptibility to counterfeiting. Well-made and particularly well regarded native crafts, such as Navajo rugs, Zuni jewelry, and Pomo baskets, often sell for high prices. Reasons for the high prices vary but include the desire of buyers to own an authentic Indian piece as well as the fact that the items in question are painstakingly and precisely made by highly skilled workers who in many cases use ancient techniques and all-natural materials. Knockoffs of these items, inferior in every way, can easily be produced for a fraction of the cost. When the copies are labeled as such no theft is being committed, since buyers who cannot afford or who do not wish to pay for the real thing may wish instead to obtain a less expensive copy.

However, far more usual than honest labeling are the cases in which cheap copies are misrepresented as authentic, either by unscrupulous dealers or, less likely, by reputable dealers in error. Fraudulent producers and marketers often go to great lengths to deceive the public, who in some cases do not realize that they are paying for fakes. Due to the multifaceted nature of native arts and crafts, sales of counterfeit items hurt the people in many ways. The sheer financial loss can be crippling, both in terms of immediate loss and of damage to the reputation of the industry as a whole. Furthermore, counterfeits are an affront to native people personally, since they represent yet another assault on their culture and traditions.

The Indian Arts and Crafts Act of 1990 is meant to offer some protection to native artisans and craftspeople by criminalizing the misrepresentation of Indian-produced goods and products or, where this activity has always been illegal, by sharply increasing the penalties. Any Indian, tribe, or member of an Indian arts and crafts organization can bring legal action against and receive compensation from a person or persons engaged in misrepresenting native arts or crafts. This act will certainly not stop all counterfeiting of Indian arts and crafts, but it is designed to deter such actions by making them federal crimes. Enforcement of the law, of course, is another matter, one that bears directly on the will of Congress to appropriate necessary funds for inspections and investigations. To date, enforcement has generally been considered lax.

INDIAN ARTS AND CRAFTS ACT
Public Law 101-644 [H.R. 2006]
November 29, 1990
Indian Arts and Crafts Act of 1990
An Act to expand the powers of the Indian Arts and Crafts Board, and for other purposes.
Be it enacted by the Senate and House of Representatives of the United States of America in Congress assembled,

Title I—Indian Arts and Crafts
Sec. 101. <25 USC 305 note> Short Title.
This title may be cited as the "Indian Arts and Crafts Act of 1990".
(Deletions)

Sec. 103. Referral for Criminal and Civil Violations.
The Act entitled "An Act to promote the development of Indian arts and crafts and to create a board to assist therein, and for other purposes" (25 U.S.C. 305 et seq.) is amended by adding at the end of the following:

"Sec. 5. <25 USC 305d> (a) The Board may receive complaints of violations of section 1159 of title 18, United States Code, and refer complaints of such violations to the Federal Bureau of Investigation for appropriate investigation. After reviewing the investigation report, the Board may recommend to the Attorney General of the United States that criminal proceedings be instituted under that section.
"(b) The Board may recommend that the Secretary of the Interior refer the matter to the Attorney General for civil action under section 6."

Sec. 104. Criminal Penalty for Misrepresentation of Indian Produced Goods and Products.
(a) In General.—Section 1159 of title 18, United States Code, is amended to read as follows:
Misrepresentation of Indian produced goods and products
"(a) It is unlawful to offer or display for sale or sell any good, with or without a Government trademark, in a manner that falsely suggests it is Indian produced, an Indian product, or the product of a particular Indian or Indian tribe or Indian arts and crafts organization, resident within the United States.
"(b) Whoever knowingly violates subsection (a) shall—

"(1) in the case of a first violation, if an individual, be fined not more than $250,000 or imprisoned not more than five years, or both, and, if a person other than an individual, be fined not more than $1,000,000; and

"(2) in the case of subsequent violations, if an individual, be fined not more than $1,000,000 or imprisoned not more than fifteen years, or both, and, if a person other than an individual, be fined not more than $5,000,000.

"(c) As used in this section—

"(1) the term 'Indian' means any individual who is a member of an Indian tribe, or for the purposes of this section is certified as an Indian artisan by an Indian tribe;

"(2) the terms 'Indian product' and 'product of a particular Indian tribe or Indian arts and crafts organization' has the meaning given such term in regulations which may be promulgated by the Secretary of the Interior;

"(3) the term 'Indian tribe' means—

"(A) any Indian tribe, band, nation, Alaska Native village, or other organized group or community which is recognized as eligible for the special programs and services provided by the United States to Indians because of their status as Indians; or

"(B) any Indian group that has been formally recognized as an Indian tribe by a State legislature or by a State commission or similar organization legislatively vested with State tribal recognition authority; and

"(4) the term 'Indian arts and crafts organization' means any legally established arts and crafts marketing organization composed of members of Indian tribes.

"(d) In the event that any provision of this section is held invalid, it is the intent of Congress that the remaining provisions of this section shall continue in full force and effect."

(b) Conforming Amendment.—The item relating to section 1159 in the table of sections for chapter 53 of title 18, United States Code, is amended to read as follows: "1159. Misrepresentation of Indian produced goods and products."

Sec. 105. Cause of Action for Misrepresentation of Indian Produced Goods and Products.

The Act entitled "An Act to promote the development of Indian arts and crafts and to create a board to assist therein, and for other purposes" (25 U.S.C. 305 et seq.) (as amended by section 3) is further amended by adding at the end of the following:

"SEC. 6. <25 USC 305e> (a) A person specified in subsection (c) may, in a civil action in a court of competent jurisdiction, bring an action against a person who offers or displays for sale or sells a good, with or without a Government trademark, in a manner that falsely suggests it is Indian produced, an Indian product, or the product of a particular Indian or Indian tribe or Indian arts and crafts organization, resident within the United States, to—

"(1) obtain injunctive or other equitable relief; and

"(2) recover the greater of—

"(A) treble damages; or

"(B) in the case of each aggrieved individual Indian, Indian tribe, or Indian arts and crafts organization, not less than $1,000 for each day on which the offer or display for sale or sale continues.

"(b) In addition to the relief specified in subsection (a), the court may award punitive damages and the costs of suit and a reasonable attorney's fee.

"(c)(1) A civil action under subsection (a) may be commenced—

"(A) by the Attorney General of the United States upon request of the Secretary of the Interior on behalf of an Indian who is a member of an Indian tribe or on behalf of an Indian tribe or Indian arts and crafts organization; or

"(B) by an Indian tribe on behalf of itself, an Indian who is a member of the tribe, or on behalf of an Indian arts and crafts organization.

"(2) Any amount recovered pursuant to this section shall be paid to the individual Indian, Indian tribe, or Indian arts and crafts organization, except that—

"(A) in the case of paragraph (1)(A), the Attorney General may deduct from the amount recovered the amount for the costs of suit and reasonable attorney's fees awarded pursuant to subsection (b) and deposit the amount of such costs and fees as a reimbursement credited to appropriations currently available to the Attorney General at the time of receipt of the amount recovered; and

"(B) in the case of paragraph (1)(B), the amount recovered for the costs of suit and reasonable attorney's fees pursuant to subsection (b) may be deducted from the total amount awarded under subsection (a)(2).

"(d) As used in this section—

"(1) the term 'Indian' means any individual who is a member of an Indian tribe; or for the purposes of this section is certified as an Indian artisan by an Indian tribe;

"(2) the terms 'Indian product' and 'product of a particular Indian tribe or Indian arts and crafts organization' has the meaning given such term in regulations which may be promulgated by the Secretary of the Interior;

"(3) the term 'Indian tribe' means—

"(A) any Indian tribe, band, nation, Alaska Native village, or other organized group or community which is recognized as eligible for the special programs and services provided by the United States to Indians because of their status as Indians; or

"(B) any Indian group that has been formally recognized as an Indian tribe by a State legislature or by a State commission or similar organization legislatively vested with State tribal recognition authority; and

"(4) the term 'Indian arts and crafts organization' means any legally established arts and crafts marketing organization composed of members of Indian tribes.

"(e) In the event that any provision of this section is held invalid, it is the intent of Congress that the remaining provisions of this section shall continue in full force and effect."

Sec. 106. Penalty for Counterfeiting Indian Arts and Crafts Board Trademark.

Section 1158 of title 18, United States Code, is amended by striking "be fined not more than $500 or imprisoned not more than six months, or both; and" and inserting "(1) in the case of a first violation, if an individual, be fined not more than $250,000 or imprisoned not more than five years, or both, and, if a person other than an individual, be fined not more than $1,000,000; and (2) in the case of subsequent violations, if an individual, be fined not more than $1,000,000 or imprisoned not more than fifteen years, or both, and, if a person other than an individual, be fined not more than $5,000,000; and (3)".

Sec. 107. <25 USC 305e Note> Certification of Indian Artisans.

For the purposes of section 1159 of title 18, United States Code, and section 6 of the Act entitled "An Act to promote the development of Indian arts and crafts and to create a board to assist therein, and for other purposes" (25 U.S.C. 305 et seq.) an Indian tribe may not impose a fee in certifying an individual as an Indian artisan. For the purposes of this section, the term "Indian tribe" has the same meaning given such term in section 1159(c)(3) of title 18, United States Code.

DECLARATION OF WAR AGAINST EXPLOITERS OF LAKOTA SPIRITUALITY

INTRODUCTION

A non-native walks into a diner and sits down next to an Indian. He watches as the Indian eats a bowl of soup, two hamburgers, a plate of French fries, a large salad, an order of potato salad, a bowl of ice cream, and a piece of pie. "Boy," he says to the Indian, "I sure wish I had your appetite." The Indian looks at him and replies, "You took my land, my wealth, my culture, the bones of my ancestors, and even my religion. Now you want my appetite too?"

The story may bring a smile but only an ironic one. As this Declaration of War clearly illustrates, the feeling experienced by at least some Indian people over the practice of spiritual exploitation is deep and strong. Although the document is signed by only three people and refers specifically only to the Lakota people (it was ratified by the Dakota-Lakota-Nakota Nation in 1993), its sentiments have been echoed by the many thousands of native people who speak out against similar acts. Readers should also refer to the "Representation" entry in the Contemporary Issues section, in which the issues of spiritual exploitation and other forms of misrepresentation are discussed in greater detail.

Unfortunately, as the document itself makes clear, instances of this kind of activity are all too common. Furthermore, not all perpetrators are evil. There are people, of course, Indians included, who ruthlessly exploit native customs and traditions in order to make money to gain power over others. However, just as common are those people who consider themselves either great friends of or highly respectful toward native people and who honestly believe that what they do—for example, trying to imitate Indian ceremonialism—honors native traditions. This document makes it clear that they are sadly mistaken.

Nevertheless, it is important to recognize the bind in which many non-natives find themselves. Established "mainstream" religions, such as Christianity and Judaism, have failed large numbers of people. Even some people who accept elements of these religions find a sort of neopaganism, or what they perceive as "Indian religion," to be very compelling. Like all complex ideas, the various forms of native religion, spirituality, and ceremonialism are poorly understood by almost all outsiders (and not a few insiders!). In a way that is perhaps typically "American," people latch on to one or two ideas without much study or thought about the people they may be dishonoring. It all seems harmless—a group gets together for a "sweatlodge," they do a bit of reading about some native ceremony and attempt to imitate it, or they embrace the concept of tribalism and adopt an "Indian name" to draw themselves closer to a culture they think they admire. Apart from the true charlatans, who are always social parasites, these people may have only the loftiest motives in mind when they initiate such activities.

The truth, however, is that there are real people alive, not mythic Indians of the past, whose culture and traditions—whose very religion—they are caricaturing. It is as if non-Catholics were in the habit of dressing approximately like priests and conducting their version of the Mass—they may be doing it out of a sincere affinity for the ritual, but Catholics are not likely to feel good about it. Casual imitation leads inexorably to parody and exploitation. Where profit is involved, such imitation is considered doubly reprehensible. Especially considering the fact that not only Lakota but practically every native culture has been systematically raped and pillaged by non-natives, the latter would be advised to consider this context and to err on the side of respect.

"Unspeakable indignity," "horror," and "outrage" are powerful words, but doubters have only to substitute their own sacred symbols and practices for those named by the authors of this document in order to understand why such words are used. The attack on native spirituality is real, multifaceted, pervasive, and ongoing. This Declaration of War helps to mobilize Lakota, Nakota, and Dakota people, as well as other native people, to resist and continue to protest such actions. The stakes are high: As the authors say, they include the ability of "our children and our children's children [to] survive and prosper in the sacred manner intended for each of our respective peoples by our Creator."

DECLARATION OF WAR AGAINST EXPLOITERS OF LAKOTA SPIRITUALITY

WHEREAS we are the conveners of an ongoing series of comprehensive forums on the abuse and exploitation of Lakota spirituality; and

WHEREAS we represent the recognized traditional spiritual leaders, traditional elders, and grassroots advocates of the Lakota people; and

WHEREAS for too long we have suffered the unspeakable indignity of having our most precious Lakota ceremonies and spiritual practices desecrated, mocked and abused by non-Indian "wannabes," hucksters, cultists, commercial profiteers and self-styled "New Age shamans" and their followers; and

WHEREAS with horror and outrage we see this disgraceful expropriation of our sacred Lakota traditions has reached epidemic proportions in urban areas throughout the country; and

WHEREAS our precious Sacred Pipe is being desecrated through the sale of pipestone pipes at flea markets, powwows, and "New Age" retail stores; and

WHEREAS pseudo-religious corporations have been formed to charge people money for admission into phony "sweatlodges" and "vision quest" programs; and

WHEREAS sacrilegious "sundances" for non-Indians are being conducted by charlatans and cult leaders who promote abominable and obscene imitations of our sacred Lakota sundance rites; and

WHEREAS non-Indians have organized themselves into imitation "tribes," assigning themselves make-believe "Indian names" to facilitate their wholesale expropriation and commercialization of our Lakota traditions; and

WHEREAS academic disciplines have sprung up at colleges and universities institutionalizing the sacrilegious imitation of our spiritual practices by students and instructors under the guise of educational programs in "shamanism"; and

WHEREAS non-Indian charlatans and "wannabes" are selling books that promote the systematic colonization of our Lakota spirituality; and

WHEREAS the television and film industry continues to saturate the entertainment media with vulgar, sensationalist and grossly distorted representations of Lakota spirituality and culture which reinforce the public's negative stereotyping of Indian people and which gravely impair the self-esteem of our children; and

WHEREAS individuals and groups involved in "the New Age Movement," in "the men's movement," in "neo-paganism" cults and in "shamanism" workshops all have exploited the spiritual traditions of our Lakota people by imitating our ceremonial ways and by mixing such imitation rituals with non-Indian occult practices in an offensive and harmful pseudo-religious hodgepodge; and

WHEREAS the absurd public posturing of this scandalous assortment of psuedo-Indian charlatans, "wannabes," commercial profiteers, cultists and "New Age shamans" comprises a momentous obstacle in the struggle of traditional Lakota people for an adequate public appraisal of the legitimate political, legal and spiritual needs of real Lakota people; and

WHEREAS this exponential exploitation of our Lakota spiritual traditions requires that we take immediate action to defend our most precious Lakota spirituality from further contamination, desecration and abuse;

THEREFORE WE RESOLVE AS FOLLOWS:

1. We hereby and henceforth declare war against all persons who persist in exploiting, abusing and misrepresenting the sacred traditions and spiritual practices of our Lakota, Dakota and Nakota people.
2. We call upon all our Lakota, Dakota and Nakota brothers and sisters from reservations, reserves, and traditional communities in the United States and Canada to actively and vocally oppose this alarming take-over and systematic destruction of our sacred traditions.
3. We urge our people to coordinate with their tribal members living in urban areas to identify instances in which our sacred traditions are being abused, and then to resist this abuse, utilizing whatever specific tactics are necessary and

sufficient—for example demonstrations, boycotts, press conferences, and acts of direct intervention.

4. We especially urge all our Lakota, Dakota, and Nakota people to take action to prevent our own people from contributing to and enabling the abuse of our sacred ceremonies and spiritual practices by outsiders; for, as we all know, there are certain ones among our own people who are prostituting our spiritual ways for their own selfish gain, with no regard for the spiritual well-being of the people as a whole.

5. We assert a posture of zero-tolerance for any "white man's shaman" who rises from within our own communities to "authorize" the expropriation of our ceremonial ways by non-Indians; all such "plastic medicine men" are enemies of the Lakota, Dakota and Nakota people.

6. We urge traditional people, tribal leaders, and governing councils of all other Indian nations, to join us in calling for an immediate end to this rampant exploitation of our respective American Indian sacred traditions by issuing statements denouncing such abuse; for it is not the Lakota, Dakota and Nakota people alone whose spiritual practices are being systematically violated by non-Indians.

7. We urge all our Indian brothers and sisters to act decisively and boldly in our present campaign to end the destruction of our sacred traditions, keeping in mind our highest duty as Indian people: to preserve the purity of our precious traditions for our future generations, so that our children and our children's children will survive and prosper in the sacred manner intended for each of our respective peoples by our Creator.

Wilmer Stampede Mesteth; (Oglala Lakota);
Traditional Spiritual Leader & Lakota Culture Instructor;
Oglala Lakota College,
Pine Ridge, South Dakota

Darrell Standing Elk; (Sicangu Lakota);
President, Center for the SPIRIT,
San Francisco, California, and
Pine Ridge, South Dakota

Phyllis Swift Hawk; (Kul Wicasa Lakota);
Tiospaye Wounspe Waokiye;
Wanblee, South Dakota

NATIVE AMERICAN HOUSING ASSISTANCE AND SELF-DETERMINATION ACT (1996)

INTRODUCTION

This act of Congress grew out of and partially replaced the landmark Indian Self-Determination and Educational Assistance Act of 1975. At least on paper, that piece of legislation had committed the government to renounce top-heavy, paternalistic management of Indian affairs (as well as its termination efforts, of course, although those, which originated in the form of House Concurrent Resolution 108 of the 83rd Congress, were not officially abandoned until 1988) and launched the period of tribal self-determination. That is, for the first time federally recognized Indian tribes were to be actively involved not only in planning policy but, by way of contracts with federal authorities, in administering and evaluating programs. Barring another radical shift, which seems unlikely despite recent congressional efforts in that direction, federal Indian policy will continue to evolve within this general framework toward greater self-determination for the tribes.

The Native American Housing Assistance and Self-Determination Act of 1996 is the most recent such piece of federal legislation. To be sure, it reiterates the government's right to "plenary power over the field of Indian affairs. . . ." It also reaffirms that the United States has a trust responsibility for the tribes and recognizes the government's obligation to meet its responsibilities under that trust relationship "in a manner that recognizes the right of Indian self-determination and tribal self-governance by making such assistance available directly to the Indian tribes. . . ."

Specifically, the act lays out a program for the improvement of housing on Indian reservations and Alaska Native villages that is marked by a considerable degree of flexibility and local autonomy. Indian tribes or tribal or native village authorities are required to create various statements of needs, goals, objectives, and programs, including budgets, to meet the needs of its low-income population for adequate housing. In addition to taking into account a litany of criteria and variables, such statements, which must be updated regularly, must demonstrate the involvement of a mix of public, private, and nonprofit entities. For its part, the government agrees to provide certain funds and otherwise facilitate the realization of the tribal plans.

The actual result of this legislation has been mixed. The act has the virtue of bringing order to the complex and often ambiguous federal housing programs. It contains important provisions for compliance and oversight that relate to both the government and, more importantly, to the tribes themselves. It is also the first housing law grounded in the federal trust responsibility, and in separating Indian housing from public housing, it provides a unique opportunity to address some of the historic inequities that plague the former.

However, economic conditions on most reservations and Alaska Native villages remain generally poor. With the unemployment rate as high as it is in those places, many native people cannot afford to buy or rent their own housing without assistance. Even with assistance, however, such as that provided by this act, a significant amount of reservation and Alaska Native village housing is considered substandard, if it exists at all. The number of decent housing units needed in Indian country is considered to exceed 90,000. The challenge to Congress is to fund the act's provisions in full, whereas the tribes must be capable of creating and properly overseeing successful housing programs. This act is an important step in the process of addressing the need for safe, clean, and affordable housing for Indians and Alaska Natives. Time will tell whether or not other necessary steps are taken as well.

NATIVE AMERICAN HOUSING ASSISTANCE AND SELF-DETERMINATION ACT

United States Public Laws
104th Congress—Second Session
Public Law 104-330 [H.R. 3219]
October 26, 1996
Native American Housing Assistance and Self-Determination Act of 1996
An Act
To provide Federal assistance for Indian tribes in a manner that recognizes the right of tribal self-governance, and for other purposes.
Be it enacted by the Senate and House of Representatives of the United States of America in Congress assembled,

Section 1. <25 USC 4101 note> Short Title and Table of Contents.
   (a)   Short Title.—This Act may be cited as the "Native American Housing Assistance and Self-Determination Act of 1996".

   (Deletions)
   The Congress finds that—

   (1)   the Federal Government has a responsibility to promote the general welfare of the Nation—
       (A)   by using Federal resources to aid families and individuals seeking affordable homes in safe and healthy environments and, in particular, assisting responsible, deserving citizens who cannot provide fully for themselves because of temporary circumstances or factors beyond their control;
       (B)   by working to ensure a thriving national economy and a strong private housing market; and

(C) by developing effective partnerships among the Federal Government, State, tribal, and local governments, and private entities that allow government to accept responsibility for fostering the development of a healthy marketplace and allow families to prosper without government involvement in their day-to-day activities;

(2) there exists a unique relationship between the Government of the United States and the governments of Indian tribes and a unique Federal responsibility to Indian people;

(3) the Constitution of the United States invests the Congress with plenary power over the field of Indian affairs, and through treaties, statutes, and historical relations with Indian tribes, the United States has undertaken a unique trust responsibility to protect and support Indian tribes and Indian people;

(4) the Congress, through treaties, statutes, and the general course of dealing with Indian tribes, has assumed a trust responsibility for the protection and preservation of Indian tribes and for working with tribes and their members to improve their housing conditions and socioeconomic status so that they are able to take greater responsibility for their own economic condition;

(5) providing affordable homes in safe and healthy environments is an essential element in the special role of the United States in helping tribes and their members to improve their housing conditions and socioeconomic status;

(6) the need for affordable homes in safe and healthy environments on Indian reservations, in Indian communities, and in Native Alaskan villages is acute and the Federal Government should work not only to provide housing assistance, but also, to the extent practicable, to assist in the development of private housing finance mechanisms on Indian lands to achieve the goals of economic self-sufficiency and self-determination for tribes and their members; and

(7) Federal assistance to meet these responsibilities should be provided in a manner that recognizes the right of Indian self-determination and tribal self-governance by making such assistance available directly to the Indian tribes or tribally designated entities under authorities similar to those accorded Indian tribes in Public Law 93-638 (25 U.S.C. 450 et seq.).

Sec. 3. <25 USC 4102> Administration Through Office of Native American Programs.

The Secretary of Housing and Urban Development shall carry out this Act through the Office of Native American Programs of the Department of Housing and Urban Development.

Sec. 4. <25 USC 4103> Definitions.

For purposes of this Act, the following definitions shall apply:

(Deletions)

(12) Indian tribe.—
   (A) In general.—The term "Indian tribe" means a tribe that is a federally recognized tribe or a State recognized tribe.
   (B) Federally recognized tribe.—The term "federally recognized tribe" means any Indian tribe, band, nation, or other organized group or community of Indians, including any Alaska Native village or regional or village corpo-

ration as defined in or established pursuant to the Alaska Native Claims Settlement Act, that is recognized as eligible for the special programs and services provided by the United States to Indians because of their status as Indians pursuant to the Indian Self-Determination and Education Assistance Act of 1975.

(C) State recognized tribe.—

   (i) In general.—The term "State recognized tribe" means any tribe, band, nation, pueblo, village, or community—

      (I) that has been recognized as an Indian tribe by any State; and

      (II) for which an Indian Housing Authority has, before the effective date under section 107, entered into a contract with the Secretary pursuant to the United States Housing Act of 1937 for housing for Indian families and has received funding pursuant to such contract within the 5-year period ending upon such effective date.

(Deletions)

Sec. 102. Indian Housing Plans.

(a) Plan Submission.—The Secretary shall provide—

   (1) for an Indian tribe to submit to the Secretary, for each fiscal year, a housing plan under this section for the tribe;

   (2) for the tribally designated housing entity for the tribe to submit the plan as provided in subsection (d) for the tribe; and

   (3) for the review of such plans.

(b) 5-Year Plan.—Each housing plan under this section shall be in a form prescribed by the Secretary and shall contain, with respect to the 5-year period beginning with the fiscal year for which the plan is submitted, the following information:

   (1) Mission statement.—A general statement of the mission of the Indian tribe to serve the needs of the low-income families in the jurisdiction of the Indian tribe during the period.

   (2) Goals and objectives.—A statement of the goals and objectives of the Indian tribe to enable the tribe to serve the needs identified in paragraph (1) during the period.

   (3) Activities plan.—An overview of the activities planned during the period including an analysis of the manner in which the activities will enable the tribe to meet its mission, goals, and objectives.

(c) 1-Year Plan.—A housing plan under this section for an Indian tribe shall be in a form prescribed by the Secretary and contain the following information relating to the upcoming fiscal year for which the assistance under this Act is to be made available:

   (1) Goals and objectives.—A statement of the goals and objectives to be accomplished during that period.

   (2) Statement of needs.—A statement of the housing needs of the low-income Indian families residing in the jurisdiction of the Indian tribe and the means by which such needs will be addressed during the period, including—

      (A) a description of the estimated housing needs and the need for assistance for the low-income Indian families in the jurisdiction, including a description of the manner in which the geographical distribution of assistance is consistent with the geographical needs and needs for various categories of housing assistance; and

(B) a description of the estimated housing needs for all Indian families in the jurisdiction.

(3) Financial resources.—An operating budget for the recipient, in a form prescribed by the Secretary, that includes—

(A) an identification and a description of the financial resources reasonably available to the recipient to carry out the purposes of this Act, including an explanation of the manner in which amounts made available will leverage additional resources; and

(B) the uses to which such resources will be committed, including eligible and required affordable housing activities under title II and administrative expenses.

(4) Affordable housing resources.—A statement of the affordable housing resources currently available and to be made available during the period, including—

(A) a description of the significant characteristics of the housing market in the jurisdiction, including the availability of housing from other public sources, private market housing, and the manner in which such characteristics influence the decision of the recipient to use grant amounts to be provided under this Act for rental assistance, production of new units, acquisition of existing units, or rehabilitation of units;

(B) a description of the structure, coordination, and means of cooperation between the recipient and any other governmental entities in the development, submission, or implementation of housing plans, including a description of the involvement of private, public, and nonprofit organizations and institutions, and the use of loan guarantees under section 184 of the Housing and Community Development Act of 1992, and other housing assistance provided by the Federal Government for Indian tribes, including loans, grants, and mortgage insurance;

(C) a description of the manner in which the plan will address the needs identified pursuant to paragraph (2);

(D) a description of the manner in which the recipient will protect and maintain the viability of housing owned and operated by the recipient that was developed under a contract between the Secretary and an Indian housing authority pursuant to the United States Housing Act of 1937;

(E) a description of any existing and anticipated homeownership programs and rental programs to be carried out during the period, and the requirements and assistance available under such programs;

(F) a description of any existing and anticipated housing rehabilitation programs necessary to ensure the long-term viability of the housing to be carried out during the period, and the requirements and assistance available under such programs;

(G) a description of all other existing or anticipated housing assistance provided by the recipient during the period, including transitional housing, homeless housing, college housing, supportive services housing, and the requirements and assistance available under such programs;

(H) a description of any housing to be demolished or disposed of, a timetable for such demolition or disposition, and any other information required by the Secretary with respect to such demolition or disposition;

(I) a description of the manner in which the recipient will coordinate with tribal and State welfare agencies to ensure that residents of such housing will be provided with access to resources to assist in obtaining employment and achieving self-sufficiency;

(J) a description of the requirements established by the recipient to promote the safety of residents of such housing, facilitate the undertaking of crime prevention measures, allow resident input and involvement, including the establishment of resident organizations, and allow for the coordination of crime prevention activities between the recipient and tribal and local law enforcement officials; and

(K) a description of the entity that will carry out the activities under the plan, including the organizational capacity and key personnel of the entity.

(5) Certification of compliance.—Evidence of compliance which shall include, as appropriate—

(A) a certification that the recipient will comply with title II of the Civil Rights Act of 1968 in carrying out this Act, to the extent that such title is applicable, and other applicable Federal statutes;

(B) a certification that the recipient will maintain adequate insurance coverage for housing units that are owned and operated or assisted with grant amounts provided under this Act, in compliance with such requirements as may be established by the Secretary;

(C) a certification that policies are in effect and are available for review by the Secretary and the public governing the eligibility, admission, and occupancy of families for housing assisted with grant amounts provided under this Act;

(D) a certification that policies are in effect and are available for review by the Secretary and the public governing rents charged, including the methods by which such rents or homebuyer payments are determined, for housing assisted with grant amounts provided under this Act; and

(E) a certification that policies are in effect and are available for review by the Secretary and the public governing the management and maintenance of housing assisted with grant amounts provided under this Act.

(d) Participation of Tribally Designated Housing Entity.—A plan under this section for an Indian tribe may be prepared and submitted on behalf of the tribe by the tribally designated housing entity for the tribe, but only if such plan contains a certification by the recognized tribal government of the grant beneficiary that such tribe—

(1) has had an opportunity to review the plan and has authorized the submission of the plan by the housing entity; or

    (2) has delegated to such tribally designated housing entity the authority to submit a plan on behalf of the tribe without prior review by the tribe.

  (e) Coordination of Plans.—A plan under this section may cover more than 1 Indian tribe, but only if the certification requirements under subsection (d) are complied with by each such grant beneficiary covered.

  (f) Plans for Small Tribes.—

    (1) Separate requirements.—The Secretary may—

        (A) establish requirements for submission of plans under this section and the information to be included in such plans applicable to small Indian tribes and small tribally designated housing entities; and

        (B) waive any requirements under this section that the Secretary determines are burdensome or unnecessary for such tribes and housing entities.

    (2) Small tribes.—The Secretary may define small Indian tribes and small tribally designated housing entities based on the number of dwelling units assisted under this title by the tribe or housing entity or owned or operated pursuant to a contract under the United States Housing Act of 1937 between the Secretary and the Indian housing authority for the tribe.

  (g) Regulations.—The requirements relating to the contents of plans under this section shall be established by regulation, pursuant to section 106.

(Deletions)

Title II—Affordable Housing Activities
Sec. 201. <25 USC 4131> National Objectives and Eligible Families.

  (a) Primary Objective.—The national objectives of this Act are—

    (1) to assist and promote affordable housing activities to develop, maintain, and operate affordable housing in safe and healthy environments on Indian reservations and in other Indian areas for occupancy by low-income Indian families;

    (2) to ensure better access to private mortgage markets for Indian tribes and their members and to promote self-sufficiency of Indian tribes and their members;

    (3) to coordinate activities to provide housing for Indian tribes and their members with Federal, State, and local activities to further economic and community development for Indian tribes and their members;

    (4) to plan for and integrate infrastructure resources for Indian tribes with housing development for tribes; and

    (5) to promote the development of private capital markets in Indian country and to allow such markets to operate and grow, thereby benefiting Indian communities.

  (b) Eligible Families.—

    (1) In general.—Except as provided under paragraph (2), assistance under eligible housing activities under this Act shall be limited to low-income Indian families on Indian reservations and other Indian areas.

    (2) Exception to low-income requirement.—A recipient may provide assistance for homeownership activities under section 202(2), model activi-

ties under section 202(6), or loan guarantee activities under title VI to Indian families who are not low-income families, to the extent that the Secretary approves the activities pursuant to such section or title because there is a need for housing for such families that cannot reasonably be met without such assistance. The Secretary shall establish limits on the amount of assistance that may be provided under this Act for activities for families who are not low-income families.

(3) Non-indian families.—Notwithstanding paragraph (1), a recipient may provide housing or housing assistance provided through affordable housing activities assisted with grant amounts under this Act for a non-Indian family on an Indian reservation or other Indian area if the recipient determines that the presence of the family on the Indian reservation or other Indian area is essential to the well-being of Indian families and the need for housing for the family cannot reasonably be met without such assistance.

(4) Preference for tribal members and other Indian families.—The Indian housing plan for an Indian tribe may require preference, for housing or housing assistance provided through affordable housing activities assisted with grant amounts provided under this Act on behalf of such tribe, to be given (to the extent practicable) to Indian families who are members of such tribe, or to other Indian families. In any case in which the applicable Indian housing plan for an Indian tribe provides for preference under this paragraph, the recipient for the tribe shall ensure that housing activities that are assisted with grant amounts under this Act for such tribe are subject to such preference.

(5) Exemption.—Title VI of the Civil Rights Act of 1964 and title VIII of the Civil Rights Act of 1968 shall not apply to actions by Indian tribes under this subsection.

Sec. 202. <25 USC 4132> Eligible Affordable Housing Activities.

Affordable housing activities under this title are activities, in accordance with the requirements of this title, to develop or to support affordable housing for rental or homeownership, or to provide housing services with respect to affordable housing, through the following activities:

(1) Indian housing assistance.—The provision of modernization or operating assistance for housing previously developed or operated pursuant to a contract between the Secretary and an Indian housing authority.

(2) Development.—The acquisition, new construction, reconstruction, or moderate or substantial rehabilitation of affordable housing, which may include real property acquisition, site improvement, development of utilities and utility services, conversion, demolition, financing, administration and planning, and other related activities.

(3) Housing services.—The provision of housing-related services for affordable housing, such as housing counseling in connection with rental or homeownership assistance, establishment and support of resident organizations and resident management corporations, energy auditing, activities related to the provision of self-sufficiency and other services, and other services related to assisting owners, tenants, contractors, and other entities, participating or seeking to participate in other housing activities assisted pursuant to this section.

(4) Housing management services.—The provision of management services for affordable housing, including preparation of work specifications, loan processing, inspections, tenant selection, management of tenant-based rental assistance, and management of affordable housing projects.

(5) Crime prevention and safety activities.—The provision of safety, security, and law enforcement measures and activities appropriate to protect residents of affordable housing from crime.

(6) Model activities.—Housing activities under model programs that are designed to carry out the purposes of this Act and are specifically approved by the Secretary as appropriate for such purpose.

Sec. 203. <25 USC 4133> Program Requirements.

(a) Rents.—

    (1) Establishment.—Subject to paragraph (2), each recipient shall develop written policies governing rents and homebuyer payments charged for dwelling units assisted under this Act, including the methods by which such rents and homebuyer payments are determined.

    (2) Maximum rent.—In the case of any low-income family residing in a dwelling unit assisted with grant amounts under this Act, the monthly rent or homebuyer payment (as applicable) for such dwelling unit may not exceed 30 percent of the monthly adjusted income of such family.

(b) Maintenance and Efficient Operation.—Each recipient who owns or operates (or is responsible for funding any entity that owns or operates) housing developed or operated pursuant to a contract between the Secretary and an Indian housing authority pursuant to the United States Housing Act of 1937 shall, using amounts of any grants received under this Act, reserve and use for operating assistance under section 202(1) such amounts as may be necessary to provide for the continued maintenance and efficient operation of such housing. This subsection may not be construed to prevent any recipient (or entity funded by a recipient) from demolishing or disposing of Indian housing referred to in this subsection, pursuant to regulations established by the Secretary.

(c) Insurance Coverage.—Each recipient shall maintain adequate insurance coverage for housing units that are owned or operated or assisted with grant amounts provided under this Act.

(d) Eligibility for Admission.—Each recipient shall develop written policies governing the eligibility, admission, and occupancy of families for housing assisted with grant amounts provided under this Act.

(e) Management and Maintenance.—Each recipient shall develop policies governing the management and maintenance of housing assisted with grant amounts under this Act.

(Deletions)

Sec. 205. <25 USC 4135> Low-Income Requirement and Income Targeting.

(a) In General.—Housing shall qualify as affordable housing for purposes of this Act only if—

    (1) each dwelling unit in the housing—

        (A) in the case of rental housing, is made available for occupancy only by a family that is a low-income family at the time of their initial occupancy of such unit; and

(B)   in the case of housing for homeownership, is made available for purchase only by a family that is a low-income family at the time of purchase; and

(2)   except for housing assisted under section 202 of the United States Housing Act of 1937 (as in effect before the date of the effectiveness of this Act), each dwelling unit in the housing will remain affordable, according to binding commitments satisfactory to the Secretary, for the remaining useful life of the property (as determined by the Secretary) without regard to the term of the mortgage or to transfer of ownership, or for such other period that the Secretary determines is the longest feasible period of time consistent with sound economics and the purposes of this Act, except upon a foreclosure by a lender (or upon other transfer in lieu of foreclosure) if such action—

(A)   recognizes any contractual or legal rights of public agencies, nonprofit sponsors, or others to take actions that would avoid termination of low-income affordability in the case of foreclosure or transfer in lieu of foreclosure; and

(B)   is not for the purpose of avoiding low-income affordability restrictions, as determined by the Secretary.

(b)   Exception.—Notwithstanding subsection (a), housing assisted pursuant to section 201(b)(2) shall be considered affordable housing for purposes of this Act.

(Deletions)

Sec. 207. <25 USC 4137> Lease Requirements and Tenant Selection.

(a)   Leases.—Except to the extent otherwise provided by or inconsistent with tribal law, in renting dwelling units in affordable housing assisted with grant amounts provided under this Act, the owner or manager of the housing shall utilize leases that—

(1)   do not contain unreasonable terms and conditions;

(2)   require the owner or manager to maintain the housing in compliance with applicable housing codes and quality standards;

(3)   require the owner or manager to give adequate written notice of termination of the lease, which shall be the period of time required under State, tribal, or local law;

(4)   specify that, with respect to any notice of eviction or termination, notwithstanding any State, tribal, or local law, a resident shall be informed of the opportunity, prior to any hearing or trial, to examine any relevant documents, records, or regulations directly related to the eviction or termination;

(5)   require that the owner or manager may not terminate the tenancy, during the term of the lease, except for serious or repeated violation of the terms or conditions of the lease, violation of applicable Federal, State, tribal, or local law, or for other good cause; and

(6)   provide that the owner or manager may terminate the tenancy of a resident for any activity, engaged in by the resident, any member of the household of the resident, or any guest or other person under the control of the resident, that—

(A)   threatens the health or safety of, or right to peaceful enjoyment of the premises by, other residents or employees of the owner or manager of the housing;

       (B)   threatens the health or safety of, or right to peaceful enjoyment of their premises by, persons residing in the immediate vicinity of the premises; or

       (C)   is criminal activity (including drug-related criminal activity) on or off the premises.

  (b)   Tenant Selection.—The owner or manager of affordable rental housing assisted with grant amounts provided under this Act shall adopt and utilize written tenant selection policies and criteria that—

    (1)   are consistent with the purpose of providing housing for low-income families;

    (2)   are reasonably related to program eligibility and the ability of the applicant to perform the obligations of the lease; and

    (3)   provide for—

       (A)   the selection of tenants from a written waiting list in accordance with the policies and goals set forth in the Indian housing plan for the tribe that is the grant beneficiary of such grant amounts; and

       (B)   the prompt notification in writing of any rejected applicant of the grounds for any rejection.

Sec. 208. <25 USC 4138> Availability of Records.

  (a)   Provision of Information.—Notwithstanding any other provision of law, except as provided in paragraph (2), the National Crime Information Center, police departments, and other law enforcement agencies shall, upon request, provide information to Indian tribes or tribally designated housing entities regarding the criminal conviction records of adult applicants for, or tenants of, housing assisted with grant amounts provided to such tribe or entity under this Act for purposes of applicant screening, lease enforcement, and eviction.

  (b)   Exception.—A law enforcement agency described in paragraph (1) shall provide information under this paragraph relating to any criminal conviction of a juvenile only to the extent that the release of such information is authorized under the law of the applicable State, tribe, or locality.

  (c)   Confidentiality.—An Indian tribe or tribally designated housing entity receiving information under this section may use such information only for the purposes provided in this section and such information may not be disclosed to any person who is not an officer, employee, or authorized representative of the tribe or entity or the owner of housing assisted under this Act, and who has a job-related need to have access to the information for the purposes under this section. For judicial eviction proceedings, disclosures may be made to the extent necessary. The Secretary shall, by regulation, establish procedures necessary to ensure that information provided under this section to any tribe or entity is used, and confidentiality is maintained, as required under this section.

(Deletions)

Sec. 502. <25 USC 4181> Termination of Indian Housing Assistance under United States Housing Act of 1937.

  (a)   Termination of Assistance.—After September 30, 1997, financial assistance may not be provided under the United States Housing Act of 1937 or pursuant to any commitment entered into under such Act, for Indian housing developed or operated pursuant to a contract between the Secretary and an Indian housing authority, unless such assistance is provided from amounts made available for fiscal year 1997 and pursuant to a commitment entered into before September 30, 1997.

(b) Termination of Restrictions on Use of Indian Housing.—After September 30, 1997, any housing developed or operated pursuant to a contract between the Secretary and an Indian housing authority pursuant to the United States Housing Act of 1937 shall not be subject to any provision of such Act or any annual contributions contract or other agreement pursuant to such Act, but shall be considered and maintained as affordable housing for purposes of this Act.

Sec. 503. <25 USC 4182> Termination of New Commitments for Rental Assistance.

After September 30, 1997, financial assistance for rental housing assistance under the United States Housing Act of 1937 may not be provided to any Indian housing authority or tribally designated housing entity, unless such assistance is provided pursuant to a contract for such assistance entered into by the Secretary and the Indian housing authority before such date. Any such assistance provided pursuant to such a contract shall be governed by the provisions of the United States Housing Act of 1937 (as in effect before the date of the effectiveness of this Act) and the provisions of such contract.

(Deletions)

Sec. 601. <25 USC 4191> Authority and Requirements.

(a) Authority.—To such extent or in such amounts as provided in appropriations Acts, the Secretary may, subject to the limitations of this title (including limitations designed to protect and maintain the viability of rental housing units owned or operated by the recipient that were developed under a contract between the Secretary and an Indian housing authority pursuant to the United States Housing Act of 1937), and upon such terms and conditions as the Secretary may prescribe, guarantee and make commitments to guarantee, the notes or other obligations issued by Indian tribes or tribally designated housing entities with tribal approval, for the purposes of financing affordable housing activities described in section 202.

(b) Lack of Financing Elsewhere.—A guarantee under this title may be used to assist an Indian tribe or housing entity in obtaining financing only if the Indian tribe or housing entity has made efforts to obtain such financing without the use of such guarantee and cannot complete such financing consistent with the timely execution of the program plans without such guarantee.

(c) Terms of Loans.—Notes or other obligations guaranteed pursuant to this title shall be in such form and denominations, have such maturities, and be subject to such conditions as may be prescribed by regulations issued by the Secretary. The Secretary may not deny a guarantee under this title on the basis of the proposed repayment period for the note or other obligation, unless the period is more than 20 years or the Secretary determines that the period causes the guarantee to constitute an unacceptable financial risk.

(d) Limitation on Outstanding Guarantees.—No guarantee or commitment to guarantee shall be made with respect to any note or other obligation if the total outstanding notes or obligations of the issuer guaranteed under this title (excluding any amount defeased under the contract entered into under section

602(a)(1)) would thereby exceed an amount equal to 5 times the amount of the grant approval for the issuer pursuant to title III.

Speaker of the House of Representatives.
Vice President of the United States and President of the Senate.

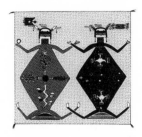

Resolution of the Tribal Council of the Confederated Salish and Kootenai Tribes to Oppose the Human Genome Diversity Project and Condemn Unethical Genetic Research on Indigenous Peoples (1998)

Introduction

By adopting the resolution presented here, the Salish and Kootenai Tribes have taken a clear and unequivocal stand on an issue of great concern to most people in the world (although they do not yet know it) and in particular to indigenous people. This issue is the granting of patents on biological material such as genes, plants, and animals, including humans. The Tribes have taken this position because, with indigenous, environmental, and religious groups around the world, they have found this activity to be a direct threat to and assault on both indigenous people and the natural order of life.

Under the general rubric of the Human Genome Diversity Project (HGDP), blood and tissue samples will be collected from hundreds of indigenous groups around the world for genetic study. Scientists maintain that this project may result in greater knowledge about human evolution. They also hope to use the information to discover cures to various diseases, especially, perhaps, those suffered disproportionately by indigenous people themselves. Another goal is to preserve for posterity or future scientific study the "cell lines" of native groups that may be headed for extinction.

Opposition to the HGDP has coalesced around a number of different points. Many native people make the point that the resources that are going into saving the genes of indigenous people would be far better used by saving the people themselves, that is, by providing access to clean water, vaccinations, and public health programs. In terms of finding answers to cosmological questions, native people note that they themselves have very few such questions and that the use of their genes in the service of passing "scientific" judgment on their beliefs is insulting and nonproductive. Many groups view "biopiracy" as just a more sophisticated form of storing their ancestors' remains in museums and scientific institutions. Furthermore, given the history of non-native treatment of indigenous people, many native groups wonder whether new genetic-based theories will be used to dispossess them even further of their rights and their land.

Neither are claims of possible medical benefits convincing. Native groups point out first of all that discovering medical applications does not fall within the purview of the HGDP's mission. In any case, any medicines that might be developed by private companies would almost certainly be too expensive for most native people to afford. The question of who stands to profit from this sort of activity is another point of contention, since it seems clear that, in this new version of the Gold Rush, "bioprospectors" will be able to stake legal claims on and profit from the genetic resources of indigenous people. There are well-established legal precedents in the United States that allow individuals to patent human genes. Few people doubt that the exploitation of the genetic resources of the Third and Fourth Worlds will mainly profit agribusiness and giant pharmaceutical companies.

Other objections center on the issue of access to and ownership of the genetic material. Access cannot be tightly controlled, and the possibility exists for people to create biological weapons that target specific human communities. The ownership issue already has a history. In 1990, for instance, the California Supreme Court ruled that donors do not have a property right to tissues or genetic material removed from their bodies. Furthermore, the question of "informed consent" and its potential for abuse raises red flags, especially, again, given past histories of treaty and other such "negotiations."

Many indigenous people object to the patenting of human life, as well as genetic engineering in general, on religious grounds. There is a strong belief in the responsibility to ensure the continuity of the natural order of all life, which, in any case, is strongly linked with the needs and hopes of indigenous people. This resolution makes the point that, for the Tribes as well as for native people all over the world, buying, selling, owning, altering, or patenting any life forms is "contrary to recognized human values and moral principles . . . and [violates] international codes of ethics. . . ." The Tribes demand immediate cessation of such activities and call upon the rest of the world, especially the U.S. government and private organizations, to actively support this position.

RESOLUTION OF THE TRIBAL COUNCIL OF THE CONFEDERATED SALISH AND KOOTENAI TRIBES OF THE FLATHEAD RESERVATION, MT

A Resolution to Oppose the Human Genome Diversity Project and Condemning Unethical Genetic Research on Indigenous Peoples

BE IT RESOLVED BY THE TRIBAL COUNCIL OF THE CONFEDERATED SALISH AND KOOTENAI TRIBES THAT; scientific research and genetic exploitation of indigenous peoples represents the greatest threat to American Indians since the European colonization of the Americas, and

WHEREAS, the Tribal Council has the authorities and duty to protect the health, security and general welfare of the Confederated Tribes; and

WHEREAS, the Confederated Salish and Kootenai Tribes support the Indigenous Peoples Coalition on Biopiracy in their efforts to stop genetic piracy and human rights violations against indigenous peoples throughout the world, and

WHEREAS, we declare absolute opposition to the Human Genome Diversity Project or other studies that violate the genetic integrity of indigenous peoples, and demand the immediate suspension of any activities to collect genetic samples, cell lines, or data of indigenous peoples, including our deceased ancestors; and

WHEREAS, we demand the fullest cooperation of any government agency or independent research institute for the return of all genetic materials, cell lines, and data they may have in their possession to the appropriate governing authorities of Tribal Governments; and

WHEREAS, we oppose any attempt to monopolize or commercialize the genetic samples, cell lines, or data derived from the cell lines of indigenous peoples, through the application of intellectual property law and patent systems; and

WHEREAS, we demand the international scientific community condemn any research that has been carried out contrary to recognized human values and moral principles, and that violates the international codes of ethics described in the Nuremberg Code and the World Medical Association Declaration of Helsinki; and

WHEREAS, federal law recognizes Tribal Governments as sovereigns with the primary authority to deny access to, refuse to participate in, or to authorize any removal of genetic materials from our peoples and our lands. The ethical principle of "individual informed consent" is also applicable, and is secondary to Tribal Governmental consent; and

WHEREAS, we demand that scientific endeavors be prioritized and resources allocated to support and improve social, economic and environmental conditions of indigenous peoples in their homelands, thereby, directly improving health conditions and raising the overall quality of life; and

WHEREAS, we demand an immediate moratorium on collections and/or patenting of genetic materials from indigenous peoples and their resources by any scientific project, health organization, government, independent agency, or individual researcher;

NOW THEREFORE, BE IT RESOLVED BY THE CONFEDERATED SALISH AND KOOTENAI TRIBES THAT, we demand that the United States Government and any private sector organizations cease participation, funding and other types of assistance to the Human Genome Diversity Project, or any related research projects which seek to research the genome of indigenous peoples; and finally

BE IT FURTHER RESOLVED THAT, we denounce the integrity of the report by the Committee on Human Genome Diversity of the National Research Council which gives biased and unethical endorsement to the Human Genome Diversity Project while acknowledging the "lack of a sharply defined proposal that it could evaluate."

Certification

The foregoing resolution was duly adopted by the Tribal Council of the Confederated Salish and Kootenai Tribes on the 15th day of January, 1998, with a vote of 10 for, 0 opposed, and 0 not voting, pursuant to the authority vested in it by Article VI, Section 1 (a), (c),(i) and (u) of the Tribal Constitution and Bylaws; said Constitution adopted and approved under Section 16 of the Act of June 18, 1934 (48 Stat. 984), as amended.

Signed,
Michael T. Pablo
Chairman of the Tribal Council

Attest:
Joseph E. Dupuis
Executive Secretary

RESOLUTION BY AN ALLIANCE OF FIRST NATIONS AND OTHER GROUPS ON A MORATORIUM ON SALMON FARMING IN BRITISH COLUMBIA (1997)

INTRODUCTION

The "Natural Resource Control" entry in the Contemporary Issues section suggests the importance of fishing, especially for salmon, to Indian tribes of the Northwest and the Columbia River plateau. A long, difficult, and expensive battle culminated in a major court victory (*United States* v. *State of Washington,* 1974) that affirmed the tribes' treaty rights to a significant extent. While ongoing non-native opposition— including the placement of salmon on the Endangered Species List—has forced the tribes to continue the legal struggle, in general they have reestablished their fisheries and restored salmon to its rightful place in their religious practice and spirituality.

First Nations living farther north along the Pacific coast have had similar problems with their salmon fishery. Indeed, in some ways they are worse off than Indians living in the United States. The latter could at least bring suit based on treaty violations, whereas Indians in British Columbia do not generally have treaties, since British Columbia traditionally refused to treat with First Nations. At this late date, First Nations are still trying to work out just settlements with the British Columbia government to compensate them for years of neglect at best and abuse at the worst (see the book's introduction, for example, for a reference to the Nisga'a treaty).

All along the British Columbia coast, including the territory of the Musgamagw Tsawataineuk Tribal Council (Broughton Archipelago) and other First Nations, the salmon aquaculture industry is causing a great deal of harm to the environment and, of course, to native resources and life. Because the industry uses open-cage systems, the ocean floor in places is covered with up to four feet of antibiotic residue and fecal fallout. Industry practices have encouraged the transfer of disease from farmed fish to wild stock, harming salmon fisheries from British Columbia to as far away as Norway. Such practices have even forced animals to change their migration patterns. For example, the high-frequency noise used to keep seals from attacking the penned salmon has kept away orcas, the seals' main predators, who would naturally migrate into the region.

The toxic mix of fecal fallout and antibiotic residue is poisoning local shellfish beds that are an important source of food for First Nations people. Other foods collected near netcage operations are also poisoned; their use constitutes an increased health risk. The entire picture—environmental degradation, diseased and decreased wild stock, and disruption of natural animal cycles—has led to a loss of access to and a crisis in the traditional fisheries for First Nations people.

The situation is so dangerous that even the powerful salmon aquaculture industry was unable to stop a coalition of First Nations and non-native environmentalists and other concerned groups from forcing the provincial government to enact a moratorium on the practice pending a formal governmental review. The review, completed in 1997, was labeled fundamentally flawed and its suggested regulatory changes a joke by the coalition, which calls in the document presented here for the moratorium to be maintained until real solutions are found.

Despite the fact that over 95 percent of First Nations in British Columbia support the moratorium and the call for regulations with teeth, the future does not look hopeful. The industry provides jobs to a region in need of jobs (just how many jobs is unclear: Opponents believe even the modest industry figure of 2,700 to be wildly exaggerated), and pressure is mounting for a repeal of the moratorium. As a result of a chronically overcrowded docket, court challenges are years away. Indians in British Columbia are only about 3 percent of the population, and their efforts to salvage their fisheries, so central to their way of life, and to prevent profound environmental and health risks, for others as well as for themselves, do not hold much political weight.

RESOLUTION PASSED BY BRITISH COLUMBIA ALLIANCE
ON SALMON FARMING, SEPTEMBER 1997

Whereas, the natural wild salmon of the Pacific Northwest are a sacred resource of all Canadians that deserve protection and conservation;

Whereas, the First Nations of British Columbia have relied upon the fisheries and pristine coastal waters since time immemorial as a source of food and cornerstone of culture;

Whereas, Canada and British Columbia recognize and affirm the constitutional rights of First Nations to fish, second only to conservation;

Whereas, the Salmon Aquaculture Review lists 1800 pages of problems associated with open salmon net cages and 49 recommendations that are Band-Aids for the problems but are not a solution;

Therefore the following First Nations, Environmental organizations, and individuals call upon Canada and B.C. to maintain the moratorium on salmon farming in B.C. waters until:

1. safe closed loop containment systems replace the existing 80 open net cage systems, and

2. Interim Measures Agreements or treaties regarding fisheries resources are in place for B.C.'s coastal First Nations.

Representation:

Musgamagw Tswataineuk Tribal Council
Kwa-wa-aineuk First Nation
Kwicksutaineuk First Nation
Tsawataineuk First Nation
'Namgis First Nation
Kwakiutl District Council
Nuu-Chau- Nulth Tribal Council
Ahousat First Nation
Tla-o-qui-aht First Nation
Heilstuk First Nation
Kitkatla First Nation
Whe-la-la-U Area Council
BC Aboriginal Fisheries Commission
Nicola Valley Watershed Fisheries
Kwakiutl Territorial Fisheries Commission
Comox Strathcona Regional District
Electoral Area "A" Mount Waddington Regional District
David Suzuki Foundation
Sierra Legal Defence Fund
Georgia Strait Alliance
Alberni Environmental Coalition
Friends of Clayoquot Sound
Sierra Club of BC
Wild Fish First Society
Western Canada Wilderness Committee
Wave Length
Concerned Sointula residents
Concerned Port Alberni residents

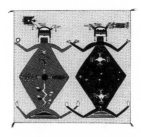

CONFEDERATED NATIVE COURT
JUDGMENT AND REASONS (1997)

INTRODUCTION

For their own reasons, both the U.S. and Canadian governments strongly encouraged officially recognized native groups to create nontraditional political structures, such as constitutions, band councils (Canada), and tribal councils (United States). Many constitutions also provide for a judicial branch that functions very nearly like that of the dominant society (see examples drawn from tribal constitutions in the Contemporary Profiles of Tribes and Groups section). However, today there are Indian courts and there are Indian courts. Even though many tribes and First Nations have created nontraditional structures to satisfy federal officials, they continue to recognize the authority—in some cases, the preeminent authority—of traditional structures such as elders' councils and hereditary chiefs. Among some groups the two systems coexist relatively harmoniously; for others they conflict. Charges that federally recognized entities are overly responsive to non-native pressure are not uncommon, yet the decisions of traditional governments and courts suffer from limited effectiveness because they are routinely ignored by federal authorities.

The judgment presented here was generated by a court that is neither traditional nor federally acknowledged. More precisely, its authority is not recognized by either the U.S. or Canadian governments, yet it is traditional, in a way, since its members have chosen to convene it based on authority granted by their own people. The four groups represented—Mohegan, Passamaquoddy, Mi'gmaq, and Algonquin—are sovereign and independent nations, yet they share a common language family, Algonquian, as well as some cultural traditions. Each signatory is considered fully as legitimate and authoritative among their people as are legally appointed or elected judges by non-native governments.

In fact, this is one of the points the document seeks to make: Based on fundamental and universally recognized legal principles, this court is every bit as legitimate as—in fact, more legitimate than—courts of either the United States or Canada. The judges base their claim to jurisdiction on prima facie evidence, but, in the event that "newcomer" courts do not agree with their conclusion, the judges further claim the right, also based on fundamental legal principles, to jointly submit the issue to an independent and impartial third party. Finally, reserving for themselves legal prerogatives usually claimed by non-native courts, the judges offer "newcomer" courts the opportunity to contest the judgment in person.

The text that follows the brief judgment lays out, using language and with a perspective not usually seen by non-natives, the reasons for the court's conclusions. I have included their references to specific international and constitutional laws in order to inform readers more thoroughly as to both historical background and contemporary legal proceedings. On the whole it is a remarkable document, one that should give pause to anyone who conceives of native rights in simplistic terms. The implications of the judges' conclusions are extremely inconvenient for non-native North Americans, yet to ignore them is to risk conceding, as few people are willing to do, that "might equals right," that genocide is justifiable, and that the rule of law is no law at all.

CONFEDERATED NATIVE COURT JUDGMENT AND REASONS

(Mohegan a.k.a. Mahican a.k.a. Mohecan Court, Richelieu River East, Quebec, Canada, Lake Chaplain East, Vermont, U.S.A. and Quebec, Canada and the Hudson River, New York, Vermont, Massachusetts and Connecticut, U.S.A.)

(Passamaquoddy Court, St. Croix River, Maine, United States and New Brunswick, Canada)

(Mi'gmaq Court, Chaleur Bay/Restigouche River, Quebec and New Brunswick, Canada)

(Algonquin Court, Ottawa and Lower St. Lawrence Rivers, Quebec and Ontario, Canada)

IN THE MATTER OF court jurisdiction under natural law in and over the unceded Indian territories of the Hudson, St. Croix, Chaleur Bay, Ottawa and lower St. Lawrence River Drainage Basins and Estuaries;

AND IN THE MATTER OF court jurisdiction under international and constitutional law's confirmation of natural law pursuant to Magna Carta, 1215, Sublimus Deus, 1537, Statute of Frauds, 1670, Mohegan Indians v. Connecticut, 1704, Cherokee Nation v. Georgia, 1831, Regina v. Cadien, 1838, and the Convention for the Prevention and Punishment of the Crime of Genocide, 1948.

Between:
Mohegan Court, Passamaquoddy Court, Mi'gmaq Court and Algonquin Court Native Courts

and:

Supreme Court of the United States and Supreme Court of Canada Newcomer Courts

Judgment

UPON TAKING judicial notice of the suppression and genocide of the native people caused by the prematurely assumed jurisdiction of the newcomer courts, and in accordance with the accompanying reasons for judgment, this native court declares:

1. Court jurisdiction prima facie territorially is vested in the native courts and precluded from the newcomer courts; and
2. That in the event the newcomer courts are unable to agree with and help to uphold this declaration of right, this court invites the newcomer courts to join with this court in referring the contested jurisdictional issue for independent and impartial third party court adjudication in the international arena; or, in the alternative
3. That in the event the newcomer courts or their governments wish to submit evidence, law or argument to this native court so as to deny the premises, findings or law as expressed herein or in the accompanying reasons for judgment, they are welcome to do so upon notifying this court of that intent.

February 2, 1997.

"Sachem Ron Roberts"
Sachem Judge, Mohegan

"Gary Metallic Sr."
Sagamaq Judge, Mi'gmaq

"John Stevens"
Sagamore Judge, Passamaquoddy

"William Commanda"
Ogima Judge, Algonquin

Reasons for Judgment

Humankind can, so easily as just doing it, choose to turn away from the Injustice Way of the past. And set its future course upon the Justice Way.

To this native court, as we hope and trust the newcomers' courts will learn to understand and respect, the Justice Way is one and the same as the Nature Way or the Native Way. It is the way of natural law.

Until recently when native people spoke of the Nature Way or the Native Way, there was hardly any basis for a communicative connection with the newcomers. The newcomers seemed unable to hear. It was rather like what Friedrich Wilhelm Nietzsche said:

> No one can draw more out of things, books included, than he already knows. A man has no ears for that to which experience has given him no access.

When the newcomers began laying waste the forests of the new world some natives could hear the sounds of the trees screaming in the face of the onslaught. But they do not hear. And if they were told, they dismissed the stories as fanciful. Yet science now discloses that plants do communicate and the medium appears to be sounds or chemicals beyond the normal reach of human sensory perception. We are told that when giraffes eat the leaves of acacia trees, the trees downwind produce chemicals that make their leaves inedible. Native medicine people could hear, sense or feel the resonances of dimensions of reality beyond the imagination of the newcomers, who dismissed their accounts as hallucinations or charlatanry. Yet since Einstein and Picasso, mathematicians, physicists, musicians and

artists have ventured far beyond abstractionism and the theory of relativity—
into quantum mechanics, unified field theory and hyperspace—making some of
the "wildest dreams" of the ancient magicians and prophets seem like simple
foresight.

Science, education and knowledge have evolved to the point where humanity is
on the brink of discovering what it already knew, before the alienation of humankind
from nature: there is a unity and a harmony that science no less than religion can
suspect or feel even if not quite yet fully understand.

If that intuition can be translated into experience for modern humankind, it will
be in virtue of tapping into the collective unconscious that unites humanity at its genetic roots. It will entail a rediscovery native people have never lost, but which was
once common for all of humanity, before the sense of awe based upon respect was su-
perseded by the conceit of the dominance of nature.

The native prophecies forecast this time. They also forecast that when this
time did come humankind and nature would be on the cusp of annihilation and
despoliation.

Before the European invasion of North America, native society was true to its
natural law principles. People, earth, sky and water were free and unpolluted. The jurisdiction of the native courts helped to maintain this condition; for the native
courts oversaw the application in practice of the natural law principles.

In contrast with the prominence of the court function the government function
was relatively minor, except in time of war. In peacetime it was not thought necessary
to survival in good health for native society to be very much engaged in the making
of new and detailed laws. Rather, the harmonious application in practice of the old
laws, the finite set of natural law principles, sufficed to maintain the balance.

After the European invasion the policy and practice of some of the newcomers
was to covet the earth, sky and water by eradicating, or at least transforming, native
society. The aboriginal people became victims of genocide; and the earth, sky and
water of genocide's companion: ecocide.

Since native society was held together by the court function, eradicating or
transforming native society meant suppressing native society's court function. The
specific way has been to substitute, prematurely and therefore illegally, the jurisdiction of the newcomers' own courts, and in a complementary and distracting way to
foster native preoccupation with new governmental functions.

To this end, the newcomer governments and courts in the United States and
Canada constitute and promote Indian governments that are federally organized,
recognized and funded, to the virtual exclusion of the native courts in the traditional jurisdiction context. These federally organized and recognized native governments function as the newcomers' agents in the application of federal law. That application is in many regions illegal, because premature, and of genocidal and
ecological consequence.

By being premature, the territorial application of federal law can be contrary to
natural law, international law and constitutional law. It depends upon whether the
native people have consented and ever since the European invasion began has been,
the specific legal means for ascertaining the consent.

Furthermore, the sufficiency of the consent—the evidence and deliberation of
its existence—is itself governed by specific positive law.

In essence, territory is off-limits to newcomers until it has been purchased by the
newcomers' governments from the natives. And purchase is a question of mixed fact
and law.

This court finds, based upon judicial notice, there has been no such purchase relative to the territories encompassed by the Ottawa, St. Lawrence and Hudson River drainage systems, Manhattan Island aside. And certainly there has been no third party adjudication of this issue.

The axis geographically described by the Ottawa, St. Lawrence and Hudson River drainage systems marks the riverine highway system that united the Algonkian-speaking linguistic family of north eastern North America, including what became known as the Mohegans, the Passamaquoddies, the Mi'gmaqs and the Algonquins. To the west lie the territories of the Iroquois-speakers. Of the Algonkian family of native nations, the Mohegans represent the southern reach, the Algonquins the northern and the Passamaquoddies and Mi'gmaqs the central and eastern. Together they are a natural collective entity of affiliated people, united not only by language but by genetics, history, culture and shared institutions for dispute resolution—the council fire system—such as represented by this native court.

The territories of each of the confederated native courts speaking collectively and in solidarity by means of these reasons for judgment remain unceded. So far as known to the oral history and personal knowledge, which together define this court's experience and understanding, there has been no purchase.

The New Brunswick region of the Passamaquoddy territory has not even arguably been ceded by the Passamaquoddies. As for their Maine region, the Maine Settlement purchase of 1980 was induced by fraud, duress and undue influence. The Passamaquoddies were coerced into signing by the fraudulent misrepresentation that they were not entitled to third party adjudication, but rather were at the mercy of their jurisdictional adversaries: the governments and courts of the newcomers. For this reason the Maine Settlement is unenforceable against objecting natives.

The Mi'gmaqs, Gespegewaqi District, which takes in the Restigouche River/Chaleur Bay drainage know the Gaspe region of Quebec and the northern region of New Brunswick, were coerced in 1779 into signing a peace and friendship treaty that does not even purport to be a purchase. And that signing was done under the newcomers' threat that 10 Mi'gmaqs being held hostage literally would be murdered if the signing were not done. That treaty therefore also is not relevant to the jurisdiction issue raised and addressed in these reasons for judgment.

There is no purchase even arguably referable to either the Hudson River drainage basin of the Mohegans or to the Ottawa and St. Lawrence River drainage basin of the Algonquins.

Since the courts of the natives and the courts of the newcomers equally are interested in the answer to the purchase question, each court system, including this court, equally is biased in addressing and resolving it. For this reason, the law is that this question can only be answered as to any given territory by an outsider—an independent and impartial third party court—one the existence of whose jurisdiction does not itself turn upon a prejudgment of the very issue in contention: which court system, native or newcomer, has jurisdiction?

The assumption by the newcomers' courts that they have the jurisdiction to decide the question of their own jurisdiction when in competition with the jurisdiction of the natives' courts, is the means to the genocide and the ecocide. That assumption is how those crimes against humanity and nature are perfected, in North America. And because of the influence of the United States and Canada upon world affairs, the successful and consistent apprehension of those crimes in the global village will not occur unless and until those crimes are apprehended here, at home.

By this route we arrive at the actual identity of the natural law principles. 1st and greatest, because all others depend upon it for their continuity and integrity, is this principle of third party adjudication.

In native society those performing the court function often, but not always, were hereditary personages. If a particular eldest child of the arbitrating family were not inclined or predisposed well to implement the function, alternative persons could and would be substituted.

But always adjudication was implemented with the advice, guidance and wisdom of the elders, those in whom was reposed the sacred trust of civilization: the continuity of the genealogical information, history, traditions and values. The carrying out of this court function was not meant to be profitable. It was a burden, a responsibility, a duty, and a privilege.

The crucial feature was that the person doing the deciding not be interested, in the sense of either advantaged or disadvantaged by the resolution of the issue in dispute. Sometimes there were issues that transcended whole communities. For this reason, among others such as social and economic reasons, communities were associated. The so-called Indian confederacies served this function, both as courts of appeal from individual community resolutions, as well as in the capacity of courts of first instance relative to disputes that efficiently could not be approached at the community level. Great councils met, at which the wisdom of the communities was pooled, and applied.

Even though native people have experienced an inconsistency between principle and practice at the hands of the newcomers, we understand that the legal heritage of the newcomers is the same as ours on the 1st principle of natural law: third party adjudication. We are informed that in Roman Law it was said *nemo potest esse simul actor et judex* (no one can be at once suitor and judge). Reputedly, the philosopher David Hume stated in reference to the principle of third party adjudication: "Here then is the origin of civil government and society." We concur.

This then is the 1st principle of natural law: third party adjudication. And what is natural law?—the law that is both anterior and superior to all other forms of law, a set of legal principles rooted in the nature and reason of humankind. This is the law to which the suppressed native North Americans' courts hold true.

The time has come for the native courts, with respect, to remind the newcomers' courts of the natural law basis for all law, for the good of all natives and newcomers alike, and for the health of their shared environment.

It is not necessary to achieve this purpose that this court oppose any native government that is carrying out modern governmental functions, for there is no conflict between this court's ancient jurisdiction and the functions of modern native governments. Modern native governments by definition do not assert, never asserted, and could not in terms of their own constitutions ever have asserted, the ancient court traditional function. From the outset of their organization, recognition and funding by the newcomers' governments, the modern federally recognized native governments have been motivated and funded to steer native society away from exercising its traditional court function vis-a-vis yet unceded native territory. From the outset, the suppression of the native court function has been the excuse used to pretend there was judicial vacuum into which the newcomers need for adjudication [fell]. From the outset, as the alternative to continuing the more direct form of genocide by wholesale outright killing, this judicial usurpation by the newcomers' courts has been the modus operandi of the genocide in North America.

For this reason the jurisdiction of this native court supplements and complements, but does not intend to compete with the modern native governmental function. To the extent that the jurisdiction of this native court competes or conflicts with any other jurisdiction, it is with the usurped jurisdiction of the newcomers' courts, and then relative only to territory that has not been purchased by the newcomers from the natives in accordance with natural law, international law and constitutional law.

Since natural law is at the root of all law the primary mandate of this court, when exercising its jurisdiction, is to implement the 4 principles of natural law relative to territory that has not, in its view, or in the view of the independent and impartial third party adjudicator under the 1st principle of natural law, been ceded to the newcomer governments in accordance with the following 3 principles of natural law.

The 2nd great principle of natural law is that truth is the summit of being, and justice is the application of truth to affairs.

3rd, respect is the imperative of being, and law worthy of the name is the application of respect to affairs.

4th, law begets liberty if but only if the law is based upon the 1st, 2nd and 3rd principles:—if, but only if, the system of third party adjudication implements justice as applied truth and law as applied respect. Otherwise, law begets nothing more than the illusion of order, but which inherently is unstable. Inevitably it leads to disorder, for life without liberty is offensive to the human condition and will, eventually, be rebelled against.

This is what the rule of law means, at least to the native people organized in their traditional native courts.

All of these principles of natural law as traditionally implemented by the native courts are mirrored in the newcomers' international law and constitutional law, which binds the newcomers' courts. But before engaging the details of the substantive provisions of that international law and constitutional law, it is absolutely crucial to comprehend exactly the specific legal sense in which the newcomers' courts are indeed well and truly bound.

So far as we are aware, no jurist has expressed this status with greater legal precision than E. V. Dicey, in a lecture given to the Harvard School of Law, published in 1920. He stated:

> Judge-made law is subject to certain limitations. It can not openly declare a new principle always take the form of a deduction from some legal principle whereof the validity is admitted, or the application or interpretation of some statutory enactment. It can not override statutory law. The courts may, by a process of interpretation, indirectly limit or possibly extend the operation of a statute, but they can not set a statute aside. Nor have they in England ever adopted the doctrine which exists, one is told, in Scotland, that a statute may be obsolete by disuse. It can not from its very nature override any established principle of judge-made law.

Dicey's legal point, with which this native court agrees, is that when addressing established natural law, international law and constitutional law, the judges of all courts of law are bound to respect and to apply the previously ascertained constitutive law.

Law that by intent is definitive of the character of the social contract upon which the society is premised, is, once declared for the first time, thereafter continuous. It continues until the people of the society or of the group of societies as a whole, change it, by due process. The change process does not number among its legitimate mechanisms judicial departure from, or willful blindness to, the established law.

This process of fundamental and constitutive change is not left up to panels called judges. Theirs is to apply previously established law, once it has been established. If they are first upon the scene of any given issue, judges can declare constitutive law, such as by recognizing certain principles, which is the essential mechanism of the common law. But thereafter, once the law has for the first time been ascertained, whether by originating statute or common law declaration, the constitutive natural law, international law and constitutional law is not subject to judicial change. Only statutory repeal is competent to that sort of profound change; judicial activism is not. Even less, are judicial assumptions made in a condition of unawareness of the previously established constitutive law.

This point of jurisdictional competence was settled, in terms of the Anglo-American legal tradition, by the original and authoritative precedent of *Campbell* v. *Hall* (1774), 98 er 848. In this, Lord Mansfield, speaking for the imperial Privy Council of Great Britain, held that once the king by exercise of the royal prerogative has conceded constitutive rights or liberties, such as in that case pursuant to the Royal Proclamation of 7 October 1763, thereafter the royal prerogative is exhausted upon the conceded issue. If at any future time the conceded rights or liberties are to be repealed or altered in a profound particular (as contrasted with merely regulated or extended in a more cosmetic sense) the repeal or alteration can only be by way of international convention or statutory constitutional enactment.

In the Anglo-American legal tradition the newcomers' court function traces its root to that same royal prerogative as was held in *Campbell* v. *Hall* inherently to be limited to recognizing existing law, but not to repealing previously established law. The kings' courts were created pursuant to the prerogative to administer laws, not to substitute themselves for the people as lawmakers. As *Campbell* v. *Hall* makes apparent, even the king himself could not directly take back the native rights conceded under the Royal Proclamation of 1763.

All the more so is it impossible for the king's courts to achieve indirectly that which the king could not achieve directly. And what applies to the king's courts applies to any and all other courts, for the limitation is inherent in the court function.

If it were not so limited courts would be rulers of the people, making their own law, rather than servants of the people administering the peoples' law.

The simple point is that natural law, international law and constitutional law rights, once conceded, cannot easily be withdrawn by tyrants or substitute tyrants. The withdrawing, if it is to occur at all, can only be achieved by the people. The form of the withdrawal can only be by way of formal international law convention and constitutional law repeal. This feature is common to native and newcomer law and government, and is probably a universal characteristic of democratic human social organization.

The familiar example of this process is the American Revolution that ended the first British Empire. The American colonists felt that constitutive rights and liberties were guaranteed them under previously established natural law, international law and constitutional law. They reasoned that the king and his courts were departing from that previously established law, and that this departure forfeited the jurisdiction of that king and those courts. The issue was taken to the people, who apparently supported it by the Declaration of Independence, which acknowledged the forfeiture, and made the former subject colonies into independent sovereign states. Great Britain acknowledged this by the Peace of Paris.

A war was necessary to perfect the change vis-a-vis America, because at that time there was no tribunal established to carry out the function of third party between Great Britain and the Continental Congress of the associated states, which is to say as between the people of the British Isles and the people of Great Britain in America. The rule of law had not, apparently, at that juncture in world history evolved a judicial institution capable independently and impartially of resolving the disagreement by peaceable judgment in lieu of war. History repeated itself with the American Civil War.

Today, Canada is facing the same kind of challenge: that posed by the prospect of Quebec secession, and the reassertion of yet unceded native sovereignty. No states are threatening to secede from the United States, but the issue of native sovereignty remains vital there no less than in Canada.

The question, therefore, becomes whether the rule of law and its administrators sufficiently have matured in the interval since the Civil War to allow reason to supplant force majeure as the resolution mechanism.

The issue of jurisdictional competence is so very central and important to this question because an erroneous assumption appears to have crept into and to have infected the North American judicial system, with disastrous consequences for the moral structure and physical integrity of North American society in general. Setting affairs right, now, depends upon examining that erroneous character of that assumption in light of existing natural, international and constitutional law, and correcting the identified mistake. This is the purpose, ultimately, of the present renewal of the long-suppressed jurisdiction of the native court system, as represented by these reasons for judgment.

Existing natural law, international law and constitutional law more adequately should have tempered the newcomers' conduct toward both the native North Americans and the North American environment. Lamentably, the newcomers often have been and in some regions still are in breach of natural, international and constitutional law. When the newcomers systematically and in a coordinated fashion breach the natural, international and constitutional law in any given region, they do so by applying domestic rules of conduct that pretend to be law, but which are not really law, precisely because they conflict with the anterior and superior natural law, international law and constitutional law.

When this occurs the rule of law is in abeyance, overrun by mere policy and practice masquerading as law. To the extent that this anti-law domestic "law" is allowed to supersede the consensus of natural law, international law and constitutional law, the rule of law is negated, and the harmonious survival of humankind in nature is jeopardized.

A right is that which the law permits one human or a group of humans to do, and which obliges others not to interfere with the doing. The most basic right in natural law is the natural concomitant of the 3rd principle of natural law: respect is the imperative of being, and law worthy of the name is the application of respect to affairs. Thus, the basic right of those humans first on territory is the right to be respected by subsequent newcomers, in terms of the first occupants' original jurisdiction and possession.

The counterbalancing obligation upon the newcomers is to respect the first right, specifically by not assuming original jurisdiction and possession. Newcomers legally can derive all or a portion of the original right, by purchase. But they cannot, legally, have the original right simply by assuming in policy and practice that the first humans are not vested with it. To do so would be to deny the humanity of those first humans, which breaks the 3rd principle of natural law. Again, respect is the imperative of being, and law worthy of the name is the application of respect to affairs.

It would be beneficial for all of humanity were the newcomers' society in North America now to address and correct its historic breach of the existing law. Society can do this by conforming to the existing law, or by due process repealing or amending the existing law. It can adopt a combination of both devices. But society cannot, legally, do this by having its courts rise above the existing law.

To do that strikes an unmistakable and undeniable posture of opportunism and lawlessness, of might being right; a posture that is so close to the heart of the society as to set a standard which negates the moral structure which makes and keeps the society a society. It is in this sense that Hume was being precise for legal purposes when he identified the true application of law under the system of third party adjudication as "the origin of civil government and society."

North American society leads humanity's evolutionary advance in the field of human and environmental rights, and neither genocide nor ecocide will be apprehended generally in the world so long as the leading exponents of its apprehension, the United States and Canada, continue to stonewall the issue at home. The addressing of this issue, in accordance with the rule of law, will signal a new beginning for humanity, a rational basis upon which to have hope for the harmonious survival of humankind in nature. With the passing of the genocide can pass from history the ecological assault upon the planet, that excess which arises in consequence of the same immature, immoderate and uncontrolled attitude in human society as that which results in the genocide.

For these purposes the native people presently feel the need to reinstitute, in practice, their original natural law right of jurisdiction, at least in regions where Indian treaties relinquishing that original right either have not yet been made or, if made, made invalidly, such as under fraud, duress or undue influence, or where there has been a failure of consideration.

Specifically, the natives upon the remaining unpurchased lands propose to exercise their inherent and never-surrendered right of court jurisdiction, so as to declare the nature of existing law, and to order the repair of its breach in various ways. Most importantly, they expect and will invite the courts of the newcomers to show comity, reciprocally by assisting with the enforcement of such native court judgments, as against the newcomer courts' own people, the newcomers.

It is conceivable that the newcomers' courts on this continent may disagree with these reasons for judgment that existing law precludes their assumption of jurisdiction relative to territory that has not been purchased by the newcomers from the natives.

But it is not open to the newcomers' courts to pretend to abrogate unto themselves the third party jurisdiction function. The newcomers' courts are not third parties. They are interested parties. If the rule of law is to function at all, it will only be in virtue of both the newcomers' and the natives' courts submitting the impasse for third party adjudication.

When that happens vis-a-vis North America, humankind will have made an evolutionary advance of structural consequence. Human evolution has moved beyond genetic mutation. Its future lies in the evolution of human institutions. Preeminent among these institutions is the rule of law administered by third party adjudication: the pragmatic guarantor of justice as applied truth, of law as applied respect, and of order as dependably stabilized liberty.

The natives wish it to be well understood that by identifying the truth and seeking respect in this fashion they do not seek to dispossess the trespassing newcomers, whose governments and courts have in the past usurped the natives' original jurisdiction and thereby denied the natives' humanity.

The natives and their traditional courts accept the facts of history as being irreversibly albeit illegally accomplished, but nevertheless seek for the future a more balanced native and newcomer relationship, one that more faithfully conforms, in alternative ways, with the spirit of the law and justice which all too often has been breached. In contemplation is a viable and modern service economy, in place and in stead of the illegally destroyed aboriginal economy, in circumstances where the new economy respects the integrity and the sanctity of the land, in perpetuity.

This native court turns now to the details of the international law and constitutional law. ...

(deletions)

As can be seen several of those applications for leave to appeal to the Supreme Court of Canada had arisen when the Supreme Court of British Columbia and the Court of Appeal for British Columbia held that the case of *Delgamuukw* v. *Attorney General of British Columbia* supposedly had addressed and resolved the jurisdictional point of law. That conclusion had been disputed by Dr. Clark on behalf of the native traditionalists on the ground the court jurisdiction point of law had not been raised in the Delgamuukw case. In the lower courts the attorneys general of British Columbia and Canada informed the judges that the Delgamuukw case had addressed and resolved the issue. Later, when one of the Delgamuukw appellants therefore sought to have the constitutional question of court jurisdiction addressed in the Supreme Court of Canada appeal in that case, the same attorneys general did a 180° about-face, and asserted that the lower courts in Delgamuukw had not even so much as touched upon the court jurisdiction issue.

This matter arose in the Supreme Court of Canada when, in the summer of 1995, legal counsel Bruce Clark was also retained as counsel by one of the appellants in the said Delgamuukw case. Leave to appeal had already been granted in the Supreme Court of Canada in that case. Clark's brief was to raise the same jurisdictional point of law as that for which leave to appeal had been denied, as unimportant, in all the other cases. For this purpose he made an application to state the jurisdictional issue as a constitutional question.

On September 12, 1995 the application to state the constitutional question was denied, on the ground that the point of law had not been raised in the courts below in the Delgamuukw case, and so could not be raised for the first time on the appeal in the Supreme Court of Canada.

In sum, by the summer/fall of 1995 it was apparent that when natives raise the court jurisdiction issue it will not be addressed by newcomer courts, no matter how it is raised. No procedural stone has been left unturned. When they try to appeal this judicial willful blindness, the Supreme Court of Canada treats the issue as not important, and denies leave to appeal. When leave is already obtained, as in the Delgamuukw case, the Supreme Court of Canada will not address the issue because the issue was not vetted in the courts below. But the Supreme Court of Canada knows that the issue is never going to be vetted by the courts below it. It had just seen the evidence of this.

Between the refusals in July and September by the Supreme Court to address the jurisdiction issue, the Registrar of the Supreme Court reported Bruce Clark to the bar association, in an attempt to have him disbarred for having insulted the court by raising the point of law. In fact, some 23 other complaints were made by or on behalf of the several judges before whom Clark had raised the point. Rather than address the law publicly, the judges worked behind the scenes to secure the disbarment of Clark for raising the law, in effect to silence the messenger in order to evade the issue.

On June 19, 1996 the bar association ruled (a) that genocide is a fact and (b) that the judges should have addressed the law. The attempt by the judges to have Clark disbarred failed.

On January 17, 1997 the Supreme Court of Canada agreed to hear the point of law argued by Dr Clark on behalf of the Mi'gmaq Nation, but refused to hear it argued on behalf of the Algonquin Nation. The only difference was that an Indian Act band opposed the Algonquin traditionalists' application, but no Indian Act band opposed the Mi'gmaq application. The context is the constitutional reference concerning the legal right, if any, of Quebec to secede from the Canadian union. The traditional natives' point is that the Court has no jurisdiction to address the question vis-a-vis that portion of Quebec that is still unpurchased Indian territory.

In reaction to the above noted pattern of unconscionable judicial stonewalling of the legal issue, and in reaction to the ongoing genocide that continues because of that stonewalling, some native traditionalists of the appellants and others occupied an armed but nevertheless defensive position at Gustafsen Lake in northern British Columbia. On August 25, 1995 they sent out from their redoute-under-police-siege a single demand that read as follows:

> The Sundancers at Gustafsen Lake have one demand: that the petition dated January 3, 1995 be addressed publicly by an independent and impartial third party tribunal, one that is neither Canadian nor Indian, such as the special constitutional court established by Queen Anne at the request of the Mohegan Indians to which court the petition is addressed: (a) is the popular assumption that the Canadian courts and police have jurisdiction legal? (b) or is that assumption criminally treasonable, fraudulent and complicitous in the genocide of the aboriginal peoples of Canada as alleged in the petition?

Rather than allow that question of law as requested to go for resolution to the constitutionally designated independent and impartial third party tribunal in accordance with the rule of law, the natives' resistance was overcome by the police. Accordingly, the Gustafsen Lake demonstrators are now facing trial in the Supreme Court of British Columbia. By way of ensuring that their point of law would not be raised and defended by the natives' legal counsel Bruce Clark, the only lawyer ready, willing and able to do so, the British Columbia Law Society, which is to say the union that represents the lawyers who themselves are criminally assuming jurisdiction in British Columbia, denied an occasional appearance certificate allowing Bruce Clark to act on the issue of law in British Columbia. Rather than listen to Bruce Clark's application that he nevertheless be permitted to address the court *amicus curae* on the point of law, on behalf of his pro bono clients, the arrested Gustafsen Lake accused persons, a judge of the Provincial Court of British Columbia sent Dr Clark in police custody to a psychiatric hospital for the criminally insane, for assessment for "mental disorder", for raising the point of law.

That judge and the members of the Law Society and Legal Aid Society and the police then steered the native clients to British Columbia lawyers labouring under a profound conflict of interest with the issue, a conflict that effectively preempts the point of law, and charged Bruce Clark with criminal contempt of court, and with assault police for symbolically resisting arrest on this charge.

When the traditionalist British Columbia native Harold Pascal, who had just heard the Supreme Court of Canada hold that the Delgamuukw case was irrelevant to the court jurisdiction issue, returned to British Columbia from Ottawa after the September 12th hearing in 1995, he was informed on March 28, 1996 by another judge, in a case in which Mr Pascal was charged with driving without a licence, that the Delgamuukw case had resolved the court jurisdiction issue, the very issue the Supreme Court of Canada had just on September 12, 1995 ruled the Delgamuukw case did not address and did not resolve.

In order to apprehend the crime of complicity in genocide by the newcomers' legal establishment, several of the native participants in the Gustafsen Lake armed Indian standoff previously had sought third party adjudication. That is, on January 3, 1995 they had petitioned Queen Elizabeth—for essentially the same relief as granted by Queen Anne to the Mohegans in similar circumstances in 1704.

This constitutional remedy of third party adjudication as constitutively provided by Queen Anne for the protection of the native right is alleged by the native traditionalists to be the preeminent "existing aboriginal right;" indeed, it is the aboriginal right without which no other serious and weighty aboriginal rights have genuine hope; for without third party adjudication the newcomers' courts will decide in the newcomers' favour. Since the third party court had already been constituted in response to the 1704 petition, the 1995 petition did not ask the present Queen, Elizabeth, to exercise a creative legislative function. All that the 1995 petition asked was that Queen Elizabeth exercise an administrative function—to appoint a fresh panel of independent and impartial judges to sit upon the existing third party court—in order to address the dispute whether the land was still under native jurisdiction, or had been purchased and so fell under newcomer jurisdiction. The corollary question raised by the 1995 petition was whether the premature assumption of jurisdiction by the newcomer courts constitutes misprision of treason and fraud and complicity in genocide.

The government of Canada instructed Queen Elizabeth not to act upon the 1995 petition, thus suborning her into complicity in the continuity of said crimes. Indeed, the police admitted to Dr Clark that their instructions from their superiors were not that the native traditionalists were wrong on the law, but, rather, that regardless, there was no way Canada would permit access to an independent and impartial third party court ever to address the law.

To assist in this stonewalling process the police engaged in what they are recorded as admitting to be a conscious "smear and misinformation campaign."

Part of the smear and misinformation campaign included distribution of a Canadian Security and Intelligence Service report that Dr Clark had been paid 5 million dollars by the Bulgarian government to destabilize North America by raising the jurisdiction issue. There is no evidence whatsoever to substantiate that report, and this court is satisfied that it is insupportable and incredible. It is conceivable, although not proven, that the false report was part of the acknowledged smear and misinformation campaign, and may have contributed to the Queen's reticence to do her constitutional duty in reference to the right of third party adjudication.

Although obliged by constitutional law to act, Queen Elizabeth followed the constitutional convention of not acting relative to Canadian affairs without the consent of the Canadian government. The Queen refused to respond to the petition dated January 3, 1995. By this means policy and practice was permitted to override contrary law. The rule of law was proven to be a hoax. The Queen, whose essential justification for being head of state is to uphold the rule of law and constitutional integrity, was made a party to the travesty.

In these circumstances, it is naive and disingenuous to pretend that any North American court constituted by and for the newcomers' society can possibly be independent and impartial with respect to the jurisdiction issue, upon which issue turns the judges' own culpability for complicity in genocide contrary to the Convention for the Prevention and Punishment of the Crime of Genocide, 1948.

The only ray of light and hope, so far, has been the decision of Judge Bolan of the Ontario Court (General Division). On October 18, 1996 in the matter of *Regina* v. *Verna Friday* Mr Justice Bolan declined to conduct a criminal trial against the accused native woman. As grounds, he said that he had acted as a lawyer in a region adjacent to territory alleged to be unpurchased Indian territory. Secondly, he held that the nature of the jurisdiction issue, its connection to the crime of genocide precluded justice being seen to be done if any judge accused of that crime were to conduct the trial. All Ontario judges are accused of that crime, because virtually every part of Canada is either on unpurchased Indian territory, or adjacent to it.

The case of *Regina* v. *Verna Friday* arose when the accused and other traditionalists entered Indian government offices in order to seize documents for court purposes. The documents indicated that the Indian government was collaborating with the police to conceal, from the courts, evidence of the fraud of the Attorney General of Ontario and the police. The police refused to assist with securing the evidence, in favour of working with the collaborating natives and the courts to conceal it. Judge Bolan, to his credit, and the salvation of the integrity of the rule of law, declined to try the case.

There are no judicial decisions dealing directly with the court jurisdiction issue since that which culminated in the Order in Council (Great Britain) of 9 March 1704 in the matter of *Mohegan Indians* v. *Connecticut*. There is nothing even remotely arguably amounting to a repeal of the previously established natural law, international law and constitutional law.

Only two cases in North America even touched upon the court jurisdiction. The above noted case of *Cherokee Nation* v. *Georgia*, 5 Peter's 1 (United States Supreme Court, 1831) dealt with the question whether the Supreme Court itself could stand in the shoes of the Privy Council, so as to be the third party adjudicator. The Cherokees argued in the affirmative. They did not want to be in the Georgia courts any more than had the Mohegans wanted to be in the Connecticut courts. But the American Revolution had intervened, so as seemingly to have cut off access to the British Privy Council. Article 3 section 2 of the American Constitution allows the US Supreme Court to be the court of first instance, much like the Standing Commission Court constituted for state versus state and Indian versus state boundary and jurisdiction disputes in the 1700s.

In the Cherokee case the Supreme Court held that while it could function as the third party adjudicator vis-a-vis state versus state disputes, it could not similarly do so relative to Indian versus state boundary and jurisdiction disputes. The Supreme Court was wise. It is not independent and impartial relative to Indian versus state boundary and jurisdiction disputes. Its own jurisdiction and therefore the culpability of its judges for complicity in genocide is directly in issue in Indian versus state boundary and jurisdiction disputes. By deciding that it did not have first instance jurisdiction, the Supreme Court did not decide that the newcomer courts below it do have that jurisdiction. All that it decided was the question it was asked to decide: does the Supreme Court itself have that jurisdiction as a court of first instance.

The only other case to have touched upon the jurisdiction issue, so far as is known at this time, has been the unreported Quebec decision in *Regina* v. *Cadien* in 1838. In this, Sir James Reid instructed a criminal jury that if it should find that the accused were an Indian, and if it appeared that the crime occurred upon unpurchased Indian territory, then the jury could not have jurisdiction.

When all that is relevant to the issue of native rights in North America that can be said, has been said, it is apparent that principle and practice have taken different roads. Principle has taken the high road, practice the low. And the crucial perception is not to allow the volume, the detail, the ingenious character of the fraud perpetrated by the practice to obscure the simple fact of the fraud. The fraudulent practice is not self-legitimizing. It is not evidence of the law, but of the breach of the law.

For 500 years, the consensus of natural law, international law and constitutional law has been straightforward and unvarying. The law, what it actually says, has remained true to itself, and to the human species and to the environment that the law exists to serve. But what the newcomers have actually done, that is the opposite of what the law says should have been done.

All along the law has said that because the natives were here first, and are humans. Until territory has been purchased from them by the newcomers, the natives have the territorial jurisdiction.

In some regions, it is true, the newcomers' governments did make proper and valid written purchases, and can produce them to prove it.

But in many other regions the newcomers' governments simply allowed in the lawyers, the judges and the police before the purchase validly was completed. Thus the legal establishment acted as a unit—to perfect the greatest and most massive fraud in human history.

Like a finely tuned machine the lawyers, judges and police successfully have thus held the law at bay in North America, equally in the United States and Canada and, so far at least, have been able to get away with it, not because they legally were capable of changing the law, but rather because illegally they abused their usurped jurisdiction to stonewall the law.

When the legal establishment prematurely, and therefore illegally, invaded any given region, the legal establishment immediately entrenched itself and consolidated its own position. The newcomer lawyers hung up their shingles and started doing land deals and certifying titles. They themselves lived in houses and raised families upon territory not yet purchased, as required by law, from the natives. When natives complained, to whom could they turn for legal redress? The judges were, and still are, elevated lawyers. Like the newcomer lawyers, the newcomer judges themselves, physically, and literally, were and are trespassers upon the yet unpurchased territory. So were, and are, the newcomer police.

If and when the natives complain, the mass of complaints fall upon the lawyers' psychologically pre-programmed ears. If and when the natives turn to the common law remedy of self-help, they are arrested as trouble makers, and taken before judges who are in a profound conflict of interest. They end up stigmatized, trivialized and discredited as criminals.

No illustration could be clearer, plainer or more poignant than that remarked above as provided by the Supreme Court of Canada, which court itself physically and literally is situate upon territory that has never been purchased from the Algonquin speakers of the Ottawa Valley drainage basin. When the traditional government of the Algonquin nation challenged that trespass, in the course of applying to intervene in the reference regarding Quebec secession, on January 17, 1997 the Supreme Court of Canada denied that nation intervener status. It did so on the basis of allowing an objection made by a federally organized, recognized and funded Indian Act government, located only on one small portion of the vast Algonquin traditional territory. The particular federally organized native government objected to the intervention of the traditional government which, in contrast, was not federally recognized. Indeed, the practical purpose of federal organization and recognition has been to preclude and to silence the traditional form of government. In sum, the federal government illegally placed both the Supreme Court of Canada and the objecting native puppet government upon the yet unpurchased territory of the hereditary government of the Algonquin Nation. Then, the two trespassing usurpers, the Court and its native collaborator, acted in concert so as to exclude the position of the traditional government. In this fashion the literal trespass of the Supreme Court of Canada upon yet unpurchased native territory has been obscured. The transparently false illusion is that the Supreme Court of Canada might be independent and impartial with regard to the Mi'gmaq intervention which it did permit.

The consequence is that each of the 4 founding principles of natural law that constitute the basis of international law and constitutional law are negated. The newcomer court system in North America, from top to bottom, is not and can not possibly be an independent and impartial third party adjudicator.

By pretending to be, the truth is preempted and therefore justice as applied truth is precluded. The net result is that law as applied respect, in this situation meaning respect for the humanity of the natives, is also precluded. The "law and order" that results is law and order without truth and respect, which is injustice and tyranny, the antithesis of liberty. The consequence is genocide and ecocide.

In such a situation the newcomer society of the perpetrators is victimized along with the native society of the victims. As the slave owner is debased by the institution of slavery, so also is the society inflicting genocide itself inflicted.

In North America the corruption of the society thus begins at the top. The people at the bottom, the ordinary newcomers and natives, speak through the natural law, the international law and the constitutional law. The consensus of that law is a projection of their collective good will. But their voice is not heard—because the legal establishment at the top of the society will not listen to the law. The lawyers, judges and police have usurped jurisdiction, and they employ the usurped jurisdiction to stonewall the law.

The message reaches to every office, every boardroom, every schoolyard, every place of worship, everywhere: might is right.

This message corrupts. It eats at the heart and sinew of the society, of all the societies, newcomer and native alike, for even the native society is conscripted into aiding and abetting its own genocide.

If the newcomers' courts cannot agree upon the merits of these reasons, the disagreement between their contrary reasoning and this court reasoning must, under existing law, be submitted for third party adjudication in the international arena.

All that we therefore ask the newcomers' courts to do is not to set upon us and our people the newcomers' police, in place and in stead of submitting the dispute, if any, between us as courts, to the third part adjudication of yet a third court system.

If, when objectively applying the rule of law as an independent and impartial outsider, the third party finds that this native court is wrong, we can live with that. We are prepared to abide by the rule of law, and ask only the same of the newcomers and their courts.

What we can no longer bear to live with, for the injustice of it is causing anguish that spells genocide and ecocide, is the denial of our right both of jurisdiction and third party adjudication to vindicate it.

Therefore, all that we ask the newcomers' courts in comity to do is recognize and affirm that at law natives have rights to arguably yet unceded territory, plus the right to third party adjudication of the question whether it is in fact ceded. We therefore invite the newcomers' courts: "Agree with this native court, or at least let an independent and impartial third party objectively decide our disagreement, in accordance with the rule of law."

Once that fair and just solution has been declared by both native and newcomer court systems, the people of both cultures and their politicians can move onward and upward toward agreeing upon the identity of the third party adjudicator for the promising millennium ahead. The era of the Native Way, the Nature Way, the Justice Way will have been reconstituted, for the good of all humankind and its environment.

Eventually the question will occur whether, as an alternative to respecting natural law, international law and constitutional law as it presently exists, that law can and should be repealed. In anticipation, this native court has at this time only to repeat that any repeal is a matter for the people by international convention and constitutional amendment.

Taking the last mentioned form of law, constitutional law, the question will be:—could the United States and Canadian constitutions, legally, be amended so as to increase the newcomers' original claim of sovereignty? Recall, the claim by newcomers to sovereignty inceptively was restricted to what the United States Supreme Court in the 1832 case of *Worcester* v. *Georgia* termed the preemptive right to purchase:

> [Discovery] could not affect the rights of those already in possession ... It gave the exclusive right to purchase, but did not found that right on a denial of the right of the possessor to sell. ... This was the exclusive right of purchasing such lands as the natives were willing to sell. ... The Indian nations possessed a full right to the lands they occupied, until that right should be extinguished by the United States, with their consent....it is the King's order to all his governors and subjects to treat the Indians with justice and humanity, and to forebear all encroachments on the territories allotted to them...Far from asserting any right of dominion over them, Congress resolved, "that the securing and preserving the friendship of the Indian nations appears to be a subject of the utmost moment to these colonies." ... Have the numerous treaties which have been formed with them ... been nothing more than an idle pageantry? ... Except by compact we have not even claimed a right of way through Indian lands. ... What is a treaty? The answer is, it is a compact formed between two nations or communities, having the right of self government.

In fact, as we have seen, there has never been legislative constitutional amendment to increase the original claim of the preemptive right of purchase to the greater right of eminent domain and American Congressional or Canadian Parliamentary omnipotence. But could there be such a constitutional amendment? The answer depends upon whether constitutional law is valid if unilaterally it departs from natural law and international law in a fundamental particular. Could, for example, the constitutional law of any country validly be amended so as to permit in future the genocide of any group?

The natural law and international law precluding genocide is based upon the identical principles as those which underlie the constitutional law perception that the newcomers' claim of sovereignty originally and inherently is limited to the pre-emptive right of purchase. To embrace the concept that the constitutions of the United States and Canada could provide for the compulsory taking of previously unpurchased territory, a constitutional amendment would be the equivalent in law of an amendment expressly authorizing genocide.

This equation between compulsory taking and genocide is literal and not merely metaphorical. Since native culture is autochthonous, which is to say springing from the land itself, the compulsory taking of the land necessarily constitutes the taking of the culture. The taking of the culture necessarily imposes "serious bodily or mental harm" within the meaning of article 2(b) of the Convention for the Prevention and Punishment of the Crime of Genocide, 1948.

Arguably, pre-War Germany might have amended the German constitution to legalize the holocaust, prior to 1948. However, it is not arguable that any country could do so subsequent to 1948. Today it universally is accepted that constitutional law is invalid to the extent that it departs from natural law and international law in a profound and fundamental particular. This is true even as to countries that may not have ratified the Convention for the Prevention and Punishment of the Crime of Genocide, 1948.

Thus we witness in the world today ad hoc courts prosecuting genocide relative to such countries as Bosnia-Herzegovina and Rwanda. A fortiori, it would not be credible to argue that countries such as Canada and the United States, which have ratified the convention, could amend their constitutions so as to permit genocide.

This is the reason that third party adjudication genuinely is, as natural law holds and Hume has said, "the origin of civil government and society." The constitutions can not directly be amended to permit genocide.

But, as the Law Society of Upper Canada in the case of *Law Society* v. *Clark* on June 19, 1996 held:—"genocide against the aboriginal people is a fact." Since that fact does exist, and this native court does take judicial notice of that fact based upon the oral history and personal knowledge of its native judges, in the absence of constitutional amendment permitting the genocide the genocide can exist only in consequence of the complementary fact that the legal establishment of North America does not prevent the genocide by implementing the law precluding it.

The genocide in North America has existed and will continue to exist, if at all, not because of any direct constitutional amendment but, rather, because the constitution indirectly has been suspended by those in society in whom is reposed the sacred trust to uphold the constitution: the lawyers, judges and police.

The newcomers' legal establishment in North America is guilty of "genocide" within the meaning of article 3(e) of the Convention for the Prevention and Punishment of the Crime of Genocide, 1948. That crime will continue to exist as a fact not only in North America, but by extension elsewhere in the world, unless and until the usurped monopoly of the North American legal establishment over unpurchased Indian territory is broken. Genocide will remain a fact until the natives' natural law, international law and constitutional law right to third party adjudication is respected.

The legal establishment of North America is in the profoundest possible conflict of interest. It has an interest in upholding the integrity of the rule of law. But it has a conflicting interest in evading accountability for its own complicity in genocide for derogating from the substance of the law.

When the North American judiciary of the newcomers permits the former interest to override the latter interest, on that day humankind will have made an evolutionary advance of structural significance. That day will dawn when the newcomer judiciary listens to, and actually hears, the traditional native judiciary.

We have, therefore, attempted, by publishing these reasons for judgment, to allow the traditional native voice to be heard.

February 2, 1997.

"Sachem Ron Roberts"
Sachem Judge, Mohegan

"Gary Metallic Sr."
Sagamaq Judge, Mi'gmaq

"John Stevens"
Sagamore Judge, Passamaquoddy

"William Commanda"
Ogima Judge, Algonquin

Bibliography

Anderson, Terry. *Sovereign Nations or Reservations?* San Francisco: Pacific Research Institute for Public Policy, 1995.

Bachman, Ronet. *Death and Violence on the Reservation.* New York: Auburn House, 1992.

Bataille, Gretchen, and Kathleen Mullen Sands. *American Indian Women.* Lincoln: University of Nebraska Press, 1984.

Bean, Lowell John. *The Ohlone Past and Present.* Menlo Park: Ballena Press, 1994.

Benedek, Emily. *The Wind Won't Know Me: A History of the Navajo-Hopi Land Dispute.* Norman: University of Oklahoma Press, 1999.

Campbell, Maria. *Halfbreed.* Lincoln: University of Nebraska Press, 1982.

Capoeman, Pauline, ed. *Land of the Quinault.* Taholah, Wash.: Quinault Indian Nation, 1990.

Carillo, Jo, ed. *Readings in American Indian Law: Recalling the Rhythm of Survival.* Philadelphia: Temple University Press, 1998.

Champagne, Duane, ed. *The Native North American Almanac.* Detroit: Gale Research, 1994.

Chance, Norman. *The Inupiat and Arctic Alaska.* Fort Worth: Holt, Rinehart and Winston, 1990.

Churchill, Ward. *Fantasies of the Master Race: Literature, Cinema, and the Colonization of American Indians.* San Francisco: City Lights Books, 1998.

———. *Indians Are Us?* Monroe, Me: Common Courage Press, 1994.

Crozier-Hogle, Lois, ed. *Surviving in Two Worlds.* Austin: University of Texas Press, 1997.

Crum, Steven. *Native America: Portrait of the Peoples.* Detroit: Visible Ink Press, 1994.

———. *The Road on Which We Came.* Salt Lake City: University of Utah Press, 1994.

Davis, Mary. *Native America in the Twentieth Century.* New York: Garland Publishing, 1994.

Eichstaedt, Peter. *If You Poison Us.* Santa Fe: Red Crane Books, 1994.

Gonzales, Mario, and Elizabeth Cook-Lynn. *The Politics of Hallowed Ground: Wounded Knee and the Struggle for Indian Sovereignty.* Urbana and Chicago: University of Illinois Press, 1999.

Harjo, Joy, and Gloria Bird, eds. *Reinventing the Enemy's Language: Contemporary Native Women's Writings of North America.* New York: W. W. Norton, 1998.

Hauptman, Laurence. *The Iroquois Struggle for Survival*. Syracuse: Syracuse University Press, 1986.

Hoxie, Frederick, ed. *Encyclopedia of North American Indians*. Boston: Houghton Mifflin, 1996.

Jacobs, Sue-Ellen, Wesley Thomas, and Sabine Lang, eds. *Two-Spirit People*. Urbana: University of Illinois Press, 1997.

Jaimes, M. Annette. *The State of Native America*. Boston: South End Press, 1992.

Jennings, Francis, ed. *The History and Culture of Iroquois Diplomacy*. Syracuse: Syracuse University Press, 1985.

Johnson, Troy, Joane Nagel, and Duane Champagne, eds. *American Indian Activism*. Urbana and Chicago: University of Illinois Press, 1997.

Keller, Robert H., and Michael F. Turek. *American Indians and National Parks*. Fayetteville: University of Arkansas Press, 1998.

Klein, Laura, and Lilian Ackerman, eds. *Women and Power in Native North America*. Norman: University of Oklahoma Press, 1995.

Kroeber, Karl, ed. *American Indian Persistence and Resurgence*. Durham and London: Duke University Press, 1994.

Lang, Sabine, and John L. Vantine (trans.). *Men as Women, Women as Men: Changing Gender in Native American Cultures*. Austin: University of Texas Press, 1998.

Lazarus, Edward. *Black Hills/White Justice*. New York: HarperCollins Publishers, 1992.

Leitch, Barbara. *A Concise Dictionary of Indian Tribes of North America*. 2d rev. ed. Algonac, Mich.: Reference Publications, 1997.

Leroux, Odette, Marion E. Jackson, and Minnie Aodla Freeman. *Inuit Women Artists*. Seattle: University of Washington Press, 1994.

Leuthold, Steven. *Indigenous Aesthetics: Native Art, Media and Identity*. Austin: University of Texas Press, 1998.

Morrison, R. Bruce, and C. Roderick Wilson. *Native Peoples: The Canadian Experience*. 2d ed. Toronto: McClelland and Stewart, 1995.

Nahohai, Milford, and Elisa Phelps. *Dialogues with Zuni Potters*. Zuni, N.M.: Zuni A:shiwi Publishing, 1995.

Nielsen, Marianne O., and Robert A. Silverman, eds. *Native Americans, Crime, and Justice*. Boulder: Westview Press, 1996.

Northwest Renewable Resources Center. "Restoration of the Tribal Land Base: Land Acquisition and Consolidation Methods," Quinault Project. Northwest Renewable Resources Center, Seattle, 1989. Photocopy.

O'Brien, Sharon. *American Indian Tribal Governments*. Norman: University of Oklahoma Press, 1989.

Ostler, James, Marian Rodee, and Milford Nahohai. *Zuni: A Village of Silversmiths*. Zuni, N.M.: Zuni A:shiwi Publishing, 1996.

Paterek, Josephine. *Encyclopedia of American Indian Costume*. Santa Barbara: ABC-CLIO, 1994.

Peltier, Leonard. *Prison Writings: My Life Is My Sundance*. New York: St. Martin's Press, 1999.

Peterson, Jacqueline, ed. *The New Peoples: Being and Becoming Métis*. Winnipeg: University of Manitoba Press, 1996.

Powers, Marla. *Oglala Women*. Chicago: University of Chicago Press, 1986.

Pritzker, Barry. *Native Americans: An Encyclopedia of History, Culture, and Peoples.* Santa Barbara and Denver: ABC-CLIO, 1998.

Reddy, Marlita, ed. *Statistical Record of Native North Americans.* Detroit: Gale Research, 1993.

Sarris, Grag. *Mabel McKay: Weaving the Dream.* Berkeley: University of California Press, 1994.

Sider, Gerald. *Lumbee Indian Histories.* Cambridge: Cambridge University Press, 1993.

Sovereign Injustice: Forcible Inclusion of the James Bay Crees and Cree Territory into a Sovereign Québec. Nemaska, Québec: Grand Council of the Crees, 1995.

Sturtevant, William, ed. *Handbook of North American Indians.* Washington, D.C.: Smithsonian Institution, 1978–.

Thompson, William. *Native American Issues.* Santa Barbara: ABC-CLIO, 1996.

Trimble, Stephen. *The People.* Santa Fe: School of American Research Press, 1993.

Washburn, Wilcomb. *Red Man's Land/White Man's Law.* 2d ed. Norman: University of Oklahoma Press, 1971.

Wells, Robert, Jr. *Native American Resurgence and Renewal.* Metuchen, N.J.: Scarecrow Press, 1994.

Wilkins, David E. *American Indian Sovereignty and the U.S. Supreme Court: The Masking of Justice.* Austin: University of Texas Press, 1997.

Wright, J. V. *A History of the Native People of Canada.* Hull, Québec: Canadian Museum of Civilization, 1995.

Wunder, John, ed. *Recent Legal Issues for American Indians, 1968 to the Present* (Native Americans and the Law 4). Lincoln: University of Nebraska Press, 1998.

———. *Native American Cultural and Religious Freedoms* (Native Americans and the Law 5). Lincoln: University of Nebraska Press, 1998.

———. *Native American Sovereignty* (Native Americans and the Law 6). Lincoln: University of Nebraska Press, 1998.

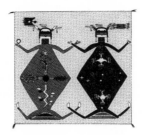

APPENDIX 1:

FEDERALLY RECOGNIZED TRIBES
AS OF DECEMBER 21, 1998

Absentee-Shawnee Tribe of Indians of Oklahoma

Agua Caliente Band of Cahuilla Indians of the Agua Caliente Indian Reservation, California

Ak Chin Indian Community of the Maricopa (Ak Chin) Indian Reservation, Arizona

Alabama-Coushatta Tribes of Texas

Alabama-Quassarte Tribal Town, Oklahoma

Alturas Indian Rancheria, California

Apache Tribe of Oklahoma

Arapahoe Tribe of the Wind River Reservation, Wyoming

Aroostook Band of Micmac Indians of Maine

Assiniboine and Sioux Tribes of the Fort Peck Indian Reservation, Montana

Augustine Band of Cahuilla Mission Indians of the Augustine Reservation, California

Bad River Band of the Lake Superior Tribe of Chippewa Indians of the Bad River Reservation, Wisconsin

Barona Group of Capitan Grande Band of Diegueno Mission Indians. *See* Capitan Grande Band of Diegueno Mission Indians of California, Barona Group

Bay Mills Indian Community of the Sault Ste. Marie Band of Chippewa Indians, Bay Mills Reservation, Michigan

Bear River Band of the Rohnerville Rancheria, California

Berry Creek Rancheria of Maidu Indians of California

Big Lagoon Rancheria, California

Big Pine Band of Owens Valley Paiute Shoshone Indians of the Big Pine Reservation, California

Big Sandy Rancheria of Mono Indians of California

Big Valley Rancheria of Pomo and Pit River Indians of California

Blackfeet Tribe of the Blackfeet Indian Reservation of Montana

Blue Lake Rancheria, California

Bridgeport Paiute Indian Colony of California

Buena Vista Rancheria of Mewuk Indians of California

Burns Paiute Tribe of the Burns Paiute Indian Colony of Oregon

Cabazon Band of Cahuilla Mission Indians of the Cabazon Reservation, California

Cachil DeHe Band of Wintun Indians of the Colusa Indian Community of the Colusa Rancheria, California

Caddo Indian Tribe of Oklahoma

Cahto Indian Tribe of the Laytonville Rancheria, California

Cahuilla Band of Mission Indians of the Cahuilla Reservation, California

Campo Band of Diegueno Mission Indians of the Campo Indian Reservation, California

Capitan Grande Band of Diegueno Mission Indians of California, Barona Group of the Barona Reservation, California

Capitan Grande Band of Diegueno Mission Indians of California, Viejas (Baron Long) Group of the Viejas Reservation, California

Catawba Indian Nation (also known as Catawba Tribe of South Carolina)

Cayuga Nation of New York

Cedarville Rancheria, California

Chemehuevi Indian Tribe of the Chemehuevi Reservation, California

Cher-ae Heights Indian Community of the Trinidad Rancheria, California

Cherokee Nation of Oklahoma

Cheyenne-Arapaho Tribes of Oklahoma

Cheyenne River Sioux Tribe of the Cheyenne River Reservation, South Dakota

Chickasaw Nation, Oklahoma

Chicken Ranch Rancheria of Mewuk Indians of California

Chippewa-Cree Indians of the Rocky Boy Reservation, Montana

Chitimacha Tribe of Louisiana

Choctaw Nation of Oklahoma

Citizen Potawatomi Nation, Oklahoma

Cloverdale Rancheria of Pomo Indians of California

Cocopah Tribe of Arizona

Coeur D'Alene Tribe of the Coeur D'Alene Reservation, Idaho

Cold Springs Rancheria of Mono Indians of California

Colorado River Indian Tribes of the Colorado River Indian Reservation, Arizona and California

Comanche Indian Tribe, Oklahoma

Confederated Salish and Kootenai Tribes of the Flathead Reservation, Montana

Confederated Tribes and Bands of the Yakama Indian Nation of the Yakama Reservation, Washington

Confederated Tribes of the Chehalis Reservation, Washington

Confederated Tribes of the Colville Reservation, Washington

Confederated Tribes of the Coos, Lower Umpqua and Siuslaw Indians of Oregon

Confederated Tribes of the Goshute Reservation, Nevada and Utah

Confederated Tribes of the Grand Ronde Community of Oregon

Confederated Tribes of the Siletz Reservation, Oregon

Confederated Tribes of the Umatilla Reservation, Oregon

Confederated Tribes of the Warm Springs Reservation of Oregon

Coquille Tribe of Oregon

Cortina Indian Rancheria of Wintun Indians of California

Coushatta Tribe of Louisiana

Cow Creek Band of Umpqua Indians of Oregon

Coyote Valley Band of Pomo Indians of California

Crow Creek Sioux Tribe of the Crow Creek Reservation, South Dakota

Crow Tribe of Montana

Cuyapaipe Community of Diegueno Mission Indians of the Cuyapaipe Reservation, California

Death Valley Timbi-sha Shoshone Band of California

Delaware Tribe of Indians, Oklahoma

Delaware Tribe of Western Oklahoma

Dry Creek Rancheria of Pomo Indians of California

Duckwater Shoshone Tribe of the Duckwater Reservation, Nevada

Eastern Band of Cherokee Indians of North Carolina

Eastern Shawnee Tribe of Oklahoma

Elem Indian Colony of Pomo Indians of the Sulphur Bank Rancheria, California

Elk Valley Rancheria, California

Ely Shoshone Tribe of Nevada

Enterprise Rancheria of Maidu Indians of California

Fort Belknap Indian Community of the Fort Belknap Reservation of Montana

Fort Bidwell Indian Community of the Fort Bidwell Reservation of California

Fort Independence Indian Community of Paiute Indians of the Fort Independence Reservation, California

Fort McDermitt Paiute and Shoshone Tribes of the Fort McDermitt Indian Reservation, Nevada and Oregon

Fort McDowell Mohave-Apache Community of the Fort McDowell Indian Reservation, Arizona

Fort Mojave Indian Tribe of Arizona, California, and Nevada

Fort Sill Apache Tribe of Oklahoma

Gila River Indian Community of the Gila River Indian Reservation, Arizona

Grand Traverse Band of Ottawa and Chippewa Indians of Michigan

Greenville Rancheria of Maidu Indians of California

Grindstone Indian Rancheria of Wintun-Wailaki Indians of California

Guidiville Rancheria of California

Hannahville Indian Community of Wisconsin Potawatomie Indians of Michigan

Havasupai Tribe of the Havasupai Reservation, Arizona

Ho-Chunk Nation of Wisconsin (formerly known as the Wisconsin Winnebago Tribe)

Hoh Indian Tribe of the Hoh Indian Reservation, Washington

Hoopa Valley Tribe, California

Hopi Tribe of Arizona

Hopland Band of Pomo Indians of the Hopland Rancheria, California

Houlton Band of Maliseet Indians of Maine

Hualapai Indian Tribe of the Hualapai Indian Reservation, Arizona

Huron Potawatomi, Inc., Michigan

Inaja Band of Diegueno Mission Indians of the Inaja and Cosmit Reservation, California

Ione Band of Mewok Indians of California

Iowa Tribe of Kansas and Nebraska

Iowa Tribe of Oklahoma

Jackson Rancheria of Mewuk Indians of California

Jamestown S'Klallam Tribe of Washington

Jamul Indian Village of California

Jena Band of Choctaw Indians, Louisiana

Jicarilla Apache Tribe of the Jicarilla Apache Indian Reservation, New Mexico

Kaibab Band of Paiute Indians of the Kaibab Indian Reservation, Arizona

Kalispel Indian Community of the Kalispel Reservation, Washington

Karuk Tribe of California

Kashia Band of Pomo Indians of the Stewarts Point Rancheria, California

Kaw Nation, Oklahoma

Keweenaw Bay Indian Community of L'Anse and Ontonagon Bands of Chippewa Indians of the L'Anse Reservation, Michigan

Kialegee Tribal Town, Oklahoma

Kickapoo Traditional Tribe of Texas

Kickapoo Tribe of Indians of the Kickapoo Reservation in Kansas

Kickapoo Tribe of Oklahoma

Kiowa Indian Tribe of Oklahoma

Klamath Indian Tribe of Oregon

Kootenai Tribe of Idaho

La Jolla Band of Luiseño Mission Indians of the La Jolla Reservation, California

La Posta Band of Diegueno Mission Indians of the La Posta Indian Reservation, California

Lac Courte Oreilles Band of Lake Superior Chippewa Indians of the Lac Courte Oreilles Reservation of Wisconsin

Lac du Flambeau Band of Lake Superior Chippewa Indians of the Lac du Flambeau Reservation of Wisconsin

Lac Vieux Desert Band of Lake Superior Chippewa Indians of Michigan

Las Vegas Tribe of Paiute Indians of the Las Vegas Indian Colony, Nevada

Little River Band of Ottawa Indians of Michigan

Little Traverse Bay Bands of Odawa Indians of Michigan

Los Coyotes Band of Cahuilla Mission Indians of the Los Coyotes Reservation, California

Lovelock Paiute Tribe of the Lovelock Indian Colony, Nevada

Lower Brule Sioux Tribe of the Lower Brule Reservation, South Dakota

Lower Elwha Tribal Community of the Lower Elwha Reservation, Washington

Lower Sioux Indian Community of Minnesota Mdewakanton Sioux Indians of the Lower Sioux Reservation in Minnesota

Lummi Tribe of the Lummi Reservation, Washington

Lytton Rancheria of California

Makah Indian Tribe of the Makah Indian Reservation, Washington

Manchester Band of Pomo Indians of the Manchester-Point Arena Rancheria, California

Manzanita Band of Diegueno Mission Indians of the Manzanita Reservation, California

Mashantucket Pequot Tribe of Connecticut

Mechoopda Indian Tribe of Chico Rancheria, California

Menominee Indian Tribe of Wisconsin

Mesa Grande Band of Diegueno Mission Indians of the Mesa Grande Reservation, California

Mescalero Apache Tribe of the Mescalero Reservation, New Mexico

Miami Tribe of Oklahoma

Miccosukee Tribe of Indians of Florida

Middletown Rancheria of Pomo Indians of California

Minnesota Chippewa Tribe, Minnesota (Six component reservations: Bois

Forte Band [Nett Lake]; Fond du Lac Band; Grand Portage Band; Leech Lake Band; Mille Lacs Band; White Earth Band)

Mississippi Band of Choctaw Indians, Mississippi

Moapa Band of Paiute Indians of the Moapa River Indian Reservation, Nevada

Modoc Tribe of Oklahoma

Mohegan Indian Tribe of Connecticut

Mooretown Rancheria of Maidu Indians of California

Morongo Band of Cahuilla Mission Indians of the Morongo Reservation, California

Muckleshoot Indian Tribe of the Muckleshoot Reservation, Washington

Muskogee (Creek) Nation, Oklahoma

Narragansett Indian Tribe of Rhode Island

Navajo Nation of Arizona, New Mexico, and Utah

Nez Perce Tribe of Idaho

Nisqually Indian Tribe of the Nisqually Reservation, Washington

Nooksack Indian Tribe of Washington

Northern Cheyenne Tribe of the Northern Cheyenne Indian Reservation, Montana

Northfork Rancheria of Mono Indians of California

Northwestern Band of Shoshoni Nation of Utah (Washakie)

Oglala Sioux Tribe of the Pine Ridge Reservation, South Dakota

Omaha Tribe of Nebraska

Oneida Nation of New York

Oneida Tribe of Wisconsin

Onondaga Nation of New York

Osage Tribe, Oklahoma

Otoe-Missouria Tribe of Indians, Oklahoma

Ottawa Tribe of Oklahoma

Paiute Indian Tribe of Utah

Paiute-Shoshone Indians of the Bishop Community of the Bishop Colony, California

Paiute-Shoshone Indians of the Lone Pine Community of the Lone Pine Reservation, California

Paiute-Shoshone Tribe of the Fallon Reservation and Colony, Nevada

Pala Band of Luiseno Mission Indians of the Pala Reservation, California

Pascua Yaqui Tribe of Arizona

Paskenta Band of Nomlaki Indians of California

Passamaquoddy Tribe of Maine

Pauma Band of Luiseño Mission Indians of the Pauma and Yuima Reservation, California

Pawnee Indian Tribe of Oklahoma

Pechanga Band of Luiseño Mission Indians of the Pechanga Reservation, California

Penobscot Tribe of Maine

Peoria Tribe of Indians of Oklahoma

Picayune Rancheria of Chukchansi Indians of California

Pinoleville Rancheria of Pomo Indians of California

Pit River Tribe, California (includes Big Bend, Lookout, Montgomery Creek, and Roaring Creek Rancherias and XL Ranch)

Poarch Band of Creek Indians of Alabama

Pokagon Band of Potawatomi Indians of Michigan

Ponca Tribe of Indians of Oklahoma

Ponca Tribe of Nebraska

Port Gamble Indian Community of the Port Gamble Reservation, Washington

Potter Valley Rancheria of Pomo Indians of California

Prairie Band of Potawatomi Indians, Kansas

Prairie Island Indian Community of Minnesota Mdewakanton Sioux Indians of the Prairie Island Reservation, Minnesota

Pueblo of Acoma, New Mexico

Pueblo of Cochiti, New Mexico

Pueblo of Isleta, New Mexico

Pueblo of Jemez, New Mexico

Pueblo of Laguna, New Mexico

Pueblo of Nambe, New Mexico

Pueblo of Picuris, New Mexico

Pueblo of Pojoaque, New Mexico

Pueblo of Sandia, New Mexico

Pueblo of San Felipe, New Mexico

Pueblo of San Ildefonso, New Mexico

Pueblo of San Juan, New Mexico

Pueblo of Santa Ana, New Mexico

Pueblo of Santa Clara, New Mexico

Pueblo of Santo Domingo, New Mexico

Pueblo of Taos, New Mexico

Pueblo of Tesuque, New Mexico

Pueblo of Zia, New Mexico

Puyallup Tribe of the Puyallup Reservation, Washington

Pyramid Lake Paiute Tribe of the Pyramid Lake Reservation, Nevada

Quapaw Tribe of Indians, Oklahoma

Quartz Valley Indian Community of the Quartz Valley Reservation of California

Quechan Tribe of the Fort Yuma Indian Reservation, California and Arizona

Quileute Tribe of the Quileute Reservation, Washington

Quinault Tribe of the Quinault Reservation, Washington

Ramona Band or Village of Cahuilla Mission Indians of California

Red Cliff Band of Lake Superior Chippewa Indians of Wisconsin

Red Lake Band of Chippewa Indians of the Red Lake Reservation, Minnesota

Redding Rancheria, California

Redwood Valley Rancheria of Pomo Indians of California

Reno-Sparks Indian Colony, Nevada

Resighini Rancheria, California (formerly known as the Coast Indian Community of Yurok Indians of the Resighini Rancheria)

Rincon Band of Luiseño Mission Indians of the Rincon Reservation, California

Robinson Rancheria of Pomo Indians of California

Rosebud Sioux Tribe of the Rosebud Indian Reservation, South Dakota

Round Valley Indian Tribes of the Round Valley Reservation, California (formerly known as the Covelo Indian Community)

Rumsey Indian Rancheria of Wintun Indians of California

Sac and Fox Nation of Missouri in Kansas and Nebraska

Sac and Fox Nation, Oklahoma

Sac and Fox Tribe of the Mississippi in Iowa

Saginaw Chippewa Indian Tribe of Michigan, Isabella Reservation

St. Croix Chippewa Indians of Wisconsin, St. Croix Reservation

St. Regis Band of Mohawk Indians of New York

Salt River Pima-Maricopa Indian Community of the Salt River Reservation, Arizona

Samish Indian Tribe, Washington

San Carlos Apache Tribe of the San Carlos Reservation, Arizona

San Juan Southern Paiute Tribe of Arizona

San Manuel Band of Serrano Mission Indians of the San Manuel Reservation, California

San Pasqual Band of Diegueno Mission Indians of California

Santa Rosa Band of Cahuilla Mission Indians of the Santa Rosa Reservation, California

Santa Rosa Indian Community of the Santa Rosa Rancheria, California

Santa Ynez Band of Chumash Mission Indians of the Santa Ynez Reservation, California

Santa Ysabel Band of Diegueno Mission Indians of the Santa Ysabel Reservation, California

Santee Sioux Tribe of the Santee Reservation of Nebraska

Sauk-Suiattle Indian Tribe of Washington

Sault Ste. Marie Tribe of Chippewa Indians of Michigan

Scotts Valley Band of Pomo Indians of California

Seminole Nation of Oklahoma

Seminole Tribe of Florida, Dania, Big Cypress, Brighton, Hollywood, and Tampa Reservations

Seneca-Cayuga Tribe of Oklahoma

Seneca Nation of New York

Shakopee Mdewakanton Sioux Community of Minnesota (Prior Lake)

Sheep Ranch Rancheria of Mewuk Indians of California

Sherwood Valley Rancheria of Pomo Indians of California

Shingle Springs Band of Miwok Indians, Shingle Springs Rancheria (Verona Tract), California

Shoalwater Bay Tribe of the Shoalwater Bay Indian Reservation, Washington

Shoshone-Bannock Tribes of the Fort Hall Reservation of Idaho

Shoshone-Paiute Tribes of the Duck Valley Reservation, Nevada

Shoshone Tribe of the Wind River Reservation, Wyoming

Sisseton-Wahpeton Sioux Tribe of the Lake Traverse Reservation, South Dakota

Skokomish Indian Tribe of the Skokomish Reservation, Washington

Skull Valley Band of Goshute Indians of Utah

Smith River Rancheria, California

Soboba Band of Luiseño Mission Indians of the Soboba Reservation, California

Sokaogon Chippewa Community of the Mole Lake Band of Chippewa Indians, Wisconsin

Southern Ute Indian Tribe of the Southern Ute Reservation, Colorado

Spirit Lake Tribe, North Dakota (formerly known as the Devils Lake Sioux Tribe)

Spokane Tribe of the Spokane Reservation, Washington

Squaxin Island Tribe of the Squaxin Island Reservation, Washington

Standing Rock Sioux Tribe of North and South Dakota

Stillaguamish Tribe of Washington

Stockbridge-Munsee Community of Mohican Indians of Wisconsin

Summit Lake Paiute Tribe of Nevada

Suquamish Indian Tribe of the Port Madison Reservation, Washington

Susanville Indian Rancheria, California

Swinomish Indians of the Swinomish Reservation, Washington

Sycuan Band of Diegueno Mission Indians of California

Table Bluff Reservation—Wiyot Tribe, California

Table Mountain Rancheria of California

Te-Moak Tribes of Western Shoshone Indians of Nevada (Four constituent bands: Battle Mountain Band, Elko Band, South Fork Band, and Wells Band)

Thlopthlocco Creek Tribal Town, Oklahoma

Three Affiliated Tribes of the Fort Berthold Reservation, North Dakota

Tohono O'odham Nation of Arizona

Tonawanda Band of Seneca Indians of New York

Tonkawa Tribe of Indians of Oklahoma

Tonto Apache Tribe of Arizona

Torres-Martinez Band of Cahuilla Mission Indians of California

Tulalip Tribes of the Tulalip Reservation, Washington

Tule River Indian Tribe of the Tule River Reservation, California

Tunica-Biloxi Indian Tribe of Louisiana

Tuolumne Band of Mewuk Indians of the Tuolumne Rancheria of California

Turtle Mountain Band of Chippewa Indians of North Dakota

Tuscarora Nation of New York

Twentynine Palms Band of Luiseño Mission Indians of California

United Auburn Indian Community of the Auburn Rancheria of California

United Keetoowah Band of Cherokee Indians of Oklahoma

Upper Lake Band of Pomo Indians of Upper Lake Rancheria of California

Upper Sioux Indian Community of the Upper Sioux Reservation, Minnesota

Upper Skagit Indian Tribe of Washington

Ute Indian Tribe of the Uintah and Ouray Reservation, Utah

Ute Mountain Tribe of the Ute Mountain Reservation, Colorado, New Mexico, and Utah

Utu Utu Gwaitu Paiute Tribe of the Benton Paiute Reservation, California

Viejas (Baron Long) Group of Capitan Grande Band of Diegueno Mission Indians. *See* Capitan Grande Band of Diegueno Mission Indians, Viejas (Baron Long) Group

Walker River Paiute Tribe of the Walker River Reservation, Nevada

Wampanoag Tribe of Gay Head (Aquinnah) of Massachusetts

Washoe Tribe of Nevada and California (Carson Colony, Dresslerville Colony, Woodfords Community, Stewart Community, and Washoe Ranches)

White Mountain Apache Tribe of the Fort Apache Reservation, Arizona

Wichita and Affiliated Tribes (Wichita, Keechi, Waco, and Tawakonie), Oklahoma

Winnebago Tribe of Nebraska

Winnemucca Indian Colony of Nevada

Wyandotte Tribe of Oklahoma

Yankton Sioux Tribe of South Dakota

Yavapai-Apache Nation of the Camp Verde Indian Reservation, Arizona

Yavapai-Prescott Tribe of the Yavapai Reservation, Arizona

Yerington Paiute Tribe of the Yerington Colony and Campbell Ranch, Nevada

Yomba Shoshone Tribe of the Yomba Reservation, Nevada

Ysleta del Sur Pueblo of Texas

Yurok Tribe of the Yurok Reservation, California

Zuni Tribe of the Zuni Reservation, New Mexico

Native Entities within the State of Alaska Recognized and Eligible to Receive Services from the U.S. Bureau of Indian Affairs

Village of Afognak

Native Village of Akhiok

Akiachak Native Community

Akiak Native Community

Native Village of Akutan
Village of Alakanuk
Alatna Village
Native Village of Aleknagik
Algaaciq Native Village (St. Mary's)
Allakaket Village
Native Village of Ambler
Village of Anaktuvuk Pass
Yupiit of Andreafski
Angoon Community Association
Village of Aniak
Anvik Village
Arctic Village (*See* Native Village of Venetie Tribal Government)
Asa'carsarmiut Tribe (formerly Native Village of Mountain Village)
Native Village of Atka
Village of Atmautluak
Atqasuk Village (Atkasook)
Native Village of Barrow Inupiat Traditional Government (formerly Native Village of Barrow)
Beaver Village
Native Village of Belkofski
Village of Bill Moore's Slough
Birch Creek Village
Native Village of Brevig Mission
Native Village of Buckland
Native Village of Cantwell
Chalkyitsik Village
Native Village of Chanega (also known as Chenega)
Village of Chefornak
Chevak Native Village
Chickaloon Native Village
Native Village of Chignik
Native Village of Chignik Lagoon
Chignik Lake Village
Chilkat Indian Village (Kluckwan)
Chilkoot Indian Association (Haines)
Chinik Eskimo Community (Golovin)
Native Village of Chistochina
Native Village of Chitina
Native Village of Chuathbaluk (Russian Mission, Kuskokwim)
Chuloonawick Native Village
Circle Native Community
Village of Clark's Point
Native Village of Council

Craig Community Association
Village of Crooked Creek
Curyung Tribal Council (formerly Native Village of Dillingham)
Native Village of Deering
Native Village of Diomede (also known as Inalik)
Village of Dot Lake
Douglas Indian Association
Native Village of Eagle
Native Village of Eek
Egegik Village
Eklutna Native Village
Native Village of Ekuk
Ekwok Village
Native Village of Elim
Emmonak Village
Evansville Village (also known as Bettles Field)
Native Village of Eyak (Cordova)
Native Village of False Pass
Native Village of Fort Yukon
Native Village of Gakona
Galena Village (also known as Louden Village)
Native Village of Gambell
Native Village of Georgetown
Native Village of Goodnews Bay
Organized Village of Grayling (also known as Holikachuk)
Gulkana Village
Native Village of Hamilton
Healy Lake Village
Holy Cross Village
Hoonah Indian Association
Native Village of Hooper Bay
Hughes Village
Huslia Village
Hydaburg Cooperative Association
Igiugig Village
Village of Iliamna
Inupiat Community of the Arctic Slope
Iqurmuit Traditional Council (formerly Native Village of Russian Mission)
Ivanoff Bay Village
Kaguyak Village
Organized Village of Kake
Kaktovik Village (also known as Barter Island)

Village of Kalskag
Village of Kaltag
Native Village of Kanatak
Native Village of Karluk
Organized Village of Kasaan
Native Village of Kasigluk
Kenaitze Indian Tribe
Ketchikan Indian Corporation
Native Village of Kiana
Agdaagux Tribe of King Cove
King Island Native Community
Native Village of Kipnuk
Native Village of Kivalina
Klawock Cooperative Association
Native Village of Kluti Kaah (also known as Copper Center)
Knik Tribe
Native Village of Kobuk
Kokhanok Village
New Koliganek Village Council (formerly Koliganek Village)
Native Village of Kongiganak
Village of Kotlik
Native Village of Kotzebue
Native Village of Koyuk
Koyukuk Native Village
Organized Village of Kwethluk
Native Village of Kwigillingok
Native Village of Kwinhagak (also known as Quinhagak)
Native Village of Larsen Bay
Levelock Village
Lesnoi Village (also known as Woody Island)
Lime Village
Village of Lower Kalskag
Manley Hot Springs Village
Manokotak Village
Native Village of Marshall (also known as Fortuna Ledge)
Native Village of Mary's Igloo
McGrath Native Village
Native Village of Mekoryuk
Mentasta Traditional Council (formerly Mentasta Lake Village)
Metlakatla Indian Community, Annette Island Reserve
Native Village of Minto
Naknek Native Village

Native Village of Nanwalek (also known as English Bay)
Native Village of Napaimute
Native Village of Napakiak
Native Village of Napaskiak
Native Village of Nelson Lagoon
Nenana Native Association
New Stuyahok Village
Newhalen Village
Newtok Village
Native Village of Nightmute
Nikolai Village
Native Village of Nikolski
Ninilchik Village
Native Village of Noatak
Nome Eskimo Community
Nondalton Village
Noorvik Native Community
Northway Village
Native Village of Nuiqsut (also known as Nooiksut)
Nulato Village
Native Village of Nunapitchuk
Village of Ohogamiut
Village of Old Harbor
Orutsararmuit Native Village (also known as Bethel)
Oscarville Traditional Village
Native Village of Ouzinkie
Native Village of Paimiut
Pauloff Harbor Village
Pedro Bay Village
Native Village of Perryville
Petersburg Indian Association
Native Village of Pilot Point
Pilot Station Traditional Village
Native Village of Pitka's Point
Platinum Traditional Village
Native Village of Point Hope
Native Village of Point Lay
Native Village of Port Graham
Native Village of Port Heiden
Native Village of Port Lions
Portage Creek Village (also known as Ohgsenakale)
Pribilof Islands Aleut Communities of St. Paul and St. George Islands
Qagan Toyagungin Tribe of Sand Point Village

Rampart Village
Village of Red Devil
Native Village of Ruby
Saint George (*See* Pribilof Islands Aleut Communities of St. Paul and St. George Islands)
Native Village of Saint Michael
Saint Paul (*See* Pribilof Islands Aleut Communities of St. Paul and St. George Islands)
Village of Salamatoff
Native Village of Savoonga
Organized Village of Saxman
Native Village of Scammon Bay
Native Village of Selawik
Seldovia Village Tribe
Shageluk Native Village
Native Village of Shaktoolik
Native Village of Sheldon's Point
Native Village of Shishmaref
Native Village of Shungnak
Sitka Tribe of Alaska
Skagway Village
Village of Sleetmute
Village of Solomon
South Naknek Village
Stebbins Community Association
Native Village of Stevens
Village of Stony River
Takotna Village
Native Village of Tanacross

Native Village of Tanana
Native Village of Tatitlek
Native Village of Tazlina
Telida Village
Native Village of Teller
Native Village of Tetlin
Central Council of the Tlingit and Haida Indian Tribes
Traditional Village of Togiak
Native Village of Toksook Bay
Tuluksak Native Community
Native Village of Tuntutuliak
Native Village of Tununak
Twin Hills Village
Native Village of Tyonek
Ugashik Village
Umkumiute Native Village
Native Village of Unalakleet
Qawalangin Tribe of Unalaska
Native Village of Unga
Village of Venetie (*See* Native Village of Venetie Tribal Government)
Native Village of Venetie Tribal Government (Arctic Village and Village of Venetie)
Native Village of Wainwright
Native Village of Wales
Village of White Mountain
Wrangell Cooperative AssociationYakutat Tlingit Tribe

APPENDIX 2:
FIRST NATIONS IN CANADA
AS OF MARCH 19, 1999

Region	Province	Band Name	Comments/Exceptions
Alberta	AB	Alexander	
Alberta	AB	Alexis	
Alberta	AB	Athabasca Chipewyan First Nation	
Alberta	AB	Beaver First Nation	
Alberta	AB	Beaver Lake	
Alberta	AB	Bigstone Cree Nation	
Alberta	AB	Blood	
Alberta	AB	Chipewyan Prairie First Nation	
Alberta	AB	Cold Lake First Nations	
Alberta	AB	Dene Tha'	
Alberta	AB	Driftpile First Nation	
Alberta	AB	Duncan's	
Alberta	AB	Enoch Cree Nation #440	
Alberta	AB	Ermineskin	
Alberta	AB	Fort McKay First Nation	
Alberta	AB	Fort McMurray #468 First Nation	
Alberta	AB	Frog Lake	
Alberta	AB	Heart Lake	
Alberta	AB	Horse Lake First Nation	
Alberta	AB	Kapawe'no First Nation	
Alberta	AB	Kehewin Cree Nation	
Alberta	AB	Little Red River Cree Nation	
Alberta	AB	Loon River Cree	
Alberta	AB	Louis Bull	
Alberta	AB	Lubicon Lake	
Alberta	AB	Mikisew Cree First Nation	
Alberta	AB	Montana	
Alberta	AB	O'Chiese	
Alberta	AB	Paul	

(continues)

Region	Province	Band Name	Comments/Exceptions
Alberta	AB	Peigan Nation	
Alberta	AB	Saddle Lake	
Alberta	AB	Samson	
Alberta	AB	Sawridge	
Alberta	AB	Siksika Nation	
Alberta	AB	Sturgeon Lake	
Alberta	AB	Sucker Creek	
Alberta	AB	Sunchild First Nation	
Alberta	AB	Swan River First Nation	
Alberta	AB	Tallcree	
Alberta	AB	Tsuu T'Ina Nation	
Alberta	AB	Whitefish Lake	
Alberta	AB	Woodland Cree First Nation	
Alberta		Bearspaw	Part of Stoney First Nation
Alberta		Chiniki	Part of Stoney First Nation
Alberta		Stoney	Has three subgroups
Alberta		Wesley	Part of Stoney First Nation
Atlantic	NB	Big Cove	
Atlantic	NB	Buctouche	
Atlantic	NB	Burnt Church	
Atlantic	NB	Eel Ground	
Atlantic	NB	Eel River	
Atlantic	NB	Fort Folly	
Atlantic	NB	Indian Island	
Atlantic	NB	Kingsclear	
Atlantic	NB	Madawaska Maliseet First Nation	
Atlantic	NB	Oromocto	
Atlantic	NB	Pabineau	
Atlantic	NB	Red Bank	
Atlantic	NB	Saint Mary's	
Atlantic	NB	Tobique	
Atlantic	NB	Woodstock	
Atlantic	NF	Miawpukek	
Atlantic	NS	Acadia	
Atlantic	NS	Afton	
Atlantic	NS	Annapolis Valley	
Atlantic	NS	Bear River	
Atlantic	NS	Chapel Island First Nation	
Atlantic	NS	Eskasoni	
Atlantic	NS	Horton	
Atlantic	NS	Membertou	
Atlantic	NS	Millbrook	
Atlantic	NS	Pictou Landing	
Atlantic	NS	Shubenacadie	
Atlantic	NS	Wagmatcook	
Atlantic	NS	Whycocomagh	

(continues)

Region	Province	Band Name	Comments/Exceptions
Atlantic	PE	Abegweit	
Atlantic	PE	Lennox Island	
British Columbia	BC	Adams Lake	
British Columbia	BC	Ahousaht	
British Columbia	BC	Aitchelitz	
British Columbia	BC	Alexandria	
British Columbia	BC	Alexis Creek	
British Columbia	BC	Ashcroft	
British Columbia	BC	Beecher Bay	
British Columbia	BC	Blueberry River First Nations	
British Columbia	BC	Bonaparte	
British Columbia	BC	Boothroyd	
British Columbia	BC	Boston Bar First Nation	
British Columbia	BC	Bridge River	
British Columbia	BC	Burns Lake	
British Columbia	BC	Burrard	
British Columbia	BC	Campbell River	
British Columbia	BC	Canim Lake	
British Columbia	BC	Canoe Creek	
British Columbia	BC	Cape Mudge	
British Columbia	BC	Cayoose Creek	
British Columbia	BC	Chawathil	
British Columbia	BC	Cheam	
British Columbia	BC	Chehalis	
British Columbia	BC	Chemainus First Nation	
British Columbia	BC	Cheslatta Carrier Nation	
British Columbia	BC	Coldwater	
British Columbia	BC	Columbia Lake	
British Columbia	BC	Comox	
British Columbia	BC	Cook's Ferry	
British Columbia	BC	Cowichan	
British Columbia	BC	Da'naxda'xw First Nation	
British Columbia	BC	Ditidaht	
British Columbia	BC	Doig River	
British Columbia	BC	Douglas	
British Columbia	BC	Ehattesaht	
British Columbia	BC	Esketemc	
British Columbia	BC	Esquimalt	
British Columbia	BC	Fort Nelson First Nation	
British Columbia	BC	Fountain	
British Columbia	BC	Gingolx First Nation	
British Columbia	BC	Gitanmaax	
British Columbia	BC	Gitanyow	
British Columbia	BC	Gitlakdamix	
British Columbia	BC	Gitsegukla	
British Columbia	BC	Gitwangak	
British Columbia	BC	Gitwinksihlkw Village Government	
British Columbia	BC	Glen Vowell	
British Columbia	BC	Gwa'Sala-Nakwaxda'xw	

(continues)

Region	Province	Band Name	Comments/Exceptions
British Columbia	BC	Gwawaenuk Tribe	
British Columbia	BC	Hagwilget Village	
British Columbia	BC	Halalt	
British Columbia	BC	Halfway River First Nation	
British Columbia	BC	Hartley Bay	
British Columbia	BC	Heiltsuk	
British Columbia	BC	Hesquiaht	
British Columbia	BC	High Bar	
British Columbia	BC	Homalco	
British Columbia	BC	Hupa¢asath First Nation	
British Columbia	BC	Huu-ay-aht First Nations	
British Columbia	BC	Iskut	
British Columbia	BC	Kamloops	
British Columbia	BC	Kanaka Bar	
British Columbia	BC	Katzie	
British Columbia	BC	Ka:'yu:'k't'h'/Che:k:tles7et'h' First Nations	
British Columbia	BC	Kispiox	
British Columbia	BC	Kitamaat	
British Columbia	BC	Kitasoo	
British Columbia	BC	Kitkatla	
British Columbia	BC	Kitselas	
British Columbia	BC	Kitsumkalum	
British Columbia	BC	Klahoose First Nation	
British Columbia	BC	Kluskus	
British Columbia	BC	Kwadacha	
British Columbia	BC	Kwakiutl	
British Columbia	BC	Kwantlen First Nation	
British Columbia	BC	Kwaw-kwaw-Apilt	
British Columbia	BC	Kwayhquitlum First Nation	
British Columbia	BC	Kwiakah	
British Columbia	BC	Kwicksutaineuk-ah-kwaw-ah-mish	
British Columbia	BC	Lakahahmen	
British Columbia	BC	Lakalzap	
British Columbia	BC	Lake Babine Nation	
British Columbia	BC	Lake Cowichan First Nation	
British Columbia	BC	Lax-kw'alaams	
British Columbia	BC	Lheidli T'enneh	
British Columbia	BC	Little Shuswap Lake	
British Columbia	BC	Lower Kootenay	
British Columbia	BC	Lower Nicola	
British Columbia	BC	Lower Similkameen	
British Columbia	BC	Lyackson	
British Columbia	BC	Lytton	
British Columbia	BC	Malahat First Nation	
British Columbia	BC	Mamalilikulla	
British Columbia	BC	Matsqui	
British Columbia	BC	McLeod Lake	
British Columbia	BC	Metlakatla	

(continues)

414

Region	Province	Band Name	Comments/Exceptions
British Columbia	BC	Moricetown	
British Columbia	BC	Mount Currie	
British Columbia	BC	Mowachaht/Muchalaht	
British Columbia	BC	Musqueam	
British Columbia	BC	N'Quatqua	
British Columbia	BC	Nadleh Whuten	
British Columbia	BC	Nak'azdli	
British Columbia	BC	Namgis First Nation	
British Columbia	BC	Nanoose First Nation	
British Columbia	BC	Nazko	
British Columbia	BC	Nee-Tahi-Buhn	
British Columbia	BC	Neskonlith	
British Columbia	BC	New Westminster	
British Columbia	BC	Nicomen	
British Columbia	BC	Nooaitch	
British Columbia	BC	North Thompson	
British Columbia	BC	Nuchatlaht	
British Columbia	BC	Nuxalk Nation	
British Columbia	BC	Okanagan	
British Columbia	BC	Old Massett Village Council	
British Columbia	BC	Oregon Jack Creek	
British Columbia	BC	Osoyoos	
British Columbia	BC	Oweekeno	
British Columbia	BC	Pacheedaht First Nation	
British Columbia	BC	Pauquachin	
British Columbia	BC	Pavilion	
British Columbia	BC	Penelakut	
British Columbia	BC	Penticton	
British Columbia	BC	Peters	
British Columbia	BC	Popkum	
British Columbia	BC	Prophet River Band	
British Columbia	BC	Qualicum First Nation	
British Columbia	BC	Quatsino	
British Columbia	BC	Red Bluff	
British Columbia	BC	Saik'uz First Nation	
British Columbia	BC	St. Mary's	
British Columbia	BC	Samahquam	
British Columbia	BC	Saulteau First Nations	
British Columbia	BC	Scowlitz	
British Columbia	BC	Seabird Island	
British Columbia	BC	Sechelt	
British Columbia	BC	Semiahmoo	
British Columbia	BC	Seton Lake	
British Columbia	BC	Shackan	
British Columbia	BC	Shuswap	
British Columbia	BC	Shxw'ow'hamel First Nation	
British Columbia	BC	Siska	
British Columbia	BC	Skawahlook First Nation	
British Columbia	BC	Skeetchestn	
British Columbia	BC	Skidegate	

(continues)

415

Region	Province	Band Name	Comments/Exceptions
British Columbia	BC	Skookumchuck	
British Columbia	BC	Skowkale	
British Columbia	BC	Skuppah	
British Columbia	BC	Skwah	
British Columbia	BC	Skway	
British Columbia	BC	Sliammon	
British Columbia	BC	Snuneymuxw First Nation	
British Columbia	BC	Soda Creek	
British Columbia	BC	Songhees First Nation	
British Columbia	BC	Soowahlie	
British Columbia	BC	Spallumcheen	
British Columbia	BC	Spuzzum	
British Columbia	BC	Squamish	
British Columbia	BC	Squiala First Nation	
British Columbia	BC	Stellat'en First Nation	
British Columbia	BC	Stone	
British Columbia	BC	Sumas First Nation	
British Columbia	BC	Tahltan	
British Columbia	BC	Takla Lake First Nation	
British Columbia	BC	T'it'kit	
British Columbia	BC	Tla-o-qui-aht First Nations	
British Columbia	BC	Tlatlasikwala	
British Columbia	BC	Tl'azt'en Nation	
British Columbia	BC	Tl'etinqox-t'in Government Office	
British Columbia	BC	Tlowitsis Tribe	
British Columbia	BC	Tobacco Plains	
British Columbia	BC	Toosey	
British Columbia	BC	Toquaht	
British Columbia	BC	Tsartlip	
British Columbia	BC	Tsawataineuk	
British Columbia	BC	Tsawout First Nation	
British Columbia	BC	Tsawwassen First Nation	
British Columbia	BC	Tsay Keh Dene	
British Columbia	BC	Tseshaht	
British Columbia	BC	Tseycum	
British Columbia	BC	T'Sou-ke First Nation	
British Columbia	BC	Tzeachten	
British Columbia	BC	Uchucklesaht	
British Columbia	BC	Ucluelet First Nation	
British Columbia	BC	Ulkatcho	
British Columbia	BC	Union Bar	
British Columbia	BC	Upper Nicola	
British Columbia	BC	Upper Similkameen	
British Columbia	BC	West Moberly First Nations	
British Columbia	BC	Westbank First Nation	
British Columbia	BC	Wet'suwet'en First Nation	
British Columbia	BC	Whispering Pines/Clinton	
British Columbia	BC	Williams Lake	

(continues)

Region	Province	Band Name	Comments/Exceptions
British Columbia	BC	Xeni Gwet'in First Nations Government	
British Columbia	BC	Yakweakwioose	
British Columbia	BC	Yale First Nation	
British Columbia	BC	Yekooche	
Manitoba	MB	Barren Lands	
Manitoba	MB	Berens River	
Manitoba	MB	Birdtail Sioux	
Manitoba	MB	Bloodvein	
Manitoba	MB	Brokenhead Ojibway Nation	
Manitoba	MB	Buffalo Point First Nation	
Manitoba	MB	Canupawakpa Dakota First Nation	
Manitoba	MB	Chemawawin First Nation	
Manitoba	MB	Cross Lake First Nation	
Manitoba	MB	Dakota Plains	
Manitoba	MB	Dakota Tipi	
Manitoba	MB	Dauphin River	
Manitoba	MB	Ebb and Flow	
Manitoba	MB	Fairford	
Manitoba	MB	Fisher River	
Manitoba	MB	Fort Alexander	
Manitoba	MB	Fox Lake	
Manitoba	MB	Gamblers	
Manitoba	MB	Garden Hill First Nations	
Manitoba	MB	God's Lake First Nation	
Manitoba	MB	God's River	
Manitoba	MB	Grand Rapids First Nation	
Manitoba	MB	Hollow Water	
Manitoba	MB	Jackhead	
Manitoba	MB	Keeseekoowenin	
Manitoba	MB	Lake Manitoba	
Manitoba	MB	Lake St. Martin	
Manitoba	MB	Little Black River	
Manitoba	MB	Little Grand Rapids	
Manitoba	MB	Little Saskatchewan	
Manitoba	MB	Long Plain	
Manitoba	MB	Mathias Colomb	
Manitoba	MB	Mosakahiken Cree Nation	
Manitoba	MB	Nisichawayasihk Cree Nation	
Manitoba	MB	Northlands	
Manitoba	MB	Norway House Cree Nation	
Manitoba	MB	O-Chi-Chak-Ko-Sipi First Nation	
Manitoba	MB	Opaskwayak Cree Nation	
Manitoba	MB	Oxford House	
Manitoba	MB	Pauingassi First Nation	
Manitoba	MB	Peguis	
Manitoba	MB	Pine Creek	
Manitoba	MB	Poplar River First Nation	

(continues)

Region	Province	Band Name	Comments/Exceptions
Manitoba	MB	Red Sucker Lake	
Manitoba	MB	Rolling River	
Manitoba	MB	Roseau River	
Manitoba	MB	St. Theresa Point	
Manitoba	MB	Sandy Bay	
Manitoba	MB	Sapotaweyak Cree Nation	
Manitoba	MB	Sayisi Dene First Nation	
Manitoba	MB	Shamattawa First Nation	
Manitoba	MB	Sioux Valley Dakota Nation	
Manitoba	MB	Split Lake Cree	
Manitoba	MB	Swan Lake	
Manitoba	MB	Tootinaowaziibeeng Treaty Reserve	
Manitoba	MB	War Lake First Nation	
Manitoba	MB	Wasagamack First Nation	
Manitoba	MB	Waterhen	
Manitoba	MB	Waywayseecappo First Nation Treaty Four—1874	
Manitoba	MB	Wuskwi Sipihk First Nation	
Manitoba	MB	York Factory First Nation	
North-West Territories	NT	Acho Dene Koe	
North-West Territories	NT	Aklavik	
North-West Territories	NT	Behdzi Ahda" First Nation	
North-West Territories	NT	Dechi Laot'i First Nations	
North-West Territories	NT	Deh Gah Gotie Dene Council	
North-West Territories	NT	Deline	
North-West Territories	NT	Deninu K'ue First Nation	
North-West Territories	NT	Dog Rib Rae	
North-West Territories	NT	Fort Good Hope	
North-West Territories	NT	Gameti First Nation	
North-West Territories	NT	Gwicha Gwich'in	
North-West Territories	NT	Hay River Dene	
North-West Territories	NT	Inuvik Native	
North-West Territories	NT	Jean Marie River Dene	
North-West Territories	NT	Ka'a'gee Tu First Nation	
North-West Territories	NT	Liidlii Kue First Nation	
North-West Territories	NT	Lutsel K'e Dene	
North-West Territories	NT	Nahanni Butte	
North-West Territories	NT	Pehdzeh Ki First Nation	
North-West Territories	NT	Salt River First Nation #195	
North-West Territories	NT	Sambaa K'e (Trout Lake) Dene	
North-West Territories	NT	Tetlit Gwich'in	
North-West Territories	NT	Tulita Dene	
North-West Territories	NT	West Point First Nation	
North-West Territories	NT	Wha Ti First Nation	
North-West Territories	NT	Yellowknives Dene First Nation	
Ontario	MN, USA	Northwest Angle No. 33	
Ontario	ON	Albany	Has two subgroups: Fort Albany and Kashechewan

(continues)

Region	Province	Band Name	Comments/Exceptions
Ontario	ON	Alderville First Nation	
Ontario	ON	Algonquins of Pikwakanagan	
Ontario	ON	Anishinabe of Wauzhushk Onigum	
Ontario	ON	Aroland	
Ontario	ON	Attawapiskat	
Ontario	ON	Batchewana First Nation	
Ontario	ON	Bearskin Lake	
Ontario	ON	Beausoleil	
Ontario	ON	Big Grassy	
Ontario	ON	Big Island	
Ontario	ON	Brunswick House	
Ontario	ON	Caldwell	
Ontario	ON	Cat Lake	
Ontario	ON	Chapleau Cree First Nation	
Ontario	ON	Chapleau Ojibway	
Ontario	ON	Chippewas of Georgina Island	
Ontario	ON	Chippewas of Kettle and Stony Point	
Ontario	ON	Chippewas of Mnjikaning First Nation	
Ontario	ON	Chippewas of Nawash First Nation	
Ontario	ON	Chippewas of Sarnia	
Ontario	ON	Chippewas of the Thames First Nation	
Ontario	ON	Constance Lake	
Ontario	ON	Couchiching First Nation	
Ontario	ON	Curve Lake	
Ontario	ON	Deer Lake	
Ontario	ON	Dokis	
Ontario	ON	Eabametoong First Nation	
Ontario	ON	Eagle Lake	
Ontario	ON	Flying Post	
Ontario	ON	Fort Severn	
Ontario	ON	Fort William	
Ontario	ON	Garden River First Nation	
Ontario	ON	Ginoogaming First Nation	
Ontario	ON	Grassy Narrows First Nation	
Ontario	ON	Gull Bay	
Ontario	ON	Henvey Inlet First Nation	
Ontario	ON	Hiawatha First Nation	
Ontario	ON	Iskatewizaagegan #39 Independent First Nation	
Ontario	ON	Kasabonika Lake	
Ontario	ON	Kee-Way-Win	
Ontario	ON	Kingfisher	
Ontario	ON	Kitchenuhmaykoosib Inninuwug	
Ontario	ON	Lac Des Milles Lacs	
Ontario	ON	Lac La Croix	

(continues)

419

Region	Province	Band Name	Comments/Exceptions
Ontario	ON	Lac Seul	
Ontario	ON	Lake Nipigon Ojibway First Nation	
Ontario	ON	Lansdowne House	
Ontario	ON	Long Lake No. 58 First Nation	
Ontario	ON	Magnetawan	
Ontario	ON	Martin Falls	
Ontario	ON	Matachewan	
Ontario	ON	Mattagami	
Ontario	ON	McDowell Lake	
Ontario	ON	Michipicoten	
Ontario	ON	Mishkeegogamang	
Ontario	ON	Missanabie Cree	
Ontario	ON	Mississauga	
Ontario	ON	Mississaugas of Scugog Island First Nation	
Ontario	ON	Mississaugas of the Credit	
Ontario	ON	Mohawks of Akwesasne	
Ontario	ON	Mohawks of the Bay of Quinte	
Ontario	ON	Moose Cree First Nation	
Ontario	ON	Moose Deer Point	
Ontario	ON	Moravian of the Thames	
Ontario	ON	Munsee-Delaware Nation	
Ontario	ON	Muskrat Dam Lake	
Ontario	ON	Naicatchewenin	
Ontario	ON	Naotkamegwanning	
Ontario	ON	New Post	
Ontario	ON	Nibinamik First Nation	
Ontario	ON	Nicickousemenecaning	
Ontario	ON	Nipissing First Nation	
Ontario	ON	North Caribou Lake	
Ontario	ON	North Spirit Lake	
Ontario	ON	Northwest Angle No. 37	
Ontario	ON	Ochiichagwe'babigo'ining First Nation	
Ontario	ON	Ojibway Nation of Saugeen	
Ontario	ON	Ojibways of Onegaming	
Ontario	ON	Ojibways of Pic River First Nation	
Ontario	ON	Ojibways of Sucker Creek	
Ontario	ON	Oneida Nation of the Thames	
Ontario	ON	Pays Plat	
Ontario	ON	Pic Mobert	
Ontario	ON	Pikangikum	
Ontario	ON	Poplar Hill	
Ontario	ON	Rainy River	
Ontario	ON	Red Rock	
Ontario	ON	Rocky Bay	
Ontario	ON	Sachigo Lake	
Ontario	ON	Sagamok Anishnawbek	

(continues)

Region	Province	Band Name	Comments/Exceptions
Ontario	ON	Sandpoint	
Ontario	ON	Sandy Lake	
Ontario	ON	Saugeen	
Ontario	ON	Seine River First Nation	
Ontario	ON	Serpent River	
Ontario	ON	Shawanaga First Nation	
Ontario	ON	Sheguiandah	
Ontario	ON	Sheshegwaning	
Ontario	ON	Shoal Lake No. 40	
Ontario	ON	Six Nations of the Grand River	Has 13 tribes/sub-groups
Ontario	ON	Slate Falls Nation	
Ontario	ON	Stanjikoming First Nation	
Ontario	ON	Temagami First Nation	
Ontario	ON	Thessalon	
Ontario	ON	Wabaseemoong Independent Nations	
Ontario	ON	Wabauskang First Nation	
Ontario	ON	Wabigoon Lake Ojibway Nation	
Ontario	ON	Wahgoshig	
Ontario	ON	Wahnapitae	
Ontario	ON	Wahta Mohawk	
Ontario	ON	Walpole Island	
Ontario	ON	Wapekeka	
Ontario	ON	Wasauksing First Nation	
Ontario	ON	Washagamis Bay	
Ontario	ON	Wawakapewin	
Ontario	ON	Webequie	
Ontario	ON	Weenusk	
Ontario	ON	West Bay	
Ontario	ON	Whitefish Lake	
Ontario	ON	Whitefish River	
Ontario	ON	Whitesand	
Ontario	ON	Wikwemikong	
Ontario	ON	Wunnumin	
Ontario	ON	Zhiibaahaasing First Nation	
Ontario		Bay of Quinte Mohawk	Part of Six Nations
Ontario		Bearfoot Onondaga	Part of Six Nations
Ontario		Deleware	Part of Six Nations
Ontario		Kashechewan	Part of Albany First Nation
Ontario		Konandaha Seneca	Part of Six Nations
Ontario		Lower Cayuga	Part of Six Nations
Ontario		Lower Mohawk	Part of Six Nations
Ontario		Niharondasa Seneca	Part of Six Nations
Ontario		Oneida	Part of Six Nations
Ontario		Onondaga Clear Sky	Part of Six Nations
Ontario		Tuscarora	Part of Six Nations
Ontario		Upper Cayuga	Part of Six Nations

(continues)

421

Region	Province	Band Name	Comments/Exceptions
Ontario		Upper Mohawk	Part of Six Nations
Ontario		Walker Mohawk	Part of Six Nations
Québec	QC	Abénakis de Wôlinak	
Québec	QC	Algonquins of Barriere Lake	
Québec	QC	Betsiamites	
Québec	QC	Conseil de la Première Nation Abitibiwinni	
Québec	QC	Cree Nation of Chisasibi	
Québec	QC	Cree Nation of Mistissini	
Québec	QC	Cree Nation of Wemindji	
Québec	QC	Eagle Village First Nation—Kipawa	
Québec	QC	Eastmain	
Québec	QC	Innu Takuaikan Uashat Mak Mani-Utenam	
Québec	QC	Kahnawake	
Québec	QC	Kanesatake	
Québec	QC	Kitcisakik	
Québec	QC	Kitigan Zibi Anishinabeg	
Québec	QC	La Nation Micmac de Gespeg	
Québec	QC	Les Atikamekw de Manawan	
Québec	QC	Listuguj Mi'gmaq First Nation Council	
Québec	QC	Long Point First Nation	
Québec	QC	Micmacs of Gesgapegiag	
Québec	QC	Mingan	
Québec	QC	Montagnais de Natashquan	
Québec	QC	Montagnais de Pakua Shipi	
Québec	QC	Montagnais de Schefferville	
Québec	QC	Montagnais de Unamen Shipu	
Québec	QC	Montagnais du Lac St.-Jean	
Québec	QC	Montagnais Essipit	
Québec	QC	Naskapi of Quebec	
Québec	QC	Nation Anishnabe du Lac Simon	
Québec	QC	Nation Huronne Wendat	
Québec	QC	Nemaska	
Québec	QC	Obedjiwan	
Québec	QC	Odanak	
Québec	QC	PremiFre Nation Malecite de Viger	
Québec	QC	PremiFre Nation de Whapmagoostui	
Québec	QC	Timiskaming	
Québec	QC	Waskaganish	
Québec	QC	Waswanipi	
Québec	QC	Wemotaci	
Québec	QC	Wolf Lake	
Saskatchewan	SK	Ahtahkakoop	
Saskatchewan	SK	Beardy's and Okemasis	

(continues)

Region	Province	Band Name	Comments/Exceptions
Saskatchewan	SK	Big River	
Saskatchewan	SK	Birch Narrows First Nation	
Saskatchewan	SK	Black Lake	
Saskatchewan	SK	Buffalo River Dene Nation	
Saskatchewan	SK	Canoe Lake	
Saskatchewan	SK	Carry the Kettle	
Saskatchewan	SK	Clearwater River Dene	
Saskatchewan	SK	Cote First Nation 366	
Saskatchewan	SK	Cowessess	
Saskatchewan	SK	Cumberland House Cree Nation	
Saskatchewan	SK	Day Star	
Saskatchewan	SK	English River First Nation	
Saskatchewan	SK	Fishing Lake First Nation	
Saskatchewan	SK	Flying Dust First Nation	
Saskatchewan	SK	Fond du Lac	
Saskatchewan	SK	Gordon	
Saskatchewan	SK	Hatchet Lake	
Saskatchewan	SK	Island Lake First Nation	
Saskatchewan	SK	James Smith	
Saskatchewan	SK	Joseph Bighead	
Saskatchewan	SK	Kahkewistahaw	
Saskatchewan	SK	Kawacatoose	
Saskatchewan	SK	Keeseekoose	
Saskatchewan	SK	Key	
Saskatchewan	SK	Kinistin	
Saskatchewan	SK	Lac La Ronge	
Saskatchewan	SK	Little Black Bear	
Saskatchewan	SK	Little Pine	
Saskatchewan	SK	Lucky Man	
Saskatchewan	SK	Makwa Sahgaiehcan First Nation	
Saskatchewan	SK	Mistawasis	
Saskatchewan	SK	Montreal Lake	
Saskatchewan	SK	Moosomin	
Saskatchewan	SK	Mosquito–Grizzly Bear's Head	
Saskatchewan	SK	Muscowpetung	
Saskatchewan	SK	Muskeg Lake	
Saskatchewan	SK	Muskowekwan	
Saskatchewan	SK	Nekaneet	
Saskatchewan	SK	Ocean Man	
Saskatchewan	SK	Ochapowace	
Saskatchewan	SK	Okanese	
Saskatchewan	SK	One Arrow	
Saskatchewan	SK	Onion Lake	
Saskatchewan	SK	Pasqua First Nation #79	
Saskatchewan	SK	Peepeekisis	
Saskatchewan	SK	Pelican Lake	
Saskatchewan	SK	Peter Ballantyne Cree Nation	
Saskatchewan	SK	Pheasant Rump Nakota	

(continues)

Region	Province	Band Name	Comments/Exceptions
Saskatchewan	SK	Piapot	
Saskatchewan	SK	Poundmaker	
Saskatchewan	SK	Red Earth	
Saskatchewan	SK	Red Pheasant	
Saskatchewan	SK	Sakimay	
Saskatchewan	SK	Saulteaux	
Saskatchewan	SK	Shoal Lake of the Cree Nation	
Saskatchewan	SK	Standing Buffalo	
Saskatchewan	SK	Star Blanket	
Saskatchewan	SK	Sturgeon Lake First Nation	
Saskatchewan	SK	Sweetgrass	
Saskatchewan	SK	Thunderchild First Nation	
Saskatchewan	SK	Wahpeton Dakota Nation	
Saskatchewan	SK	Waterhen Lake	
Saskatchewan	SK	White Bear	
Saskatchewan	SK	Whitecap Dakota/Sioux First Nation	
Saskatchewan	SK	Witchekan Lake	
Saskatchewan	SK	Wood Mountain	
Saskatchewan	SK	Yellow Quill	
Saskatchewan		Muskoday First Nation	
Yukon	BC	Dease River	Located in BC, administered by the Yukon
Yukon	BC	Taku River Tlingit	Located in BC, administered by the Yukon
Yukon	YT	Carcross/Tagish First Nations	
Yukon	YT	Champagne and Aishihik First Nations	
Yukon	YT	First Nation of Nacho Nyak Dun	
Yukon	YT	Kluane First Nation	
Yukon	YT	Kwanlin Dun First Nation	
Yukon	YT	Liard River	
Yukon	YT	Little Salmon/Carmacks First Nation	
Yukon	YT	Ross River	
Yukon	YT	Selkirk First Nation	
Yukon	YT	Ta'an Kwach'an	
Yukon	YT	Teslin Tlingit Council	
Yukon	YT	Tr'on dëk Hwëch'in	
Yukon	YT	Vuntut Gwitchin First Nation	
Yukon	YT	White River First Nation	

APPENDIX 3:
INDIAN GROUPS WHO
HAVE PETITIONED FOR FEDERAL
RECOGNITION, UNRECOGNIZED
AS OF MARCH 2, 1999

Abenaki:
    Cowasuck Band—Abenaki People, MA
    St. Francis/Sokoki Band of Abenakis of VT
Accohannock Indian Tribal Association, Inc., MD
Adais. *See* Caddo
Adams County, Ohio. *See* Shawnee Nation, Ohio Blue Creek Band
Ahon-to-ays Ojibwa Band, also known as Rocky Boy Ojibway Band, MT
Alleghenny Nation (Ohio Band), OH
American Cherokee Confederacy. *See* Southeastern Cherokee Confederacy, Inc.
American Indian Council of Mariposa County, CA. *See* Southern Sierra Miwuk Nation
Amonsoquath Tribe of Cherokee, MO
Ani-Stohini/Unami Nation, VA
Ani Yvwi Yuchi, CA (#175)
Antelope Valley Paiute Tribe, CA. *See also* Washoe/Paiute of Antelope Valley, CA
Apache:
    Choctaw-Apache Community of Ebarb, LA

The People of LaJunta (Jumano/Mescalero), TX
Apalachee Indian Tribe, LA
Apalachee Indians of Louisiana, LA
Apalachicola Band of Creek Indians, FL

Beaver Creek Band of Pee Dee Indians, SC
Biloxi
    Tunica-Biloxi
    Biloxi, Chitimacha Confederation of Muskogees, Inc.
Black River. *See* Chippewa: Swan Creek Black River Confederated Ojibwa Tribes, Inc.
Blue Creek Band. *See* Shawnee Nation, Ohio Blue Creek Band of Adams County
Brotherton Indians of Wisconsin
Burt Lake Band of Ottawa and Chippewa Indians, Inc., MI

Caddo Adais Indians, Inc., LA
California Tribal Council. *See* Gabrielino/Tongva Indians of California Tribal Council
Calusa-Seminole Nation of Santa Cruz, California, CA

Canoncito Band of Navajos, NM

Carmel Mission Indians. *See* Coastanoan Band of Carmel Mission Indians

Carrizo. *See* Tribal Council of the Carrizo/Comecrudo Nation of Texas

Chalola. *See* Tinoqui-Chalola Council of Kitanemuk and Yowlumne Tejon Indians

Chaubunagungamaug Band of the Nipmuck Nation, MA

Cheraw. *See* Lumbee Tribe of Cheraw Indians

Cherokee:

American Cherokee Confederacy. *See* Southeastern Cherokee Confederacy

Amonsoquath Tribe of Cherokee, MO

Cane Break Band of Eastern Cherokees

Cherokee Indians of Georgia

Cherokee Indians of Hoke County (NC)

Cherokee Indians of Robeson and Adjoining Cos. (NC)

Cherokee Nation of Alabama, AL

Cherokee Nation West: Southern Band of the Eastern Cherokee Indians of Missouri and Arkansas, MO

Cherokee-Powhattan Indian Association

Cherokees of Jackson Co., AL

Cherokees of Southeast Alabama

Chickamauga Cherokee Indian Nation of AR and MO

Dahlonega Cherokees. *See* Cherokee: Georgia Tribe of Eastern Cherokees, Inc. GA

Etowah Cherokee Nation, TN

Georgia Tribe of Eastern Cherokees, Inc., GA

Indians of Person County, NC

Langley Band of the Chickamogee Cherokee Indians of the Southeastern U.S., AL

Lost Cherokee of Arkansas and Missouri, AR

Northern Cherokee Nation of Old Louisana Terr., MO

Northern Cherokee Tribe of Indians, MO

Northwest Cherokee Wolf Band

Red Clay Intertribal Indian Band

Sac River and White River Bands of the Chickamauga-Cherokee Nation of Arkansas and Missouri, Inc.

Southern Band of the Eastern Cherokee Indians of Missouri and Arkansas

Southeastern Cherokee Confederacy (also known as SECC)

SouthEastern Indian Nation

Tuscola United Cherokee Tribe of FL and AL, Inc.

Western Arkansas Cherokee Tribe, AR

Western Cherokee Nation of Arkansas and Missouri, AR

Chi-cau-gon Band of Lake Superior Chippewa of Iron County, MI

Chickahominy Indian Tribe, VA

Chickamauga Cherokee Indian Nation of AR and MO. *See also* Sac River and White River Bands of the Chickamauga-Cherokee Nation of Arkansas and Missouri, Inc.

Chickamogee Cherokee Indians. *See* Langley Band of the Chickamogee Cherokee Indians of the Southeastern U.S.

Chicora Indian Tribe of SC

Chicora-Siouan Indian People, SC. *See* Chicora-Waccamaw Indian People, SC

Chicora-Waccamaw Indian People, SC

Chilkat. *See* Katallah-Chilkat Tlingit Tribe of Alaska

Chilkoot Kaagwaantaan Clan, AK

Chinook Indian Tribe/Chinook Nation, WA

Chippewa:

Ahon-to-ays Ojibwa Band, also known as Rocky Boy Ojibway Band

Burt Lake Band

Chi-cau-gon Band of Lake Superior Chippewa of Iron County, MI

Christian Pembina Chippewa

Consolidated Bahwetig Ojibwas and Mackinac Tribe, MI

Kah-Bay-Kah-Nong (Warroad Chippewa)

Lake Superior Chippewa of Marquette, Inc., MI

Little Shell Band of North Dakota

Little Shell Tribe of Montana

Mackinac Bands of Chippewa and Ottawa Indians, MI

The Displaced Elem Lineage Emancipated Members, CA

Drowning Creek Tuscarora. *See* Tuscarora: Tuscarora Indian Tribe, Drowning Creek Reservation

Dunlap Band of Mono Indians, CA

Duwamish Indian Tribe, WA

Eastern Cherokee Indians. *See* Cherokee Nation West: Southern Band of the Eastern Cherokee Indians of Missouri and Arkansas

Eastern Pequot Indians of CT. *See also* Paucatuck Eastern Pequot of CT

Edisto:
Four Hole Indian Organization, SC
SouthEastern Indian Nation, GA

Edisto Tribe, SC. *See* Four Hole Indian Organization/Edisto Tribe

Elem. *See* The Displaced Elem Lineage Emancipated Members

Eno-Occaneechi Tribe of Indians, NC

Esselen:
Esselen Tribe of Monterey County, CA
Ohlone/Costanoan-Esselen Nation, CA
Esselen Tribe of Monterey County, CA

Etowah Cherokee Nation, TN

Euchee. *See* Yuchi

Faircloth Indians. *See* Coree Indians

Federated Coast Miwok, CA

Federation: Moorish Science Temple of America, Inc., MD

Fernandeno/Tataviam Tribe, CA

Florala Creek. *See* Principal Creek Indian Nation East of Mississippi

Florida Tribe of Eastern Creek Indians, FL

Four Hole Indian Organization/Edisto Tribe, SC

Gabrieleno Band of Mission Indians, CA

Gabrielino: *See also* Coastal Gabrieleno Dieguено Band of Mission Indians
Gabrielino/Tongva Indians of California Tribal Council, CA
Gabrielino/Tongva Tribal Council, CA

Golden Hill Paugussett Tribe, CT

Grand River Bands of Ottawa Indians (formerly Grand River Band Ottawa Council), MI

Green River Area, TN. *See* Ani Yvwi Yuchi

Haliwa-Saponi Indian Tribe, Inc., NC

Hassanamisco Band. *See* Nipmuc Nation, Hassanamisco Band

Hattadare Indian Nation, NC

Hatteras Tuscarora Indians, NC

Hayfork Band of Nor-El-Muk Wintu Indians, CA. *See* Nor-Rel-Muk Nation

High Plains Indians, NC. *See* Indians of Person Co.

Hoke County Cherokees. *See* Cherokee Indians of Hoke County, Inc.

Honey Lake Valley. *See* Wadatkuht Band of the Northern Paiutes of the Honey Lake Valley

Houma:
Biloxi, Chitimacha Confederation of Muskogees, Inc.
Point au Chene Indian Tribe
United Houma Nation

Huron Potawatomi, Inc., also known as Nottawaseppi Huron Potawatomi Band, MI

Idaho Delaware. *See* Delawares of Idaho, Inc.

Indian Canyon Band of Coastanoan/Mutsun Indians of CA

Indiana Miami. *See* Miami Nation of Indians of the State of Indiana, Inc.

Indians of Person County, NC (formerly Cherokee-Powhattan Indian Association)

Ish Panesh Band of Mission Indians. *See* Ish Panesh United Band of Indians

Ish Panesh United Band of Indians, CA (formerly Oakbrook Park Chumash)

Jena Band of Choctaws, LA

Juaneno Band of Mission Indians, CA

Jumano. *See* People of LaJunta

Kaagwaantaan. *See* Chilkoot Kaagwaantaan Clan

Kah-Bay-Kah-Nong (Warroad Chippewa), MN

Kansas Wyandot. *See* Wyandot Nation of Kansas

Katallah-Chilkat Tlingit Tribe of Alaska

Kaweah Indian Nation, Inc., NC:
See also United Lumbee Nation of North Carolina and America

Kern Valley Indian Community, CA

Kispoko. See Upper Kispoko Band of the Shawnee Nation

Kitanemuk. See Tinoqui-Chalola Council of Kitanemuk and Yowlumne Tejon Indians

Konkow Valley Band of Maidu, CA

Kussoo. See Four Hole Indian Organization/Edisto Tribe

LaJunta. See People of LaJunta

Lake Superior Chippewa of Marquette, Inc., MI

Langley Band of the Chickamogee Cherokee Indians of the Southeastern U.S., AL

Lenni-Lenape: See also Delaware
Nanticoke Lenni-Lenape Indians, NJ
Ramapough Mountain Indians, NJ

Little Shell Band of North Dakota

Little Shell Tribe of Chippewa Indians of Montana

LMC. See Lower Muskogee Creek Tribe East of the Mississippi

Lost Cherokee of Arkansas and Missouri, AR

Lower Muskogee Creek Tribe-East of the Mississippi (also known as LMC), GA

Loyal Shawnee, OK

LRDA. See Lumbee Regional Development Association, Inc.

Lumbee:
Kaweah Indian Nation, Inc.
Lumbee Regional Development Association
Lumbee Tribe of Cheraw Indians
United Lumbee Nation of North Carolina and America

MaChis Lower Alabama Creek Indian Tribe, AL

Mackinac. See Consolidated Bahwetig Ojibwas and Mackinac Tribe

Mackinac Bands of Chippewa and Ottawa Indians, MI

Maidu:
Konkow Valley Band of Maidu
Maidu Nation, CA
Maidu Tribe of Greenville Rancheria, CA
North Eastern Maidu. See Maidu Nation
Plumas Co. Indians. See Maidu Nation T'si-akim Maidu

Manso. See Piro/Manso/Tiwa Indian Tribe of the Pueblo of San Juan de Guadelupe

Mariposa:
American Indian Council of Mariposa County, CA
Chukchansi Yokotch Tribe of Mariposa, CA

Mashpee Wampanoag, MA

Match-e-be-nash-she-wish Band of Pottawatomi Indians, MI (formerly Gun Lake Village Band of Ottawas) (formerly United Nation of Chippewa, Ottawa, and Potawatomi)

Mattaponi:
Mattaponi Tribe (Mattaponi Indian Reservation), VA
Upper Mattaponi Tribe, Inc. (formerly Uppper Mattaponi Tribal Association, Inc.)

Mdewakanton. See Mendota Mdewakanton Dakota Community

Meherrin Indian Tribe, NC

Meherrin Tribe, NC

Mendota Mdewakanton Dakota Community, MN

Mescalero. See People of LaJunta

Miami:
Miami Nation of Indians of the State of Indiana, Inc.
North Eastern U.S. Miami Inter-Tribal Council, OH
Miami Nation of Indians of the State of Indiana, Inc.

Mission Indian:
Coastal Gabrieleno Diegueno Band of Mission Indians
Coastanoan Band of Carmel Mission Indians
Gabrieleno Band of Mission Indians
Ish Panesh Band of Mission Indians

Juaneno Band
San Luis Rey Band
Mississippi Band of Chicasaw Indians, MS
Miwok:
　Federated Coast Miwok
　Southern Sierra Miwuk Nation
Mohegan:
　Mohegan Tribe and Nation, CT
　Western Mohegan Tribe and Nation of
　　New York, NY
Monacan Indian Tribe, Inc., VA
Mono:
　Dunlap Band
　Mono Lake Indian Community
Montauk Indian Nation, NY
Montaukett Tribe of Long Island, NY
Monterey. See Esselen: Esselen Tribe of
　Monterey County
Moorish Science Temple of America, Inc.
　See Federation: Moorish Science Tem-
　ple of America, Inc.
MOWA Band of Choctaw Indians, AL
Muncie. See Delaware-Muncie, KS
Munsee–Thames River Delaware, CO
Muskogee. See Creek
Mutsun:
　Costanoan Ohlone Rumsen-Mutsun
　　Tribe, CA
　Indian Canyon Band (CA)
Muwekma Indian Tribe. See Ohlone/
　Coastanoan Muwekema Tribe
Muwekma Indian Tribe, CA. See also
　Ohlone/Costanoan Muwekma Tribe

Nanticoke Indian Association, DE
Nanticoke Lenni-Lenape Indians, NJ
Natchez-Kussoo Indians. See Four Hole
　Indian Organization/Edisto Tribe
Navajo. See Canoncito Band of Navajos
Nehantic Tribe and Nation, CT
Niantic. See Nehantic
Nipmuc Nation, Hassanamisco Band,
　MA
Nipmuc Tribal Council of Massachusetts.
　See Chaubunagungamaug Band of the
　Nipmuc Nation
Nor-El-Muk Band of Wintu Indians. See
　Nor-Rel-Muk Nation
Nor-Rel-Muk Nation, CA
North Eastern Maidu. See Maidu Nation

North Eastern U.S. Miami Inter-Tribal
　Council, OH
Northern Cherokee Nation of Old
　Louisiana Territory, MO
Northern Cherokee Tribe of Indians, MO
Northern Paiutes. See Wadatkuht Band of
　the Northern Paiutes of the Honey
　Lake Valley
Nottawaseppi Huron Potawatomi Band.
　See Huron Potawatomi, Inc.

Oakbrook Chumash People. See Ish
　Panesh Band of Mission Indians
Oakbrook Park Chumash. See Ish Panesh
　Band of Mission Indians
Occaneechi:
　Eno-Occaneechi Tribe of Indians
　Occaneechi Band of Saponi Nation
　Occaneechi Band of Saponi Nation, NC
Odawa/Ottawa:
　Gun Lake Village Band. See Match-e-
　　be-nash-she-wish Band of Pot-
　　tawatomi Indians
　Grand River Bands of Ottawa Indians
　Mackinac Bands of Chippewa and Ot-
　　tawa Indians
　United Nation. See Match-e-be-nash-
　　she-wish Band of Pottawatomi Indi-
　　ans
Ohio Band. See Alleghenny Nation
Ohio Blue Creek Band. See Shawnee Na-
　tion, Ohio Blue Creek Band of Adams
　County
Ohio Shawnee. See Piqua Sept of Ohio
　Shawnee Indians
Ohlone:
　Costanoan Ohlone Rumsen-Mutsun
　　Tribe, CA
　Muwekma Indian Tribe, CA
　Ohlone/Costanoan-Esselen Nation, CA
　Ohlone/Costanoan Muwekma Tribe,
　　CA
Ohlone/Costanoan-Esselen Nation, CA
Ohlone/Costanoan Muwekma Tribe, CA.
　See Muwekma Indian Tribe
Ojibwa. See Chippewa
Oklewaha Band of Yamassee Seminole In-
　dians, FL
Old Louisiana Territory. See Northern Cher-
　okee Nation of Old Louisiana Territory

Osceola. *See* Oklewaha Band of Yamassee Seminole Indians

Ouichita. *See* Revived Ouichita Indians of AR and America

Paiutes:
    Antelope Valley Paiute Tribe, CA
    Pahrump Band
    San Juan Southern Paiute
    Wadatkuht Band of the Northern Paiutes of the Honey Lake Valley
    Washoe/Paiute of Antelope Valley, CA
Paucatuck Eastern Pequot Indians of CT
Paugussett. *See* Golden Hill Paugussett Tribe
Pahrump Band of Paiutes, NV
PeeDee:
    Beaver Creek Band of Pee Dee Indians, SC
    PeeDee Indian Association, Inc., SC
PeeDee Indian Association, Inc., SC
Penateka. *See* Comanche Penateka Tribe
People of LaJunta (Jumano/Mescalero), TX
Pequot:
    Eastern Pequot Indians of CT
    Paucatuck Eastern Pequot of CT
    Southern Pequot Tribe
Piedmont Indian Association, SC
Piqua Sept of Ohio Shawnee Indians, OH
Piro/Manso/Tiwa Indian Tribe of the Pueblo of San Juan de Guadalupe, NM (formerly Tiwa Indian Tribe)
Piscataway-Conoy Confederacy and Sub-Tribes, Inc., MD
Plumas Co. Indians. *See* Maidu Tribe of Greenville Rancheria
Pokanoket Tribe/and Bands. *See* Pokanoket/Wampanoag Federation/Wampanoag Nation/Pokanoket Tribe/and Bands
Pokanoket/Wampanoag Federation/Wampanoag Nation/Pokanoket Tribe/and Bands, RI
Pocasset Wampanoag Indian Tribe, MA
Potawatomi:
    Huron Potawatomi, Inc.
    Match-e-be-nash-she-wish Band of Pottawatomi Indians
    Nottawaseppi Huron Potawatomi Band. *See* Huron Potawatomi, Inc.
    Potawatomi Indian Nation, Inc.

Potawatomi Indians of Indiana and Michigan
United Nation of Ottawa, Chippewa, and Potawatomi. *See* Match-e-be-nash-she-wish Band of Pottawatomi Indians
Powhatan Renape Nation, NJ
Powhattan. *See* Indians of Person County Indians
Principal Creek Indian Nation East of Mississippi, AL (also known as Florala Creeks)
Pueblo of San Juan de Guadalupe. *See* Piro/Manso/Tiwa Indian Tribe of the Pueblo of San Juan de Guadalupe

Ramapough Mountain Indians, Inc., NJ
Rappahannock. *See* United Rappahannock Tribe, Inc.
Red Clay Inter-tribal Indian Band, TN
Renape. *See* Powhatan Renape Nation
Revived Ouachita Indians of AR and America
Rocky Boy Ojibway Band. *See* Ahon-to-ays Ojibwa Band
Rogue—Table Rock. *See* Confederated Tribes: Rogue—Table Rock and Associated Tribes, Inc.
Rumsen:
    Costanoan Ohlone Rumsen-Mutsun Tribe, CA
    Costanoan-Rumsen Carmel Tribe, CA

Sac River and White River Bands of the Chickamauga-Cherokee Nation of Arkansas and Missouri, Inc., MO
St. Francis/Sokoki Band of Abenakis of Vermont
Salinan Tribe of Monterey County, CA
Salinan Nation, CA
Samish Tribe of Indians, WA
San Juan de Guadalupe Tiwa. *See* Piro/Manso/Tiwa Indian Tribe of the Pueblo of San Juan de Guadalupe
San Juan Southern Paiute Tribe (also known as San Juan Paiutes), AZ
San Luis Rey Band of Mission Indians, CA
Santee Tribe, White Oak Indian Community, SC

Saponi:

Eno-Occaneechi, NC

Haliwa Saponi, NC

Occaneechi Band of Saponi Nation, NC

Saponi Nation of Ohio, OH

Saponi Nation of Ohio, OH

Schaghticoke Indian Tribe, CT

Seaconke Wampanoag Tribe, RI

Seminole:

Calusa Seminole Nation of Santa Cruz, CA

Cox-Osceola Indian Reservation

Oklewaha Band of Yamassee Seminole Indians, FL

Seminole Nation of Florida (also known as Traditional Seminole)

Shasta Nation, CA

Shawnee:

Loyal Shawnee, OK

Piqua Sept of Ohio Shawnee Indians, OH

Shawnee Nation, Ohio Blue Creek Band of Adams County, OH

Shawnee Remnant Band, OH

United Tribe of Shawnee Indians, KS

Upper Kispoko Band of the Shawnee Nation, IN

Shawnee Nation U.K.B, IN (formerly Shawnee Nation, United Remnant Band, OH)

Shinnecock Tribe, NY

Siouan:

Chicora-Waccamaw Indian People, SC (formerly Chicora-Siouan Indian People, SC)

Waccamaw Siouan Development Association, Inc., NC

Waccamaw-Siouan Indian Association, SC

Siuslaw. See Confederated Tribes: Rogue —Table Rock and Associated Tribes, Inc.

Snohomish Tribe of Indians, WA

Snoqualmie Indian Tribe, WA

Snoqualmoo Tribe of Whidbey Island, WA

Sokoki. See St. Francis/Sokoki Band of Abenakis of VT

Southeastern Cherokee Confederacy, Inc. (also known as SECC), GA (known

since 1996 as American Cherokee Confederacy). See also: Northwest Cherokee Wolf Band; Red Clay Inter-Tribal Indian Band

SouthEastern Indian Nation, GA

Southern Band of the Eastern Cherokee Indians. See Cherokee Nation West: Southern Band of the Eastern Cherokee Indians of Missouri and Arkansas

Southern Pequot Tribe, CT

Southern Sierra Miwuk Nation, CA

Steilacoom Tribe of Indians, WA

Stohini. See Ani-Stohini/Unami Nation, VA

Table Rock. See Confederated Tribes: Rogue—Table Rock and Associated Tribes, Inc.

Tap Pilam: The Coahuiltecan Nation, TX

Tataviam. See Fernandeno/Tataviam Tribe

Tchinouk Indians, OR

Tejon. See Tinoqui-Chalola Council of Kitanemuk and Yowlumne Tejon Indians

Thames River Delaware. See Munsee–Thames River Delaware

Tinoqui-Chalola Council of Kitanemuk and Yowlumne Tejon Indians, CA

Tiwa Indian Tribe (also known as San Juan de Guadalupe), NM. See Piro/Manso/Tiwa Indian Tribe of the Pueblo of San Juan de Guadalupe

Tlingit. See Katalla-Chilkat Tlingit Tribe of Alaska

Tolowa Nation, CA

Tongva. See Gabrielino

Traditional Seminole. See Seminole Nation of Florida

T'si-akim Maidu, CA

Tribal Council of the Carrizo/Comecrudo Nation of Texas, TX

Tsimshian Tribal Council, AK

Tsnungwe Council, CA

Tuscarora:

Hatteras Tuscarora

Tuscarora Hoke Co. See Cherokee Indians of Hoke County, Inc.

Tuscarora Indian Tribe, Drowning Creek Reservation, NC

Tuscarora Nation of the Kautanoh. As of 1999, umbrella group for Tus-

carora Tribe of NC, Tuscarora Nation of North Carolina, Cherokee Indians of Hoke County, Inc.
Tuscarora Nation of North Carolina
Tuscola United Cherokee Tribe of FL and AL, Inc., FL

Unami. *See* Ani-Stohini/Unami Nation, VA
United Houma Nation, Inc., LA
United Lumbee Nation of NC and America, CA. *See also* Kaweah Indian Nation, CA
United Nation of Chippewa, Ottawa, and Potawatomi. *See* Match-e-be-nash-she-wish Band of Pottawatomi Indians
United Rappahannock Tribe, Inc., VA
United Tribe of Shawnee Indians, KS
Upper Kispoko Band of the Shawnee Nation, IN
Upper Mattaponi Tribe, Inc., VA (formerly Upper Mattaponi Indian Tribal Association, Inc.)

Waccamaw:
    Chicora Waccamaw Indian People, SC
    Waccamaw Siouan Development Association, Inc., NC
    Waccamaw-Siouan Indian Association, SC
Wadatkuht Band of the Northern Paiutes of the Honey Lake Valley
Wampanoag:
    Mashpee Wampanoag
    Pocasset Wampanoag Indian Tribe, MA
    Pokanoket/Wampanoag Federation/Wampanoag Nation/Pokanoket Tribe/and Bands
    Seaconke Wampanoag Tribe
Wampanoag Nation. *See* Pokanoket/Wampanoag Federation/Wampanoag Nation/Plkanoket Tribe/and Bands
Warroad Chippewa. *See* Kah-Bay-Kah-Nong
Washoe/Paiute of Antelope Valley, CA

Western Arkansas Cherokee Tribe, AR
Western Cherokee Nation of Arkansas and Missouri, AR
Western Mohegan Tribe and Nation of New York, NY
Whidbey Island, WA. *See* Snoqualmoo Tribe of Whidbey Island
White Oak Indian Community. *See* Santee Tribe, White Oak Indian Community
White River Band. *See* Sac River and White River Bands of the Chickamauga-Cherokee Nation of Arkansas and Missouri, Inc.
Winnebago. *See* Council for the Benefit of Colorado Winnebagos, CO
Wintoon Indians, CA
Wintu:
    Hayfork Band of Nor-El-Muk Wintu Indians
    Nor-El-Muk Band of Wintu Indians
    Nor-Rel-Muk Nation
    Wintoon Indians
Wintu Indians of Central Valley, CA
Wintu Tribe, CA
Wolf Band. *See* Northwest Cherokee Wolf Band
Wukchumni Council, CA
Wyandot Nation of Kansas, KS

Yamassee. *See* Oklewaha Band of Yamassee Seminole Indians
Yokayo, CA
Yokotch. *See* Chukchansi Yokotch Tribe of Coarsegold; Chukchansi Yokotch Tribe of Mariposa
Yosemite. *See* American Indian Council of Mariposa County
Yowlumne. *See* Tinoqui-Chalola Council of Kitanemuk and Yowlumne Tejon Indians
Yuchi:
    Ani Yvwi Yuchi, CA
    Yuchi Tribal Organization, OK
Yvwi. *See* Ani Yvwi Yuchi

APPENDIX 4: MAP OF FEDERAL INDIAN LANDS AS OF 1992

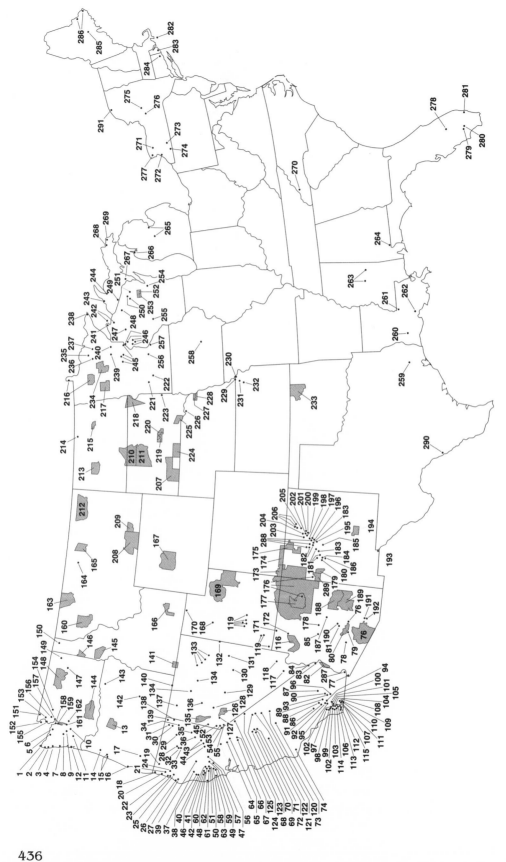

Legend

1. Makah I.R.
2. Ozette I.R.
3. Quileute I.R.
4. Hoh I.R.
5. Lower Elwha I.R.
6. Jamestown Klallam I.R.
7. Quinault I.R.
8. Skokomish I.R.
9. Squaxin I.R.
10. Nisqually I.R.
11. Chehalis I.R.
12. Shoalwater Bay I.R.
13. Warm Springs I.R.
14. Grande Ronde I.R.
15. Siletz I.R.
16. Coos, Lower Umpqua & Siuslaw
17. Cow Creek of Umpqua I.R.
18. Smith River Rancheria
19. Karok I.R.
20. Resighini Rancheria
21. Yurok I.R.
22. Big Lagoon Rancheria
23. Trinidad Rancheria
24. Hoopa Valley I.R.
25. Blue Lake Rancheria
26. Table Bluff Rancheria
27. Rohnerville Rancheria
28. Big Bend Rancheria
29. Lookout Rancheria
30. Alturas Rancheria
31. XI Rancheria
32. Roaring Creek Rancheria
33. Montgomery Creek Rancheria
34. Likely Rancheria
35. Susanville Rancheria
36. Greenville Rancheria
37. Round Valley I.R.
38. Laytonville Rancheria
39. Grindstone Creek Rancheria
40. Redwood Valley Rancheria
41. Sherwood Valley Rancheria
42. Coyote Valley Rancheria
43. Enterprise Rancheria
44. Berry Creek Rancheria
45. Reno Sparks I.R.
46. Upper Lake Rancheria
47. Colusa Rancheria
48. Robinson Rancheria
49. Cortina Rancheria
50. Sulpher Bank Rancheria
51. Big Valley Rancheria
52. Carson Colony I.R.
53. Dresslerville Colony I.R.
54. Woodfords Indian Community
55. Washoe I.R.
56. Shingle Springs Rancheria
57. Rumsey Rancheria
58. Middletown Rancheria
59. Dry Creek Rancheria

60. Pinoleville Rancheria
61. Hopland Rancheria
62. Manchester Rancheria
63. Stewarts Point Rancheria
64. Jackson Rancheria
65. Sheep Ranch Rancheria
66. Chicken Ranch Rancheria
67. Tolumne Rancheria
68. Northfork Rancheria
69. Big Sandy Rancheria
70. Table Mountain Rancheria
71. Cold Springs Rancheria
72. Santa Rosa Rancheria
73. Tule River I.R.
74. Santa Ynes I.R.
75. Annette Island I.R...
76. Papago I.R.
77. Cocopah I.R.
78. Gila Bend I.R.
79. Maricopa I.R.
80. Gila River I.R.
81. Salt River I.R.
82. Colorado River I.R.
83. Chemehuevi I.R.
84. Fort Mojave I.R.
85. Yavapai I.R.
86. San Manuel I.R.
87. Twentynine Palms I.R.
88. Morongo I.R.
89. Agua Caliente I.R.
90. Cabazon I.R.
91. Saboba I.R.
92. Ramona I.R.
93. Augustine I.R.
94. Santa Rosa I.R.
95. Cahuilla I.R.
96. Torres-Martinez I.R.
97. Pechanga I.R.
98. Pala I.R.
99. Pauma I.R.
100. Los Coyotes I.R.
101. La Jollai I.R.
102. Rincon I.R.
103. San Pasqual I.R.
104. Mesa Grande I.R.
105. Santa Ysabel I.R.
106. Inaja-Cosmit I.R.
107. Capitan Grande I.R.
108. Cuyapaipe I.R.
109. Manzanita I.R.
110. Campo I.R.
111. La Posta I.R.
112. Sycuan I.R.
113. Jamul I.R.
114. Barona Rancheria
115. Viejas I.R.
116. Hualapai I.R.
117. Las Vegas Colony I.R.
118. Moapa River I.R.

119. Paiute I.R.
120. Lone Pine Rancheria
121. Fort Independence I.R.
122. Big Pine Rancheria
123. Bishop Rancheria
124. Benton Paiute I.R.
125. Bridgeport Rancheria
126. Walker River I.R.
127. Yerington I.R.
128. Fallon Colony and I.R.
129. Yomba I.R.
130. Duckwater I.R.
131. Ely Colony I.R.
132. Goshute I.R.
133. Te-Moak I.R.
134. Winnemucca Colony I.R.
135. Pyramid Lake I.R.
136. Lovelock Colony I.R.
137. Summit Lake I.R.
138. Cedarville Rancheria
139. Fort Bidwell I.R.
140. Fort McDermitt I.R.
141. Duck Valley I.R.
142. Burns Paiute Colony I.R.
143. Umatilla I.R.
144. Yakima I.R.
145. Nez Perce I.R.
146. Couer D'Alene I.R.
147. Spokane I.R.
148. Colville I.R.
149. Kalispel I.R.
150. Kootenai I.R.
151. Noosack I.R.
152. Lummi I.R.
153. Upper Skagit I.R.
154. Sauk Suiattle I.R.
155. Swinomish I.R.
156. Stillaguamish I.R.
157. Tulalip I.R.
158. Port Gamble I.R.
159. Port Madison I.R.
160. Flathead I.R.
161. Puyallup I.R.
162. Muckleshoot I.R.
163. Blackfeet I.R.
164. Rocky Boys I.R.
165. Fort Belknap I.R.
166. Fort Hall I.R.
167. Wind River I.R.
168. Skull Valley I.R.
169. Unitah and Ouray I.R.
170. Northwestern Shoshoni I.R.
171. Kaibab I.R.
172. Havasuapi I.R.
173. Ute Mountain I.R.
174. Southern Ute I.R.
175. Jicarilla I.R.
176. Navajo I.R. (3)
177. Hopi I.R.

178. Camp Verde I.R.
179. Ramah Navajo I.R.
180. Acoma I.R.
181. Laguna I.R. (3)
182. Zai I.R. (2)
183. Santa Ana I.R.
184. Canoncito I.R.
185. Isleta I.R.
186. Alamo Navajo I.R.
187. Payson Community I.R.
188. Fort Apache I.R.
189. San Carlos I.R.
190. Fort McDowell I.R.
191. Pascua Yaqui I.R.
192. San Xavier I.R.
193. Ysleta Del Sur I.R.
194. Mescalero I.R.
195. Sandia I.R.
196. San Felipe I.R.
197. Santo Domingo I.R.
198. Cochiti I.R.
199. San Idlefonso I.R.
200. Tesuque I.R.
201. Nambe I.R.
202. Pojoaque I.R.
203. Santa Clara I.R.
204. San Juan I.R.
205. Picuris I.R.
206. Taos I.R. (2)
207. Pine Ridge I.R.
208. Crow I.R.
209. Northern Cheynne I.R.
210. Standing Rock I.R.
211. Cheyenne River I.R.
212. Fort Beck I.R.
213. Fort Bethold I.R.
214. Turtle Mountain I.R.
215. Devils Lake I.R.
216. Red Lake I.R. (2)
217. White Earth I.R.
218. Lake Traverse I.R.
219. Lower Brule I.R.
220. Crow Creek I.R.
221. Upper Sioux I.R.
222. Lower Sioux I.R.
223. Flandreau I.R.
224. Rosebud I.R.
225. Yankton I.R.
226. Sante Sioux I.R.
227. Winnebago I.R.
228. Omaha I.R.
229. Sac and Fox I.R.
230. Iowa I.R.
231. Kickapoo I.R.
232. Potawatomi I.R.
233. Osage I.R.
234. Leech Lake I.R.
235. Bois Forte I.R.
236. Deer Creek I.R.

237. Vermillion Lake I.R.
238. Grand Portage I.R.
239. Sandy Lake I.R.
240. Fond Du Lac I.R.
241. Red Cliff I.R.
242. Bad River I.R. (2)
243. Ontonagon I.R.
244. L'Anse I.R.
245. Mille Lacs I.R. (4)
246. St. Croix I.R. (5)
247. Lac Courte Oreilles I.R.
248. Lac Du Flambeau I.R.
249. Lac Vieux Desert I.R.
250. Sokaogon Chippewa I.R. (2)
251. Potawatomi I.R.
252. Menominee I.R.
253. Stockbridge I.R.
254. Oneida I.R.
255. Winnebago I.R.
256. Shakopee I.R.
257. Prarie Island I.R.
258. Sac and Fox I.R.
259. Alabama-Coushatta I.R.
260. Coushatta I.R.
261. Tunica-Biloxi I.R.
262. Chitimacha I.R.
263. Mississippi Choctaw I.R.
264. Poarch Creek I.R.
265. Isabella I.R. (2)
266. Grand Traverse I.R.
267. Hannahville I.R.
268. Bay Mills I.R.
269. Sault Saint Marie I.R.
270. Cherokee I.R.
271. Tonawanda I.R.
272. Cattaraugus I.R.
273. Oil Springs I.R.
274. Allegany I.R.
275. Oneida I.R.
276. Onondaga I.R.
277. Tuscarora I.R.
278. Brighton I.R.
279. Big Cypress I.R.
280. Miccosukee I.R.
281. Hollywood I.R.
282. Wamponoag I.R.
283. Narragansett I.R.
284. Mashantucket Pequot I.R.
285. Pennobscot I.R.
286. Passamaqouddy I.R. (2)
287. Fort Yuma I.R.
288. Jemez I.R.
289. Zuni I.R.
290. Texas Kickapoo I.R.
291. St. Regis I.R.

Note: Several reservations have been added to the federal system since this map was created in 1992.
Source: Adapted from Indian Lands Map, 1992. Compiled by the Handbook of North American Indians (Smithsonian Institution) in cooperation with the Bureau of Indian Affairs, prepared by the U.S. Geological Survey.

INDEX